Grajewo Poland Memorial (*Yizkor*) Book
Translation of *Grayeve Yisker-Bukh*

**Translation Project Coordinators
Evelyn Fine and Shelly Levin**

This is a translation from:
Grayeve Yisker-Bukh (Grajewo Memorial Book)
Editor: Dr. George Gorin, New York
Originally Published by:
United Grayever Relief Committee, 1950
In Yiddish and English, 311 pages.

Published by JewishGen

An Affiliate of the Museum of Jewish Heritage - A Living Memorial to the Holocaust
New York

Grajewo Poland Memorial *(Yizkor)* Book
Translation of *Grayeve Yisker-Bukh*

Copyright © 2014 by JewishGen, Inc.
All rights reserved.
First Printing: May 2014, Iyar 5774

Translation Project Coordinators: Evelyn Fine and Shelly Levin
Layout Editor: Joel Alpert
Cover Design: Jan R. Fine
Publicity: Sandra Hirschhorn
Yiddish and Hebrew Consultant: Josef Rosin
Technical Consultant: Hank Mishkoff

This book may not be reproduced, in whole or in part, including illustrations in any form (beyond that copying permitted by Sections 107 and 108 of the U.S. Copyright Law and except by reviewers for public press), without written permission from the publisher.

Published by JewishGen, Inc.
An Affiliate of the Museum of Jewish Heritage
A Living Memorial to the Holocaust
36 Battery Place, New York, NY 10280

"JewishGen, Inc. is not responsible for inaccuracies or omissions in the original work and makes no representations regarding the accuracy of this translation. Digital images of the original book's contents can be seen online at the New York Public Library Web site."

The mission of the JewishGen organization is to produce a translation of the original work and we cannot verify the accuracy of statements or alter facts cited.

Printed by CreateSpace.

Library of Congress Control Number (LCCN): 2014939755
ISBN: 978-1-939561-22-0 (paperback: 358 pages, alk. paper)

Cover image from the original Yiddish Yizkor Book:
The Shul, Besmedresh and *Oheves Khesed* [Love of Charity] –
Drawn by A. D. Fishbeyn
Back Cover Credit:
A part of the Grayeve Cemetery and the little lake, looking from River Street -
Drawn by A. D. Fishbeyn

JewishGen and the Yizkor-Books-in-Print Project

This book has been published by the **Yizkor-Books-in-Print Project,** as part of the **Yizkor Book Project** of **JewishGen, Inc.**

JewishGen, Inc. is a non-profit organization founded in 1987 as a resource for Jewish genealogy. Its website [www.jewishgen.org] serves as an international clearinghouse and resource center to assist individuals who are researching the history of their Jewish families and the places where they lived. JewishGen provides databases, facilitates discussion groups, and coordinates projects relating to Jewish genealogy and the history of the Jewish people. In 2003, JewishGen became an affiliate of the **Museum of Jewish Heritage - A Living Memorial to the Holocaust** in New York.

The **JewishGen Yizkor Book Project** was organized to make more widely known the existence of Yizkor (Memorial) Books written by survivors and former residents of various Jewish communities throughout the world. Later, volunteers connected to the different destroyed communities began cooperating to have these books translated from the original language—usually Hebrew or Yiddish—into English, thus enabling a wider audience to have access to the valuable information contained within them. As each chapter of these books was translated, it was posted on the JewishGen website and made available to the general public.

The **Yizkor-Books-in-Print Project** began in 2011 as an initiative to print and publish Yizkor Books that had been fully translated, so that hard copies would be available for purchase by the descendants of these communities and also by scholars, universities, synagogues, libraries, and museums.

These Yizkor Books have been produced almost entirely through the volunteer effort of researchers from around the world, assisted by donations from private individuals. The books are printed and sold at near cost, so as to make them as affordable as possible. Our goal is to make this important genre of Jewish literature and history available in English in book form, so that people can have the personal histories of their ancestral towns on their bookshelves for themselves and for their children and grandchildren.

A list of all published translated Yizkor Books can be found at:
http://www.jewishgen.org/Yizkor/ybip.html

Lance Ackerfeld, Yizkor Book Project Manager

Joel Alpert, Yizkor-Books-in-Print Project Coordinator

This book is presented by the
Yizkor Books in Print Project
Project Coordinator: Joel Alpert

Part of the
Yizkor Books Project of JewishGen, Inc.
Project Manager: Lance Ackerfeld

These books have been produced solely through volunteer effort of individuals from around the world. The books are printed and sold at near cost, so as to make them as affordable as possible.

Our goal is to make this history and important genre of Jewish literature available in English in book form so that people can have the near-personal histories of their ancestral towns on their bookshelves for themselves and for their children and grandchildren.

Any donations to the Yizkor Books Project are appreciated.

Please send donations to:
Yizkor Book Project
JewishGen
36 Battery Place
New York, NY 10280

JewishGen, Inc. is an affiliate of the
Museum of Jewish Heritage
A Living Memorial to the Holocaust

Title Page of Original Yiddish Yizkor Book

גראַיעװע
יזכּור=בוך

•

רעדאַקציע:

דר. ג. גאָרין, פאָרזיצער

הײמאַן בלום

סאָל פישבײן

•

אַרויסגעגעבן פון

פאַראײניקטן גראַיעװער הילפס־קאָמיטעט

ניו־יאָרק, 1950

From the Original Yizkor Book

GRAYEVO
MEMORIAL BOOK

Published by the

UNITED GRAYEVER RELIEF COMMITTEE

IRVING SAPIRSTEIN, Sec'y

1655 Monroe Ave, Bronx, N. Y.

Printed in the United States of America by
The Shoulson Press, 227 West 17th Street, New York 11, N. Y.

Foreword for the Publication of the Translation

This translation project was a labor of love. My father, Isaac Fine, was born in Grajewo in 1914. He miraculously escaped World War II, later joining the US Army to help liberate Europe. As I grew up he told me stories of his childhood, drew maps of his town, and drew me in to a previous time. He guarded the Yizkor Book of his town as a reminder of his lost life, his lost family.

I visited the city in 1998. Much of it is intact. The devastation of the Holocaust occurred so quickly that most buildings remained. After studying Yiddish in Vilnius in 2009 I embarked upon the task of working on translating the book. Donations from friends and family made this project possible. I was assisted by Shelly Levin. Many thanks to Yiddish translators Tina Lunson and Miriam Leberstein for their tireless work. Thanks too, to friends around the world for help in translating occasional Hebrew, Aramaic and Polish passages. And thanks to Hank Mishkoff for capturing and digitizing all original photos.

Evelyn Fine, Translation Project Coordinator

April 18, 2014

Historic Background

Jewish people have been living in Grajewo, a small town in the province of Bialystok, Poland since the latter half of the 17th century. The 1765 census counted 83 Jewish people and by 1857, the number had grown to 1,457 when they comprised 76% of the entire population of Grajewo. At the turn of the twentieth century the population was 4,336, but this fell to just 2,834 by 1921, when the percentage of Jews had decreased to 39% of the population.

Anti-Semitism, from both the political establishment and the general population was common throughout contemporary Europe. Development of significant anti-Jewish outbreaks in Grajewo occurred in 1933. During the Soviet occupation, between September 1939 and June 1941, Jewish businesses were nationalized. The capture of Grajewo on 22 June 1941 by the Germans marked the beginning of the devastation and horrors thrust upon the Jewish population. Within a few months, 1,600 to 2,000 Jews had been sent to the transit camp at Bogosza and on to the extermination camps at Treblinka and Auschwitz.

The United Grayever (Grajewo) Relief Committee memorialized the Jewish Community of Grajewo by publishing the original Yiddish Yizkor Book in 1950. Now it is available in English for future generations to learn of their past. It is fitting that my father would have been 100 years old this year.

Evelyn Fine, Translation Project Coordinator

April 18, 2014

Dedication for the Publication of the Translation

This book is dedicated to my family members who were murdered, along with all of the Shoah victims of Grajewo and the vicinity, as well as to all descendants of the survivors.

Evelyn Fine

Acknowledgements for the Publication of the Translation

This book would not have seen the light of day in English without the dedication and hard work of Evelyn Fine and Shelly Levin. The Yizkor-Books-in-Print Project is grateful to them for making this publication possible.

Location of Grajewo in Poland Today

Geopolitical Information:

Grajewo is located at 53°39' North Latitude and 22°27' East Longitude 114 mi NNE of Warsaw in Poland.

Alternate names for the town are: Grajewo (Polish), Grayavah (Yiddish), Graevo (Russian), Grayeve, and Grayevo.

	Town	District	Province	Country
Before WWI (c. 1900):	Grajewo	Szczuczyn	Łomża	Russian Empire
Between the wars (c. 1930):	Grajewo	Szczuczyn	Białystok	Poland
After WWII (c. 1950):	Grajewo			Poland
Today (c. 2000)	Grajewo			Poland

Nearby Jewish Communities:
- Szczuczyn 8 miles SW
- Wąsosz 11 miles SSW
- Rajgród 12 miles ENE
- Ełk 13 miles NNW
- Goniądz 17 miles SE
- Radziłów 17 miles S
- Stawiski 23 miles SSW
- Trzcianne 24 miles SSE
- Jedwabne 26 miles SSW
- Augustów 26 miles ENE
- Kolno 27 miles SW
- Sztabin 27 miles E
- Raczki 27 miles NNE
- Suchowola 27 miles E
- Knyszyn 30 miles SE

Notes to the Reader:

Within the text the reader will note "{34}" standing ahead of a paragraph. This indicates that the material translated below was on page 34 of the original book. However, when a paragraph was split between two pages in the original book, the marker is placed in this book after the end of the paragraph for ease of reading.

Also please note that all references within the text of the book to page numbers, refer to the page numbers of the original Yizkor Book.

The English spelling of many of the family names contained herein have been approximated by the translators and may be different depending upon the translator.

Family Notes

Table of Contents

Table of Contents 2
   Foreword 4
First Part: 6
Once, once… 6
   Midnight 7
   Grayeve from the Past 8
   Our Hometown, Grayeve 16
   Grayeve – Aspiring and Dreaming 29
   Images and Figures of *Grayeve* 40
Second Part: 59
Community and Life-Style 59
   The Zionist Movement in Grayeve 59
   Workers' Organizations in Grayeve 89
   An Encounter Between Grayevers in Siberia 102
   Grayeve Dzshegtshares 106
   Hasidism in Grayeve 125
   Hepner's Suspender Factory 133
   Grajewo 136
Third Part: 151
The Holocaust 151
   History of the Grayeve Ghetto 153
   A Grayeve Partisan Recounts 188
   Shtutzin – Grayeve to the Last Breath 191
   The Violent Death of the Jews of Shtutzin 195
   The Violent Death of the Jews of Kolna 197
   The Pogroms in Radzshilov [Radzilow] 199
Fourth Part: 206
Grayeve Jews in America 206
   A Word from the Chairman of the 206
   United Grayever Relief Committee 206
   The Grayever Relief Committee in New York 210
   The United Grayever Relief Committee 218
   Grayever Branch 35 of the Workmen's Circle 227
   The Grayever Branch 56 233
   of the Jewish People's Fraternal Order 233
   The Shtutziner and Grayever Shul in New York 234
   The Grayever Landsleit in Chicago 237
   Letters and Documents from Grayeve 239
   From American Joint Distribution Committee, Warsaw 252
Fifth Part: 253
Grayeve Writers and Scholars 253
   Grayeve Jews in Eretz-Yisroel 253
   The Three Grayevans in Jerusalem: 258
   Dr. Emmanuel Olshvanger, Dr. Tsvi Voyslavski, Ari Ibn-Zahav 258
   Avrom Mordkhe Piurko 261
   Memories of Avrom-Mordkhe Piurko 265
   Prof. Shimen Rabidovitsh 267
   About the illustrations of A. D. Fishbeyn: 270
In Holy Remembrance 274

English Section 300
　The Story of Grayevo 300
　History of the Grayevo Ghetto 311
Table of Contents of the Original Yizkor Book　　　　　　　　　　336

[Page 7]

Foreword
Translated by Tina Lunson

With sorrowful hearts and mournful spirits we stand by the unveiling of this modest memorial for the sanctified and martyred, our murdered fathers and mothers, sisters and brothers, comrades and friends from our old hometown, Grayeve [Grajewo].

Only a few Grayeve Jews were saved from the Nazi murderers, only a few remained alive to tell of the destruction. In Grayeve, as in hundreds of other towns and villages in Poland, there is no longer one Jew. Consequently, it took several years after Hitler's devastating inundation until we felt the courage and gathered the strength to erect this memorial – a *Grayever Yizker-Bukh*. [Grayeve Memorial Book]

A town with a Jewish community of several thousand souls, Grayeve in the last decades of her life demonstrated response to, and absorption in the social, cultural and political currents and ambitions of the large creative Jewish settlement in Poland. Little Grayeve also published a number of distinguished Yiddish and Hebrew writers, scholars and community leaders, of whom a significant number, along with other sons of the town, in time emigrated to America, *Erets Yisroel* and other lands. The *Grayeve Yizker-Bukh* was entirely written with our own energies and is presented as both a monograph of our annihilated community and a certain reflection of the life of the Grayeve *landslayt* [countrymen] in America and Israel.

Of course, in most of the treatises of the book one hears the wail of mourners: in the memoirs, the tone of funeral oratory and eulogy, and there is necessarily lament in the descriptions of the Holocaust. For the writers and publishers of this book, the *Khurbm* [destruction] *Grayeve*, like the overall tragedy of the Jews in Europe, is bound up with personal tragedy, with sorrow for their families and close ones.

There are also here and there repetitions in descriptions about the same matters, events and persons. But the repetition completes the description and all together they create a picture of its bonds and ways of life, its needs, ambitions and struggles, its joys and sorrows, disappointments and achievements. Together, everything relates how much we have lost, the inestimable loss!

There are also in this book descriptions and documents of the Jewish *Khurbm* in the neighboring towns around *Grayeve* – *Shtshutshin* [Szczuczyn], Radzshilov [Radzilow], Kolne [Kolno] and others, the towns that always partnered with Grayeve and enjoyed its society and culture. May the *landslayt* from the annihilated Jewish towns, like the surviving remnant wherever they are found, consider the *Grayever Yizker-Bukh* as a memorial to their most loved and dearest, both for those mentioned in the book and for those not mentioned.

We extend a warm hand and a *yasher-keyekh* [may your strength grow] to all the *landslayt* who sent in materials for the *Yizker-Bukh*. At the same time we beg the pardon of our dear *landslayt* whose articles could not, for technical reasons be included in the book.

We are especially grateful to our hometown poet Nakhman Rapp, one of the small number of Grayeve Jews who remained in Poland and who sensed the difficult and painful mission to investigate and describe just a small part of the destruction of Grayeve. The poet himself lost his closest friends in Grayeve, and by a miracle survived in the Soviet Union. After the bloody, devastating Nazi inundation he went back to Poland, but in his hometown he found no living Jewish soul (or even any dead ones), as he relates in his history of the Grayeve ghetto and as he eulogized it in his book of poems *Funken in ash* [*Sparks in the Ashes*], published in Wroclaw in 1947. The description by Rapp, which we print in this book, is certainly an important addition to the history of the Jewish *Khurbm* and martyrdom under the Nazis, as are also the documents from the Jewish Historical Committee in Bialystok, which we print here. For the English-reading children and relatives of our *landslayt*, we print a shortened overview of N. Rapp's description and also an introduction to the book by Dr. G. Gorin.

With bowed heads and wringing hands we stand at this modest memorial for our slaughtered Grayeve community. *Khaval al d'avdin v'la mishtak'khin.* [A pity for our loss of those who are no longer with us]. May this *Yizker-Bukh* be a lasting reminder for the *landslayt* of *Grayeve* and vicinity to unite their strengths through the Grayeve Aid Committee and other organizations that help to build and strengthen Jewish community life. May this *Grayever Yizker-Bukh* be a reminder from generation to generation that the survival of the Jewish people is eternally inseparable from the ideals: "end of days," social heritage, peoples' freedom and world peace.

Editorial colleagues of the United Grayeve Aid Committee

Dr. G. Gorin, Chairman

Hayman Blum

Sh. Y. Fishbeyn

New York, April 15, 1950

[Page 8]

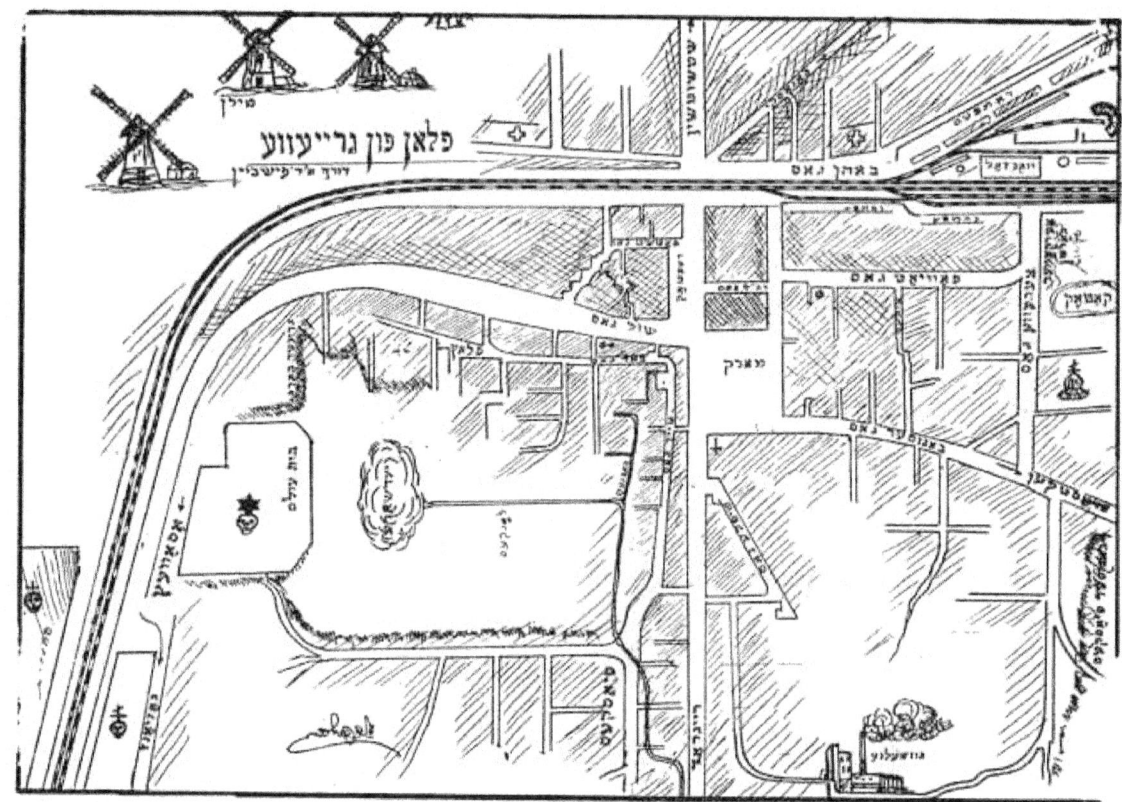

Map of Grajewo

First Part:

Once, once…

Midnight
Nakhman Rapp (Wroclaw)
Translated by Tina Lunson

The doors are closed and the shutters chained,
I am alone in my dark room,
I see my fracture as in a dark mirror –
I perform an empty, decimated *seyder*.

I pour no ash on my head, like my granddad,
I tear no *kries**, like my father –
Too heavy the pain, too enormous the loss
That I could patch it with *kries.**

But now at midnight in my lonely room,
I don't shy from friends or from enemies now,
The night may hear my curse, my oath,
The night can drink the lament from my face.

O, who damned the hours, the moments,
When they flung my brothers into the pits?
O, who lamented, when over the shores
The bloody flood drowned out all flesh?

The prayers of our fathers and mothers,
O, who heard in their last gasp:
Master of the universe, avert, don't delay,
Jealous and avenging – you God of revenge…

I search my conscience for a peg, a splinter,
I search in people's eyes for only a spark
At least to remind in a sacred shiver
Of kindness and pity, a little flame, just a wink …

With thousands of hands I cover my wounds,
So the sun will not see them, no friend would know,
And I keep them bound before the foe,
Because his appearance would tear up my heart.

Only now in the dark sadness of the room,
I don't shy from friends or from enemies now,
The night may hear my curse, my oath,
The night can drink the lament from my face.

***kries:** tear in clothing for mourning

[Page 11]

Grayeve from the Past
Historical Notes

By Sh. Y. Fishbeyn

Translated by Tina Lunson

Grayeve, in *Lomzhe* [Łomża] province, is located four *viorsts* [a viorst is approximately 0.6 mile/1 kilometer] from the German border, near the eastern Prussian town of *Prostken* [Prostki].

The river Lenk (which we called "Kosherove"), along which Grayeve was built, runs from the lakes in southern Prussia to the old Polish fortress *Osovyets* [Osowiec].

The fortunate geographic position and other factors give us sufficient grounds to suppose that Grayeve has a long history of hundreds of years behind it. There are also signs of an old Jewish settlement in Grayeve. But apparently, the Jews never imagined that we would ever have to publish "Yizker-bikher" about the hundreds of Jewish towns and villages of Poland. . . there are very few remaining birth certificates and letters of pedigree from our annihilated settlements. We try now to restore their old historical footsteps; receive the echo of their development and the reflections of their past.

How Old is Grayeve?

Chroniclers usually attend to events of a general character or events of historical significance in connection with given places and towns. As regards to smaller towns or villages, their history is considered according to official documents and unofficial information as well as in relationship to the events in the surrounding towns.

[Page 12]

According to the Polish encyclopedia "*Slownik Geograficzni, Krulewstwa Polska,*" the towns of *Shtutzin* [Szczuczyn] and Lomzhe were mentioned in the years 1326 and 1340, respectively. The village *Raigrod* [Rajgród] was mentioned as early as the 12th century. The towns were usually mentioned in their earliest period through the activities of the Catholic religion or because of the building of a church. In the later periods events of a general character were recorded.

It is implied that Grayeve is as old as the towns around it, such as Lomzhe and Shtutzin in the north and Raigrod in the south.

The first time that Grayeve is mentioned in *Slownik Polski* [Polish Dictionary] is in connection with a wooden church that was built in Grayeve in 1497. Grayeve is mentioned later in 1725, when a brick church was built.

Until the construction of the king's postal highway in 1800 that extended from *Kovne* [Kaunas] to *Varshe* [Warsaw], Grayeve was insignificant in comparison to Shtutzin and Raigrod. Provisions such as oil, salt and so on were driven along a sand road to *Bogushe* [Bogusze] or Shtutzin. With the construction of the postal highway Grayeve became a pass-through center for freight transport from *Ogustove* [Augustów] and Raigrod through Grayeve to Lomzhe and Warsaw.

From as far away as Ogustove, in the agricultural hinterland of the country, merchants drove around and bought up products from the villages. The products were loaded in big covered wagons (wagons with linen stretched over them). The caravans of covered wagons were pulled by three pairs of horses – through Grayeve and on to Lomzhe for unloading at the big market. Inns and resting places were created in Grayeve, as mostly people rested and changed horses there. The number of merchants, purveyors and artisans multiplied. Grayeve came even with and rose above the neighboring towns.

The Jewish Community in Grayeve

The *Encyclopedia Judaica* reports that in 1856 there was a population of two thousand people in Grayeve, 1,457 Jews and 551 Poles. One can also deduce that the Grayeve Jewish settlement was as old as the surrounding settlements and that its Jewish institutions like *bote-medroshim* [Houses of Study] had existed in Grayeve for the last several hundred years. It was reported that the old beys-medresh was already a very old building 75 years ago. People who were in Grayeve when the old shul was pulled down in 1899 believe that the old shul – judging from the heavy, massive stones of its construction – had existed for at least a hundred years.

[Page 13]

Jewish administrative affairs had already been conducted by the Jewish community council for a long time. Every year around *Peysakh* [Passover] time representatives assembled delegates from each beys-medresh or Hasidic prayer room, for the goal of choosing a manager for the council. The right to choose the delegates belonged only to those who had businesses or property; craftsmen or laborers who did not have any property were not entitled to take part in the voting for delegates.

The representatives of all the bote-medroshim selected "guardians" and trustees who, together with the *rov* ["rabbi"] and *dayan* [Jewish judge], constituted the administration of the council. The town council was maintained by a tax that was imposed on the purchase of meat. The tax was called *"koropke"* [tax]. The taxes were imposed on the entire Jewish community, although the general community did not have voting rights.

Unfortunately the Grayeve record book was not saved, so the facts about council administration in the very early time are not known. But it is known by the information of evidence about that time, that in 1885 the guardians were Meylekh Vaks, Avrom Yankl Zshmievski, Leybl Levit, Yesokher Podbelski, Tutelman.

The community built the bathhouse in 1888. The first bathhouse attendant was Shleyme the bather; after him was Borekh Mordkhe and later his son-in-law Mayer.

When the old shul was torn down in 1899, work began on building the new shul. In addition to the community administration, a special committee for building the shul was created. The committee was headed by Elye Vierzshblovski. Certain facts about a few families from an earlier period are also known. So it is known that in 1837, a Grayeve Jew was active as a "doctor," who was called Yisrolke the *rofe* [doctor], Meylekh Vaks' father-in-law.

[Page 14]

Already in the previous century there were several tanneries in Grayeve that produced fine leather. As early as 1840 the family Mayir Fishbeyn – Orushe's son-in-law – operated tanneries that employed many workers. Mayir Orushe's sold leather in Danzig into his 70's.

In addition to trade, the Jews in Grayeve were an integral part of the general economy of the area. Jewish artisans worked and served the villages as well as the town. Jewish blacksmiths made plows, forged wagons, made harrows and scythes and shoed the horses; wheelwrights made wagons, barrels, wheels. Shoemaking, tailoring, carpentry, cap making, bakeries and saw-making were entirely Jewish pursuits in Grayeve. The same went for millers, barbers and wagon drivers. The latter served as transporters. Thus Grayeve was a very constructive, productive society.

Mayir Orushe's Fishbeyn, born
in Grayeve in 1798, died in 1898

Grayeve in the Polish Rebellion

After the illegal partition of Poland in 1795, especially after the Vienna Congress of the then great powers Russia, Germany and Austria, a part of Poland became known as Russian Poland.

In the great rebellion of Poles' struggle for Polish liberation in 1831, a Polish resistance army was concentrated around the large forest on the way from Grayeve to Raigrod under the leadership of Polish patriot Dombrowski.

To counter the rebels of the Grayeve area, the Russian government sent an army of 8,000 infantrymen, 2,000 artillerymen and thousands of cavalry soldiers. This was a large army for that time, which indicates the seriousness of the rebellion.

[Page 15]

It is also known that two Grayeve Jews were punished by the tsarist government for their participation and aid to the rebels. They were Leyzer Hepner and Dovid Kolko.

In the *History of the Jews in Poland and Russia*, Professor Dubnow [Shimen Dubnow 1860-1941] writes that in 1825 the Grand Duke Pawlowicz, who was appointed by Alexander the First to govern over Poland, issued a decree that Jews were forbidden to locate in an area within 50 viorsts of the western border unless the Jew had immoveable property. The Jews defended themselves against this brutal decree with every possible way and although it is not known how many Jews were driven out of the border towns by the decree, it is certain that the normal life and growth of the Jewish settlements in the border towns, including Grayeve, was much disturbed. That cruel law was only repealed in 1862 under the rule of Alexander the Second.

The *Encyclopedia Judaica* notes that in 1862, Jews in Poland were forbidden to be estate managers and to settle in Grayeve. That shows while the decree to drive Jews out of Grayeve and other border towns had been repealed, new Jewish immigrants were still prohibited from settling in Grayeve.

Grayeve, a trade center

The laying of the train line Brisk-Litovsk-Grayeve was finished around 1874. Grayeve then emerged on the map as an important trade town. Direct connections between Russia and Germany opened through Grayeve. Raw materials from Russia and industrial products from Germany passed through and were delivered to Grayeve.

Agricultural products from the entire area around Grayeve as well as from Ukraine and Russia were directed through Grayeve. Grayeve merchants traveled to Russia to buy horses, geese, grain, flax and so on and exported them through Grayeve to Germany. A Russian train went into Germany twice a day and twice a day a German train came into Grayeve. Big warehouses were built. Trade was expanded, a chamber of commerce was established and a duty house. Shipping bureaus were established, offices, and Grayeve became a central point in trade between Russia and Germany.

[Page 16]

With the rise in foreign trade big Jewish offices developed, with shipping houses and banks. Well known among the among the prominent Grayeve Jews were the business houses of Yezsherski, Vierzshblovski, Olshvanger, Zilbershteyn, Levin, Beynish Kolko, Bialystotski, Markus, Tutelman, Knorozovski and others.

In 1892, some of the mentioned wealthy men decided that praying in the old beys-medresh with all the craftsmen, paupers and wagon drivers did not suit them. And since the shul was not heated and moreover no one could pray there in the summer, the clerks and upcoming rich men decided to build a beys-medresh for themselves. That is how the new beys-medresh came to be built.

The *Slownik Geograficzni, Krulewstwa Polska*, edited in 1881, reports that in 1876 the exports through the Grayeve commercial center amounted to eight and a half million rubles and the imports, thirteen and a half million rubles, for a total of 22 million rubles worth going through Grayeve in one year; and the trade grew from year to year.

Grayeve had a large factory for rubber and suspenders, which was taken over by Hepner in 1896. In the production of suspenders the factory at one time employed 50 Jews in a combined total of 200 workers.

Grayeve also had a factory for the production of chemical fertilizer and glue for carpenters. The factory was called "the bone factory," because the bones of cattle were used in the production of the chemical fertilizer.

A factor contributing to trade in the town was the garrison for cavalry soldiers quartered in Grayeve in 1890, and consisting of eight squadrons totaling 1,200 people. Jewish merchants arranged provisions for the soldiers. The general providing for the soldiers increased the prosperity of the town.

There was also a big, modern schnapps factory in Grayeve. The factory belonged to the local gentry Jegelski and the manager was a Jew by the name of Khaym Bernzon.

[Page 17]

In Grayeve there was a glove factory too, which belonged to Kolken and in which Jewish women worked. The gloves were sent to be sold in the larger cities.

In the area of education there were, besides *khedarim* [Jewish religious schools] also a town school under the direction of Khenine Gron. In 1882 the school functioned under Gron and also had as teachers Feltin and Rotshild. Later the school was taken over by the teacher Shatski.

In 1890 the Grayeve area saw large military maneuvers of the regiments of the whole region. General Graf Szuwalow came from Warsaw to lead the maneuvers. Three delegations went out from the city to receive the elevated guests. The delegations were made up of the Russian, Polish and Jewish populations. The Jewish delegation consisted of elected proprietors from town led by Rov Eliahu Aron Milikovski. As was the custom, the delegation carried bread and salt on a silver tray. When they arrived at the reception the Jewish delegation was not allowed in. The wealthy Grayeve Jews Yezsherski and Vierzshbalovski reported the incident to the German press and the Berlin *Tageblatt* [German newspaper published in Berlin, 1872-1939] wrote very critically about it. Some time later Szuwalow called for the Grayeve council, by way of the Lomzhe governor, to send him the silver tray.

With the growth of commerce, industry and artisanry, the population of Grayeve grew as well. The *Slownik* reports that in 1880 there was already a population of 5,000 people in Grayeve, and in 1897 the population had grown to a total of 4,336 Jews and 3,315 Poles – a town of 8,000 people.

The physical appearance of the town changed with the construction of the train line. The neighborhood of the train station and the warehouses had previously been swamps. The entire quadrant was dried out and in place of the swamps a lovely market and a duty house were built besides the warehouses and train station. New streets were laid out and the town bloomed, so that by the end of the 19th century Grayeve had become an eminent, productive and commercial town.

[Page 18]

Bibliography:

1. *History of the Jews in Poland and Russia*, Professor Dubnow
2. *Slownik Geograficzni, Krulewstwa Polska*
3. *Encyclopedia Judaica*
4. Facts collected from private individuals:
a. Mr. Maks Vaks
b. Leon Beylis in Mount Vernon
c. Mrs. Sore Rivke Fishbeyn

A part of the Grayeve cemetery and the little lake, looking from River Street

Drawing by A. D. Fishbeyn

[Page 19]

Our Hometown, Grayeve
By Mayer Vaser
Translated by Tina Lunson

Dedicated to my dear life companion Manye (Miriam), killed in Treblinka, in August 1942; my only child Hanushe (Hinde), killed in Treblinka in August 1942 at the age of 16; my brother Gershon, who died in the Warsaw Ghetto in August 1940, and his wife, killed in Treblinka; my sister Khave Kantorovitsh and her husband Heshl and two boys, who perished along with all the Byalistok Jews; my brother Eliahu and his wife and two boys, killed in Treblinka; my sister Tsivie, killed along with all the Grayeve Jews.

A town like any town, one of over 600 "Jewish" towns and villages in the land of Poland.

The Jewish settlement in Poland was more than 800 years old before the Second World War. The Jews in Poland live through various times, good and bad. Apparently more were bad than good, but they always moved ahead.

Polish Jewry had a reputation in the larger world, wherever a Jew was found. In old times past, it was famous for scholars, loving kindness and good works. In the last few generations modern Jewish culture and literature arose in that place. Over a period of hundreds of years, Jewish Poland influenced all the Jewish settlements in the world.

The Jewish settlement in Poland also significantly affected its non-Jewish surroundings. But it was influenced in no small part by those same surroundings. Ideas of national and social freedom struck deep roots. Jewish youth threw themselves into the struggle to realize the thousand-year dreams of Jew and human with Hasidic fervor and self-sacrifice.

Then the Second World War began. Poland was destined to be the first flooded by the German-Hitlerist wave, which continued to roll over the countries of Europe with frightening impetus. It did not take long for the Hitlerist animals to tear out by the roots the ebullient Jewish settlement in Poland and to annihilate all the Jews there. Of the more than six million Jews killed during the Hitler slaughter in the ghettos, death camps and gas chambers of Majdanek, Treblinka, Sobibor, Oświęcim (Auschwitz) and others, approximately half of them were Jews from Poland.

[Page 20]

The pre-war settlement of more than three and a half million Jews in Poland is no more. The great majority of towns and villages where Jews had lived for centuries were now *"Judenrein"* ["clean of Jews"].

Our hometown Grayeve shared that same bitter fate. Our nearest and dearest were also driven in the death march of millions of victims – our blood brothers and sisters, fathers and mothers. Their huge, unknown common grave is leveled off with the ground. No kind of gravestone, no kind of marker indicates the place of their murder.

We want to recall them in the most unassuming way. We want to try to record their life, their joys and sorrows, concerns and celebrations in the times before the bloody flood.

With its own face

Although it was a small town, Grayeve distinguished itself from its surroundings. Grayeve had its peculiarities, which separated it from the other surrounding towns larger and smaller than Grayeve. The particular face of Grayeve was formed over time. But at the turn of this century the physiognomy of the town was already clear and definite. And that period until the First World War we will record here.

Two factors had a decided effect on the development of Grayeve. First, the nearness of the German border: in total about 4 viorsts (a little more than 2 American miles) separated Grayeve from the Prussian border town of *Prostken* [Prostki]. Second, because of the train junction with Germany, Grayeve became a transit point for lively traffic in international trade.

Grayeve was the last train station of the big southeast train line that ran from Odessa by the Black Sea, through Kiev and Ukraine, cut through Polesia (*Brisk* [Brest, Belarus]) and then through *Byalistok* [Białystok] and ended in Grayeve.

Not one of the surrounding towns had a train junction. Not even the larger provincial capitols – *Lomzhe* [Łomża] on one side and *Suvalk* [**Suwałki**] on the other side – had a train junction until well into the 1890's. Thus Grayeve became the transit center for merchandise that arrived by train for all the towns and villages near and far. From there, the merchandise was distributed to the surrounding towns by large and small wagons and covered wagons.

[Page 21]

How did Jews make a living?

Export

The most important thing in the life of Grayeve was the border. All kinds of grains were exported through Grayeve to Germany, from as far away as deep Russia and Ukraine. Of those Grayeve Jews who took part in the grain export, the following names remain in my memory: Shtrausberg, the Bufenshteyns, Meyshe Ayzik Vaynshteyn, and Borkovski. Lumber was exported as well, raw and finished, that came from the Polesia forests.

In general the export was diverse. So for example, mushrooms from the Belorussian forests were exported. Grayeve Jews – the brothers Ravidovitsh, Yankl Ginzburg, Nosn Frank and others made a profit from it. Kempner and his sons exported flax. Crayfish were also exported. But eggs, especially goose eggs, took the top place in exports. Horses also held an important place in export.

The geese were brought from Russia. During the summer almost everyday whole trains went by with tens of cars loaded with geese. On the German side of the border the geese had to go through quarantine. If the inspector found even a couple of sick geese in a car, the whole car was sent back to Grayeve. In such cases the merchants often tried to drive the geese along the highway through *Bogushe* [Bogusze] to Prostken, where the inspection was not so strict.

Among the geese dealers were Yankl Vadovski, Leyb Vanovitsh, Rinkovski, Yudeinski and others.

[Page 22]

The horse export developed very significantly. Grayeve horse dealers used to travel deep into Russia to buy horses raised on the broad Russian steppes. Whole trainloads, with eight horses to a car, went through Grayeve to Germany. Some of the exported horses went beyond Germany to other countries. During the English-Boer War (1899) thousands of horses that had been bought for the English Army passed through Grayeve.

The rise and development of the Grayeve horse trade was very curious. For tens of years Grayeve Jews traveled to Germany to sell grease for wagons. From one season to another, from after Peysakh until Sukes [the festival of booths] and from after Sukes until Peysakh, Grayeve *dzshegtshares* [tar dealers] traveled around among the villages of Prussia and other German territories in their covered wagons, in order to buy up their goods. They made their living that way. Gradually the more enterprising of the dzshegtshares went into horse dealing and worked their way up very well. Specific horse dealers were Yamshun with his partner Shimer, Bialishevski, Vayslovski,

Kalinovski. One of the horse dealers, Kurlender, settled in *Breslev* [**Braslaw**] where he possessed his own large horse stable.

Import

A large role in Grayeve's development was played by the import of foreign goods that passed the Grayeve border and through the customs house on the way to Russia. The goods were quite varied, but the majority consisted of machines and parts for machines for Russian industry. The import of herring played a specific role, being shipped to Poland, *Belorussia* [Belarus] and even further. Over many years carloads of dynamite for the coal mines in southern Russia and for the oil wells in the Caucasus passed over the border.

A number of shipping offices sprang up around the import of foreign goods. Their work was to calculate the border tariff for the customs and to send the goods further on to their places of destination. However the Russian tariff was very complicated. It took long years until an employee could specialize as a declarer of the border tariff.

[Page 23]

The shipping offices were in Jewish hands. The most important of them were: N. Yezsherski, the brothers Levin, Eliahu Verzshbalovski, Alshvanger and Fayfenzilber, Yudl Bialistotski. Beynish Kolko and Mayer Zilbershteyn were partly involved. A large number of youths from among the wealthier class were employed in those offices. Verzshbalovski and Yezsherski were bankers during that same time, representatives of large banks in Warsaw.

In contrast to export, which Grayeve Jews ran with their own hands and responsibility, their role in import was a more limited one. It consisted only of the function of handling the border tariffs and sending the merchandise further on.

The Secret Border Trade

A wide-branching illegal trade went on around the border. A couple hundred people were drawn into it. Various goods were smuggled in from Germany that way, beginning with warm underwear and other merchandise up to German lottery tickets and even revolvers for the Polish and Russian revolutionaries and for Jewish self-defense against pogroms around 1905.

In the morning dozens of people – men, women and even children – would travel by train to Prussia and then return laden with illegal goods. The border patrol and the overseers at the customs house were usually bribed and they turned a blind eye. But there were also cases of failure, with arrests and prosecutions.

Besides the train, smuggling also went on through the border by the village Bogushe. A highway that started at the edge of town, at the end of Bogushe Street, led to the border point. Tens of wagons with passengers drove back and forth. It was not a secret to anyone that a large part of the passengers came back loaded with illegal goods.

[Page 24]

Another place was used for illegal emigration through the border. Tens of thousands of Jewish émigrés stole across the border around Grayeve on their way to America. Among the illegal immigrants were also revolutionaries, and not only Jews. So, for example, it is known that the eventual president of the Polish republic between the two world wars, Moszcicki, stole the border at Bogushe in his young revolutionary years.

Industry

Grayeve did not possess any special industry. However at times, thanks to the proximity of Grayeve to the border, efforts were made to establish factories that would be supplied with raw materials brought from Germany, and not necessarily by "kosher" means. Several such efforts succeeded. The enterprises became established and later did not need to receive raw materials smuggled over the border.

At the beginning of the 1880s a certain Aronson started a weaving factory, for silk ribbons. In the later years the factory was moved to *Byalistok*, where it existed for many years.

At about that same time a factory for manufacturing rubber products, like elastic bands for shoes, suspenders, and sock-bands, was created in Grayeve. The founders were Leyzer Hepner and his son Leybl Meyshe, and son-in-law Hersh Vaser. Another partner in the factory was a German Jew Zalinger from *Lik* (Prussia) [Ełk, Prussia]. After several years they had to give up the factory. It was taken over by a Suvalk banker, Pokroiski. Because Pokroiski got entangled in his banking business, the factory was auctioned off in 1896. Then it was bought by one of it founders, Leybl Meyshe (Volf) Hepner.

Over a period of several years Hepner was able to improve the condition of the factory. In time it became one of the most modern and largest in its field in Europe. It employed almost 300 workers. Most of the workers, weavers, spinners and so on, were not Jews. Jewish workers worked only in the ready-made department that manufactured suspenders and sock-halters. Jews also worked in the box department and in making crates.

In the 1890s Yosl Bialostotski built a chemical factory that was crowned in the mouth of the folk as the "bone mill." The factory used bones in the manufacture of glue and also fertilizer. In hindsight, that factory was one of the first in the great land of the tsar.

[Page 25]

The brothers Rinkovski established an umbrella factory. That factory supported Jews. Leyble Yokhson also started a similar factory.

In 1905 Berl Gershuni founded a factory for mother-of-pearl buttons. He employed tens of workers, mostly non-Jews.

In the latter years a certain Shtaygman built a steam mill. There was also a tannery in Grayeve, which belonged to Leybl Levit and his son Tuvia.

Trade

The entire internal town trade was in Jewish hands. Of the large number of shops that filled the market square on all four sides and parts of Highway Street, Raigrod Street, Shul Street and others, only a few were not Jewish.

They were mostly small shops for the needs of the town people, the majority of them Jews, and of the surrounding village population. On market days, Tuesday and Friday, the peasants brought grain, potatoes, eggs and fowl into town to sell, and also wood and peat for heating. With the money that they earned they bought what they needed for their own households in the Jewish shops.

The fairs were very lively. Hundreds of peasant wagons filled the market, the Shul Street and all the surrounding streets. Besides the already-mentioned village products, the peasants then brought cows and horses to sell. The buyers were once again Jews. And in the Jewish shops, as in the market trade, there were good proceeds from the peasants.

Among the shops there were a row of larger ones, for example, the fabric shops of Etl Mishkovski, Zerekh Elkan, the ironmonger Avrom Yankl Zshmievski, the bakery and delicatessen of Sapirshteyn and Vigodski.

Providing products for the military took its own place – there was a troop of cavalry and a brigade of border patrol stationed nearby.

[Page 26]

The Grayeve Jews Leyzer Hepner and his son Leybl Meyshe and son-in-law Hersh Vaser built the barracks for the troops. Leybl Meyshe Hepner later also built the buildings for the administration of the border patrol and living quarters for the officers. Meyshe Babkovski built the barracks for the border patrol.

The largest proportion of products for the military was provided by Jewish contractors: Bernshteyn, Dorn, Kats, Epshteyn, Burshteyn, and others.

The Grayeve Jews Knarzovski, Meyshe Shaye Zshmievski and Babkovski, as building contractors, erected government buildings, bridges and roads in various towns and regions.

For many years Grayeve merchants leased ponds, both on this side of the border, like *Tatshilova* [Toczyłowo] and on the Prussian side. Issakar Koptshovski and Mayer Novinski – both sons-in-law of the first and oldest wealthy Grayever, Podbielski – kept ponds for fishing in the famous Prussian Mazur Lakes.

Crafts

Crafts were also almost exclusively in Jewish hands. First the tailors, among them the best tradesmen in the area: Meyshe Mendl Kureyvovski and his son Yankl Yudke; Hamburg, Avrom Itsik and others. There were no non-Jewish tailors in Grayeve. The same for the shoemakers: Lozshe, Tuvia, Shepsl, Shimon, Gershon (with the exception of one Laskovski). Most of them worked to order, but there were also some who worked for the market.

Besides tailors, shoemakers and cap-makers, there were carpenters, locksmiths, tinsmiths, painters, masons, wheelwrights and blacksmiths. The latter consisted of whole "dynasties" of grandfathers, fathers and grandchildren. The bakers were also Jews, among them Moti Abramski, Peysakh Starozshinski, Rutke Bagish and her sons Gedalye and Shaye Leyzer, Langus, Efroym Zeligzon, Mikhl Tsibulski and others. There were watchmakers, Levi Tenenboym and Ziberski. Both worked together with their sons. And of course there was the goldsmith Levin. Also the butchers and fishers were Jews.

The number of wagon-drivers and porters was large. Some of the wagon-drivers distributed the goods from the train to the surrounding towns.

[Page 27]

Outside the town there were several Dutch windmills. The mills served mostly the peasants. They also made rye flour for the bakers. Two of the windmills belonged to the brothers Avrom-Itskhak and Khaym Katsprovski. Leybl Tutlman, Markus and others brought better wheat flour by train from Russia.

Intellectual Life

Considering it was such a small town, its intellectual life was very multi-hued. People not only prayed in the Large Shul, in the *bote-medroshim* [Houses of Study] and in the Hasidic *shtiblekh* [small house of prayer used by Hasidim], they also studied with gusto. There were a number of scholars in town, who were known far around.

The education of the younger generation was mostly observant orthodox. Besides the *khedarim* [Jewish religious schools] there was also a Talmud Torah and a small yeshiva.

Thanks to their connections to the larger world, Grayeve, earlier than the surrounding towns, was infected with the spirit of the *haskole* [Jewish enlightenment movement]. The first *maskilim* [proponents of the Jewish enlightenment movement] were Knarzovski, Avrom Mordkhe Piurka, Leybl Kolko, and others.

Piurka was really a great scholar and knowledgeable in all the wisdom of Judaism. He was also a Hebrew writer and master of Hebrew grammar.

A class of Jewish girl pupils before the First World War

[Page 28]

As a teacher of Hebrew, he planted a love for the language of the prophets in a large number of the youth. He demonstrated much knowledge and initiative in collecting and giving out Hebrew textbooks. He put his meager earnings to use in publishing the first children's journal in Hebrew, "Gan sheashuim." Unable to obtain a permit for the journal from the tsarist government, he initially had to have it printed in Lik (Prussia). By the way, there was still no printing press in Grayeve then. Later, A. M. Piurka himself established a printing press – that was incidentally the only Jewish press in the entire region – and a Jewish book dealership.

Khibes Tsien – Zionism

The rise of *khibes tsien*[1] found a reverberation in Grayeve. In the 1890s there were about 80 *khovevi-tsien* [members of khibes tsien] in Grayeve, who paid the three rubles a year every year to the *Odessa Committee*[2] of the *khovevi-tsien*. Indeed those members built the foundation of the first Zionist organization in Grayeve, *Bney tsien* [Children of Zion]. Already at the *First Zionist Congress*[3] in Basel, the Grayeve Zionists were represented by their own delegates, Beynush Kolko and Ravidovitsh.

The orthodox Jews had, as everywhere, initially looked askance at the Zionists. There were disputes and feuds. The Rov Mileykovski (later rov in Kharkov) used to try to smooth things out, but without success.

A significant role in the development of Zionism in Grayeve was played by Yankev Olshvanger (died as a young doctor) and his brother Alek (been in Israel for many years). While they were still university students, coming home for holidays and vacations, they arranged lectures on Zionist topics. Elimelekh Pomerants also played a certain role.

The Libraries

Grayeve also had the first Yiddish-Hebrew library in the area. The foundation was laid by one Grinboym, an employee in Yezsherski's office. He contributed his own library of a few hundred books, mostly Hebrew. He also set his own residence at the library's disposal (in Yamshun's house).

[Page 29]

The library became the gathering place for the Zionists. Non-Zionist youths who were wearied by the difficult questions that Jewish life and life in general brought up, also came there.

In time there came a division of thinking. Some of the youth then tried to establish another library. But that was not so easy, because one had to first get a permit from the police authorities. They convinced Eliahu Vaks, who was "kosher" in the eyes of the police that the request should be made in his name. But the further development of general events in 1905, it seems, upset the realization of the plan.

As usual, there was also a shadow-side to intellectual life in Grayeve. It was the conflict around rabbis, Jewish judges and slaughterers; between *misnagdim* [opponents of Hasidism] and Hasidim; then between orthodox and Zionist that would from time to time overheat their dispositions. Also the standard disagreements between fathers and children; between young and old were vividly reflected in Grayeve. All that could not noticeably weaken the intensive intellectual life that, in hindsight, pushed our town forward relative to the neighboring towns.

As regards living together with the non-Jewish neighbors in that time, it was initially not bad. Active anti-Semitism only began in 1912, after the elections to the fourth Russian parliament, when Jewish voters in Warsaw elected the Polish socialist Jagelo. From then on, one could notice continually worsening relationships in Grayeve too. The whole Lomzhe region in time became – especially between the two world wars – one of the most poisonous nests of anti-Semitism in half-fascist, pre-war Poland.

Workers' Movement

The first efforts to draw the Jewish worker into community life were made in 1901-1902. This was done by several young Zionists, led by Elimelekh Pomerants.

[Page 30]

In those days the workers, actually the handworkers' associations – tailors, shoemakers, carpenters and so on – worked from before dawn until late at night. They took short breaks to pray and to eat. On Thursdays they often worked the entire night. Also Shabes night after *havdole* [the end of Shabbat, separating it from regular weekdays], they went back to work until midnight.

At first the only goal was to draw the workers into the circle of the Zionist movement. An attic room was rented in Meylekh Vaks' house. Shabes and holidays they prayed there in their own *minyon* [prayer quorum of 10 Jewish adult men]. Discussions of Zionist themes were also held there.

At that time there was already a powerful revolutionary, socialist movement going on among the Jewish workers and the youth in almost all the towns and villages of the Pale. Individual socialists and revolutionaries showed up in Grayeve too. They were workers from other towns – carpenters, printers, who were working temporarily in Grayeve. There were a few Grayeve workers too, who had worked in larger towns like Byalistok or Warsaw, and also students. But the town as such – the workers and the youth in general – were still little touched by the revolutionary, socialistic current of that time.

A change took place by degrees. As a consequence of the defeats in the Russian-Japanese war in 1904-1905, the air in the huge land of the tsar was laden with social gunpowder. A revolutionary wave poured everywhere over the country.

Then one could notice a change in the mood among the Grayeve youth in general and the workers in particular. The leadership of the Grayeve *poale-tsien*[4] was taken over by the young Zionist idealist, Mordkhe Rembelinker. They began to devote more attention to the unmet needs and wants of the workers.

Strikes and Clashes

In the summer of 1905 there were strikes, the main one by the tailors' association. ☐During a strike in the tailoring workshop of Yankl Yudke Kureyvovski there was a sharp physical clash and the police were called in.

[Page 31]

The police looked on the workers with suspicion. One had to watch out for a "good eye" from every policeman and gendarme. Because of this the gatherings of the poale-tsien had to be held in the forest outside the town. [4*]

Mordkhe Rembelinker

Elimelekh Pomerants
Hebrew teacher and Zionist activist

A series of strikes by the non-Jewish workers took place in Hepner's elastic factory. And the Jewish workers – stitchers and others – went out on strike too. But an event occurred that was characteristic for many Jewish manufacturers in that time.

[Page 32]

Hepner had no choice but to give in to the demands of the weavers and of the other non-Jewish workers. But he stubbornly refused even to negotiate with the striking Jewish workers. The strike lasted for weeks. Recognizing that he could not break the strike, the manufacturer closed the division where the Jewish workers had worked (ready-made). He shipped the work off to Warsaw to be finished. This was a terrible blow for tens of Jewish workers and their families, who were left hungry because of the truculence and powerfulness of a Jewish manufacturer. One of the leaders of the strike was Itshe Vilenski, a quilter who died along with the martyrs of the Warsaw Ghetto.

Political Awakening

Within the poale-tsien itself, individual members who were not happy with the apolitical and exclusively Zionist character of the organization, began to break off. The dissatisfied members found themselves under the strong impression of the revolutionary activity of the *Bund*[5], which among Jews played the leading role in the struggle against tsarism in the area of the Pale of Settlement.

At the end of the summer, Abush Kolko (son of Beynish Kolko) returned to Grayeve. All of 18 years old, he already had a "history" behind him. For his sympathies to the revolutionary movement and the Bund, he had earlier been expelled from the Suvalk *gimnazye* [secondary school]. He then became an employee in a pharmacy in one of the weaving towns near Moscow (apparently *Ivanova-Voznesensk* [Ivanovo]). Kolko was arrested during a strike by the local weavers. Because he was a minor he was shipped home under police supervision.

The disaffected among the poale-tsien grouped themselves around Kolko. Along with the writer of these lines (who used to help Rembelinker in the poale-tsien), the dissatisfied youth tried to win over the entire organization to their side. However they ran into resistance from Rembelinker, Antshkovski and others.

[Page 33]

During Sukes 1905 proclamations from the Bund suddenly appeared on the streets, on the walls, and also in the bote-medroshim. They caused a great stir. A Bund organization was also created, which quickly won over a large part of the poale-tsien. Endless discussions went on between the two organizations. Lengthy open discussion groups were also held, with the participation of representatives of both organizations who had been brought back from outside (Byalistok).

The failure of the revolution in 1905 was accompanied by a frightful political reaction. Abush Kolko was arrested in Grayeve and taken to the Lomzhe jail. A case was made against him to include all of his "sins." After a year in jail he was sentenced to hard labor for two years and eight months and then to deportation to Siberia. This "milder" sentence was motivated by his youth. In 1912 he escaped from the place of his deportation place in Siberia, and came to America where he remained until 1917. From then on he was in the Soviet Union.

The reaction also drove the Grayeve workers' movement underground. But the kindled flame was not entirely extinguished. Years later, at the first opportunity, the movement came to the surface again.

* * *

That is how life appeared in our hometown in those times. It was not an expansive life. It did not lack for worries and frequent trouble, but there were also joys; it was intellectually and socially on the rise.

It is hard to make peace with the thought that today there is no trace left in Grayeve, that the German Hitlerite hordes killed all the Jews in Grayeve and that the town of our childhood and youth, where a robust Jewish life pulsed, is now "Judenrein."

We Grayever, sown all over the world, will surely hold in our hearts the memory of our dearest and nearest – fathers and mothers, sisters, and brothers, relatives and friends, of all the Grayeve Jews who were savagely annihilated by the cruel assassins.

Footnotes

1 *khibes tsien:* associations of proto-Zionist study groups formed in Europe from about 1880 until 1902-1903, after which they merged into the Zionist movement.
2 *Odessa Committee:* "The Society for the Support of Jewish Farmers and Artisans in Syria and Palestine," was a pre-Zionist charitable organization which supported immigration to Eretz Israel and helped Jews engage in productive work, particularly in the field of agriculture.
3 *First Zionist Congress*: organized by Theodor Herzl and held in Basel, Switzerland on 29 Aug 1897. Its main goal was to establish a home for the Jewish people in Eretz Israel.
4 *Poale-Tsion:* movement of Marxist Zionist Jewish workers in the Russian empire active around the turn of the 20th century.
4* [written by author, M.V.] Of the *poale-tsien* of that time Heyman Blum, Sam Krinski, Rafoel Kats, Hershl Zaydenburg, Philip Buzman, Beni Bagish, Adom Taytelboym, and others are now in America.
5 *Bund*: Jewish Labor Bund was a secular anti-Zionist socialist party in the Russian empire active around the turn of the 20th century. They focused primarily on furthering the rights and status of the Jewish proletariat

[Page 34]

The shul, besmedresh and *oheves khesed* [love of charity] – drawn by A. D. Fishbeyn

[Page 35]

Grayeve – Aspiring and Dreaming
By Professor Shimen Rabidovitsh
A Chapter of Memoirs
Translated by Tina Lunson

What I am writing here about is our common birthplace, the sacred community Grayeve, based on my youthful impressions up to the year 1914. We left Grayeve exactly the fifth week of the First World War, as did many other families "*biezshenes*," or refugees, as they were called. Since 1914 I have to my great regret, not visited Grayeve. I regret very deeply that I did not in these 30 years accept a proposal to make a lecture tour across Poland, because I would certainly have visited the town of my youth.

The Grayeve Jewish community in the years before the First World War was naturally like all small provincial communities in the *Lomzhe* [Łomża] province and the neighboring areas: economically an average community, mainly merchants and shopkeepers, a few artisans and quite a few pious, exemplary Jews. Grayeve was different in certain respects, in that it was a border town and there was daily and very lively contact with Eastern Prussia (*Prostken* or *Prostki* as Grayeve Jews called it; *Lik* [Ełk] to *Kenigsberg* [Kaliningrad] where Grayevers used to visit the professors; *Kranz* [Kręsk] where the rich went in summer "to the baths"), on one side and with the large Jewish center of *Byalistok* [Białystok] on the other side.

[Page 36]

Although geographically Grayeve was certainly Poland, its Jewish settlement belonged intellectually and linguistically to *Lite* [Ashkenazi Lithuania]. It was typically *Litvish* [Lithuanian Yiddish dialect] in its style of learning (such as Talmud study).

The Grayeve community was religiously orthodox through and through with an overwhelming majority of *misnagdim* [opponents of Hasidism]. There were also two large Hasidic prayer rooms, *Kotsk*[1] and *Ger*[2]; and there were also a few individual followers of other Hasidic *rabeim* [Hasidic rabbis]. Not one Jewish shop was open on Shabes (except for Shvarts' pharmacy, but what Grayeve Jew would go to buy ordinary things not necessary for saving a life?). Since the majority of the shops were Jewish and the Poles from the surrounding villages only came to Grayeve when there was something to buy, the Shabes rest in Grayeve was total, in the strictest sense of the word. Even the somewhat free youth, who began to be bold in Grayeve shortly before 1914 –including several students of *gimnazyes* [secondary schools] who came back to their home town for vacation – did not dare to go out on the street carrying a stick on Shabes. Perhaps the Jewish doctors were a little more lenient in that respect – the doctor and the pharmacist in every Jewish town enjoyed a bit of a "privileged" position concerning the religious lifestyle and one was often not as strict with them.

Of the Grayeve wigmakers – there were a total of four Jewish wigmaker shops – it seems that one or two had the "courage" to edge in on Shabes a little (but really just a little) after the *shames* [beadle] Zalman Zmude the Lame, had already shouted out from the main streets of Grayeve *"In shul arayn!"* [Get into shul!], which always sounded like *"In-el-shul-arayn."* Why they chose a limping beadle for that strenuous function, I really do not know. (Grayeve beadles are a chapter unto themselves.)

Even the small circle of shippers and their employees, some of whom had to go to the train station on Shabes and desecrate it in public, were officially and practically *besmedresh* [house of study] Jews. They did not pray in the congregation every day, maybe not even every Monday and Thursday [when Torah is read], but Rosheshone, interim days, Purim, not to even mention Shabes and holidays, they were in the study-house in their *taleysim* [prayer shawls] with all the other Grayeve Jews, and some even with a talis over his head, like the others.

In that detail Jewish Grayeve had the same face as most Jewish towns in Russia, especially the small towns with a compact Jewish population. So Grayeve's Jewishness was total, with a set way of life; a Jewishness of "when you lie down and when you rise up...." [from the *Shema* - the basic tenet of Judaism], from the first day of birth when *kheyder* [Jewish religious school] boys came to the child-bed to read the *krishma*[3] and receive a packet of nuts and sweets; until the funeral in the cemetery at the end of Shul Street which was the horror of every Grayeve Jewish child, especially during long winter evenings at school and even more so going home in the moonless nights. (The gas lamps in the middle of the Grayeve market square near the pump were installed much later.)

[Page 37]

2

The social and political life of the Grayeve community was not highly developed, as in the majority of the provincial towns of the same type. The few *maskilim* [followers of the Jewish Enlightenment] in Grayeve lived as the other Jews. The revolutionary spirit at the beginning of the century found a weak echo among the Grayeve youth, especially when compared with, for example, the great mobility and activity of various Jewish circles in not-so-distant Byalistok (which had Jewish factories, Jewish industrialists and workers). Only a small part of Grayeve artisans, especially the younger ones and a few intellectuals – that is, a few gimnazye and other students, but they were very few in number, limited to only a few families in town – got carried away by the waves of the distant revolutionary movement. As far as I recall, there was no actual organized Jewish socialist party of a certain scope, like the "*Bund*"[4] or *Poalei Tsion*.[5] A few individuals received illegal literature from Byalistok and other places, which they spread a little among the artisans and the youth; and a small circle of "left" young people used to gather in the cemetery particularly on Tishebov when all the Jews go to that "good place," to visit their ancestors' graves. The police did not suspect that those few young people went there for a completely different reason.

Grayeve had many societies and charity organizations, like other Jewish towns.

[Page 38]

Shortly before the war the Jews had begun to organize a kind of collective lending society, a cooperative bank, which was needed to help and protect the Jewish merchant against the Polish boycott and the agricultural expansionism of their competitors.

Relatively, the most touching political group was *Khibat Tsion* [lovers of Zion] movement which also found a lively response in Grayeve. However, the founding of "political Zionism," by Theodore Herzl probably shocked a lot of the earlier, older proponents of the idea of a settlement in Erets Yisroel.

3

As I am writing a page in a chapter about "Zionism in Grayeve" I must connect it to my father, Reb [Mr.] Khaym Itsik of blessed memory, although I do not intend to write my father's biography, and certainly not my own autobiography. However, my father was the "head of Zionism" in Grayeve and so involved all of his days, that I cannot separate them. He was sent as a delegate from the Lomzhe province to the 7th Zionist Congress [Basel Switzerland, 1905] – after Herzl's death, when the question of Uganda was discussed. My father belonged to the naysayers, although the *mizrakhi* [religious Zionist party] under the leadership of *Rov* ["Rabbi"] Reynes said "yes" to Uganda.

The overwhelming majority of Grayeve Jews were very apathetic toward Zionism, uninterested, or neutral. The more conscious, intelligent leaders of the orthodoxy were even strongly opposed, passively or actively. My father told me that the contemporary Rov Eliahu Aron Milikovski – the author of *Oheli Aron* [Aaron's tents] printed his book in Grayeve. He later became rov in Kharkov and eventually head of the *beys-din* [Jewish court] in Tel Aviv, where he passed away after having reached a great old age – had initially been sympathetic, but later under moral pressure from the direction of Rov Khaym Brisker, the greatest Talmud authority in Russia at the time, became estranged from Zionism. His follower, Rov Moyshe Avigdor Amiel (later lived in Antwerp and then became the head rabbi in Tel Aviv) stood at a distance from Zionism until the war years.

[Page 39]

I recall that the Zionist preacher and religious writer Rov Itsik Nisnboym in *Varshe* [Warsaw] had even written to my father in 1913 that Rov Amiel – then a candidate for the Grayeve rabbinate – was no sympathizer of Zionism. In the war years Rov Amiel joined the mizrakhi and became one of its most important ideologues and spiritual leaders.

Even as a young child I often came up against opposition to Zionism from many religious Jews in Grayeve. What they did not dare say to my father's face they told me while I was sitting with them by the big oven in the new besmedresh studying Talmud. To them, Zionism and heresy were synonymous. My father would probably have been strongly persecuted if he had not been a true God-fearing Jew who constantly studied in the besmedresh. He was the only Jewish merchant in Grayeve who went every day before dawn to the first *minyen* [prayer quorum of 10 Jewish adult men], to pray and study a page of Talmud before making his daily visit to his granary office in Prostken. The great respect the ultra-orthodox Grayeve Jews had for the head of the Zionists in their town somewhat counterbalanced the orthodox opposition to Zionism and prevented it from taking on radical forms. However, my father was not completely kosher in the eyes of those very pious Jews. "Reb Khaym Itsik is a little caught up in the story," they would say amongst themselves, and I would often hear it in the new besmedresh in Grayeve, where I spent a large part of my youth.

Not only was our home the "*tsienistish*" [Zionist] center in Grayeve, so was our granary. Residing for many years among my father's goods, were the remains of the first library in Grayeve, which the Zionists had founded on *Shtutzin* [Szczuczyn] Street. It was in the granary in a dark brown bookcase before I was even able to read, where I first saw *Hashliakh*[6] [The Emissary] and *Akhiasaf*[6] and other Hebrew publications. As I came to understand, the library was closed soon after its founding because of fear of the Grayeve police (Zionist societies were not legalized in Russia and Poland at the time). The holdings were hidden in the chief Zionist's granary until shortly before the War when a small Yiddish-Hebrew lending library was founded again in Grayeve.

[Page 40]

The meetings of the leading Zionists in town took place in our home. There were no official elections among the Grayeve Zionists. "Parliamentary procedure" had not evolved in little towns like Grayeve, but people knew exactly who the chief Zionist was and his most active colleagues. The Grayeve police knew that as well and often made house searches, rummaging through all the cupboards, desk drawers and bookcases ("*savantkes*" in Grayeve Yiddish). Even if they found no *sheklim* [coins] or National Fund collection boxes, it still had to cost five or ten rubles [in bribes] to prevent them from making a "protocol" against father. As we use to say, "That's how the story went." It is hard to say whether the house searches resulted from denunciations. It was enough for some kind of Zionist speaker or Erets Yisroel messenger [*meshulekh*] (as we called it then, their modern heirs are now called *shlikhim*) to visit us and stay overnight, to result in two or three policemen turning our whole house upside down. Initially we were terrified, but then we became accustomed to these uninvited visitors. As a result, my father kept the Zionist literature, collection boxes and other heretical materials on the other side of the border at his granary in Prostken for security reasons.

4

How easy it is to be a Zionist today. The younger generation cannot imagine how hard it was during those years in our Grayeve. The Bund had little influence on the artisans or on the youth because then, only a few had been influenced by socialism. The strong hand of the Grayeve police was able to defeat much of their influence. They were "real *goyim*" [Gentiles, non-Jews], that is to say that they were indeed on the take. The greatest difficulty for Zionism was the traditional apathy of the middle class, which was the majority of the Grayeve community council in addition to the ideological opposition of the *Kovne* [Kaunas, Lithuania] "black office"[7] and other militant orthodox circles.

[Page 41]

After many battles my father for example, was allowed on the *bime* [Torah-reading platform] in the new besmedresh on *Shabes nakhamu* ["Shabes of comfort" after Tishebov] and Shimshen the beadle was allowed to recite the prayer of blessing for the Odessa "Council for the Settlement in Erets Yisroel." This eventually became a custom in the other Grayeve bote-medroshim. Later my father was also "allowed" to recite the laments for Zion and "God of Zion" on Tishebov morning. The others who recited the laments began to feel this was a "monopoly" of the chief Zionist and thus a great triumph for the small handful of Zion-dreamers in Grayeve. Among them I would especially like to mention: Khaym Katsperovsken, a miller and an excellent prayer leader for *Rosheshone* ["head of the year" or commonly known as the Jewish New Year], whom we used to call Khaym-nigune-milrah because when he sang *zokhreynu lekhaym* [remember us to life] the accents were on the last syllables. There was also Yankev Yehoshue Kharmin, whose nickname in Grayeve was Storazum. He was the Zionist school teacher to whom my father gave strong moral support and whose kheyder he sent all 5 of his sons. This was considered a "modern" religious school since we studied from Shnayder's text book Beys seyfer, which was more contemporary than what they studied in other Grayeve khedarim.

There was also Elimelekh Pomerants the dear and devoted Hebrew teacher (I also studied with him one semester); Hershl Koptshilovski, a very great idealist, a fine person and a son of one of the finest families in Grayeve. He died in the First World War on the road between Shtutzin and Grayeve. Other notable names include: Berl Rozen, Faynshteyn, Zeydke Berman, Khinkovski, my uncle Mordkhe Rembelinker, Gevirtsman, the younger Tzvi Vislovski, Dr. Shaul Olshvanger, a dear Hebraist and son of the family who produced several Jewish scholars and Zionist activists (Emanuel Olshvanger, Alek Olshvanger in Erets Yisroel, my friend Eliahu Olshvanger now living in Switzerland who was gifted with a treasury of wisdom and love of the holy language, although he was long considered a Yiddishist. Before I left for America, Eliahu came to London and begged me, almost decreed that I not go to America, but to Erets

Yisroel). Dr. Shaul Olshvanger, like all of his brothers brought a new atmosphere to Grayeve. They combined in themselves Russian and German culture and to this day still occupy a special place in the history of Grayeve intelligentsia.

[Page 42]

At age fifteen I once went to Dr. Olshvanger as a patient for one single reason: I wanted the pleasure and honor of being medically examined by someone who spoke Hebrew. The fifty kopecks from my "private fund" were well worth it, even though I did not then need a doctor. What a luxury for a young Hebraist in Grayeve to be able to enjoy!

5

I will briefly describe the main activities of the small Zionist group in Grayeve. They consisted mostly of collecting money and propaganda – in today's language, the struggle to recognize the commandment to settle Erets Yisroel; presenting verses and quotations from the *Mishne* [2nd century BCE collection and oral interpretations of Jewish law] to show that Erets Yisroel was "kosher." In fact, many of the holidays were used for intensive Zionist effort. On Tishebov they collected money for *keren kayemet leyisroel* [Jewish National Fund]. "*Sheklim*" were sold the whole year and prior to the Zionist Congresses. All the pledges were for Erets Yisroel on Shabes nakhamu. A separate activity was developed for the month of *Elul*[8] for selling *esroygim* [citrons used for *Sukes*, the festival of booths]. The most observant of the observant used to agitate strongly against esroygim from Erets Yisroel because the Jewish colonists were generally heretics and they did not observe the sabbatical year of rest. Instead of Erets Yisroel, they imported esroygim from Corfu – but right afterward there was a pogrom against Jews in Corfu. In the month of Elul the Grayeve bote-medroshim began seething with the esroygim question.

I used to go around to the bote-medroshim nailing up long proclamations using every source of the holy literature that it wasn't a sin to buy an Erets Yisroel esreg, but rather the opposite; it was a very great *mitsve* [commandment]. It was even written: "and you shall take from your own" and so on. I went to the trouble of nailing up the proclamation on the doors of the bote-medroshim – the only publicity center in old Grayeve – and our pious opponents ripped them down, just as they tore down every announcement about Zionist speakers such as Nisenboym or Yevzerov, who used to come to Grayeve. Even the word *"matef"* ["speaker"] was a thorn in their eyes.

[Page 43]

Why just matef and not *magid* [preacher] or *darshen* [orator]? My rebi, Rov Berele (a grandson of Yudke the coachman, who traveled the "line" between Grayeve and Lomzhe) used to tell me, it is not for nothing that they are called matef, because it is written, "for floating you shall be floated and those who floated you shall be floated" [Mishne: a metaphor for someone who killed a person and whose head was seen floating in the river].

We did not need to concern ourselves with announcements. My father would order a couple hundred Erets Yisroel esroygim and *lulovim* [palm branches] from Odessa or Varshe and the last two weeks before Sukes our house became partly an esroygim market: cases of esroygim wrapped in special esreg batting – their fragrance and color still live in my memory – and the children ran the business and wove the rings to hold the lulavim. One Grayeve specialist taught us how to "clean" esroygim, that is, to rub off their imperfections. It was not always successful. The stem often broke off during that operation and the esreg would never find a buyer. We also used to make "propaganda" so that Jews would come to us, assuring them that such flawless beauties as ours could not be found among the Corfu esroygim. Jews came and looked and scrutinized to see that the stem was whole and whether the esreg was really flawless. Grayeve Jews had time. They spent hours selecting an esreg, just as they spent time in the shops choosing foodstuffs or clothing. Naturally they bargained and haggled over an esreg, a holy thing, as they did over everyday items. Grayeve knew nothing about "fixed prices" then – and not only in Grayeve.

6

Every holiday had its own fight. On *Erev Yonkiper* [eve of Yom Kippur, the day of atonement] at the afternoon prayers there was a long table standing in the vestibule of each bes-medresh full of plates – collection bowls – with receipts for various societies: the guest and poor fund, visitors to the sick, the *Talmud Torah* [school], the home for the poor sick, a bowl for the beadle, for the besmedresh, and so on, where every Jew should throw in a contribution after praying, before going home to the final meal prior to the fast. The Zionists finally succeeded in getting permission to set out a bowl for the Odessa Committee for the Settlement in Erets Yisroel, which created a yearly report of the receipts (including the names of the donors who gave twenty kopecks or more, if I am not mistaken; it would be worth the effort to look into those reports to see if the Grayeve Jews who donated to Erets Yisroel can be found). My father gave me the assignment of ensuring there would be a bowl for Erets Yisroel in each besmedresh including the women's section. So, I became the central overseer of all the Erev-Yonkiper bowls, especially in the largest bote-medroshim: the old, the new, the shul, the guest and poor society. We did not have any rights in the Hasidic prayer houses. I spent a certain amount of time in each besmedresh to see that the Erets Yisroel bowl did not get pushed aside, because the other institutions did not look on it with friendly eyes. I also had to remind them about an accounting and a well-to-do householder, and that there is such a thing as an Erets Yisroel bowl. That is how I came to see how the Grayeve women gave charity after the afternoon prayers. The women would put three or five kopecks in a bowl and withdrew change to put into another bowl. Thus, they were able to "work" perhaps fifteen bowls with three or five kopecks and maybe put a little change back into their tear-stained kerchiefs. May they have a light-filled hereafter and may they forgive me, I would never blame them. The kopeck in those days in Grayeve was a coin worth much more than a dollar to today's American grandchildren of the poorest Grayeve families. For a kopeck – two groshen – in Grayeve you could get a lot of things, and a donation of a kopeck was a donation!

[Page 44]

We packed up the money in kerchiefs. Each besmedresh had its own kerchief; and of course we counted it before Yonkiper began. I was often late coming home for the last meal due to my supervision of the Erets Yisroel bowls in the Grayeve bote-medroshim.

Later the task became larger. In addition to the Odessa Committee we added a new bowl for the National Fund. At first the head of the Odessa Committee Menakhem Usishkin, was very much against allowing a keren kayemet leyisroel [KKL] bowl because it would result in competition. Later he agreed by necessity. At that time the leader of the Moscow Zionists Dr. Yekhiel Tshlenov, was the head of the KKL. After the First World War, as is known, Usishkin himself became the great fighter for the goals of the KKL. I do not know whether the custom of the donation bowls continued in Grayeve between the two world wars.

[Page 45]

The Grayeve Zionists also arranged special simkhes beys hashuave evenings on the interim days of Sukes. The Zionist minyen on *Shmimi Atseres* [seventh day of Sukes] and *Simkhes Toyre* [rejoicing in the Torah, the eighth day of Sukes] had a special place, which was arranged in a private home (once at old Polakevitsh and one at the very active Zionist Faynshteyns). This served as both a source of revenue for the Zionist cause because all the promissory notes went only to Erets Yisroel. This was a morale-strengthener for the group, enlivening the spirits of the small Zionist circle and fortifying them in their struggle to build up Erets Yisroel.

7

The holidays were the high points of Zionist activity in Grayeve, but that activity went on the entire year: the sale of sheklim (and Grayeve sent delegates to Zionist Congresses twice, my father to the Seventh Congress, see above, and Dr. Shaul Olshvanger to the Ninth Congress), and all sorts of collections for Erets Yisroel such as collecting money at weddings. (In competition with Tsar Nikolay's postal service, we carried around wedding invitations with KKL marks and thus had a "Jewish post" long before Medines Yisroel had created the first Jewish postal service. I introduced that postal activity for KKL during my first year in Bialystok in 1915.) The Zionist youth were happy in their role as the "hands and feet," or execution organ for Grayeve Zionism. They were not as ideologically regulated as the Zionist youth in Bialystok for example, or other large centers. They did not revolt against the "elders". It was only shortly before the First World War that an attempt was made to create a youth group and if I am not mistaken, Dr. Shmuel Ayzenshtat came to Grayeve especially for that purpose.

Shortly before the war a small group of Zionist young people also began speaking Hebrew amongst themselves and propagandized for speaking Hebrew. The poor things used to have to pay a groshen for every Yiddish word that accidentally slipped from their mouths.

[Page 46]

So it was in the Bogushe forest, along the highway between Shtutzin and *Raigrod* [Rajgród] on the way to *Kosherove* [Kędzierowo] from one direction and Shtutzin on the other, at the site of the post office, where the Grayeve youth gathered beside the train tracks. It was this location where they began to hear the sound of the old language that was revived in Erets Yisroel and in other lands

A large part of the Grayeve youth from more well-to-do homes learned Russian and German. A smaller part went to various gimnazyes in Lomzhe, Suvalk, Mariampol, Pultosk and *Vilne* [Vilnius]. Russian was not yet the main language of Grayeve youth before the First World War. At that time, there was a small group of young Yiddishists, but the majority of the enlightened youth were inclined to speak Hebrew.

Much that the Grayeve Zionists did also took place in other towns and villages in the provinces of Lomzhe, Suvalk and Grodne. The general Jewish society and the special Zionist life of Grayeve was not – and naturally could not be – as ordered as in the larger Jewish settlements like Byalistok, Varshe and so on. Yet, when one compares Grayeve life to settlements in Poland and Lithuania with the same Jewish population and way of life, one can certainly say, without any exaggeration that intellectually and culturally Grayeve Jewry stood on a higher level than other towns of the same stature.

The heirs of those Grayeve Jews up to 1914 – their children and grandchildren, wherever they are now – may be proud of the life and aspirations of their ancestors in old Grayeve. To the merit of their ancestors, may they create their own merit in Jewish life as that will be the finest memorial to our small and lovely Jewish holy community, Grayeve, may she rest in peace.

Shimen Rabidovitsh (Grayeve, Byalistok, Berlin, London, Leeds and now in Chicago)

Footnotes

5. *Kotsk:* Hasidic dynasty founded by Rebbe Menachem Mendel Morgenstern (1787–1859). The Hasidim of Kotsk focused on truth seeking rather than conformity to religious traditionalism. They were also known for their radical and controversial style of expression.
6. *Ger (Gur):* The largest Hasidic dynasty in Poland prior to the Holocaust; founded by Rabbi Yitzchak Meir Alter (1799–1866), brother-in-law of The Kotzker Rebbe. He was an insightful Torah scholar and *Halakhist* [*halakhah*: the collective basis of Jewish religious law, including Biblical, Talmudic and Rabbinic.]
7. *krias shema prayer*: affirmation and declaration of faith in one God, the original proclamation of monotheism.
8. *Bund*: Jewish Labor Bund was a secular anti-Zionist socialist party in the Russian empire active around the turn of the 20th century. They focused primarily on furthering the rights and status of the Jewish proletariat.
9. *Poalei Tsion:* Movement of Marxist Zionist Jewish workers in the Russian empire active around the turn of the 20th century.
10. *Hashliakh and Akhiasaf:* early Zionist publications written in Hebrew. They were little "journals" of a few pages, but politically very important.
11. *"black office:"* group of religious scholars who engaged in an impassioned war of writings against Zionism.
    Elul: last month of the Jewish year, dedicated to spiritual preparation for the High Holy days of Rosh Hashanah and Yom Kippur.

[Page 47]

Images and Figures of *Grayeve*
(Between the First and Second World War)

Dr. G. Gorin

Note: *This translation was generously donated by Nora Jean Levin, whose father Hirsch Bieler-Suwalski (1900-1985) translated part of this chapter for his children's benefit between 1979 and 1982. Mr. Bieler-Suwalski was born in Grajewo and left in 1919 for Leipzig, Germany. In 1936 Hirsch went to Palestine with his wife Anna and daughter Tania. The family ultimately came to the U.S. and settled in Philadelphia, PA after 1938.*

Edited by Tina Lunson and Nora Jean Levin

1
The first departure and return

It was a sunny spring day in 1921 when I, for the first time, left my beloved native city Grayeve, a feeling of longing and loss nagged in my heart thinking of my childhood years in Grayeve, where every house, every street, every fence was connected with so many memories, and everyone was a friend or an acquaintance. It was a departure not only from Grayeve, but also from my childhood.

The two were so closely tied and knitted together. In later years I often returned to find there consolation and a retreat from the strange wild world. In Grayeve, I always felt as part of the town and not as a stranger. Yet it did not look the same, when I returned for the first time. Everything looked different. The streets looked shorter, the houses lower. For the first time in my life, I was in the position to observe everything in the town objectively.

A city is like a living creature. It has a heart that feels, and has moods of melancholy and frivolity, enthusiasm and worries. It seems there were a lot of Grayeves, and each and every one of them had a different face, depending on the different circumstances.

Grayeve on a *Shabes* [Sabbath] afternoon in summer when Jews finished eating the *tsholent* [stew warmed overnight to avoid cooking on the Sabbath] was so quiet, that you could hear the rustle of a leaf on a tree. The hamlet lay drowned in thick silence under the burning sun. All stores closed, the shutters closed and chained, and the streets were empty. It was a time of delightful tranquility when the worries of the week were put aside somewhere in a distant corner to become a worry-free, benevolent and silent Grayeve.

The silence does not last long. A door opens and closes with a bang. A boy with a brass kettle in his hand runs to River Street for tea. Slowly the whole hamlet arouses from the deep slumber. This is how it was in summertime, every Saturday afternoon, year in, year out.

In the wintery Sabbath afternoons, one takes out the brass kettle and sits around the tiled oven drinking hot tea. The silence in the street is quite different. Cheerful noises are heard from the street by ice-skating boys, which disturb a bit the afternoon nap. The thick snow is soft under the feet, but the burning frost pinches the ears and nose, when Jews go to the *besmedresh* [house of study] for the *minkhe* [afternoon prayers] services.

Grayeve looks quite different during the Days of Awe and the ten days of repentance between, *Rosheshone* [Rosh Hashanah] and *Yonkiper* [Yom Kippur]. All faces are serious and deep in thought and meditation. You can feel it in the air that something is being expected. The Day of Judgment is a serious event for everybody, young and old.

I remember how my father used to pull his *talis* [prayer shawl] over his head, when the cantor reached the *unsaneh tokef* prayer [recited during the Days of Awe which speaks of the sanctity of God's Day of Judgment], as if to protect himself from terrible atrocities. I was yet so small that I could not reach the *makhzer* [prayer book for the High Holidays] on the stand, and with frightened eyes, I looked up at how a grown man cried with bitter tears, "who by fire, and who by water; who by the sword and who by the pestilence; who by hunger and who by thirst?" I understood the meaning of these gruesome deaths from the stories the rabbi used to tell us in *kheyder* [Jewish religious school], but could not imagine that such a dreadful death would befall my own father in the Hitler *gehenem* [hell; place or state of torment or suffering].

As soon as the *shoyfer* [ram's horn blown on Rosh Hashanah and Yom Kippur] is blown for the last time, everyone gives a sigh of relief and is resigned to accept the decree from above. The day-to-day routine returns, but not for long. Thereafter comes the *Sukes* [Sukkot] holidays, and everybody to his own standard enjoys the traditional festivities until *Simkhes-Toyre* [Simchat Torah], when the joyous festivities reach the climax.

After that comes the gray and cold days with the worries for the coming winter. The whole city gets ready. Homeowners buy loads of potatoes to be stored in cellars; the sheds replenished with firewood and peat. The hamlet braces itself for survival of the oncoming winter.

When again spring's mild breezes begin to blow, the heart rejoices—baking, cleaning, washing the household furnishings, airing the books, and hanging the clothing and bedding in the open air. After the long winter, when windows are pasted with paper and cotton, and the doors are always closed, the fresh air is like a toxic drink. The *shtetl* [small town] is again good-natured. People smile again in harmony with nature, grateful not only for the fact of being freed from the bondage of Egypt, but also from the severe, long and lonely winter.

There was also a Grayeve of Friday evenings and Grayeve of Saturday evenings; and a Grayeve where, when a funeral procession passed through *Shul Gas* [Synagogue Street] all the stores close in sympathy and respect for the departed; Grayeve, where a band of musicians on the way to play for a wedding are followed by small boys; Grayeve on *Tishebov* night when laments are recited for the *khurbm* [destruction]; [*Tishebov* / Tish'a B'Av is the 9th day of the month of *Ov* or *Av*; a day of mourning in commemoration of the destruction of the 1st and 2nd Temples in Jerusalem]; Grayeve, where Jews bless the new moon in a clear sky

All of these pictures of Grayeve stand before my eyes, etched in my soul. They are unforgettable, like still impressions and happenings of the childhood years which remain a part of us for the rest of our lives.

The Jews of Grayeve in general were kind-hearted people and proud of their city. Truthfully, compared to Byalistok [Bialystok] they felt a little bit inferior, they felt a little bit ashamed of their pronunciation. In Byalistok they called the Jews of Grayeve the "*Grayever plotkes*" [small fry], the accent on the hard "L." Compared to the surrounding "*shtetlekh*" [smaller villages] like Raigrod [Rajgród], Vonsosh [Wąsosz], and even *Shtutzin* [Szczuczyn], the *Grayever's* considered themselves big city stuff, with a railroad and a foreign border and communication with the big world.

In the evening when the train arrived from Byalistok, the station outside was packed with curious people standing on both sides of the exit, creating a narrow corridor through which passengers exited. One used to look them over from head to toe, especially strange faces visiting Grayeve for the first time, like a young man or girl who comes to visit. There were few secrets in Grayeve.

The station's building was very beautiful for such a small town. People used to walk in the evening on *Ban Gas* [Train Street]. In later years, they extended the avenue to the post office, with trees and benches on both sides. There the people of Grayeve enjoyed the summer evenings and discussed various topics, or just sat and gossiped about the passersby.

On Shtutzin Highway, on both sides of the road, as far to the windmills, there was another place where young people spent the evening on the grass. Romances and love affairs developed, and there the youth of the town dreamed about the big world, to which so many of them escaped to try their luck.

Boys used to play on the green hill behind the cemetery. In my eyes it was the highest mountain in the world. With beating hearts, we used to climb to the top, spreading ourselves flat on the soft, green grass. It was like a field of eternity, behind the eternal resting place of generations of the Jews of Grayeve.

2
The livelihood and working trades of the Jews of Grayeve

In the twenties, Grayeve was no longer prosperous as before the First World War. The reasons were varied: first, the general depression after the War, which existed in the country and all over the world; second, the town was no longer part of Russia as before 1914, so big commerce with Germany via Grayeve existed no more; third, the evil attitude of the new-born Polish government towards Jews and Jewish trade hit very hard. It went so far that the people nostalgically spoke about the times before the War.

As a result of the economic depression Jewish youth started to emigrate to America, *Eretz Yisroel* and France. The town had become narrower for them, and the future hopeless as ever. The older generation tried to hold on to their occupations after the war. Jewish businessmen used to travel to Byalistok, Varshe [Warsaw] and Lodzh [Łódź] for goods. Jewish artisans, who had mostly remained in the city during the time of the war, struggled to beat out a living in their workshops. A great many Jews somehow got by with the support they received from American relatives.

Trade was limited, yet some succeeded in sending carloads of lumber and other goods to Germany. They traded in train box-car loads, as they were called.

The offices which were so busy before the First World War lost a lot of their importance.

As the situation was, the Jews played the most important role in the economic life of the city. Grayeve was surrounded by many villages. Twice a week, Mondays and Fridays, were market days, and once a month there was a big fair to which Jewish merchants came from all the surrounding *shtetlekh* with their merchandise. In those days, the farmers used to bring their products for sale, and in return, buy in the stores, suits, coats, shoes, various products for the house, food etc.

Most of the Jewish stores were in the market place, on *Shul* Street and *Shtutzin* Street. In the Twenties there were but a few Christian stores.

The butcher stores were on *Bogushe* Street. They were a world in itself, exactly like the Jewish butchers were in a class by themselves. The street always smelled of blood and meat. The butchers were a crude bunch. The

Jewish women were afraid of them. They cursed and swore when a woman showed displeasure with the meat.

The fish traders used to set up every Friday in *Shul* Street, opposite the *Hasidic shtibl* [small house of prayer used by Hasidim] with barrels of fish, and Jewish women used to come to buy fish for *Shabes*. In Grayeve there were also several stores which sold nets and equipment and utensils for fishing.

Jewish artisans were represented in shoemaking, tailoring, cabinet making, carpentry, and other trade works where the owners worked alone or with a few helpers.

A typical livelihood was the trade in geese, which merchants bought up by the thousands and then drove into Germany. Many Jewish women sold fowl on a small scale. They cut the fowl in parts, wings, gizzards etc. and sold them to the housewives. I remember my grandmother, Hinde-Rifke, sitting till late at night in the winter evenings with a white shawl over her head plucking feathers for bedding. She also fried and sold *gendzene shmalts* [goose fat].

In the grain business, the Jews occupied the top positions. A few Grayeve Jews dealt in grains on a big scale, sending carloads all over the country or abroad. Milling flour was also a Jewish trade. There were several wind mills, and one ran by steam and electricity.

There were many blacksmiths in Grayeve. A horde of them dwelt on *Taykh Gas* (River Street). They had their own style of pronunciation that differed from other Grayevers. They swore their own curses and sometimes dealt a blow, so everybody was afraid; even the peasants trembled before them. The smiths also bought and sold horses.

On the plaza, in a separate neighborhood, lived the *"drotshakes"* [wirers] whose job was to wire together broken earthenware and porcelain pots. They were the poorest, living on muddy streets in low, sunken-in houses and like all the poor in Grayeve, had a lot of children running around naked and barefoot. When there were not enough broken dishes to mend, they occupied themselves with shoemaking. Of one of them was Nakhman Drotshak. They say that when the police imposed a fine for poor upkeep of his property, he gathered all the barefoot children of the neighborhood, went to the yard of the district administrator, lined them up outside the mayor's windows, and made such a heartbreaking wail that they removed the fine out of pity for the starving children.

The Tar Jews were in a class by themselves. They were immortalized in a book called *The Tar Jews* by our honorable *landsman* [someone from the same town], Ari Ibn Zahav. I will only mention them briefly. The Tar Jews you only saw in Grayeve twice a year, for *peysakh* [the holiday Passover] and the High Holy Days, when they came to visit their families. They spent all the year in Germany dealing in horses and related work. For the holidays some of them used to come down all dolled up in foreign clothing, strongly perfumed, smoothly shaved and with the *Yekisher* [German style] short haircuts, a white handkerchief in the front breast pocket, a beautiful tie with a big knot, and a mother-of-pearl tie pin and a big golden watch with a long golden chain. Those fellows had a darn good time in Germany, as you could see from their flaming faces and thick red necks. They used to speak a Germanized Yiddish, walking in the streets telling about their fabulous fortunes in *Yekeland* [nickname for Germany] and their own grandeur.

3
Interesting and tragic types in Grayeve

There were many curious and interesting characters of Grayeve. I will only tell of a few of them: Hershel *bochen-bisen*, so he was called. He was a son-in-law of a *melamed* [elementary teacher]. Hershele had a speech defect and when he prayed you could only hear him say *bochen-bisen, bochen-bisen,*" but he was a genius of a mathematician. I remember he could figure the most difficult mathematical problems in his head, faster than I could figure on paper. In one minute he could resolve difficult problems that took me an hour, using algebraic methods. Even old people used to test his abilities. They used to ask him "Hershel, I have *yortsayt* [anniversary of a death] for my grandfather who died the tenth day in the month of *Shvat*. Which day of the week was it thirty years ago when he died?" Hershel would pull his reddish beard, close the eyes and between a few *bochen-bisen* would say the exact day.

Everybody in Grayeve knew Yosl *bloz* [nickname the "blower]. He was a blacksmith and his face was always black from blowing on the fire in the smithy....

[Pages 53-68]

The following section was translated by Tina Lunson

His son Yehuda was off on some dark business and became a porter. He and Zundele, two beefy youths obstructed all the traffic at the Grayeve train station and would not allow anyone else to carry a suitcase for travelers who had stayed the night at Frank's hotel. That livelihood brought them a good income; they were well-dressed, used perfume, and ate *"landrinkes"* [unknown translation] on the street (in Grayeve in those times that was a sign of prosperity). Later Yehuda became a barber. He went around in a clean, white smock as if to demonstrate his pleasure with his "clean" profession and as if to show how high he had risen above his father Yosl of the leaky bellows.

That Yehuda set up a primitive radio, one of the first radios in Grayeve. Yosl bloz told the [study] group *Ayn Yankev* [1] about the wonderful activities of his son in these words: "Do you know what a radio is? You stick a pole in Khaye Alte's chimney and a stick in Sore Leye's chimney (those were his neighbors), you fix a wire between them, you stick a piece of tinplate in the ground, you put on a pair of ear handles and you hear music from around the whole world."

* * *

Among the tragic types in Grayeve were the "blind." These were a few families in which most of the men became blind around the age of twenty. They suffered from a disease of the optic nerve. The disease passed mostly from fathers to sons and attacked the victims around the age of 20. The blind ones went around begging from door to door. Everyone knew Itshi Pinye, Mayer Leybl and Yosl Tuvye as they went around tapping their way with a walking stick, or a young girl would lead them about. They would go into Germany to beg for charity when the "season" was poor in Grayeve. The Jews in *Prostken* [Prostki] and *Lik* [Ełk] bribed them, and gave them a certain sum of money with the condition that they leave the town so that they, the German Jews, would not be shamed in the eyes of their neighbors by these Jewish paupers from Poland. When the blind ones returned from their tour of the German provinces they divided among themselves the small things they had gotten by begging. The distribution took place in their neighborhood and often ended with fisticuffs. When the news that the blind ones were fighting arrived in the besmedresh we boys would quickly finish up shimenesre[2] and run with bated breath to Post Office Street to see the battle. The blind ones would be cursing and screaming with wild voices. They knew instinctively where their opponents were hiding. Although they could not see, they knew where to throw an iron bar, a board or a stone.

4
Social and Religious Life

All the well-known institutions that Jews supported in other towns and villages of Poland existed in Grayeve. The *lines hatsedek* society [society to care for the indigent sick] possessed a good variety of medical instruments, which Grayeve Jews often borrowed in times of illness. The lines hatsedek also had devoted volunteer members who visited the ill and sat with them at night.

The *gemiles khesed* [charitable loan society] functioned in a small measure and gave small loans without interest. The Grayeve Jews also organized a Jewish cooperative bank which conducted various transactions and also gave loans. The bank was a very useful institution for Grayeve Jewish merchants and small proprietors.

Grayeve also had a committee to ensure that guests in town were hosted for the shabes and holidays, a burial society and a number of smaller institutions.

The Grayeve proprietors were organized in a professional union. The union was especially important because of the various decrees that the Polish government issued for handworkers – particularly the guilds. A young Jewish man could not learn a trade if he could not find a craftsman, a member of a guild, to teach him. Few Jewish craftsmen were taken in as members of a guild. The situation changed very much in that regard, during the years of the Second World War.

Grayeve had a good library, housed in the "house of the people." One could find the best and most recent books in Yiddish, Hebrew and Polish for loan. The library was operated by volunteer workers; the number of books grew from year to year and Grayeve youth had the opportunity to read good literature thanks to the devotion of a small number of young people from the library management. The Bund[3] organization also had a Yiddish library, but the number of books was much smaller.

There were two types of religious education institutions in Grayeve: the old khadorim and the refashioned ones, modern religious schools.

I knew the Grayever melamed because I went to almost all of the khadorim, including the Talmud-Torah. Of course, the Grayeve melamed were not acquainted with the newest methods in pedagogy and slapping was the best way to keep discipline.

Shmaye the melamed, a broad Jew with a sparse white beard and a hot temperament, used to pinch cheeks and then look at his two fingers as if to see whether he had torn off a piece of flesh. His kheyder was in Mendl Borukh's house and we used to run from there out on the "*biel*" and hide for hours. His daughter Fradl, a pale, dried up old maid, always came to take us in and sometimes she succeeded in cooling her father's fury at his pupils.

The melamed from Raigrod was a thin, sickly Jew with a big beard, smeared with yellow stains from snuff. He drank tea all day, carved wood with a sharp little knife and made various figurines for us. He was too weak to beat the boys; he let out his anger through a Russian curse with Yiddish words mixed in. The poverty in his home was great and after his death when his children were grown, they became very active in the communist movement. One of his daughters and his son, Khaym Arye, were both put into Polish prisons for their political activity.

My melamed in the Hasidic kheyder on River Street was an angry Jew who beat and pinched his pupils. I was then nine years old and we studied the Talmud section *kidushin*[4] the entire year. On the hot summer afternoons, when our childish hearts were drawn outdoors by a world with green trees, soft grass and a clear blue sky, the *rebi* [teacher] held forth in a monotone voice on "a woman is acquired three ways." I did not understand what was being dealt with there and was not interested in the "ways." Only the older boys had roguish smiles on their faces and already knew, it seems, the "big secret." Once I got so sleepy in the stuffy air of the kheyder that I sank down to a sweet nap over the Talmud. The rebi had a sharp eye, though. He threw the hard case for his eyeglasses at me and when I woke up he served up a smack.

The Talmud-Torah was maintained by community counsel money and many poor children studied there. American support also helped the institution. There were times, right after the First War, when the children in the Talmud-Torah were given one meal a day to eat. For many of them it was their only meal, because their families were very poor.

The Talmud-Torah building

**A class of Jewish children in the town school.
The teachers: Kureivovski and Popovski**

My Talmud teacher at the Talmud Torah was Yisroel Borekh. He was a tall Jew with a sparse beard, a long nose and deep blue eyes. I do not recall his ever hitting a boy. He was a Hasid and a good person. When I visited Grayeve the last time in 1937, I happened to encounter him in the street. We had a long conversation and I was inspired by his tolerance. He told me he had hoped that I would be a *yeshive* [a Jewish school of high Talmudic learning] student, but, he easily admitted, was happy that I studied at a university because studying in any area is good knowledge and leads to an understanding of God.

Among the "modern khadorim" there was Kharmon's kheyder and Eli-Melekh Pomerants' kheyder where much more importance was put on *Tanakh* [abbreviation for *Torah, Neviim, Ksuvim*; Law, Prophets, Writings, respectively] and Hebrew as a language of daily use and not only as a holy tongue. In both of those khadorim the children also studied general subjects.

Besides the religious schools there was also a secular school in Grayeve. There were two *folks-shuln* [public schools] with Polish as the language of instruction – one for the Polish children and one for the Jewish children. In the latter, mostly Jewish girls studied; the parents did not want to send the boys to a non-Jewish school.

Grayeve also had a Polish government high school where only a small number of Jewish children studied. In the first years of the high school's existence Jewish parents did not want to send their children there, because they had to write on shabes. In later years the school introduced the *numerus clausus* (a quota) and they only accepted a few Jewish students each year – only those who had "potential."

Middle-class Jews mostly sent their children to the *Tarbut* [secular Hebrew Zionist] schools. One cannot speak of the Grayeve Tarbut schools and not mention in particular the tireless efforts of two Grayeve teachers in the area of Hebrew education. One of them was Eli-Melekh Pomerants, a veteran Zionist activist and Hebraist, who his whole life furthered activity in the area of Hebrew education and spread the use of Hebrew as an everyday language. The second was Popovski, who worked for years as a teacher in the Tarbut schools and also taught Jewish religion and Hebrew in the Polish folks-shul for Jewish children.

A class of the Tarbut School

The Tarbut School also had a number of Hebrew teachers whom the central office of the Tarbut organization in Warsaw sent to work in Grayeve. Students who graduated from the Tarbut School in Grayeve were automatically in the fourth class of the Hebrew high school in *Byalistok* [Białystok].

I was one of the first Grayeve students to travel to study in the Hebrew high school in Byalistok. In the years 1926 to 1929 there were fifteen students from Grayeve in the Byalistok Tarbut high school. Many of them later traveled abroad and studied in various universities. Grayeve then had around ten Jewish youths who studied medicine. A few of them stayed in Poland, others went out into the world because they were not allowed to practice in Poland. Grayeve young people also studied engineering, agronomy, literature and philosophy.

For the older generation, as always, an important place was occupied by the botemedroshim – the old and the new, the *Oheves khesed* [love of charity], the shul, the Hasidic shtibl and the various other non-Hasidic groups like Ayn Yankev and *Khevre mikre* [reading group].

The Grayeve shul was built at the initiative and with the help of the Vierzshbolovski family. In the 1920s the Grayeve Jews brought in an artist who decorated the ark and other parts of the shul.

We boys loved most of all to pray in the old besmedresh, especially shabes evening when it was already dark but still too early to turn on the lights, and the Jews would sit in the dark and recite psalms and sing "happy are those whose path is pure." Then we would run around and play across the benches and under the tables and the Kuliav beadle would chase us with a book in his hand and shout, "Get out of here, you scoundrels."

The Hasidic shtibl was the merriest place of all. There were many Hasidim in Grayeve. There were Kotsker[5] and Gerer[6] and a certain number were followers of others rabeim.

I cannot forget such beautiful and noble faces as Meyshe Mendl the *sheykhet* [ritual slaughterer], Alter Tsuker, Henekh Mishkovski and many others. They were pious and good-hearted Jews who brought warmth to their beliefs and happiness to their piety.

In speaking of communal institutions one must also mention the Grayeve bath-house, which was a very important factor for hygiene in the life of Grayeve Jews.

5
Grayeve Intellectuals and Youth

Here will be mentioned only some of the Jews who played an important role in the communal life of Grayeve and who exercised an influence on the development of the Grayeve Jewish settlement, especially those who were active in community work, institutions and organizations. Among those families I want to mention the family Kolko, a respectable family with many children who went off into the world and studied and excelled in various fields;

the families Ayzenshtat, Zilbershteyn, Rekhtman, Ziberski, Rinkovski, Vaks, Dr. Viner, Dr. Velikovski, Olshvanger, Verzshbolovski, Koptshovski, Galambievski, Gershtanski, Mieshonzshnik, Barkovski, Khainovski, Bialystotski, Berman, Levit, Frieda and many others.

Dr. Eliahu Vaser, an efficient and beloved community activist, was mayor of Grayeve in the time of the German occupation (1915–1918) and later, under Polish authority, vice mayor. Through his impartiality he won the trust of all levels of the Grayeve Jewish population.

Some Grayeve Jews, who were occupied in commerce or with the state, saw that their children would not be able to settle down in Poland and they sent them to study a profession in the universities. So did Abramski, Gortshitski, Vapinski, Ayzenshtat, Kureivovski, Sarna, Rubenshteyn, Antshkovski and others.

In the summer time many young people, high school and [university] students gathered in Grayeve from various cities in Poland and various universities in other countries. In the 1930s Grayeve was full of intellectual youths, especially during the summer vacations. Despite the fact that they had seen the wonder of the big world they still longingly awaited the summer to return to their little town. This was a happy youth, but also a youth interested in social problems and cultural matters, and there was always a close collaboration between the Jewish intellectuals who lived permanently in Grayeve and the students who lived in Grayeve part-time.

One of the most interesting undertakings of the Grayeve intellectuals were the literary "trials." People spent the whole summer preparing for such an undertaking. The theme of the trial was announced so that everyone would be able to prepare. The trial usually took place during the interim days of *sukes* [the festival of booths] and went on for two or three evenings. Heated discussions took place on both sides and people awaited the "sentence" in great suspense.

There was also a drama group in Grayeve and from time to time they would present a Yiddish play. That was an event for the whole night – it was usually shabes night or the end of a holiday. The event was often held in the firehouse on Bogush Street and the intermission between the acts was so long that after half the night the audience would refresh themselves with warm bagels and cakes from Branervayn's bakery. Young people from all the surrounding villages came to such cultural events, and Grayeve was very proud to play the important role of a center.

The drama club that presented *Hertsl the Aristocrat* in 1923

The drama club that presented the *Yeshive-bokher* [Yeshive student] in 1924

The drama club presenting the melodrama *Hofni and Pinkhas*
to benefit the Palestine Workers' Fund in March 1924

The Grayeve youth, regardless of political direction or social position, were restless youth. The reasons were the dissatisfaction with their environment, a striving toward the larger world, a thirst for learning and especially the insecurity and cloudy future in the small Polish town. The First World War had interrupted the stream of emigration, but soon after the war, Jewish youth tore off to other places. Some traveled to America, South Africa, Erets Yisroel and Germany.

In the time of unrest right after the retreat of the Russian Army, when Polish authority had returned, a horrible tragedy befell Jewish Grayeve, which took the lives of sixteen youths, among them the three Segalevitsh brothers. The sixteen youths had set out on the road to Lithuania, from where they hoped to sneak out into the larger world. They were captured by Poles in *Ogustove* [Augustów] and were taken back to Grayeve. On the way, in the village of Belda, the Poles brutally murdered them and all sixteen lie there in a common grave.

When the situation had stabilized in the early 1920s Grayeve had an active, politically conscious youth, well organized into various groups, both Zionist and non-Zionist. These various groupings are described in other articles in this book.

[The banner the girls are holding: "A garland for our unforgettable friends."

Below the banner: "Damashevski, Vertman, Surazki"]

A group of friends visit the common grave of 16 Grayeve Jewish youths who were murdered by the Poles in 1920, in Barglove. [Bargłów]

6
Before the Storm

My visits to Grayeve in the 1930s were not frequent: once a year or every two years. When the train would race past Ruda my heart began to beat in a faster tempo in anticipation of seeing my old home, my parents, sisters, brothers, friends and all the beloved streets and alleyways in which I had spent my childhood years. There were [the landmarks] the *mogilkes*, "close in behind the train," the second gates, the mills, Striev's photography workshop, the first gates where I could see a flash of my parents' house in the corner between Shul Street, Shtutzin Street and Market street.

One could forget the larger world when the train puffed and whistled through the last stretch of a few hundred meters. At the station I could see familiar, friendly faces; I kissed my parents and we all went home together.

The old home became more beloved with each visit. I wanted to sing and laugh and be carefree as in my childhood!

But one time in 1932 I arrived by train and the station was empty, no one was waiting for me, the streets were empty and patrolled by Polish soldiers and police. The town looked like after a pogrom – quiet, sunken in a deep gloom, shutters and windows closed.

This was the time that the hooligans *Endekes* [Polish Nationalist and Anti-Semitic Party] increased their incitement against the Jews. They had huge influence in Grayeve and that day they had incited the peasants in the market square to make a pogrom against the Jews. The previous Sunday the Grayeve priest had given a fiery anti-Semitic sermon in church and the murderous instincts had been aroused. Peasants came to that market day with axes and sticks to beat and kill Jews and they had not forgotten to bring huge sacks in which to pack up the merchandise from robbed Jewish businesses. But thanks to the vigilance of the Jewish community council a bloody pogrom against Jews was avoided.

Police and soldiers from the barracks kept order that day. Only a few Jews were badly beaten and many window panes were broken in Jewish houses. The town was calm in a few days, but one could recognize the shocked disquiet on the faces of the Grayeve Jews.

The situation in Grayeve changed for the worse. The Polish government applied every means to drive Jews out of commerce. It subsidized Polish merchants and helped to open businesses to compete with the Jews. The Endekes set up pickets at Jewish businesses and forced the peasants not to buy from Jews. In the mornings, Jews would find the doors of their businesses smeared with anti-Semitic slogans in red letters, calling on the Poles to boycott Jewish trade. The Polish government declared a moratorium for the debts of the peasants and overnight Jewish merchants had to lose possessions that the peasants owed them for merchandise.

A few Grayeve Jews left for Erets Yisroel and liquidated their businesses in Grayeve. But the majority of Jews were not able to move from the spot because of the foreign currency decree, which forbade taking money out of Poland and because of the impoverishment of Jewish trade through ruinous taxes.

The economic pressure was applied with even better technique in the later 1930s. Each time I arrived in Grayeve I found a few Jewish businesses closed and a few new Polish businesses. Poles from the area had bought Jewish houses or built new buildings.

The economic and social pressure came from all sides and as a result, Jewish poverty grew and the pressure to emigrate was stronger. Young people fled to wherever they could. Unfortunately the doors of the world gradually closed and the great Jewish masses in Grayeve could not move away and watched with horror at the black storm clouds that gathered over the skies of Hitler's Germany.

* * *

My last visit to Grayeve was in 1937, when I went to take my leave of my parents before traveling to America.

The mood in Grayeve was very heavy. All the Jews expected bad times but they did not know that they were standing over an abyss and that their days were numbered. Poles talked openly of murdering the Jews, yet Jews in Grayeve as all over Poland never anticipated and did not conceive of such a huge tragedy and such annihilation as befell them a few years later.

On that last visit I did not find many of my old friends. A few had died, others had left Grayeve. All were envious of me with my opportunity to go to America.

In that uneasy atmosphere, one summer evening came the news about Leybl Elkan's death on the battlefield in Spain. I recall how police came to Zerekh Elkan, who lived close to us, to give him the sad news. While there they insulted him and cursed him for having "a son who was a revolutionary and a Bolshevik."

Leybl Elkan, the son of a Hasid, an idealistic youth, a Pioneer – had gone to Erets Yisroel a few years earlier. From there he went back to France, and from there he joined the international brigade and fell as a hero in the fight for freedom. Many Grayeve Jews did not understand then, the significance of Leybl Elkan's falling in battle against their own bloody enemy, Hitler.

It was a double tragedy for me to part from my parents and my birthplace. I had a premonition that this was my last visit, that I would never see my parents again and never see Grayeve. It was sad for me to look at the struggle of the Jewish community. The town and the Grayeve Jews were so near to my heart and so beloved – all the men, women and children, rich and poor, I loved them all without exception and had pity for them and worried about their future.

I will never forget the July evening when late at night I left for the train accompanied by my parents, brother and sister. Tears were choking me and I felt like a person saving himself from a danger and leaving his dearest behind alone. The Grayeve streets were dark and abandoned. It was late at night and a community of Jews slept uneasily, surrounded by a hateful wrathful world, enveloped in black shadows of reaction and enmity.

I kissed by dearest and the train quickly cut through the darkness of the night, on the way to far-off America.

✱
Grayeve Pronunciation

From a treatise by M. Viner, "On Yiddish Dialects," in *Tsaytshrift* [periodical] published by the Institute for White Russian Culture, Yiddish Department, Minsk, 1925.

M. Viner writes: "The notes that I provide here present the phonetic characteristic of a number of White Russian, Lithuanian and Ukrainian dialects." The phonetic characteristics of the Grayeve pronunciation follow:

Footnotes

12. *Ayn Yankev: Ein Yaakov*: book written in the 16th century about the ethical and inspirational teachings of the Talmud.
13. *Shimenesre:* The eighteen benedictions also called "*The Amidah,*" [central prayer] that is said while standing facing toward Yerusholayim.
14. *Bund:* Jewish Labor Bund was a secular socialist organization in the Russian empire active around the turn of the 20th century, who was opposed to Zionism. They focused primarily on furthering the rights and status of the Jewish proletariat
15. *Kidushin*: Consecrate. The first part of the two-part process of Jewish marriage which creates the legal relationship.
16. *Kotsk*: Hasidic dynasty founded by Rebbe Menachem Mendel Morgenstern (1787–1859). The Hasidim of Kotsk focused on truth seeking rather than conformity to religious traditionalism. They were also known for their radical and controversial style of expression
    Ger (Gur): The largest Hasidic dynasty in Poland prior to the Holocaust and founded by Rabbi Yitzchak Meir Alter (1799–1866), brother-in-law of The Kotzker Rebbe. He was an insightful Torah scholar and Halakhist [*halakhah*: the collective basis of Jewish religious law, including Biblical, Talmudic and Rabbinic]

[Page 71]

Second Part:

Community and Life-Style

The Zionist Movement in Grayeve
Itsik Gartshitshi (M.Phil.-Tel Aviv)[1]

Translated by Miriam Leberstein

In the years when the international Zionist organization set out on the road toward the great goal of building a Jewish homeland in Erets Yisroel, in that epoch which begins with the first Zionist Congress in Basel in 1892, the Jews of Grayeve were already caught up in Zionist thought.

Like all Jewish *shtetls*, Grayeve was, in the 19th century, a town of pious, God-fearing Jews. The *besmedresh* [prayer and study house, small synagogue] was for them a fortress of Torah and piety, where they could forget their everyday worries and experience a few hours of spiritual exaltation. The Jewish holidays, which played a significant role in their lives, were connected with Jewish history and with Erets Yisroel: *Khanike*, a commemoration of Jewish heroism; *Peysakh*, a commemoration of Jewish liberation from Egypt; and *Tishabov*, a time of mourning over the destruction of the Temple. The vow that the Jewish exiles swore by the rivers of Babylon --"If I forget thee, Oh Jerusalem..." --was remembered by all Jews throughout the long generations of the Diaspora, and Grayeve Jews were no exception.

[Page 72]

We must fully appreciate the significance of that vow for the Jewish people and its land. Without the connection to Zion and the old traditions, and without the longing for the holy land, the Jewish people would have long ago disappeared as a nation on the world stage, vanished without a trace. And without the longing for Zion, Zionism would never have become a popular movement. Obviously, anti-Semitism and persecution played a significant role in this process, but these factors simply helped Zionist thought to become deeply embedded in the broad Jewish masses.

On the other hand, it is also true that strict and fanatical observance of tradition also brought about a petrifaction of Jewish life. Tradition was a thick wall which new thoughts were unable to penetrate. Still, Grayeve did not remain a backwards, unenlightened shtetl. Quite early, it entered the arena of culture, secular education, and new ideas, including Zionism. Grayeve was a border town, linked by rail and roads to Germany, and to Russia and Russian Jewry. Because of the commercial traffic through Grayeve, and its communication resources, Grayeve Jews often travelled to Germany. From time to time, Jewish youth on their way to study abroad would also pass through Grayeve. Also, many political refugees, Jews and non- Jews, would pass through Grayeve in their flight from Tsarist oppression.

It is not easy to determine the influence on the Grayeve Jews of these people who passed through the town. But we can be sure that their contact with the Jewish intelligentsia of Grayeve exercised a certain cultural influence and helped to spread the new social and political ides of the great Yiddish and Hebrew cultural centers of Kovno, Vilna, Minsk, Kiev, Odessa, Warsaw, Konigsberg, and so forth.

[Page 73]

Links with the Large Cultural Centers

As time passed, several families from the larger cities settled in Grayeve. These families had already established lively and direct cultural links between the town and the large cultural centers of Russia and abroad. The educated members of these families would correspond with friends in their former homes. One such example is the connection between the Olshvanger-Verzhbalovski family with their enlightened relatives in Russia, Lithuania, and Vienna, especially with the writer, Miriam Markl-Mozeszohn, the daughter of Shimen Verzhbalovski and the aunt of the Grayever Verzhbalovskis.

In 1927, Avraham Yeri published in Jerusalem the letters which the renowned Hebrew poet Yehude Leyb Gordon wrote to Miriam Moseszohn in the years 1868-1887. Several years earlier, Prof. B.Ts. Dinaberg published in the literary journal "*Ktuvim*" ["Writings"], letters written to her by the Hebrew writer and *Havevey Tsion* [lover of Zion, member of the organization *Hibat Tsion* (Love of Zion)], Lilienblum. From these letters one can see how much these writers loved and esteemed this intelligent woman.

Cultural and literary themes also served as the topics of long conversations when Miriam Mozeszohn came to Grayeve for extended visits. The regular participants in these conversations were: Olshvanger, who had studied at the Rabbinical Seminary in Breslau, and who had brilliantly mastered Hebrew, in addition to the most important European languages; Olshvanger's wife, who was a highly educated woman, considered to be the only woman in Grayeve who had graduated from a Russian gymnasium in the 1870's or 1880's, and who, together with her husband and sister, created a cultural atmosphere in Grayeve; and Reb [respectful term of address] Avraham Piurko, who was the Hebrew teacher for the Olshvanger children, and who later became the central and beloved figure among the educated Jews and scholars of Grayeve.

[Page 74]

It isn't difficult to imagine the enormous influence these two families had upon the cultural development of Grayeve Jewry, especially when one takes into consideration that the members of these families were populists, who, despite their high level of education, knew how to relate to the common people.

Another factor that linked Grayeve Jews to the wider world must be mentioned. These families who settled in the town were unable to provide their children with a suitable education there, and sent them to study in the larger cities. This set an example for other Jews who later also began to send their children to large yeshivas or secular schools. These were not limited to prosperous Jews, like Khaim Itsik Ravidovits. The children of poor families were also sent to study in yeshivas out of town, for example, the son of the widow Khane Bashe Vaystlovski, Dr. Tsvi Vayslavski, well-known in Erets Yisroel, and about whom I will speak further in this article. His great achievements illustrate very well the saying of our sages: "Take care of the poor children, because they will bring forth learning." These children became ambassadors of culture, through whom the Grayeve Jews – or, at least, the enlightened ones -- came into close contact with the new ideas, which, after a long struggle, were forged into the Zionist ideology and Zionism as a political movement. From all of this, it is clear that, quite early on – in the 1870's and 1880's—Grayeve was saved from the danger of petrifaction and from religious-traditionalist fanaticism.

Besides the above-mentioned Olshvanger-Verzhbalovski and Piurko families, Grayeve also had a class of merchant Jews, who were interested in secular matters and Zionist ideas and who found time to educate themselves in the literature of the enlightenment. The following such people should be mentioned: Khaim Itsik Ravidovits, Yezherski, Kahane, Kaptshavski, Beynesh Kolko, Mordkhe Rembelinker, Gvirtsman, Genakhovski, Kravtsinski, Kats, Khaim Katsprovski, Elimelekh Pomerants, Avraham-Itsik Faynshtayn, Sender Guzhik, Mordkhe Rinkovski, Markus, Shabtsi Frida, Vapinski, Ruvn Malakhovski, Henekh Raykhelzon, Itsik Gershtanski, and many more whose names I no longer remember.

[Page 75]

The First Influences Prior to the Building of Eretz-Yisroel

Apparently, Grayever Jews didn't travel to Erets Yisroel only out of longing for the holy places of the ancient land, in order to spend their life weeping, praying and studying Torah at the sacred graves and synagogues, or in order to die and be buried there, as did many aged Jews from various surrounding large and small towns, as early as the 18th century. Rather, the Jews of Grayeve understood the need to organize and to join the Hibat Tsion [Love of Zion] movement, whose goal was to aid and support the Jews who went to Erets Yisroel not to die, but to resurrect and rebuild the land.

It was undoubtedly the Hebrew weekly *Hamagid [The Preacher]*, published by David Gordon, that did the most to awaken the Jewish youth of Grayeve to the great historical events in [Zionist] Jewish life of those times: BILU [student group which took its name from the Hebrew initials of the Biblical verse, House of Jacob, let us go up]; Dr. Liev Pinsker's brochure, Autoemancipation [1882]; and the Katovitser Conference [held in Katowice, Silesia, November 1884]. From the earliest years of its publication, beginning in 1857, in Lyck, Germany, not far from the Russian border, *Hamagid* was an organ of outspoken nationalist character. It published the plans of Rabbis Tsvi Kalisher and [Yehuda] Alkaley to build Erets Yisroel upon a modern foundation. In *Hamagid* there appeared the translation of "Rome and Jerusalem" by Moses Hess. In his articles, the editor urged and warned the Jews not to engage in the conflict between the Poles and the Russians (as in 1863, at the time of the Polish uprising against Russia) but to follow their own path, that is, to build their own homeland in Erets Yisroel.

Hamagid became even more pro-Zionist after 1881, after the terrible pogroms in Russia. From that time on, it published articles by such renowned Havovei Tsion [Lovers of Zion, i.e. members of Hibat Tsion] as Pinsker, Rabbi [Shmuel] Mohilever, Rabbi Eliasberg (From Riga), Sir Laurence Oliphant, Dr. Albert Kahn (the teacher of Benjamin Edmond Rothschild), and others. Starting in 1881, Gordon became one of the most important personalities in the Hibat Tsion movement.

[Page 76]

Of course, Grayeve was the first town in Russia to receive the newspaper right after it came out, as early as the same day, because many Grayeve Jews spent the entire day in Germany. In addition, according to the report of Elimelekh Pomerants, Yudl Faynberg of Grayeve and his wife, a fervent Zionist, were in close contact with David Gordon, who thus exerted a direct influence on the town. Of course, Piurko was a loyal reader of *Hamagid*, and along with him, his many students.

In addition to these, about 15 people in Grayever, according to Pomerants' report, received *Hamalits* [*The Advocate*], published by Aleksander Tsederboym, which began to appear in 1860. (15 people subscribed, and 50 read the newspaper.) This newspaper also had a nationalist character and supported the Havevei Tsion. Among the Grayever Havovei Tsion who received *Hamalits* were Khaim Katsprovski, Ravidovits, Abraham Itsik Faynsthayn, Pomerants, Itsik Vitkievits (now in America) and others.

And when *Hatsefira* ["*Dawn*" or "*Morning*"] began to appear in 1862, it, too, found many readers in Grayeve. From my earliest childhood, I remember how the Jews would go very early to the post office, and even to the train station, in order to get their copies of *Hatsefire*, because they couldn't bear to wait for the postman to bring the paper to their homes. How much the editors of *Hatsefira* valued its circulation in Grayeve can be seen from the fact that after the first Zionist Conference in Basel in 1897, Pomerants, who was then the *Hatsefira* agent, received as a gift from Nokhem Sokolov the works of Y.L.G. [the Hebrew poet, Yehuda Leyb Gordon] and Smolenski.

The Hebrew teachers A.M. Piurko, Binyomen Goldberg, and Gran played an important role in the process of bringing Zionist thought to Grayeve. At that time, the study and writing of Hebrew were by no means identified with Zionism, as they are today.

[Page 77]

But in Grayeve, thanks to the Zionist Hebrew Press, Hebrew was synonymous with Zionism, and the Hebrew teachers were therefore very important to the movement.

At this point, we should mention the Grayever *melameds* [teachers of young children] of that time -- Simkhe-Hersh, who was pro-Zionist; and Berl the Melamed – because it very much depended on the *melamed* whether the study of the bible and of Talmud by a young child awakened a love for Erets Yisroel and a hatred of life in the Diaspora, or satisfaction with the Diaspora and indifference to Erets Yisroel.

Grayeve was also visited by *magidim* [preachers], who knew how to arouse great enthusiasm for the Hibat Tsion movement. One of these, according to Pomerants, was the *magid* Drugitshin, who repeated to the Grayeve audience the sermons of the renowned Rabbi Mohilever.

The Grayever Lovers of Zion were in close contact with Rabbi Mohilever, who was then rabbi in Bialystok. They would turn to him each time the religious fanatics in Grayeve and surrounding towns would try to obstruct various Zionist efforts, and Rabbi Mohilever had enormous influence on the Grayever Jews. The pious considered him a holy person. As for their own

Grayever rabbi, an intelligent man, and very beloved by the populace, the Zionists were reluctant to antagonize him when they felt that he didn't fulfill his obligations to the community. This can be seen in the following example:

Once, the Grayever rabbi refused, out of fear, to sign a telegram to the president of the Russian Duma [parliamentary body], urging the government to take action against pogroms in Bialystok. [Alexander] Olshvanger (Jerusalem) and [Elimelekh] Pomerants, angry at him, went off and sent the telegram with the signatures of the presiding members of the Jewish *kehile* [organized community]. (One of these, who signed reluctantly and fearfully, was the devoted Zionist Moti (Mordkhe) Abramski.) By playing his usual active role in the matter, Olshvanger risked serious consequences, since at the time he was serving in Grayeve's army regiment. The Grayever Zionists not only were not afraid to act in opposition to the rabbi's wishes, they also knew how to influence him, and to get him, not a member of Hibat Tsion, to hold sermons in the *besmedresh* in favor of Erets Yisroel.

[Page 78]

The Founding of the Havevei Tsion

It is impossible to determine precisely when and where the founding meeting of the Grayever Havevei Tsion [Lovers of Zion; alternate name for Hibat Tsion] took place. Perhaps such a meeting never even occurred. But there is no doubt that in Grayeve, as in other larger towns, the Havevei Tsion movement began soon after the pogroms of 1881. This is evidenced by the following:

Shortly before the Katovitser Conference of 1884, the council of the Warsaw Havevei Tsion decided, at the suggestion of Sh.P.Rabinovits, to publish the portrait of the esteemed birthday celebrant [Sir Moses] Montefiore [British Jewish philanthropist who supported Jewish settlement in Palestine], and to sell it in Russia and other countries. In addition to other goals (educational, financial, honoring the celebrant), this would also serve as a membership card for the Lovers of Zion movement. Each Jew who purchased the portrait would thereby declare his participation in or sympathy with the movement. Thanks to the active, energetic Lovers of Zion of Grayeve, such as Elimelekh Pomerants, Beynush Kolko, Tsvi Kaptshavski, Barkovski, Khaim Katspravski, Avraham-Itsik Faynshtayn, Elihu Vaks and others, the Jews of Grayeve responded very well, and the portrait of Montefiore, which sold there for one ruble, appeared in almost every home.

This great success was made possible in large part by the propaganda program that the Lovers of Zion group in Grayeve had developed in the several years since its inception. Grayeve also sent greetings to the birthday celebrant. The thank you note that Montefiore sent in return to Olshvanger, still remains in the Jerusalem home of his daughter, Zelma Verzhbalovski.

The small group of Havevei Tsion in Grayeve consisted mainly of young *maskilim* [followers of the Jewish Enlightenment Movement], modern Jews with modern beliefs. And although they didn't reject the Jewish religious tradition, they remained isolated, and the broad masses of religious Jews did not actively join with them, but passively supported them. The attitude toward the movement on the part of a significant segment of the town's religious Jews changed after Khaim-Itsik Ravidovits settled in Grayeve. When he arrived, the religious Jews understood that here was a strictly observant Jew, a man deeply learned in Judaism, a true scholar from the Volazhiner yeshiva.

[Page 79]

Only someone who has long immersed himself in the study of Talmud can properly appreciate the level of erudition attained by Khaim Itsik Ravidovits. One can rely on the opinion of one such authority, Rabbi Kook, as expressed in his preface to the book, *Merhavi [Interpretations by] Itsik*, which Khaim Itsik Ravidovits published in Erets Yisroel in 1929. But, as great was the joy of the religious Jews over Khaim-Itsik Ravidovits the Talmudist, equally great was their surprise when they learned that he had joined the Havevei Tsion, and had become the central figure in their circle.

After a while, many religious Jews in Grayeve followed in his steps, and signed on as members of the "Odessa Support Committee." (This was the abbreviated name of the legalized Lovers of Zion movement after 1880.) A short time later, thanks to the expansion of the activity of the Havevei Tsion under the influence of Ravidovits, even Hasidim entered the movement, as did even the so-called "practical people." (Ravidovits was not only a great religious scholar, but also a fine merchant, very successful in business, and this, apparently, attracted not a few Grayeve merchants to the movement.) As Pomerants reports in his article about Ravidovits (in *Haaretz*, [the newspaper, *The Land*], October 11, 1936), Grayeve was practically the only town in the entire area at that time, that counted 90 members of the Odessa Committee. And with the growing activity of the movement in Russia, which began with its legalization, the Grayeve Havevei Tsion also began to develop an energetic program on behalf of Erets Yisroel.

Selling Wine and Planting Trees

Pomerants repeated some of the facts in the above-mentioned article in conversations I had with him 13 years after its publication, and these were also substantiated by other Grayever Zionists living in Israel.

With money lent by Khaim Itsik Ravidovits, the Grayever Lovers of Zion bought *esrogim* [pl. of *esrog*, citron used in observing Succot] from Erets Yisroel, and sold them in Grayeve and the surrounding towns. Ravidovits not only lent the money, he went from one *besmedresh* to another, holding sermons, promoting the product, and the Havevei Tsion kept selling *esrogim* until they had driven out the *esrogim* imported from Corfu, and had become almost the sole *esrogim* dealers in the entire Lomzhe-Suwalk area.

[Page 80]

When the Carmel Society was established in Erets Yisroel in 1890, the Grayeve Hovevei Tsion, with the help of Ravidovits and others, purchased its wine, and the young people went door to door selling it, in that way forcing merchants to buy wine from Israel.

In the year 1894, the Havevei Tsion movement in Russia decided to celebrate the 70th birthday of Rabbi Shmuel Mohilever by planting a garden in Hedera, [Jewish settlement in Palestine] to be named Gan Shmuel [Shmuel's garden]. This garden had an additional, important (perhaps the primary) goal: to dry out the swamps of Hedera and in that way to combat malaria, which spread illness and death among the Hedera colonists. Grayeve played an honored role in this undertaking: Grayeve Jews planted over 100 trees, at a cost of over 600 rubles, quite a significant sum for the town.

Of course, the constructive assistance which the Havevei Tsion movement provided to the colonists through the above-mentioned undertakings were a heavy blow for the *khaluka* people in Erets Yisroel who spent their years praying and studying Torah and lived out their lonely lives thanks to the money they received from Jews in the Diaspora. [*Khaluka* was a system of free housing and subsidized living expenses that supported the religious Jewish population in pre-Zionist Palestine.] In their campaign against the Havevei Tsion, the *khaluka* people stopped at nothing, and even denounced them [to the authorities]. As a result of these denunciations, in 1894 Eliezer Ben Yehuda was arrested as a suspect in an attempt to organize an uprising by the Jews in Erets Yisroel against Turkey. This vile action by the Jerusalem *khaluka* people aroused the fury of all Jewry. And when, that same year, a *khaluka* emissary came to Grayeve to solicit funds and at the same time began to inspect *tsitsis* [fringed undergarment worn by Orthodox] to see if they were kosher, the Grayever Hovevei Tsion became enraged and under the leadership of Elimelekh Pomerants they set out throughout the town to find and throw away the *pushkes* [charity collection boxes] of Rabbi Meyer Bal Ha Nes. Very many Grayever Jews who at that time withdrew their support for the *khaluka* Jews began to sympathize with the Odessa Committee and even contributed money to the Jewish colonists in Erets Yisroel.

[Page 81]

From that time on, Grayeve became known as a town with an openly expressed Zionist character. The Grayever Zionists energetically and scrupulously carried out the decisions of the central Havevei Tsion bodies, and their ranks continued to grow broader and stronger. And if anyone, from inside or outside, tried to hinder them, they soon found ways to deflect them. When several of the so-called "political Zionists", like Beynush Kolko, Borkovski, *et al.*, who were dissatisfied with the Odessa Committee, began separately to collect money to help a family to travel to Erets Yisroel as colonists, the Grayever Havevei Tsion contacted Rabbi Mohilever, and he turned to the Grayever rabbi, demanding that he warn the opponents of the Odessa Committee not to dare to do such things. And his intervention helped.

A *"Shmite"* Year and a *Heter-Iske*

An incident occurred involving a *shmite* year, during which it is forbidden by the Torah to cultivate the fields, vineyards, or engage in other agricultural enterprises. It seems to me that this was the year 1894. Because of their difficult circumstances, the colonists in Erets Yisroel were given permission by the rabbis of the Hibat Tsion movement to engage in agricultural activities and to sell agricultural products, just as the great rabbi, Yehude Ha Nasi had done, for humanitarian and nationalist reasons. But the Shtshutshiner rabbi did not, in this case, accept the point of view of Rabbi Yehuda Ha Nasi, the creator of the Mishna. Rather, he sided with Rabbi Pinkhes Ben Yair, the fanatical opponent of Rasbi Yehuda Ha Nasi, and forbade the Shtshutishiner Jews to buy *esrogim* from Erets Yisroel that *shmita* year. And Rabbi Mohilever once again intervened at the request of the Grayever Havevei Tsion, and the Shtshutshiner rabbi had to submit.

[Page 82]

Barely a year had gone by after this victory by the Grayever Havevei Tsion over the *shmite* issue, when a new difficulty arose in the form of *heter iske* [a business document which permits one to receive interest from a loan, by restructuring it as an investment.] The second Zionist Congress in Basel had founded the Jewish Colonial Trust, and appealed to the Jewish people to help establish the financial apparatus to build the land by buying stock shares. A prominent Grayever Jew, M.B., a great Talmudist and a wealthy merchant, who was opposed to Zionism, came forward and declared to the pious Jews, that buying a share entails receiving interest, which is absolutely forbidden by the Torah. This created a threat that the sale of shares, which Dr. [Theodor] Hertzl had so wished would occur among the broad masses of the people, would fail in Zionist Grayeve.

Faced with this difficulty, the Grayever Zionists turned to [Zionist leader David] Volfson, and he immediately responded: "We may not be greatly pious, but we did provide for a *heter-iske*." Volfson's response was disseminated in all of the synagogues, and even the Grayever rabbi himself gave a sermon in favor of the Colonial Trust. The Zionists then threw themselves into selling shares, and they had colossal success. They sold over 600 shares, which brought the Colonial Trust over 6,000 rubles, quite a significant sum for a town like Grayeve. There were families that bought only one share, and others that bought two or three. Kh.I. Ravidovits bought the most shares – 25—for cash.

One can imagine the enthusiastic mood that prevailed in Grayeve during the time of the sale of the shares, so that even Dikar the Apostate, the cashier at the train station, bought two shares, and gave a down payment, and even declared himself ready to purchase the Zionist *shekel* [membership in World Zionist Organization] (according to Pomerants' article in *Hatsefire* on June 18, 1931, which appeared on the 25th anniversary of the Bialystok pogrom, in which Dikar's son died defending a Jewish girl from the pogromists.)

Illegal Zionist Activities

Thus did the Grayever Zionists carry out with zest and ardor every task set them by the Zionist organisation, whether the activity was public and legal, or whether it was forbidden by the Russian government. Indefatigable and fearless, they worked for the Jewish people and its land, Erets Yisroel.

[Page 83]

The Zionists were not scared away, and did not cease their activities, even in the years when the Zionist movement, along with other political movements in Russia, was strictly forbidden, when even participating in a meeting was to risk going to prison. The illegal meetings of that time would take place in the home of Kh. I Ravidovitsh, in the bakery, or in Mordkhe Abramski's storehouse. During these meetings, several children of parents who were at the meeting, or others, under the supervision of today's Dr. Shimen Ravidovitsh (Chicago), would stand watch on the street. And if they saw a suspicious person or a policeman approaching, they would immediately sound an alert. Papers, letters and documents would quickly be hidden, and the meeting would transform itself into an educational society which had gathered to hear lectures by Pomerants on history, by one of the Olshwangers on medicine, Katsprovski on religious rules governing commerce, or Ravidovitsh on Talmud.

Pomerants relates that in 1900 word came that all the members of the Zionist central committee in Vilna had been arrested. When the news was told to Kh.I. Ravidovitsh, and he was warned to be careful, he and Kaprovski gave the following response: "If I.L.Goldberg and his comrades can do time in prison, we have no right to save ourselves and the work must continue as before, whatever the conditions."

And the Zionist work in Grayeve did continue as before, in Hebrew, Yiddish, and Russian. They continued to sell *shekels* throughout the town, and the proceeds were sent over the border to Prostke. As before, Leybl Kats would abandon his shop and go door to door selling the Keren-Kayemet [Jewish National Fund] tokens. As before, there would be bitter arguments between the supporters of "Alt-Nay-Land" under the leadership of Katspravski, and the followers of Ahad Ha'Am [Asher Ginzberg], led by Pomerants and Hershl Kaptshavski. And, as before, the Grayeve Poali Tsion[2] [Workers of Zion, a political movement] would meet in their office in the house of Getsl the Leaseholder on Shul Street, disguising the meeting as a group coming together to study a chapter of Mishna or the Torah portion of the week. And after the meeting, they would sing the well-known Zionist songs of the time: *Mishmar HaYarden* [Guarding the Jordan]; *Al Tal v'al Matar* [Let there be no Dew nor Rain]; *Di Shvue* [The Vow]; *S'u Tsiona Nes v'Degel* [Rise up Toward Zion, Flag and Banner] and *Al Am HaDerekh* [On the Road].

[Page 84]

Children in the Zionist Movement

Like the adults, the children and youth were not scared away from the ban by the Russian government, and participated in every fund-raising effort, and went wherever they were sent.

Yashe (Yosef) Karenietski, the son of the *mashgiekh* [overseer over the laws of kashruth], (today he is called Yosef Karni and has worked since 1922 as chief bookkeeper in Vad HaLeumi [National Committee]) relates that once, when he was nine years old, he was sent to sell New Years cards door to door for Keren Kayemet. Suddenly, he noticed that Kurtselapov (I don't know if that was his real name, or only a nickname for the fat policeman) was running in his direction. He followed him from one street to another until it got dark. Not until midnight did the nine year old Yashe come home, tired and fearful.

This same Karni also relates that when he was a young boy, he, the young Shimen Ravidovitsh and their friends, were given the task of distributing the *shekel* among the Jewish soldiers serving in the Grayever regiment. And in order to carry out this assignment, they had to circulate around the barracks for hours, very fearful, until they managed secretly to sell some *shekels*.

Zionist education of the younger generation was very important in Grayeve. And the older Zionists knew how to attract the young children to the work. Avraham Ravidovitsh (Tel Aviv) recounts that the Grayeve Zionists always employed children to sell *esrogim* and *lulavs* [palm fronds used in observance of Succot] as well as to prepare the *lulavs*. But the children weren't satisfied with these jobs. Avraham and his friends would make little rings from the leftover *lulav* leaves, which they would sell to other children, giving the money to Keren Kayemet. Shifre Ravidovitsh (Shifre Levin, Afula) recounts that on the Sabbath, Kh. I. Ravidovitsh would take the children on an outing on the Shtshutshiner Road, and play with them in Hebrew.

[Page 85]

When the Hertzl Gymnasium was founded in Tel Aviv, three children left Grayeve to study in that institution: Yankev Ravidovitsh (a doctor in America); Yosef Karmin, today a very active teacher in schools in Erets Yisroel and the author of various textbooks in the field of natural history; and Yeheskl Papovski, who later became one of the most active and devoted Zionists in Grayeve and a longtime teacher in the Tarbut schools [modern Zionist schools in which Hebrew was the main language of instruction.]

Dr. Tsvi Vayslavski also did a lot to get children involved in Zionist work. Avraham Ravidovitsh relates that Dr. Vayslavski used to persuade the children to work at collecting money for Keren Kayemet and advised them on how to deal with the difficulties they encountered in that thankless task. But this wasn't Dr. Vayslavki's only, or most important, field of endeavor. In 1907 he undertook to distribute *Dos Yidishe Folk* [The Jewish People], the central organ of the Zionist movement. Later, he did a lot to distribute Hebrew periodicals and literature in Grayeve. In 1911, he was one of the most active Zionists in Grayeve. Together with Hershl Kapstovski he would organize meetings of the active Zionists: Rembelinker, Pomerants, Faynshtayn, Ravidovitsh, Rinkovski, the Olshvangers, *et. al.* (The meetings were held at the homes of Faynshtayn, Ravidovitch, Rinkovski, and at Berl Rozen's, in Yamshun's house.)

Dr. Vayslavski was at that time one of the chief speakers and gave many talks on Zionist themes. The intelligent speeches on Jewish history which he delivered to the young and to adults were very significant. These talks awoke in Grayeve's Jewish youth a love for Jewish history and literature and thus helped to form their Zionist world view. Dr. Vayslavski was then already one of the most gifted students of Prof. Yosef Kloyzner, who was then renowned for his literary activity and his talks on Jewish history in Odessa, which was at the time one of the most important centers of the renaissance movement in Hebrew literature and culture.

[Page 86]

The Role of the *Kheder-Mesukn*

[*Kheder-mesukn*: reformed, modern religious school for young children]

A special role was played by the modern *kheders*, the so-called "*khadorim-mesukonim*" run by Karmin, Piurka, Pomerants and Lis, which were well-attended by the children of Zionists as soon as they opened (about 1908). Pomerants and Lis didn't limit themselves to teaching Hebrew; they provided a broad and energetic education. The very young children at these modern *kheders* absorbed a viewpoint, consciously or unconsciously, on various Zionist problems. At the time of the language war in Erets Yisroel, before the First World War, (over whether Yiddish or Hebrew would be the language of instruction), the children of the Pomerants *kheder mesukn* were brought into the fight and energetically took the side of those who declared a strike in protest against the attempt to make Yiddish the language of instruction. And it was perhaps thanks to the children's position, that the adults organized to send money in support of the strikers. And although sending money from Russia to Erets Yisroel was a very difficult and complicated matter, the Grayever Zionists found a way to send the money through London

[Page 87]

.

The *khadorim-mesukonim* created a Zionist atmosphere in the entire town, awakened a love for the Hebrew language, and contributed much to its spread among broader segments of the Jewish population. Three years after the founding of the *kheders*, there already existed in Grayeve, according to the report of Dr. Vayslavski, quite a large number of Jewish boys and girls who understood Hebrew very well. And, as reported by many Grayever Zionists living in Israel today, the young people listened with joy and enthusiasm to lectures by Dr. Vayslavski (who was then still called Hirsh-Leyb), who already spoke a rich and literary Hebrew. And the Grayeve Zionists were great experts on that matter, since very many themselves wrote a rich, beautiful, expressive Hebrew. This can be seen by reading the speech given at one of the memorials for Herzl by Mordkhe Rembelinker, who spoke so eloquently and with such feeling, who was a true intellectual in his speech, bearing and understanding, and who, sadly, died before his time.

A group of schoolgirls from the Hebrew Tarbut School

Among the various educational endeavors carried out by the Zionists on behalf of and with the help of the young people was the founding of the Grayever library in 1912. As soon as permission was granted to open a library in the name of the Lovers of Hebrew society, Leyzer Zilbershtayn, Itsik Gershtanski and Pomerants began to work on its establishment. They purchased a large number of books in Hebrew, Yiddish, and Russian, and they opened the library in a house on the Rabbi's lane. The librarian was the daughter of Rafalovitsh the scribe. In order to strengthen the financial foundation of the new institution, the founders immediately, in its first year, mounted a production of King Lear (the first theater performance in Grayeve.) The participants were Mordkhe Rembelinker, Leyzer Zilbershtayn, Itsik Gershantski, Alte Ravidovitsh (Rechavie), *et al.*

[Page 88]

Conflicts with Rabbis and Fanatics

At the beginning of the 20th century, the Zionist movement in Grayeve was already closely tied to the international movement. The Grayeve Zionists were already sending representatives to national conferences and to the Zionist Congress. They elected Elimelekh Pomerants as their representative to the conference in Minsk in 1902, in order to propose the very important plan to conduct cultural work on two fronts: among the religious and non-religious Zionists. Pomerants fell ill and did not attend the conference and his mission was entrusted to Mr. Rutski from Gonyandz, who had also represented Grayeve and made the above-mentioned proposal (known as Ussishkin's Plan). [Menakhem Ussishkin was a member of the Executive Committee of Hibat Tsion.]

In 1903, Kh.I. Ravidovitsh was a delegate to the 6th Zionist congress in Basel and along with Tsioni Tsion [Zionists for Zion], he voted against Dr. Hertzl's Uganda Plan [to establish the Jewish homeland in East Africa.] As Pomerants relates in his article about Ravidovitsh in *Haaretz*, the Grayever Zionists, under Ravidovitsh's leadership, threw themselves into a difficult and bitter struggle against the anti-Zionist fanatics and rabbis who had gathered around the Kovner rabbi, and Rabbi Akiva Rabinovitsh, publisher of the sinister and reactionary organ, *HaPeles* [*The Scale*]. By revealing the sinister and fanatical plans of the group, the Grayever Zionists emerged from the fight victorious and Grayeve earned for itself a reputation as a fortress of Zionism.

This and other victories, in Grayeve and beyond, encouraged the Zionists even more, and from time to time, Grayeve sent emissaries to the nearby towns in order to win them over to Zionist thought.

[Page 89]

Thus, the Grayeve Zionists worked tirelessly and successfully in several areas: propaganda, selling of *shekels*, Keren Kayemet, education, and cultural work, until the outbreak of World War One (1914). Actually, until the last minute, just two days before the war broke out, and suspense grew from minute to minute, when one could already detect the smell of gunpowder in the air, and many people in Grayeve had already packed and others had even left town –in that suspenseful atmosphere Pomerants sat in Ravidovitsh's store in Prostken and organized the proceeds from the sale of *shekels* and sent them to Cologne.

In the Difficult War Years

The Grayever Zionists lived through several difficult years, years of forced inactivity and impatient expectation and waiting for the end of the war, years of deep worry over the fate of the Jewish people in Erets Yisroel. In this regard, it is appropriate to mention the following from Pomerants' article: When the news reached Bialystok that Dr. Yankev Ravidovitsh (America) had joined the Jewish division of the English army, which was fighting against Turkey on the Gallipoli front, Kh. I Ravidovitsh was visited by one of the Grayeve merchants. This man, who had a reputation as a speculator, who had profited by speculating on the need of the hungry masses, said with biting sarcasm to the worried father: "Is it really true, then, Mr. Ravidovitsh, that your son went to welcome the Messiah?"[3]

The administration of the library

Top row, from right: Yosef Karni, Khave Shtrasberg, Markus, Rokhl Piurko, Ladelski, Itsik Piurko

Bottom row, from right: Khanovski, Zalmen Sutker, Ida Shtraserg, Isakhar Kaptshavski, Leybl Ziberski, Meyer Vaks

[Page 90]

To this, Ravidovitsh answered: "Whether my son will bring the Messiah, I cannot say. But that he will not bring hunger to the Jewish masses like some Jewish merchant-speculators – of that I am entirely certain." And Ravidovitsh added: "If England would change its position and would send Jewish soldiers to the front in Erets Yisroel, I would also send my son Shimen" (today Dr. Shimen Ravidovitsh, professor at the University of Chicago.)

In summer 1915, the Germans took Bialystok and a half year later, the Jewish families who had left their beloved town in 1914, returned. The youth of Grayeve began to work energetically for the realization of their ideal, which they grew up with, which had straightened out the hunched Jewish backs, which had made them free, proud people, and filled them with self-empowerment and with love for the Jewish people, for its history, and its great cultural values.

New Youth, New Cultural Forces

New, young forces –youths aged 17-20 -- now entered the Zionist life of Grayeve. They threw themselves into the work with youthful enthusiasm. With ardor and stubbornness and with their energetic activity, they drew in the majority of Jewish youth. As soon as they returned to Grayeve, they met to reorganize Zionist work in the town. The most active among them were Yosef Karni (Jerusalem), Yeshayohu Abramski (Tel Aviv), Sholem Khanovski and Dvoyre Khanovski (Tel Aviv), Moyshe Khanovski (Ramat Gan), Borekh Khanovski, Etke Khanovski, Rokhl Piurko (Tel Aviv), Merke Khanovski, Feygl Vilenski (Sweden), Brustin, Shloyme Radam (Tel Aviv), the daughters of the Lifshits family, Menashe Furman (died in Tel Aviv), Shalakhman, Itsik Piurko (Jerusalem), Hershl Tenenboym. For a short time the following worked with them: Yisoskher Kaptshavski, Leybl Zilberski and the Shtroysberg sisters. Later, the following joined with the [Zionist] youth: Pomerants, Rembelinker, Eliezer Zilbershtayn, Faynshtayn, Gvirtsman (who literally spent everything he owned on Zionist causes). The more religious active Zionists joined *Mizrakhi*, such as Leybl Kats (died in Erets Yisroel), Ber-Velvl Khanovski, Khaim Tuvie Khanovski (died in Tel Aviv), Khenokh Raykhlson (died in Haifa), Mordkhe Abramski (died in Tel Aviv), Tutelman, Markus, et. al.

[Page 91]

The young Zionists rented a hall in Yamshun's building and began methodically and skillfully to carry out one activity after another. First, they began to recruit new members for the united Grayeve Zionist organization called Agudat Bnai Tsion [Society of the Sons of Zion]. After an energetic, house to house propaganda campaign, they succeeded in recruiting 100 new members. A. Pomerants was elected chairman; Yosef Karni, vice-chairman; Yeheskl Papovski, secretary (he wrote a splendid Hebrew, in an exceptionally beautiful handwriting); Yeshayohu Abramski, treasurer; and Mordkhe Rembelinker , representative for Keren Kayemet. When Rembelinker became very sick in 1921, Abramski became the representative for Keren Kayemet, and he developed a very active program until he made *aliyah* [emigrated to Israel] in 1926. After him, Hershl Gershtanski (Tel Aviv) took over this difficult job, and fulfilled his obligation with the same devotion until the Second World War in 1939.

A group of Zionist activists after a Keren Kayemet action

Standing, from right: **Sholem Khanovski (Karni), Etke Khanovski, Yehoshayu Abramski, Borekh Khanovski, Katshalski**

Sitting, from right: **Itke Halalit [sp.?], Menukheke, Leybl Leybl Ladelski, Malke Khanovski**

[Page 92]

The Zionist organization developed a wide range of propaganda and cultural activities, and organized public programs on Zionism and other themes, and public discussions, with the additional participation of representatives of other parties, from Grayeve and elsewhere. As I recall, the first public lecture was given by Mr. Milaykovki, who was sent by the central office of the Zionist organization in Warsaw. The public discussion evenings would often end in shouting and even in physical fighting, thus helping to crystallize the viewpoints of two opposing camps –Zionist and anti-Zionist.

In the same hall, there would also be held celebratory gatherings. One of these was to celebrate the Balfour Declaration of November 2, 1917 [in which Britain recognized the right to a Jewish homeland in Palestine]. On the day that Grayever celebrated this great event, all the stores were closed, and the entire Jewish population gathered in the *shul* [synagogue] to hear sermons and speeches. After the mass meeting in *shul*, in the evening, there was a lecture by Mr. Piantnitski from Warsaw, and discussions, with the participation of a Bundist speaker.

On Saturday evenings, a small group of educated boys and girls organized lectures and recitations that were of an especially appealing cultural character. Members of the older generation, such as Mordkhe Rembelinker, also participated. The active members of this group were: Yesoskher Kaptshavski, Leybl Ziberski, Rokhl Piurko, the Shtroysberg daughters, *et al.* They would gather together, as their fathers did, in the *besmedresh*, in the evenings and on the Sabbath, to read and to discuss various books. They would also organize public gatherings with recitations in the reading room of the library. The proceeds were donated to the library to purchase new books.

[Page 93]

In addition to this group, another group was formed in 1916, consisting of several young people who devoted themselves to studying Hebrew literature on their own, and chiefly to publishing a Hebrew weekly which appeared in pamphlet form, written in a clear, fine handwriting, and illustrated with drawings. It had stories by Leybl Goldshteyn (today the popular Hebrew author, Ari Ibn Zaav), sketches and humorous pieces about life in Grayeve, and articles about current events. The most important of the weekly's staff were, as I recall: L. Goldshteyn, Adamshteyn, Emanuel Kolko, Fayvl Shtroysberg, and Yeheskl Obiedoynski. This group would also organize lectures on Hebrew literature. The group was called Agudat HaNoar [Young People's Society]. Its members set themselves the task of disseminating Hebrew language and considered themselves patriots of Erets Yisroel and fighters for the Jewish people. Yosef Karni devoted much effort and time to this group. He supported its development, delivered lectures and published their articles and stories in his weekly.

Lectures, Theater Productions, Courses, Celebrations

After the young Zionists had returned to Grayeve, their first job was to gather the books form the library, which had disappeared during the time in which the majority of the Jewish population had abandoned Grayeve. The library, with its reading room, became the most important center for cultural work for the entire town, not excluding any [political] party or social class.

Evening classes were also established, with a limited but systematically conducted curriculum: Jewish history, Hebrew literature, and Tanakh [the Pentateuch]. The teachers were: Buzshoze, Elimelekh Pomerants, Yeheskl Popavski, and Yosef Karni. The classes were held in the Zionist offices in Berenzon's house. Youth from all classes and sectors of society studied there. Well-off students paid a monthly fee, and those who were indigent did not have to pay. Through various means, the Grayeve youth created a kind of educational fund, which covered the costs of tuition for those who couldn't pay. These classes were held for several years. In the evening, one would encounter in the streets of Grayeve boys and girls 15 to 16 years old, hurrying with Hebrew books and notebooks to the classes in the Zionist offices. After the classes, loud discussions among the student would continue until late.

[Page 94]

Out of these evening courses there began to develop activities meant for a broader audience. These included the interesting lectures given by the teacher, Buzshoze, and Leybl Godshteyn; and theatrical productions, in which not only the students and young Zionist activists participated, but also others, non-Zionists, such as Zalman Sutker. These theater productions accomplished two important goals: they served as exceptional propaganda for Zionism, and they also brought in significant sums of money, which were designated for the library and for the Zionist organization.

Every holiday and every day commemorating an event in Jewish or Zionist history, there were theater performances or evenings of recitation and readings, which created an atmosphere of Jewish culture in Grayeve. One can easily imagine the great social and nationalistic value of these performances by the young Zionists. Grayeve Jews no longer had to limit themselves to praying, studying Torah, and taking an afternoon nap on the Sabbath. There grew up a new need to get together to enjoy culture, art, and literature, and when there came a Sabbath or holiday when "nothing was happening," as they used to say in Grayeve, the individual, as well as the community, would feel he had been deprived of a somehow important and enjoyable thing. Even the religious Jews were no longer satisfied with the ways that had observed the Sabbath and holidays in former years.

After the Mizrakhi [religious Zionists] organization was established in Grayeve, there wasn't a Sabbath or holiday that the older generation didn't rush off to *shul* or to the old *besmedresh* to hear the sermons of Rabbi Emiel, which were learned in their content, and splendid in their form and style. And, like the sermons of Rabbi Emiel, the inspiring Zionists speeches that Yosl Zaydenberg gave in the *shtibls* [small Hasidic synagogue] and *besmedreshim* also attracted the people of Grayeve. From time to time, a Zionist from out of town would come to give a sermon, attracting a large audience on a weekday as well.

[Page 95]

Thanks to the expanded activity of the young Zionists and of the older generation, Grayeve became a Zionist town in the full meaning of the word. This would have been very clear to anyone who lived in Grayeve in the days of the San Remo Conference in April 1920 [at which the Allies in World War One confirmed the pledge of the Balfour Declaration concerning the establishment of a Jewish national home in Palestine] and the establishment of Keren Hayesod [United Israel Appeal; literally "the foundation fund"] in July 1920.

In the spring of San Remo, which fell on [the holiday] Lag b'omer, all the businesses were closed, even the Polish ones. The school children of Hashomer Hatsair marched to the *shul* holding national flags, accompanied by the majority of the town's Jewish population. In the *shul*, Rabbi Emiel gave a talk, and then Yosef Karni, in the name of the Grayever Zionist organization, strongly protested the arrest of [Vladimir] Jabotinksi [leader of the Revisionist Zionist movement] in Erets Yisroel. And just when the children and the older audience had left the *shul*, a demonstration spontaneously broke out, and people went off to the Bogusher Woods singing Hebrew songs. In the evening there was a festive gathering at the Zionist office, with speeches by Pomerants, Rembelinker, Yosef Zaydenberg and Yosef Karni.

At the time of the foundation of the Keren Hayesod, there occurred in the *shul*, after the speeches, and later in people's homes, that which in the Book of Exodus is called *vayisparku* [generous giving; from the verses in Exodus 32:3 *et seq.*in which the Israelites stripped off their jewelry to build the Golden Calf]. And not only the rich or well to do Grayever Jews, but also quite a few poor ones, laborers and artisans, joyfully gave as much as they could.

That same year, the opponents of Zionism, the Hasidim, were won over, and if they didn't actually join up as members, they demonstrated their sympathy by giving money to the Zionist fund. Yosef Karni relates that one Yom Kippur eve, he proposed that the Zionists visit the Hasidic *shtibls*, too, when they went out to collect money for Erets Yisroel. People laughed at him, because none of the Zionists could imagine that they would find anyone among the Hasidim who would give money. So he went alone, and to the amazement of the Zionists, he brought back from the Hasidic *shtibls* twice as much as was collected in the other houses of worship.

[Page 96]

The "Shomer Hatsair" and the "Khalutz"

With the founding of Hashomer Hatsair [The Young Guard], not only the majority of the youth, but also the majority of the children, became Zionists. The leadership of Hashomer was twofold. There were the young instructors, like Leybl and Yisroel Vaks (Tel Aviv); Yekheskl Rinkovski, that inspired speaker with his lovely, poetic language; the talented theater personality, the good and intelligent Khatskele; Yisroel Radom (Tel Aviv), Mordkhe Masenznik, *et al.* And there were the patrons, who consisted mainly of Zionists, like Leyzer and Moniak Zilbershteyn, but also of non-Zionists, like Zalmen Sutker, who devoted much work and effort to the organization.

The importance of the patrons was immeasurably great. Thanks to them, Hashomer Hatsair inspired trust in the Jewish parents, and they confidently agreed to let their children enroll in the movement. The organization grew from day to day, and expanded its activity among and on behalf of the young people (Hebrew courses, lectures on Zionist and general themes, and excursions), as well as in all areas of the general Zionist programs. Through its chorus (under the direction of Zalmen Sutker,) its sports program, its general participation, it enriched and embellished every Zionist celebration.

[Page 97]

In later years, after the movement was reorganized, the most active participants were Itsik Gartshinski (the son of Moyshe), Aron Kravtsinski (Yagur), Zishke Gartshitski (New York), Paltiel Pasternak (South America), Yisroel Kirshenboym (Haifa), *et al.* They carried out the work of Hashomer Hatsair almost until the last year before the outbreak of World War II (1939).

With Hashomer Hatsair, we actually have already entered a later stage in the development of the Zionist movement in Grayeve. We must, however, return to 1917, and give an overview of another Zionist phenomenon, a movement which didn't limit itself to raising money, to send others to Erets Yisroel, a movement which set itself the task of preparing its members spiritually and physically to make *aliyah* – that is, the Hekhaluts [Pioneer] movement, which was established in Grayeve in 1917. And it should be noted that the Hekhaluts movement in Grayeve was founded entirely independently and without the influence of the general Hekhaluts movement, which was founded by Yosef Trumpeldor in Russia after the October Revolution of 1917, and which spread to various cities of Russia, Lithuania, and Poland right after the first Hekhaluts conference in Kharkov in 1918. In 1917, there did not and could not exist, any link between Russia and the occupied areas of Poland.

A group from Hashomer Hastair
Rokhl Shidlo, Tevel Gartsitski, Rokhl Rozenboym, Yehtskl Keynun, Tsvi Kirshenbaum, Khane Gratshteyn, Shabtsi Yakubinski, Isroel Novalski

Hashomer Hatsair on an excursion to Ganiandz in 1928

[Page 98]

The history of Hekhaluts in Grayeve is as follows: In the summer of 1917, the Christian peasants in the nearby villages stopped selling their products to the Jews. Their slogan was "Jews, go to Palestine." The economic situation for the Jews was unimaginably bad. It was impossible to obtain milk, butter, eggs, meat, etc. The shortage of these products became even worse when the German military authority confiscated from the peasants every food they produced. Every well-off Jew then bought himself a cow and poultry; the poorer ones bought a goat.

A group of *khalutsim* in 1926

In order to alleviate the great want of the masses, there was established a public kitchen, in which the following were very active: Rabbi Emiel and his wife, Amtsi Piurko, the daughters of Mikhl Vilenski, Khaim-Tuvie Khanovski, *et al*. Then, the Grayeve Jews remembered that they had fields ("*doyalkes*") that could be cultivated, and a few of them began to do so, *e.g.* Nekhemie Bukovski, (Tel Aviv), Khanovski, Abramski, and Levit.

[Page 99]

But if some of the older Zionists and others found some sort of solution to their economic plight by cultivating their fields, at the same time a handful of young Zionists got together -- Shloyme Radom (Tel Aviv), Meyer Bialostotski (Tel Aviv), Azriel Ladelski (Kfar Eta), Moyshe Khanovski (Ramat Gan), and Rastigalski – and decided to study agriculture and go to Erets Yisroel. Without material help and even without moral support, they began to carry out their plan with their own resources. (The only Grayever Jew who was enthusiastic about the plan from the first, and who encouraged and invigorated the young idealists with his words was Yisroel-Yankev Grudzeminski, the bookbinder. He was also the first Grayever Jew to leave for Erets Yisroel after the war.)

They attracted several additional young people and the handful grew into a group of 14 members, among them the daughters of the scribe (for a Jewish girl of the Grayeve middle class of that time to join Hekhaluts to study agriculture and to go to Erets Yisroel was certainly a unique and even revolutionary occurrence.) They acquired a horse -- who doesn't remember the Hekhaluts' white horse? -- a wagon, several pitchforks and shovels. They rented a stable from Nosn Zilberman. They leased one garden near Masienznik (Train Street), a second on Bogusher Street, near Vaynshtayn, and somewhat later, part of a field of 10 *morg* [unit of measurement, about an acre]. Then they began to bring manure to the fields. (One can imagine how the Grayevers carried on every time they drove manure through the streets.) And they set to work, with great effort and no experience, but with youthful obstinacy.

Hashomer Hastair on an excursion in 1932

[Page 100]

Mordkhe Abramski used to lend them his horses to carry the manure, and Nekhemie Bukovski gave them very important instructions on how to cultivate the fields. The sarcastic comments by the anti-Zionists soon ceased. The idea resonated strongly with a large part of the young people, and other boys and girls began to ask to be admitted as members of Hekhaluts. But there were also the Jewish mothers who came to weep and wail over why their children were being forced to do such heavy and filthy work. As a result, the council of Hekhaluts began to accept as members only those who passed the "exam"; that is, those who weren't frightened off by having to jump into the manure bins and empty them. Every candidate had to demonstrate, in this way, that he would be able to withstand other trials and difficulties in the future.

The "Herut V'Tehiye" and "Hekhaluts Hatsair"

Several years later, after the split in Hashomer Hastair, when that fine youth organization had practically dissolved, there appeared another group of young Zionists who demonstrated just as much initiative and energy as the founders of Hekhaluts. This was the youth organization Herut V'Tehiye [Freedom and Rebirth], (although the Herut V'Tehiye did not do the kind of pioneer work that Hekhaluts had). The intellectuals of Grayeve, as well as the older Zionists, had almost nothing to do with this youth organization. But the organization had boys and girls capable of carrying out the work, who could fend for themselves. All on their own, they organized lectures on history and literature. Later, they brought in teachers from the town's Tarbut schools, Shikare and Kaplan, who, for pay, gave classes in history and cultural history. they took over the Jewish library and organized it. Yankev Shatsky,(Tel Aviv), Dovid Bialistotski (Netanya), Shloyme Bergenzon, Shloyme Fridman (the son of the "Russian" shopkeeper), *et al.*, sat for long weeks and bound, numbered, and catalogued the books. And when they saw how few books the library had, they organized (again, on their own) several theater productions (Gordin or Goldfaden plays) in Grayeve and Shtshutshin. The main participants were Reyzl Bialistotski (Netanya), the Fridmans, *et al.*). And with the proceeds they bought books every month and enriched the library. With the appearance of the new books, there came new readers, and the library once again became an important cultural center for all of Jewish Grayeve.

[Page 101]

A year after the founding of HV, I believe in 1924, there began a new Khaluts movement, Hekhaluts Hatsair, which the members of the dissolved Herut V'Tehiye later joined. In the beginning of its existence, the new Khaluts organization took in all of the Grayever youth –former students of the Tarbut schools and of *kheders*, apprentices to artisans -- who because of ideological or other reasons had not found a place in Herut V'Tehiye or in Hashomer Hatsair. The founders of the new Hekhaluts movement in Grayeve were Moyshe and Arye Elkan (Tel Aviv), Khaim Fridman, Avraham Berenzon (Dafne), Emanuel Berman (Tel Aviv), Yeshaye Stavinski (Ein Harod), Dov Marushevski (Haifa). The movement had a library named after Yosef Khaim Brener. Some of the books were donated, but most were purchased with the proceeds of various lotteries and evening events held in Grayeve and surrounding small towns.

A group of *khalutsim* on a Keren Kayemet action

[Page 102]

There was also a drama circle and a sports club with the name "Power", which often won in matches with Polish sports clubs. The members of Hekhaluts, like those of Hashomer Hatsair, would go to *hakhsore* [training farms where people prepared for *aliyah*] and a large number of them are today in Israel. In Hekhaluts, as in Hashomer Hastair, there were courses in Hebrew, there were daily talks and lectures on general, Jewish and Zionist issues, conducted by their members or by other Zionists from the town like Dovid Bialastotski or speakers who would come from other cities.

In 1929, a Revisionist party was founded in Grayeve, and connected to it, somewhat later, Betar [youth movement of the Revisionist Party]. The founders of the Revisionist party and Betar were Moyshe Ziberski (Tel Aviv), Avraham Rembelinker (Jerusalem), Elihu Verzhbalovski (Jerusalem), Atlasovits, Bobrovski (Tel Aviv). Betar conducted the same kinds of cultural and educational activities as the youth organizations previously mentioned (Hebrew courses, lectures on Zionist and general subjects) and, in keeping with Betar's ideology, very active military training for youth.

Finally, we must also mention WIZO [Women's International Zionist Organization, founded 1920, in England; pronounced "Vitso" in Hebrew] in which the most active members were: Hadasa Olshvanger, Dvore Verzhbalovski, Klare Rekhtman, the Lifshits daughters. WIZO, too, held lectures almost every week by Zelme Verzhbalovski (Jerusalem), Yekheskl Papovski, and speakers from out of town, about Jewish history, literature, and current events. The assembled women, Jewish mothers and daughters from all segments of society, would listen to the lectures with great interest and would also ask questions and participate in the discussions. It should be emphasized that that the WIZO activities served brilliantly to counteract the negative influence of the card club of the so-called Jewish "elite" of Grayeve.

[Page 103]

The bazaars held by WIZO were very well attended. They were held very frequently, and aside from enlivening the whole town, they brought in a lot of money for the Keren Kayemet. When the bazaars were held, there would be various artistic events, successfully organized by Miss Kashdim (America), who was also very active in other aspects of Zionist life in Grayeve.

Naturally, with so many youth organizations, Zionist activity in Grayeve was carried out with great energy, and almost every Zionist undertaking had a successful outcome. The youth organizations occupied themselves with Keren Kayemet and selling *shekels*, etc., and the older Zionists were thus able to devote themselves to other kinds of Zionist activities. One of these –the most important –was the Tarbut school, which, despite many difficulties and obstacles, operated from 1920 until the Second World War. There was also a kindergarten connected with the school.

A group from Hashomer Hatsair in 1929

[Page 104]

The school administration included Itsik and Frida Gershtanski (Tel Aviv), Vayner (Tel Aviv) *et al.*

It must be noted that there wasn't a single area of life in Grayeve in which the Zionists did not participate and work with all their strength for the good of the community.

The Magistrat

Grayever firefighters

Footnotes

17. Itsik Gartshitski was born in Grayeve in 1904. He studied in *kheders* [religious elementary schools], then in the Polish *gymnasiums* [academic high schools] in Bialystok and Vilna. He studied literature and philosophy in the Vilna University, which he graduated with a master's degree in philosophy. Since 1935 he has lived in Israel, where he is a teacher in a Hebrew *gymnasium*. He translated Gradenvits' history of Miuzik into Hebrew, and co-authored several Hebrew textbooks for adults. –The Editors.
18. The Poale Tsion movement in Grayeve apparently started after the Fourth Zionist Congress of 1901. It appears that as a result of the great differences of opinion, Pomerants left the General Zionists and together with Kalman Antshkovki and Berl the carpenter's son, founded the Poale Tsion in Grayeve. To this organization belonged: Moyshe Gershtanski, Rosman, Yosef Ziberski, Tikatshi, Ruven Malakhovski, Shabtsi Marushevski, Aron-Yankev Gartshitski, and many others.
    In the fortress of Gallipoli, the Turkish powers had, around 250 years earlier, imprisoned Shabtsi Tsvi, who was known as the False Messiah.

[Page 105]

Workers' Organizations in Grayeve
(Since the First World War)

Sh. Y. Fishbeyn

Translated by Miriam Leberstein

Some attempts to organize the working class, the poor, and the youth of Grayeve were made as early as the first years of this century.

The revolutionary storm that surged through the Russian Empire after the Tsarist defeat in the Russo-Japanese War in 1904 also engulfed Jewish workers and youth in the cities and *shtetlakh* [small villages] of Poland, touching down in Grayeve as well. A number of strikes occurred in the town's factories and workshops. Organizers from the *Bund*[1] began to be active, chiefly among the youth. The *Poaleii Tsion*[2] as well as the General Zionists, siphoned off the young people into their ranks, turning them away from the revolutionary organizations and struggle.

The Tsarist reaction, which so bloodily repressed the revolution of 1905, did not spare Grayeve. The first sprouts of the workers' movement were suppressed before they had a chance to take root and grow. The reaction reached its highest expression with the outbreak of the First World War. In the economic and social upheaval of the war it was clearly impossible for the working class of the small towns to organize. Only after the war, when Poland formally gained its independence, did the workers' parties throughout the country begin to develop their activities, and Grayeve also began to stir.

[Page 106]

A group of workers making cement bricks (in 1918)
From right to left: Eli Sosno, Mayer Levit, Avreml Levit, Matke Levit, Fridman, Kats, and Fishbeyn

The revolution in Russia and the uprisings in Germany and other countries resonated in Poland; a new kind of language began to be heard, new terms about social justice, workers' power, socialism, Bolsheviks, Spartacists. What meaning could this have for Grayeve, for Jews, for the youth? These questions had to be answered and made clear –but who would do that, and how?

In 1918, Grayeve had an energetic group of young people. In addition to the young people who were employed in the small workshops, there were those who were employed in public works projects. Jewish men and women worked on the building of the Ruder road and many Jewish workers were employed in the Belder Forest, in the building of a light rail train (*kolayke*), and in the barracks.

With the revival of the workers' movement in the land, the larger parties began to strengthen their position through the expansion of their activity and influence in the provincial towns. Party representatives and speakers from Warsaw began to appear in Grayeve. Speakers came from the Bund and from

Poaleii Tsion. seeking to organize separate sections for their parties though lectures, debates and agitation. At that time, the Bundist activist Lurie came from Warsaw. A gifted speaker, in the course of several weeks he gave a number of lectures on the questions of Socialism and the workers' parties. Under his influence, a non-partisan workers' club began to be organized. Among the leading activists of the club were: Yankl Margolis, Berl Sutker, Avrutin, Kaptshavski and others.

[Page 107]

The club set itself the task of conducting general cultural activities. It did not have any defined program and did not follow a specific ideology. Nor was the leadership clear about its goals. The members of the workers' club were seeking an answer to their societal problems and they had a great thirst for learning and for knowledge. Hundreds of people frequented the club premises, but no systematic educational program was ever established. Nothing at all was done in the area of trade unionism and social action.

In the winter of 1918-1919, commerce between Grayeve and Germany was re-established. Wagonloads of salt, herring and gasoline began to come into Grayeve for distribution to other towns. But this did not greatly affect the general economic conditions of the town. There was great poverty among the Jewish masses; the shortage of shoes, clothing, heating fuel and food was unbearable. In the face of this need, the leaders of the worker' club began to agitate for the creation of a cooperative to provide the needy with bread and heating fuel.

A Cooperative for Relief for the Poor

They adopted a plan, in which the well-to-do and the merchants of the town would finance a workers' relief cooperative. The executive board of the club contacted individual rich men and leaders of the town's public institutions about this matter but nothing resulted from this.

[Page 108]

The executive board then decided to bring together all the people of substance in the town in a meeting at the old *besmedresh* [prayer house] on *shabes* [Sabbath] during the day to discuss with them helping the poor people of the town. The meeting was a failure, because the people of means simply didn't show up to pray that shabes.

For the next shabes, the club leadership mobilized the membership and decided to shut all of the houses of worship, with the exception of the old besmedresh, and in that way to force the wealthy to come together in one place. When it came time to pray and the wealthy didn't arrive at the besmedresh, the executive board sent committees of envoys to the homes of the rich, to bring them to the besmedresh. Many incidents occurred in the attempt to assemble the wealthy. Some were comical, but there were also serious incidents and fights. At the Kapitser on Raigroder Street, there was even a shooting.

The town became very agitated as a result of the shabes demonstration. The wealthy were convinced that they would not be able to completely escape responsibility for the poor and agreed to contribute a significant sum of money. The club leadership then rented a store to serve as a warehouse for the purchase of food and distributed the food among the poor.

This continued until certain of the wealthy denounced the leaders of the club to the Polish authorities. They were accused of Bolshevism. As a result of the denunciations some of the leaders had to leave Grayeve and the club fell apart.

The Bund and the Poaleii Tsion Organizations

In the spring of 1919, two separate groups began to form – a Bundist one, and a Poaleii Tsionist. Each group brought in speakers from Warsaw. Lurie returned, but was met with a tepid response. Lurie did, however, organize an official Bund organization. The leaders were the Segalovitshes, Bogush and others. The Bundist organization devoted itself primarily to educational work.

[Page 109]

They frequently organized recreational events. Their drama circle mounted a series of theatrical performances. The recreational programs attracted young people who had no party affiliation.

The Poaleii Tsion brought in a speaker from Warsaw named Krol, who held a series of lectures and assisted them in the formation of their organization. Their leaders were: Striev, Krinski, Sosno, and others.

At that time, the reaction [to the revolutionary movement] was growing stronger in Poland, and the Polish government, supported by the allies, went to war against the Soviet Union. Some of the young people were drafted into the army; some emigrated. The Bundist and Poalei Tsion organizations fell apart.

The only young people remaining in the town were those who were too young for military service. Although the organized groups no longer existed, the young people continued to hold meetings and discussions, according to the traditions and programs of both parties.

The Executive Board of the Bund and Tsukunft in 1920

[Page 110]

Grayeve Workers Organization

Debates were held between the two sides in the same manner as the central organizations. It was principally the national question that divided the two groups. But despite their differences, the personal relationships between the members of the two groups were very friendly.

Arrests and Clandestine Activities

A gathering of a Jewish sports organization was attacked on the field and several of the athletes were arrested. A shabes excursion of *Hechalutz* [a Zionist youth organization] outside the town, on the Shtutziner Road, was attacked and about 40 young people were arrested. It became impossible for Jewish youth to engage in any kind of activity.

After the disintegration of the Bundist organization, a youth group was organized, called "*Tsukunft*" [The Future], which would come together in secret, to distribute leaflets and subscribe to Bundist publications. The leaders of the group were Fishbeyn, Kravtshinski and Baykovski, under the supervision of the Segalovitshes, and with the support of Dr. Elihu Vaser, the dentist, Peshe Vodovski, Ruven Bogush, and others.

[Page 111]

In April, 1919, the Tsukunft organization in Warsaw sent a charter to the writer of these lines. This meant that, based upon the existing organization in Warsaw, it was now possible to establish branches of the organization in the provinces. Dr. Elihu Vaser, Peshe Vodovski, and Sh.Y.Fishbeyn signed on the responsible parties for the new, legal organization.

At that time, a delegation from Poalei Tsion approached the young Bundists with a proposal to form a non-partisan workers' club to carry out educational activities. The question was to have been considered at a session of Tsukunft, but just at that moment, there arrived from the government in Warsaw an inquiry as to the names and addresses of the Tsukunft leadership, which signified that the club had been legalized. The Bundists were overjoyed. They immediately rented an abandoned house near the train station. They renovated it themselves, and the workers made tables and chairs.

For the grand opening, they organized a concert and dance. Hundreds of workers and sympathizers came to the celebration. The Tsukunft group no longer wanted to consider the proposed non-partisan club. The "victory" of their party precluded a joint effort by the two groups.

The Tsukunft leadership consisted entirely of young people, and so the quest for education and self-development was always on the agenda. The executive board began to organize evening courses. Active in the work of self-education were Peshe Vodovski, Yehudis Shtroysberg, Kravtshinski and others. The courses were poorly attended. It was simply physically impossible for the young workers to attend, because they worked from 12 to 14 hours a day! Agitation therefore began, to organize a trade union to fight for a shorter work day.

In the meantime, the club continued with the usual recreational activities, readings, and the distribution of brochures and newspapers. programs of both parties.

[Page 112]

Grayeve Workers Organization

In May, 1919, a regional conference of Tsukunft representatives was hold in Lomzhe [Łomża]. Representatives came from Ostrova [Ostrów Mazowiecka], Zaromb [Zaręby Kościelne].

Vizhna [Wizna], Lomzhe and Grayeve. The young Muzhinski presided over the conference. Grayeve was represented by Ben-Tsion Kolko and Fishbeyn. It turned out that there were no clubs in any towns other than Lomzhe and Grayeve.

In the spring of 1920, a youthful trade union was functioning at the Tsukunft club. They began agitating for strikes, and a special organizational apparatus was installed for that purpose.

A May First Celebration

At this time, an office of the Polish Socialist Party (P.P.S.) was operating in Grayeve, with a large membership. The leader was a worker from the former suspender factory, named Galetski. The executive board of the Tsukunft club decided to join with the Polish union to celebrate the First of May together [Labor Day -International Workers' Day].

[Page 113]

Our delegation was not cordially received. They rejected the request for a united demonstration, and would permit us to attend only as onlookers.

The Tsukunft club thus decided to hold their May First celebration at their own premises. On the eve of May First, some of the young people put up proclamations around town, explaining the significance of May First. No other organization in town did this.

In the post-war years, the Grayeve *kehile* [organized Jewish community] received aid from various organizations overseas, to be distributed among the poor. The Tsukunft club became interested in the manner in which the distribution was made; facts regarding irregularities became known. It was therefore decided to demand representation in the kehile, and two representatives were delegated to state our demands.

At the time, the kehile met at the home of Reb Amiel on Raigrader Street. They permitted us to state our grievances, and promised a response, which they did not hasten to provide.

A Strike for an 8-Hour Work Day

At the beginning of June, 1920, a strike of Jewish workers was declared in Grayeve, demanding an 8-hour work day. The strike received a broad response, despite the difficult material conditions of the young people. Besides hunger and want, the young had to contend with opposition from their parents. All the tailors, cobblers, carpenters and hat makers stopped work. There were cases of great suffering and need, especially among those workers who took their meals with their employers.

In July, 1920, Soviet forces occupied Grayeve. Widespread social activism developed among the Jewish masses. Leaders of cultural and economic action were: Shimen Kolko, Dr. Elihu Vaser, Peshe Vodovski, a teacher from the town, and others. A public kitchen was organized at the home of Etl Mishkovske in the large apartment building. The kitchen provided the poor with a meal and with bread.

At the end of September, the Soviet forces retreated, and the Polish army returned to Grayeve.

Persecution and pogroms poured down on the population. Eighteen young Grayevers were murdered in cold blood by Polish soldiers. All political work was halted, and it became impossible to conduct any kind of educational work among the Jewish masses.

[Page 114]

Radical Activities by the I.L. Perets Library

Not until 1926 did the radical youth succeed in organizing the founding of a library named in honor of I.L. Perets,[3] with its own premises for meetings, and for general recreational and educational activities. A number of Grayever youth in America took an interest in the library's activities, and sent large sums of money, which they raised through direct contributions and fundraising events.

The I.L.Perets library succeeded in buying 1,400 books, from fiction to works on social and economic matters. The leadership of the library organized a self-education group for young workers. They ran evening courses in reading and writing. They organized lectures on literature and political questions, with speakers from the larger cities.

The leadership of the I.L. Perets Library in 1927

[Page 115]

The Perets library had over 150 subscribers and hundreds of young people visited every week. It was an intellectual home for the young workers. The library's existence as a legal entity made it possible to carry on radical enlightenment among the working class. The administration ran into the same kinds of difficulties as the Tsukunft club 6 years earlier: the issue of the long working day, which made it impossible for the young people to continue with their self-education. The library thus established a trade union. After sound preparation, a strike was declared in 1927, in the needle trade. The chief demand was once again an 8-hour workday.

Arrests and Denunciations Regarding "Money from Moscow"

In connection with the tailors' strike, there occurred an incident involving the workshop of Yankl Yudke, who brought in strikebreakers from another town. The trade union sent pickets to stop the strikebreakers. The owner brought in the police, who arrested the pickets.

The enemies of the Perets library exploited the strike to denounce the leadership. They spread a rumor, that the money to establish the library had not come from America, but that the leadership had obtained money from Russia in order to "make the revolution" in Grayeve.

The Pisuldski regime in Poland generally took a dim view of the independent activities by workers, whether in the cultural or political realms. Many difficulties were placed in the way of our organization. And when the restrictions and oppression didn't scare away the library activists from continuing their work, the government switched to open persecution and arrests.

[Page 116]

In 1927, a group of young people were arrested, including the foremost, most capable activist, Khaim Arye Bartshevski, who was the intellectual leader and moving force for all radical activities in Grayeve at the time. The arrests placed the library's existence in jeopardy. In the fear that the books would be confiscated, they were hidden away in private homes. When the strike was over and the arrests had abated, the books were returned to the library, which resumed its program of wide ranging educational and cultural activities.

The whole area surrounding Grayeve marveled at the activity of Grayeve's Marxist youth, and the Grayevers had a significant influence on the nearby shtetlakh.

The trial of Khaim Arye and the others was held in Lomzhe.

A group of Left Poaleii Tsionists, in 1922

[Page 117]

The young Grayevers in America raised over $1000, and sent it to their defense committee. The trial of Khaim Arye and the others was held in Lomzhe. Khaim Arye was convicted and served several years in the Lomzhe prison. After his release he once again exercised an influence over the activities of the Perets Library. Cultural and educational activities were again carried out in the radical Socialist spirit. The young workers were encouraged to study, to read, and to understand that it is always necessary to organize and fight for the liberation of the working class.

In 1932 a joint committee was organized to distribute relief funds sent by the Grayever *landslayt* [fellow Jews, specifically those from the same town or village] in America. The Perets library (or, as it was now designated in official documents, the "Left Workers") was among the organizations that constituted the committee. The Poalei Tsion was also represented by Motl Striev, who was a prominent activist and was popular among the Jewish population of the town. In the late 1930's, Striev was elected a town councilman.

A Communist Party Organization

At the end of the 1920's, a group of Communist-leaning workers were active in the needle trades union. In the 1930's, until the eve of the Second World War, there functioned in Grayeve a Communist party organization, illegal or semi-legal, to which a sizeable number of workers and intellectuals belonged.

[Page 118]

The activity among the Jewish workers and common people was conducted through a Jewish division of the party, but it was connected organizationally to the Polish party.

The Communist organization carried out relief efforts on behalf of political arrestees through the "*Mop'r*", (the fund for political arrestees). The party had quite a broad circle of contributors to the fund, including some bourgeois elements. In addition, it distributed leaflets about various political and social issues, and carried out educational work in various ways.

In 1935 the Communist party organized a semi-legal bakers' union, to which Polish and Jewish workers belonged. In the course of its existence, until 1938, the bakers' union carried out several successful strikes.

The various workers' organizations operated in Grayeve until the Hitler invasion. Many Grayeve workers and progressive people who are living today in various countries have to thank for their development, the early education that they received through the workers' organizations in their hometown.

Among our martyrs, two well known Grayever activists fell as heroes in the struggle against Hitler's beasts: Khaim Arye Bartshevski died fighting the fascists with weapons in his hands in the *Byalistoker* [Białystoker] Ghetto and Motl Striev fell during the first days of the Hitler regime in Grayeve. As for the others, we know little about their final resistance to the persecutors.

Honor to the holy memory of the Jewish worker-heroes and martyrs!

Footnotes

19. *Jewish Labor Bund*: a secular socialist organization in the Russian empire active around the turn of the 20th century who was opposed to Zionism. They focused primarily on furthering the rights and status of the Jewish proletariat.
20. *Poaleii Tsion* Movement of Marxist Zionist Jewish workers in the Russian empire active around the turn of the 20th century
21. *Itsik Leyb Perets*: The author, (1852-1915) was one of the most influential figures of Yiddish literature. His work often expressed protest against social injustice, and he championed workers' rights and the expression of Jewish ideals through secular culture.

[Page 119]

An Encounter Between Grayevers in Siberia
Abutsh Kolko

How a Young Pole[1] from Grayeve Became a Socialist

Translated by Miriam Leberstein

From the Editors: This memoir was published under the title, "the Grayevers" in a program distributed at a ball of the "Grayever Young Men's Benevolent Association" on January 25, 1913, edited by H. Blum. The author of the memoir, Abutsh Kolko, from the distinguished Kolko family of Grayeve, fled to America to escape Tsarist persecution, and stayed there until 1917. Right after the October Revolution, he left for the Soviet Union, where he remained. [Note in the original text.]

Grayeve! My hometown! How distant and how dear you were to me during all the long days and years of my exile. In the dimness of the dark prison for those sentenced to penal servitude, the memories of my childhood and youth, so closely connected to you, awoke in me dreams of life and happiness.

Infrequent letters from friends would bring me news of Grayeve, of its small town life, of its joys and travails, of its sorrow and unrest. Days and years sped by, but throughout all that time in prison, I never met a townsman from Grayeve, with whom I could share my memories of the town and our dreams of freedom and happiness. I had already lost hope of such an encounter.

[Page 120]

I had already begun to think of myself as the "sole representative" of Grayeve in cold, faraway Siberia, until one day...

This happened in the Aleksandrov prison (Irkutsk province). I had completed my period of forced labor and was waiting for the Lena River to be opened for ships after the long winter freeze, when I would be sent with the first convoy of convicts to the farthest corner of Siberia. The prison was overcrowded. New groups of political exiles came and went every day. Rooms that were meant to hold 100 people were packed with 200, 300, and more. There was no place to breathe or rest one's head. Curses and screams in various languages and dialects rang out and reverberated.

One day, as I was sitting as usual on a cot, and for the thousandth time counting and calculating how many days and nights I would still have to languish there, a young man approached me. He looked like a Pole, and asked me, in broken Russian:

"Is it true you are Kolko from Grayeve?"

"Yes, I'm Kolko."

The young man was delighted, and warmly clasped my hand, while explaining that he was also from Grayeve, and knew me. I was happy and surprised to meet a townsman, but, no matter how much I wracked my memory, I could not remember ever having seen him. The young man noticed my perplexity:

"Yes, I know you don't recognize me, but I know you – it's because of you that I became a Socialist!"

"How so?"

I expressed my confusion. And the young man explained:

"It was in 1905. I was then only 16. I was an apprentice to the cobbler Kh[2]..., who lived on the corner of Shul Street, not far from your house. Once on a winter night, going out into the street to take a little walk after a hard 16-hour workday, I saw the police taking you out of the house, in a convoy of prisoners. I was astonished: What? *Pan* [formal term of address in Polish] Kolko's son under arrest by the police? What kind of crime did he commit? He couldn't be a thief or a murderer! Perhaps he smuggled contraband? Amazed, I ran home and told my employer, Pan Kh..., and he told me: 'Those Socialists got what they deserved!'"

[Page 121]

"That was the first time I had heard the word 'Socialists.' Not knowing its meaning, I asked my boss to explain it. Pan Kh...'s reply was brief and blunt: 'Socialists are bandits who don't want to work, who run around the streets singing songs.' This explanation didn't satisfy me. Aside from the fact that in general I didn't accept everything the boss told me as the truth, the tone of his explanation was suspicious. I began to inquire among my friends, the older workers, about the meaning of the word. The little that I learned from them made more sense to me, and my interest was aroused."

"Life then took me to Warsaw, and there I had the opportunity to become acquainted with the Socialist movement and with Socialists, and I, too, became a Socialist. That's how, after a couple of years, I wound up in prison and followed you to Siberia, and here we encountered each other. Permit me, Comrade Kolko, to shake your hand and to express my recognition that you, even if indirectly, were my teacher and my guide."

With tears of joy I clasped the hand extended to me by my new comrade, my townsman, the only other Grayever whom I ever encountered in Siberia.

[Page 122]

The approach to the train station

The market-square in 1916

Max M. Vaks and Gushe Antman, photographed in 1903, when they were serving in the musical group of the second Finlandish Regiment

Footnotes

1. *Young Pole:* Note from translator: The expression "young Pole" could also be rendered "Polish youth." In either case, the author means a Pole who is not Jewish.

    Kh: Author wrote the letter "ח" [khet] referring to the cobbler's given name.

[Page 123]

Grayeve Dzshegtshares
Chapters from the book *Dzshegtshares* [tar sellers], translated from Hebrew [into Yiddish] by the author; published by Akhiever, Warsaw 1939

Translated by Yael Chaver, Ph.D

Edited by Tina Lunson

A Grayeve tar-sellers' song:
When the husband returns

Let there be no talk of money.

He'll happily go to Lik

To buy you a satin dress.

But if you nag him

He'll abuse you.

He'll find his woman in Prussia

And you'll be in big trouble…

Isrekhag[1]

A week or two before the High Holidays, the first tar-sellers, back from Germany, would appear in Grayeve. The wealthier ones came a bit earlier, the poorer ones later. But by the last few days before the holidays, all the owners and their young apprentices were already in the town. Although they were only a few dozen, they seemed to fill the town.

[Page 124]

The apprentices were in green outfits, like those worn by the Gentiles in the Grayeve region who worked for the Germans and the Masurians and the owners wore fuzzy green hats with feathers as a sign that they were "Germans." They would wander around the market, sneak into the houses of study [bote-medroshim] and look down their noses at the provincial folks who stay close to the besmedresh stove and haven't seen the great world – Berlin, Leipzig, or Dessau.

But, wandering around Germany, they often regretted their own fate: what did they, as it were, actually see in Berlin or Dessau? What pleasure did they get out of the rich state of Prussia? They would struggle around the villages, collecting tiny sums of money, eat cooked food only on the Sabbath (and not even all of them, at that); sleep either in a barn or on their wagons and the Prussians treated them like gypsies. Poor things, what did they know of Prussia? But as soon as they sniffed the air in Grayeve, all these feelings vanished and they always boasted to the provincials about the fact that they had seen "the wide world."

In the afternoon, between the afternoon and evening prayers, small groups of craftsmen, and even storekeepers, would gather around such a tar-seller, who would sit at ease on a stone in front of a building, and talk calmly and with dignity about Aleksander-Plaza and the Königlicher Palace and about the Kaiser himself, who goes for a walk in the streets of Berlin each morning; about the evening illumination of Berlin or Leipzig, which is, for example, seven times stronger than that of Grayeve during the daytime... Another one would sit in a different nook and talk about beautiful Dresden (which he had never seen) and about the cradle of Catherine the Great that stands in the palace at Zerbst-Anhalt. The truth was that, although he had spent his whole life in Zerbst and its environs, he had never dared to go inside the palace, which was open to the public on Sundays. He had only seen the palace from the outside, from the edge of its park. And, a cradle is just a cradle – isn't it the same as if he had seen it with his own eyes?

And Grayeve's curious Jews would stand, open-mouthed, and keep asking endless questions in the deepening twilight: is the cradle made of gold; does it simply stand on the floor? And the tar-seller would answer with whatever came to his mind. God forbid, he wasn't lying.

[Page 125]

He had seen the great palace with his own eyes and the rest could be deduced, just as though he had experienced it with his own senses...

And in the evenings, you sit on the threshold or on rocks in front of the house, at open doors and the tar-sellers recount all these wonders, while old and young listen. The old listen out of curiosity, yawn and enjoy it. The young are consumed by a strange longing that draws them, as if with ropes, over there, and many of them lie sleepless later that night. They think of what they heard that evening and envy the tar-seller who wanders from town to town, but sees the wide world... Everyone knows that the tar-sellers are uneducated: a storekeeper or a merchant would not make a match with them. But on holidays, when they recount the miracles and wonders in the big, beautiful world, their lowly lineage and their trade are forgotten and they are respected out of envy. That is the only poor compensation that a tar-seller has in this world, because even a holiday is not a joyful occasion for him. If he has even a bit of feeling – and many tar-sellers have that – from the minute he sets foot in his home, he anticipates the day after the holiday, isrekhag. One of them, who understood the meaning of the term, called that day "harness up the wagon" ...

Reb [Mr.] Avrom-Khaym Eysov was one such person. He used to say that he had never felt the flavor of a true holiday since he became fully aware of life. He was an odd person: while wandering through the German villages, he would practically faint with longing for dear Grayeve, which was his only ray of light during his journeys. But the moment he set out on the way back, traveling from Dessau to Berlin and from Berlin to *Kenigsberg* [Kaliningrad], the nearer he came to his home, the sadder he became. Once he had crossed the border and taken a seat in the cart bound for Grayeve, he would become miserable to the point of weeping. Would he ever be so lucky as to travel through the forest and the sands feeling that he would never have to go back? If he were a prophet and knew how much longer he had to live; if he were able to marry off both his daughters without a dowry and his small fortune would be just enough to live on, he would stay at home once and for all.

[Page 126]

But Reb Avrom-Khaym was a clever Jew and thus knew that no one was wise enough to know what the next day would bring – would it be fire, or illness, or an actual war? For that reason one must, as the Russian peasants say, strike the iron while it's hot. As long as he can travel, a Jew who knows the meaning of the phrase "making a livelihood is as difficult for Jews as the rending of the Sea of Reeds" must never sit idle. Reb Avrom- Khaym knew himself well and knew that as long as his legs held out, he would start out on the way again the day after the holiday, and would always remain a slave to tar. That's why he was always gloomy when he came back home for a holiday.

His wife was quite different. She was busy to the end of Simkhes-Toyre (and in the spring, to the end of Peysakh), running around from one store and butcher shop to another and wasn't concerned with the end of the holiday. She would stay home all year and take care of the girls, living a meager life and worried about every penny that she took out of her savings. But the moment her husband came home, she seemed to come alive. She opened her bundle of savings, which she had collected over the previous five months and poured money over butcher shops and fish stalls.

All year round she would buy calves' lungs and liver, or a foot and tripe, with which she and the two girls would make do the whole week: sometimes stewed lungs, sometimes with vinegar; sometimes a foot with potatoes; or cold and jellied foot, never varying the diet. But when her husband came home, she would proudly enter the butcher shop, push herself among the respectable ladies and say in a rich woman's tone, "I don't like lungs, would you happen to have a whole fresh liver? Give me a pound, and don't be stingy--I don't mind if there's another quarter pound. Do you have young calf's meat? No? Then give me a piece of this rib; ribs are wonderful in soup."

The butcher laughed inwardly, but a person needs to make a living. He flattered her: "Maybe, dear lady, a foot?" It was clear that he meant to insult her, but he said it so seriously, lifting the animal's foot up to her nose, that she didn't understand it negatively: "A foot is fine," she said, "even though I really don't need it, but sometimes a relative comes for a meal, or my husband brings someone and in that case I can prepare something to eat." And so it went, on and on.

[Page 127]

She did this to annoy the ladies she would stand behind all year round, along with the dogs who waited for a bone. The same ritual would be repeated at the fish stall: "Be so kind as to show me the fish you're keeping for Anshel, the rich man; my stomach, and especially my husband's stomach, is no less aristocratic than his."

To annoy all the other women, she would fill her apron with the best produce, gesturing and moving around. In order to irritate the women who were always haughtier, she would yell to her daughters from afar, to come out and take the fish indoors as they were a heavy load. The moment she went inside her house, she would call all the neighboring women and show them the large live fish that were available in the market that day, "and not expensive at all," she would add several times.

While the mother was all agitated, the daughters were as quiet as frozen water, as though they had lost their tongues. During the year their mother would curse and constantly threaten them that she would tell their father everything. Now that their father had come, they felt as though a policeman was in the house. They knew that every time their father came home he would ask how they had behaved. The mere thought of that forced them to obey their mother. Ten times a day, she would send them to the store or the baker's, give them her and their father's shoes to shine, tell them to patch their father's shirts and old trousers that reeked of tar so badly that you could choke. In short, she couldn't let them be still for a moment. In the evenings they had to stay indoors and go to bed very early. They longed, especially on Saturdays and holidays, for the Green Hill where boys and girls would meet and have lively times, but they were afraid of their father. In actual fact, their father was not that strict, but he was religiously observant and believed the Green Hill – especially the walks to the spring – to be evil. Can you imagine worse torture for grown girls than having to stay indoors? To them, their father was a stranger, because they saw him only on holidays. If he was in a good mood he would pat one of them on the head. She would turn as red as a beet, as though a stranger had touched her.

[Page 128]

In their hearts, both girls wanted the holiday to end as soon as possible, but neither dared to say it to the other. For the first few days they accepted everything gladly – especially as their father would bring fabric for a dress or an apron – but after that they would count the days impatiently until he would leave, and both waited eagerly for the day he would go back to "Prussia."

Simkhes-Toyre [Simchat Torah] was coming.

Along with all the other Jews of the town, Reb Avrom-Khaym went to the old besmedresh on Synagogue Street, paid for the right to say half of the prayer before the procession of the Torah scrolls began and gave the right to the young religious judge, as a mark of respect. He was given one of the first turns carrying a scroll in the procession, which annoyed the other tar-sellers, although they knew that he was more important than them. He would dance and yell out, "Rejoice in the joy of the Torah," but his heart was far from joyous. At this time tomorrow he would be on the other side of the border, in Lik or perhaps in Korschen. "Rejoice" – he wanted to forget what the next day would bring, at least during the prayer. He looks at the other tar-sellers, at how they down their drinks one after the other until the drink seems to leak out of their eyes, but he was already thinking of the day after the holiday. How could he not think of the cart now, as he saw the cart-driver, whom he needed to tell to pick him up the next day? For as long as he could remember, Simkhes-Toyre was Tishebov for him… The kind-hearted Reb Avrom-Khaym, who envied no one, now envied the cart-drivers, the water-carriers, the old beadles. "Who's keeping you from becoming a cart-driver or a water-carrier?" The thought crossed his mind. And he answered himself, "Don't ask God questions."

After prayers, the entire congregation was invited to the home of the synagogue's chief trustee for *Shabes* [Sabbath] lunch. The property owners who sat in the first two rows always went, and Avrom-Khaym also had a place in the second row. He had bought it from an aunt who had inherited it from her uncle, who had no sons. But he didn't go to the shabes lunch because his mood was bad. The time was going by quickly, he told himself painfully. As he left the synagogue, a large heap of withered leaves blew across his path, and their rustling sounded like a quiet moaning, in tune with his own feelings.

[Page 129]

When he entered his house, the fragrance of the roasted goose greeted him at the door. It reminded him of his childhood, when his father was alive. He thought to himself, "If my father were alive I would not have to wander in these lands." As he opened the door he shouted "Good holiday, good year!" His wife knew this shout, which rang with stifled sorrow and always caused her to weep. She stayed in the kitchen for a long time until she was calmer, then came into the room and started serving the food. This was the only meal during which they didn't speak to each other. The girls brought and removed bowls. They ate calmly, as though their father wasn't preparing to leave for six months. But the mother changed as the evening went on. She seemed to shrink and her eyes were red, though no one saw her weeping. He, the father, just chewed his food. He didn't raise his head from the glazed bowl and thought only of one thing: this was his last meal at his own table.

In the afternoon he returned to the besmedresh and danced with the congregation, as though he were as drunk as the others. The men played games all afternoon and even after the evening prayer and he dreaded the moment when the games would stop and he would have to go back home. He especially liked the game of "cat and mouse:" the men stood in two rows and two smart yeshive students played the roles of cat and mouse. He enjoyed that game because it took a long time. When people got tired of it and wanted to leave, he told the beadle to go get some beer, and they started all over again. He wasn't the only tar-seller in the rows – apparently, the other tar-sellers also felt miserable.

When the fun was over, the tar-sellers walked along like mourners. "Who's chasing us? Why do we need to cross the border at dawn?" thought Avrom-Khaym.

[Page 130]

Other tar-sellers may have asked themselves the same question, but no one thought that it could be changed and arranged so that they could stay at home for another week. They were fearful of the competition, of lost clients. You would never know if a person told you he was going to visit a relative in Prussia, whether he was stealing across the border and snatching up your clients... A tar-seller is destined to be a wanderer.

When he came back home after the holiday fun that evening, Avrom-Khaym went straight to bed. His wife baked *khale* [challah, a twisted egg bread] and biscuits so he would have home-baked goods for a few weeks. Then she placed his patched trousers in a pillowcase, laid one bundle over the other by the door, and went to her bed. Both pretended to be asleep, but were not sleeping. She wept her heart out silently – in effect, she was an eternal *aguna* [an abandoned wife who is not divorced and therefore can't remarry] – while he sighed into his pillow, bothered by bad thoughts, thoughts about dying in a foreign country. Such thoughts exhausted him every year before leaving home. Nothing bad ever happened to him, but each time he would be sure that the thoughts were justified…

But the girls slept very well. They woke up when the cart-driver knocked at the window. When they opened their eyes they saw their mother rushing from the kitchen into the main room and back into the kitchen and their father tying the two bundles together.

"You can get up now!" their mother said, passing by the wooden sofa where they slept. Then, as if by command, they quickly got up. Their mother was saying, "So this is how you leave me with the two wild girls – I didn't want to say anything until now." But he seemed not to hear what she was saying. When the bundles were on the cart, Avrom-Khaym picked up his *tales* [prayer shawl] and *tfiln*[2], asked his wife whether she had remembered to pack the Five Books of the Torah; shook hands with his wife and the girls, not saying a word – he was choked by tears – and quickly left the house and climbed onto the cart.

[Page 131]

"Go fast!" he told the driver. "Be well!" he shouted to his wife and daughters who stood at the door. Bogushe Street is long, but it was still dark and the cart soon disappeared. The girls went back indoors and the mother stood and listened to the noise the wheels made. When the noise stopped, she went indoors.

Snowflakes started falling from the sky. Wrapped in a dream, the cart crawled through the forest on the way to the border. Avrom-Khaym bundled up against the cold and sorrow and sadly thought about the good holiday days that had gone by and about the long, bitter winter that awaited him in the foreign country.

Zundl the Scholar

When God blessed Avrom-Khaym Eysov and he became rich, he decided to choose a *yeshive* [a Jewish school of high Talmudic learning] scholar as a son-in-law. Avrom-Khaym was a smart person who thought ahead. He would always joke about the life of a tar-seller and was considered an old jokester. But he never forgot the lesson of his life-in-exile. Before considering a tar-seller as a son-in-law, he decided to go to the yeshive of *Lomzhe* [Łomża] to pick a husband for his older daughter Tsirl. A storekeeper or a merchant, or even a well-off tailor, would not consider a match with a tar-seller. As for the blacksmiths, who were numerous in Grayeve, or even a good cobbler, Avrom-Hayim wouldn't consider them for a match.

One fine autumn day, between *Rosheshone* [Rosh Hashanah] and *Yonkiper* [Yom Kippur] he went to the Lomzhe yeshive and picked out a fine boy, Zundl the Studious, of *Shtutzin* [Szczuczyn], the closest town to Grayeve in the west, two miles away. Because he had to go back to Germany the day after the holiday, he did it all fast. The betrothal document was written the day before *sukes* [Sukkot], and the wedding took place during the week of sukes. Tsirl, who used to take walks on the "Green Hill" when her father was away, and would meet boys there as well, was very offended because she had been given a husband she knew nothing about. But when she saw him the first time under the *khupe* [wedding canopy], she was happy.

[Page 132]

She realized that her father was an experienced merchant and that he knew what to buy: he was big and handsome, more handsome than all the tailors' apprentices, cobblers and carpenters, and even more than the tar-sellers who used to come down from Prussia dressed in finery.

Because Avrom-Khaym was the first tar-seller who had bought a scholar for a son-in-law, his prestige rose among the rich men in town, among the members of the rabbinical court, and even with the rabbi. But the good-for-nothings of Steam-Bath Street were not impressed. When the guests left Avrom-Khaym's house with the bride on their way to the synagogue, those guys accompanied the bride with old and new songs that they composed specifically for tar-seller weddings and drowned out the fiddles. At the khupe, Avrom-Khaym stood embittered, because the rough guys stood around and made the guests laugh so much that the marriage ceremony couldn't be performed. If they were ignored, the rascals yelled so loudly across the synagogue courtyard that they grew hoarse. They were especially loud with the song, "A tar-seller has a new servant, worthless to him and his daughter" [*hot a dzhegtshar a nayem meshores, far zikh un far der tokhter af kapores*]. But Avrom-Khaym smiled; they weren't referring to him – he had taken a yeshive-student as a son-in-law, who would sit and study and do a bit of commerce, but wouldn't be a servant.

During the "Seven Blessings" Zundl the Studious gave a learned speech. Avrom-Khaym didn't understand a crumb of the scholarly reasoning, but his eyes were full of tears when the religious judge shook the bridegroom's hand. His wife, too, who watched the speech through the cracks of the kitchen door with all the neighboring women peering in behind her, was also so astonished that she started kissing all the women. It was a powerful expression of her excitement, especially if we remember that she hated the neighbors and wanted them to die of frustration when she carried home baskets full of good food during the holiday season...

This time Avrom-Khaym left home, the day after the holiday, in calm spirits. First, it was a huge load off his mind. Second, he was leaving a man at home and not just a braggart, but a very fine guy... His wife, on the other hand, suffered. For years, with no man in the house, she had been accustomed to make do with a lung and a foot all week. But now there was a son-in-law at home and that wouldn't work. When she got used to him, she wanted to start "economizing" a bit.

[Page 133]

But Tsirl wouldn't let her do it. Once, when Zundl was in the besmedresh, mother and daughter had such a fight that people came running when they heard the shouting. If the daughter hadn't been ashamed – she didn't want her husband to know about it –the fight would have gone on for a long time. The end of the game was that the daughter wrote her father a letter and Avrom-Khaym soon wrote his wife such a letter that she nearly fainted when it was read to her. After that she improved, but stinginess is, after all, a natural trait, a passion like other passions. She would occasionally try to overcome her passion, but was never able to.

The year that Zundl lived at Avrom-Khaym's house and was supported by him nearly drove her, the wife, crazy. She had not saved money for those five months and so couldn't show off at holiday time to the ladies at the butcher shop and the fish market. She lived with this for a whole year and almost burst from frustration.

When the year of support was over, the question of a livelihood for the young couple arose. Avrom-Khaym believed that Zundl wasn't suited to be a storekeeper and Zundl was of the same opinion. But what would he do with the hundred rubles of the dowry? He lent them to his father-in-law. As soon as Avrom-Khaym left for Germany, Zundl went to Shtutzin, his home town. He had many relatives there and hoped to find something. His Tsirl stayed with her mother, because they had gotten a room for five years, in Avrom-Khaym's two-room apartment. Zundl wanted to become a teacher in the Talmud-Torah, but he couldn't get in: the teachers with good connections had finalized everything at the beginning of the year. He wanted to open a *kheyder* [Jewish religious school], but when the other kheyder-teachers found out, that dream also vanished. What could he do? His uncle, with whom he was staying, told him, "The surest livelihood is through a craft. I will teach you tanning and you will be a tanner." Zundl went pale. Why had he studied so hard in the yeshive? He had dreamed of being a rabbi and now he would become a tanner? His uncle understood that Zundl had doubts because tanning was not a very respectable occupation. He said, "Your father-in-law is a tar-seller, does that make him an unfit Jew? Shtutzin is fourteen *viorts* [one viorst = 1.06 kilometers] away from Grayeve. Who needs to know what your occupation is?

You tell your wife that you're a kheyder-teacher..." The moment he heard that he could hide it from Grayeve, he agreed. He would come to his wife for one Shabes a month, bringing some money for her and for Moshe-Berl – the child who suddenly appeared – and on Sunday he would immediately leave again to practice his nasty trade.

[Page 134]

At the beginning of *nisn* [Nissan, the 7th month of the Jewish calendar] Avrom-Khaym came home. His wife told him that Zundl had become a kheyder-teacher and was bringing Tsirl his wages. Avrom-Khaym was very pleased: over time, Zundl could become a real rabbi... During the last week before *Peysach* [Passover], when all the teachers had already left their khadorim and Zundl hadn't come, Avrom-Khaym wondered, especially as Zundl knew that his father-in-law was about to come back from far away and should be greeted. A man does everything for a livelihood, Avrom-Khaym thought, but what was a kheyder-teacher doing in Shtutzin on the eve of Peysach when his family was in Grayeve? And when his wife told him that she had dreamed that Zundl was ill, he thought no more but got into a cart and was in Shtutzin two hours later. He went to all the houses of study and the prayers groups, and didn't find him. Then he went to Zundl's uncle, the tanner. There, he saw Zundl eating in the kitchen. Seeing Zundl's clothes, and how pale he had suddenly become, Avrom-Khaym immediately understood what had happened. Zundl stood up and with bent head shook his hand. The uncle immediately appeared and said, as though answering a question, "What's the fuss? Is a tar-seller a human being and a tanner – an animal? If Zundl is a scholar, his trade won't take the pelt off him." He came into the room and sat down at the table. Avrom-Khaym's heart was racing: he had chosen a yeshive student and gotten a tanner. In order to calm him, Zundl's uncle said, "And you, Avrom-Khaym, if you're a tar-seller, aren't you smart with many good qualities?" When the uncle saw that Avrom-Khaym was listening, he added, "And Rabbi Yohanan the shoemaker and Rabbi Yehoshua the blacksmith, didn't they revive the dead?" This was the argument that craftsmen always used, when they wondered why the rich folks, many of whom knew the Talmud, looked down on craftsmen... At that point, Zundl came to himself and calmly told his father-in-law how this came about.

[Page 135]

"I did it," he concluded, "to be able to support my wife and child, and not depend on you, nomad that you are, for my living." Avrom-Khaym softened, and tried to set his son-in-law's mind at rest. Nevertheless, he believed it would be better that no one in Grayeve, and even at home, knew the truth. The two of them decided to say that he had caught a cold and was staying in bed at his uncle's house.

When they got home, Avrom-Khaym immediately put him to bed and Tsirl cared for him like a mother. When there was no one in the room, Avrom-Khaym came in to see Zundl, patted him on the head, and they both laughed at the clever idea. Zundl got up the day before Peysakh and the next day he went to synagogue with his father-in-law, dressed in a black coat and a rabbinical hat. Avrom-Khaym took great pleasure in the way everyone looked on with envy.

When the holiday week was over, Avrom-Khaym went back to his tar wagon, and Zundl – to his uncle's tannery.

On a Friday in *Tamuz* [10th month of the Jewish calendar], an event took place that determined Zundl's fate for the rest of his life. Before he went home, he would go to the Shtutzin steam bath and steam himself thoroughly. That Friday, the father of the steam-bath's owner died suddenly, and the steam bath was not heated up. Zundl gave himself a good immersion in the ritual bath, but the cold water apparently didn't dispel the bad odor of the animal skins that clung to his body. On the way to Grayeve, he had to drop off a few skins in Popov; he emptied the sack and took it with him. When he came home, he first went into the barn and hid the empty sack in a corner, to take back to Shtutzin on Sunday. Tsirl actually saw him coming out of the barn, but was ashamed to ask him what he had done there. Sitting at the Friday-night table, a bad odor came from him. Being used to it, he himself was unaware. But Tsirl felt it strongly, and even had a perverse desire to breathe it in deeply. Something in the smell was familiar, but she couldn't recollect it. At night she nearly suffocated, and couldn't sleep a wink. While he was snoring, she moved closer to him and smelled his shirt and his neck.

[Page 136]

Finally, she remembered that she would smell the same stink passing by the tannery on her way to the baker's. She jumped out of bed, got dressed and went to the barn. When she found the sack and put it to her nose, she felt extremely nauseous. She went back into the house as pale as the whitewashed wall, and wouldn't let him near her the entire Shabes.

Sunday morning, after his farewells, he sneaked into the barn to take his sack. Tsirl followed him quietly, and when he was about to leave the barn, she stepped in. "What kind of sack is that?" she asked, annoyed. He stammered. "You are a stinking tanner and not a kheyder-teacher," she let him have it very quietly so that no one outside would hear, God forbid, "I won't go on living with you!" and she ran out quickly. He stayed for a short while in the dark barn, holding the sack, confused and frightened. When he came to himself, he twisted it up and started towards the carts for Shtutzin, ashamed and pained.

The next month he washed himself properly in the steam bath and poured many ladles of hot water over his body. He climbed up to the highest bench and paid the attendant half a kopeck to give him a good thrashing with the broom. He refused to take any sack with him from Shtutzin, but when he got to Grayeve, Tsirl nevertheless wouldn't talk to him. She sat at the other side of the table during the meal and at night she lay at the edge of her bed in order to be as far away from him as possible. Neither could sleep, but they never spoke a word to each other. He wanted to ask her why she was angry at him, and remove any suspicions she might have. But he was afraid to say anything, in case his mother-in-law on the other side of the wooden wall could hear; that would be the end of him... The next day, when Tsirl was nursing the child in their room, he found a chance to talk with her. He came up to her, brought his sleeve to her nose and quietly said, "Sniff my sleeve. You must have been mistaken." She turned her head away, and when he didn't give up, she stood up with the nursing child at her breast and went into the next room, where her mother and sisters were sitting. The poor man went back to Shtutzin the next day, without having made peace with Tsirl.

[Page 137]

The mother saw that something had happened between Tsirl and Zundl. When she couldn't get anything out of Tsirl, she left it alone. "They'll make it up," she thought to herself, and remembered the folk saying, "Where two heads lie on the same cushion, a third person shouldn't intervene," overcoming her curiosity... He wasn't able to make it up with his wife even on the Shabes before the start of the month of *Elul* [the month of the Jewish year, dedicated to spiritual preparation for the High Holy Days]. On the contrary, the moment she saw him she became enraged and slept on the chest that stood near the beds. To annoy her, he left for Shtutzin Saturday night. Later he often wondered what had annoyed her... The closer it got to Rosheshone, the calmer he became. His father-in-law would come and would make peace between them. He would slap her around and she would be with him again.

Avrom-Khaym came home a week before the holiday, five days before Zundl arrived. His wife immediately told him that something had happened between Zundl and Tsirl. But Tsirl told him nothing, as though it was her mother's secret. That evening, when Tsirl had gone to bed, Avrom-Khaym went in to her and asked her sharply what had happened. Even after the wedding, Avrom-Khaym was more like an uncle to Tsirl, "an uncle who would come from Prussia for the holiday." Ashamed, she pulled her feather comforter over her eyes and said nothing. "If I whip you," he threatened her, holding the end of his belt in his hand, "you'll have to answer me." She burst out in tears, and lamenting as though over the destruction of the Temple, told him everything. "But you're a big fool," he said more softly, and left the room. The next day he saw his chance and wanted to confront her with an argument. This time she didn't weep; she opened her eyes wide – Eysov's family were famous for their large eyes – and with a resolute voice declared, "I won't live with a stinking tanner, no matter what you do to me!" Avrom-Khaym, who loved his daughters and understood them, bowed his head and made no answer. To be sure, he, too, was not pleased with his son-in-law's work, and didn't think he would do that forever.

[Page 138]

His wife sent both daughters on errands, one to the baker to roll out *matze* [matzah] with onions and the other to the market – that was the only way she could get them out of the house when their father was at home. She heard the whole story from her husband. For a time, she was angry at her son-in-law and then at her daughter. "Does she think you're Rothschild? True, it's a nasty line of work, but if you divorce from him, you have to pay back the hundred rubles." "My wife is a smart woman," thought Avrom-Khaym, because at that very moment he was also thinking about the hundred rubles he had invested in the business, which were making him a fine profit.

The next day, he sent his wife and younger daughter away and stayed at home alone with Tsirl. He played with Moshe-Berl, who lay in his cradle and laughed out loud when Avrom-Khaym touched his neck. Then he called Tsirl and asked her to make him a glass of tea. When she brought him the tea, he asked her, "And if I had gotten you a tar-seller husband, would you have been happy?" "Of course," she replied, "after all, you are a tar-seller, and even your workers don't smell and they're dressed in fine clothes." "Suppose I take Zundl with me?" he asked quietly. She was silent for a time and then answered, "Then I would have a husband. As it is, he is neither a scholar nor a tanner." He clapped her lovingly on the shoulder.

Avrom-Khaym's spirits lifted. That solution had many good features. First, he wouldn't have to return the hundred rubles; second, he needed two apprentices or one partner and one apprentice. In that case, it would be better for his apprentice Hatskel to travel with his son-in-law Zundl, who was family, after all, and an honest man besides. Third, on Saturday evenings and during the long winter days when nothing was happening, his son-in-law would study the Torah, Rashi and commentaries with him. Fourth, Tsirl and Zundl would have a peaceful life... He waited for Zundl impatiently, but was not worried, because he knew that Zundl would agree to everything he said. He told Tsirl that he had decided to take her husband with him, and she sobbed for joy.

On the way to Grayeve, Zundl rehearsed what he would tell his father-in-law. He would interject verses from the Bible and allegories from the Talmud and Midrash and the old man would teach his daughter how women should behave...

[Page 139]

When he came home, his wife greeted him very amicably, to his great astonishment. And he, the scholar and kindly man, forgot in an instant all the trouble she had caused him for months, and was happy. That very same evening, as they walked back from the synagogue, the father-in-law told the son-in-law: "I know everything. I have decided to take you with me." Zundl was stunned and remained silent. Only one thought went through his mind: would he end up a tar-seller? And Avrom-Khaym explained: "A tar-seller is a merchant, whereas a tanner is no more than a chopper, a skin-flayer. You'll be a merchant and instead of spending your life as a small tanner and a manual laborer dependent on others, you'll be a decent tar-seller, because you're a scholar. You'll be independent, my partner and my heir; after all, I have no other son." "You're both smart and kind," Zuyndl stammered his thanks, bowing his head in shame.

So as to totally uproot tanning from Zundl, Avrom-Khaym sniffed his clothes energetically and said, "You must have gone to the steam-bath, yet you still smell of carcasses. Soot, blubber, and tar are clean and have a healthy odor." "That's true," Zundl added, though he had never smelled those substances.

When they got home, they sat down at the table. "Sit next to him," Avrom-Khaym ordered Tsirl, in a fatherly manner. "Let him first go to the steam-bath," Tsirl whined, sitting down next to Zundl, and blushed.

That was the end of the quiet "tragedy" in Avrom-Khaym's house.

The day after the holiday both left Grayeve and started for Prussia. All of Grayeve was in an uproar: a yeshive student had become a tar-seller. "The old man led the young guy astray," the yeshive students said. One of the rich residents said, "Instead of raising himself to the level of his son-in-law, he pulled the son-in-law down to his own level." "He'll teach a bit of Torah to uneducated Jews. Avrom-Khaym is a good Jew and knows what he's doing," the religious judge took his side.

[Page 140]

The tar-sellers, who travelled to Prostken together and would scatter from there throughout Germany, were thunderstruck by the news. "Now that he has a scholar with him, Avrom-Khaym will monopolize all the towns," they worriedly told each other. Avrom-Khaym strolled around among them head held high, proud of his son-in-law, like a Jew who carries a Torah scroll with him on his travels...

Green-Hill Love

At a time when places to stroll were unknown in Shtutzin, Stavisk and other nearby towns, Grayeve already had two such places, where young men and women could meet. One place was the Shtutzin road, for the rich folks. The other was the Green Hill, for poorer folks. When the train station was built, that became a strolling place for all classes.

They say that the Green Hill became famous since Velvl Bok buried his oldest son there. It started by visiting family graves; boys and girls would accidentally meet there and then take walks on Shabes and holidays. That would be the meeting point. Many love affairs in Grayeve were played out there. One person would come down the hill happy and another would be downcast. Girls looked at the Green Hill longingly and mothers – fearfully. The mothers certainly did not want their daughters to slink up to the Green Hill, but the daughters couldn't stay away. It might be a lucky place, at least once. How can a mother refuse her child? The fathers were stricter in this matter. They were worried about a sad end to these "walks." Often, an old father would stroll along the cemetery fence, constantly glancing upwards, towards the Green Hill... Incidentally, a very nasty incident had already happened, but that was on the Shtutzin road, where the fancy folks strolled. Every girl of the working-class families experienced the same course of events over a short time: first, she would accidentally walk to the Green Hill with her girlfriends on Shabes. Afterwards her mother would hit her and warn her never to set foot on the cursed hill; after that, the father would hit her and moralize.

[Page 141]

The end was that she would be the winner and go there even on weekdays. What's the point of a boring life in a shtetl if a girl can't get some distance from the eyes of her parents and neighbors, and get closer to the eyes of the boys, who are full of such love and longing?

When Elkanah came back from Prussia and appeared on the Green Hill for the first time – it was the *Shabes-shuva* [Sabbath before Yom Kippur] – all the girls watched him. He had left Grayeve as a wild boy, the leader of a gang of rascals, and had come back like a thunderbolt, a rich guy, a real count. Though he was Hertzke's apprentice, he looked like a boss, more impressive than all the other tar-sellers and many of Grayeve's rich kids. He climbed the Green Hill with his uncle Fayvl's son, and asked him who every passing girl was. They finally stopped at Bok's grave. Under the tree that grew out of the grave there sat three girls, one of whom was the daughter of Mendl the baker. When they were still far away, he had heard a pleasant, delicate voice singing:

You fool, why are you annoyed,

Why the long face?

Do you want to know your history?

Come, I'll tell you.

[Translator's note: This folk song rhymes in Yiddish]

When he came close, she didn't stop singing; she glanced at him and went on singing.

He looked down at her blonde hair and white throat, and stopped as though glued to the spot. He was deep in thought and because his thoughts were strange, he didn't dare speak to her. He left along with his cousin, and didn't say a word about his feelings. As he stepped aside, the girl again began to sing. His pace slowed... The voice was carried to him like a golden thread and his heart was agitated. He passed by the girls again, walking stiffly, but something seemed to press on his shoulders, bowing him lower.

[Page 142]

He had gone to the Green Hill proud and easy-spirited, and now was coming back down beaten, heavy-hearted.

His uncle, the tailor, started seeking matches for him. "A guy like you," he said, "would suit even the Rabbi's daughter." But Elkanah's response was that no one in Prussia made matches. Each person sought out his own match.

On the holiday, after the meal, Elkanah sprayed his clothes with eau-de-cologne – at that time, only the richest girls were familiar with it – and left for the Green Hill. What can one say? One heart feels the other. Zelda, the daughter of Mendl the baker, had put on her finest dress that day, her mother's golden chain around her neck, and left with her girlfriend for the Green Hill. When the two saw each other, they both blushed. He had always fantasized about such a girl: fat, blonde, and fair. She, for her part, dreamed about a tall, handsome and rich guy – he didn't really need to be rich, but had to appear rich. That holiday afternoon, he was able to stay near her. At first he spoke briefly with her friends. Later, his cousin stayed with the two other girls and he went on ahead before them, with Zelda.

The next day, he came to visit her at home. He was daring to do something that no guy dared to do at that time. As he came in, a fragrance of perfume entered the house. This intoxicated Mendl the baker, and completely confused his wife. Both of them were very happy.

"A guy like that has to be rich," said Khaye quietly to her husband, when they both happened to go into the next room. When he left, the parents asked him to come again. Khaya told her daughter happily, "Why do we need matchmakers? God will be the matchmaker. Keep him at your side, using your brains, and don't say a word to your girlfriends..."

Elkanah would come in the morning, during the day, and at night – he was completely out of his senses. Zelda, for her part, like a sick hen, stopped eating and drinking or talking – she thought only of the handsome Elkanah. Bath-house Street was seething like the bath-house furnace: some said that he wasn't suited to her. Others said that she wasn't right for him.

[Page 143]

No one was willing to see how happy they were…

Four days went by, and Elkanah felt as though it had been four months. His uncle kept admonishing him: "Mendl is rich; all the non-Jews buy his bread. Don't let them fool you into marrying her without a dowry." Elkanah considered this and thought that his uncle was right. One marries only once in a lifetime; why shouldn't he receive a dowry? The fifth day, when he was in the back room with Zelda, unaware that her father was in the next room and separated only by a wooden wall, he started off very simply: "Zelda, do you love me?" She turned red as a beet. Who asks such questions before the wedding? When he asked her again, she answered, embarrassed, "You're a low-life…that's not a nice thing to ask." Elkanah laughed. "People of the world have a better idea of what a low-life is." She turned even redder. "Your father will give us two hundred rubles and we'll be married," he said quickly. Her heart beat fast, as though she was committing a crime, and she said quietly, "Where would Father get money?" "From the fortune he placed around your mother's neck," Elkanah smiled. Zelda looked down in embarrassment, wrapped herself in her warm shawl, and said, "All my life, my father has worked hard at night. If he's managed to save a few pennies, he needs them for his old age, after all." Mendl, who was standing glued to the wall in the next room, was very pleased and moved at his daughter's wise words. His eyes filled with tears. "If so, we can't get married," said Elkanah, and struck the table with his hand. Zelda was silent. Elkanah was certain that Zelda loved him, but that her father wouldn't give over his pennies. He became angry with himself. He stood up, like someone who had been shot, and said, "So what do you say, Zelda?" When she didn't answer, he shouted angrily, "When your father dies an unnatural death, we can get married." Zelda turned as white as chalk. She stood up and wanted to say something, but her father suddenly came into the room. He, too, was as white as though he had just emerged from a sack of flour. He stood opposite Elkanah, barely reaching his chest, and yelled, "Get out, you rascal!" Elkanah took fright, and vanished.

[Page 144]

On the following days, Zelda didn't leave the house, and Elkanah roamed around the Green Hill, in the market and through the streets as though he had lost his senses. He had confided everything to his cousin, and begged him to go and make peace for him with Mendl the baker. But his cousin was afraid even to go near Mendl's house… Bath-house Street immediately knew that something had happened between Zelda and Elkanah. Many people took pleasure in murmuring that Mendl had caught Elkanah and Zelda hugging on the wooden sofa…

Elkanah, who had come to town before the holidays ruddy and happy, left the town after the holidays pale and mournful. Reb Hertzke said that he looked ready for a coffin. Oy-oy, if only he had kept his mouth shut for a minute, he would certainly have been married today! Zelda was ashamed to show her face outside. Everyone had already envied her; she had been so close to happiness. If she hadn't annoyed him, he wouldn't have stumbled. Today, the day after the holiday, she would have been standing, in white, under the khupe ... Until today, they were both hoping that things would work out somehow. "Now Mendl, may his name be erased, will marry off his daughter," thought Elkanah. "He won't come to town again for years and will forget about me as though I were dead," thought Zelda and complained to him silently.

But if God is running matters from above, people down below have no chance of spoiling things. Elkanah didn't forget Zelda even for a minute and waited very impatiently the whole winter, until Peysakh. All the gentile girls, whom he used to toy with, were now unattractive. Zelda suffered in silence. She was too embarrassed to talk about it with her girlfriends, let alone with her mother. Her mother – and mothers, after all, see everything – saw what was happening in her Zeldale's heart. Similar things were happening to her. When she was alone with her husband, she would try to calm him and say that even an angel might stumble over a word, let alone a tar-seller. Mendl also loved his daughter and sympathized with her, but she couldn't give in. Man and wife often argued about the issue, arguments that always ended with Mendl's refusing to eat all day.

[Page 145]

When the Peysakh vacation came around, Elkanah wanted to go to Grayeve with Hertzke. When he got there, he asked his cousin fearfully whether Zelda was engaged yet. When he heard that she was still free, his heart lifted. He suddenly became the most pious of men and told himself, "It's ordained in heaven, she's waiting for me." His heart overflowed with love and longing, and he decided to go to her home and make peace with her father. It was Friday. The next day, Saturday, as soon as he reached the Green Hill with his cousin, Zelda's face shone out at him... He hadn't expected it and she didn't know that he had arrived the previous day. Both became as white as chalk. She passed him. "Zelda," he called her in a trembling voice. She couldn't control herself and turned her head towards him. Her girlfriend stopped first and she stopped as well. His cousin told the other girl, "Let's walk on our own," and Zelda was immediately alone with Elkanah...

The next day they met again on the Green Hill. She told him that she had talked with her father and that he could come to their home on the first day of Peysakh. He came to Zelda's home, bringing a silk kerchief for her mother (he had bought it in Prussia to give Zelda if she was still free) and a nice tobacco container for her father. "Forgive me, Reb Mendl," he murmured, unable to look the older man in the eye, "I didn't know what I was saying."

Mendl pretended to completely forgive Elkanah, but he secretly bore a grudge and wanted to hurt him. Elkanah was sure they would be married the day after the holiday and Zelda would finally be his. But Mendl had a different idea: "If I arrange a hasty marriage people will immediately talk and give her a bad reputation," he said. Elkanah was embarrassed to keep talking about it and remained silent.

[Page 146]

He did tell Zelda that her father was being unjust, but she shrugged her shoulders and answered, shamefacedly, "We can't interfere; after all, it's up to the parent."

The betrothal document was drawn up in the evening at the end of the holiday. Mendl wanted to set the wedding for the week of Sukes, when Elkanah would be back from Prussia. Elkanah was stunned. "May you be struck dumb, you old hound," he thought to himself. He finally mustered up his courage and said, "Torn isn't far from Grayeve, and I'll make a special trip for Shvues [Shavuot]." And so it was all decided.

Anyone But a Tar-seller

A favorite song of the Grayeve tar-sellers

If God gave you a daughter,

Don't give her to a tar-seller;

He's a nomad all his life

And she – as lonely as a stone.

Tar-seller, give her a cobbler husband,

He'll make you strong shoes;

Or a tailor – a true noble,

He'll sew you a jacket.

But don't get involved

With a rich man;

He must be out of his mind

To want your sweet daughter…

If you have no choice, a rich man will also do,

Just not a tar-seller, three times no!

He'll be in Prussia, far from her,

She'll be in Grayeve, lonely as a stone.

Footnotes

22. *Isrekhag*: Half holiday. Hebraic, literally: "bind the festival sacrifice."
23. *tfiln*: phylacteries (small boxes) filled with scripture that are strapped to the left arm and forehead for morning prayers.

[Page 147]

Hasidism in Grayeve
50 years ago
Hyman Blum

Translated by Joshua Shanes

Edited by Tina Lunson

(Recollections)

Grayeve possessed a significant Hasidic island in the great "*misnagdish* [traditional, non-Hasidic] sea" of Grayeve itself and of the surrounding *shtetlakh* [small villages], like Raigrod [Rajgród], *Ogustove* [Augustów], *Shtutzin* [Szczuczyn], *Rodzilova* [Radziłów], *Goniondzh* [Goniądz], *Trestiny* [Trzcianne], etc., where there were perhaps individual Hasidim, but no "organized Hasidism" – no Hasidic *shtiblekh* [prayer rooms].

My memories about the Hasidic ways in Grayeve are youth memories. I have lost the home-city of my early youth and will have to rely on how well my memory serves me and on discussions I have had with several people from the community who, just like me, received a Hasidic upbringing in their childhood years and for whom the Hasidic *shtibl* [prayer room] was a second home.

Grayeve in the time about which I write (the end of the nineteenth century and the beginning of the twentieth) had two Hasidic shtiblekh – the old one, on Shul Street, and the new one, on Rov's Alley.

The old shtibl remained the property of the Hasidim since the last recent failed Polish uprising against Russia, in 1863, after which the government confiscated the property of the Polish nobleman, the owner of the shtetl, and divided the houses and the surrounding fields among those who lived in the houses.

The new shtibl was founded several years after the great fire, around 1895, when Khaym Shmuel's Gerer[1] shtibl burned down.

[Page 148]

There was also an attempt at one time to find a separate Kotzker[2] shtibl, in an upper shtibl on Shul Street, but it didn't last long.

According to Mr. William Friedman, a son of Yitskhok Mayer Friedman of Atlanta, Georgia, (Moshe Nekhemye's son) the Kotzker shtibl was founded due to a clash in the new shtibl between two close friends – his father, who was a Kotzker Hasid, and Yankel Ginzburg (Avigdor's son-in-law), a Gerer hasid. This took place at the end of *shabes* [Sabbath], at the third meal. It was about whether to sing *"bnei heikhola"*[3] with a Kotzker melody or with a Gerer tune. The battle spread and the Kotzker Hasidim then split off and founded their own shtibl. With them went the Gerer Hasid Nosn Silberman (the wine maker), because the Kotzker Hasidim needed him as a good Torah reader. The above-mentioned two good friends remained enemies after that for a long time.

Most Hasidim in Grayeve went to the Gerer Rebe; a significant number – to the Kotzker Rebe. There were also several who went to other rabeim. There also arrived from time-to-time the traveling rabeim– the Kobriner [Kobryń, Belarus] and the Slonimer [Slonim, Belarus].

I was actually "reared" in the old Hasidic shtibl. It's already almost half a century since I left the shtibl, but I still remember the particular type of life in the shtibl and the interesting personalities which it contained. Therefore my memories relate to the old shtibl, but actually the difference between the old and new shtiblakh was quite small.

The Hasidic children felt quite uncomfortable with their long Hasidic frocks, Hasidic caps and long *peyes* [sidelocks]. *Misnagdish* children usually called us "skhidakes!" [4] The average person rarely spoke the word "Hasidism." Usually they used to call us "*shkidim.*"[4] The Hasidic children rarely had much to do with the misnagdish children

Hasidic children mostly lived their lives in Hasidic shtiblekh – especially on shabes and holidays, and especially at the end of shabes for the third meal, when it was dark in the shtibl, the fathers seated around the table, singing *"Bnei heikhola"* and other shabes songs, telling stories about good Jews and trying out new melodies, which were brought from the Hasidic courts. The main singers in my time were: Yehoshua Leyzer Banish, the baker; the Mishkovskes – Shlomo-Hirsch and his sons, Henokh and Moshe-Mendel, who later became the butcher in Grayeve.

[Page 149]

We, the Hasidic children, had pleasure from special holiday activities, which the misnagdish children didn't know.

One such "holiday" was *tishebov* [Tisha B'Av]. Even though everyone fasted and recited *kinos* [dirges: somber song expressing mourning or grief], we children thought of the day more as a holiday than as a day of mourning. Perhaps it was because with tishebov the mourning period of the "3 weeks" and "9 days" ended. We children, used to get good with the burrs, which we used to throw into the beards and short beards of the young Hasidim and obviously in each other's peyes.

A real "holiday" by for us was *erev peysakh* [the evening before the first Passover Seder]; the *"matso mitsve"* [the matso used for the Seder] was baked in the shtibl itself. Just over the wall from the shtibl lived Berl-Lazer, the baker. They would set long tables out in the shtibl, at which the Hasidim and their grown boys would roll and perforate the matsos while reciting psalms [*hallel:* chant of praise consisting of Psalms 113 through 118] and drinking peysakh liquor. Afterwards the matsos – which would have taken many different shapes due to inexperienced rollers – were then passed to Berl-Lazer's bakery through a hole in the wall, which was carved out specifically for this purpose. And even though we, the children, could not help with anything in the work because we were not yet *barmitsve* [bar mitzvah], we used to make enough tumult and stomp around among the adults.

The holiday had actually already begun the night before, when they used to go to the river, to the *Kosherova* [Kêdzierowo], to draw *"mayim she-lanu"* [literally, our water or "water that slept overnight"] used to bake these matsos. This was always considered by us to be a dangerous adventure. The path to the river stretched through *goyishe* [Gentile, non-Jewish] houses and we were placed in danger of being bitten by riled dogs or getting a stone in the head. But at the walk erev peysakh we felt safe, because a whole group of Jews were going and were singing Hallel all the way. Although the one God in heaven knows, that even among the grownups the heart trembled with fears under the *tales-katan* [fringed garment worn either under or over one's clothing by Orthodox Jewish males].

[Page 150]

Of course, we took an especially active part in such truly celebratory holidays like purim and *simkhes-toyre* [Simchat Torah, rejoicing in the Torah, the eighth day of sukes], when our parents allowed themselves to throw off their daily concerns and fall into the mood of joy and felt carefree.

The grown boys had their own "club" in the shtibl. They stuck together and dressed a little misnagdish, their peyes trimmed and the signs of a little beard that showed itself they cleaned up with a scissor or with a "number one *machinke*," [clippers], but this did not prevent them from joining in at "Bnei heikhola." Typically each one of these songs was sung near the beginning of each one of the shabes meals or in the *shabosim* [sabbaths] and holidays at prayers. From this group I remember: Moyshe (Morris) Elkon and his cousins, Botshe and Khaym-Yoysef; Zaydke Simkha-Hirsch's; Sholem Zaydenberg,

Khaym-Itshe Vaser, Itshe-Mayer Ayzenshtat, Mulie Zelegzon (a grandson of Paltiel's).

The Hasidic shtibl didn't only serve as a holy place, as a place for prayer and learning, but also as a center for social and charitable activities, and also as a sort of "political club."

Even though Hasidim considered the Hebrew newspapers of that time, "*Ha'tsefira*" [Hebrew periodical created in 1860's in Warsaw] and "*Ha'melits*" [the first Hebrew-language weekly to appear in tsarist Russia] to be heretical papers, this didn't prevent politics from being discussed before and after prayers, especially during the time of the English-Boer War and of the Russo-Japanese War. And every little piece of news that the above-mentioned newspapers printed found resonance in the shtibl. At the time of the Russo-Japanese war they were already reading "Ha'tsefira" in the shtibl itself. The "political club" concentrated itself around Reb Akiva, a Grayeve Jew who lived many years in Hungary and returned to Grayeve a "European." Leyzer Hepner, the rich man of the shtibl, a merchant Jew whose business led him to the larger cities of Russia and abroad, also had very weighty words; Paltiel the collector – a stunted, hunched-over Hasid who when he was older won a large award of 20,000 rubles; Zerakh Elkon a clever Jew, and several others. We, children, used to gather around them and with strained ears grab the war news and the political discussions, which would last many hours.

The "*hakhnoses orkhim*" [welcoming the guests] duties of the Hasidic shtibl consisted in hosting the frequent "guests" who slept there – Hasidic poor, who used to travel around, or went by foot, from city to city collecting charity. This was a higher class of poor, who did not go over the houses from door to door begging for pennies, but would only get their portion from a fund, into which the Hasidim paid weekly and called "general fund." As a Hasidic young boy it came to me for a brief time to be the "collector," the solicitor of the fund. The Hasidic guests, of whom most were learned, used to get their donations honorably and while they were spending a day or two in Grayeve, used to actually spend the night in the shtibl. Truthfully, the resting place was on a hard bench, but the bench stood next to a Dutch-tiled oven, in which a merry fire burnt the entire winter and spread sweet warmth over the shtibl.

[Page 151]

One could also encounter a baker spread out on the same bench during the day – having been baking bread all night, he felt much more comfortable in the quiet Hasidic shtibl than in his tumultuous house, where the customers and children would not let him sleep.

The democratic spirit among the Hasidim expressed itself in many ways. Old and young, rich and poor – with few exceptions – always addressed each other informally, using the familiar "*du*" [you, informal] and not the formal "*ir*."

At frequent small *simkhes* [celebrations], like *malva-malkas* (Saturday night meals), *yortsaytn* [anniversary of a person's death], or holidays like purim and simkhes-toyre, one felt a true sense of family, at which the boundaries were washed away not only between poor and rich, but even between scholarly and ignorant.

Among the Hasidim there were a variety of elements: important, wealthy families like the Hepners – Leyzer Hepner and his son Leybl-Moyshe, the owner of the only large factory in the city, that employed several hundred workers; and Leyzer Hepner's son-in-law, the prematurely deceased Hersh Vasser, who besides being a great Jewish scholar, was highly educated secularly, and spoke several European languages fluently, including English; the wheat merchant Weinstein (from Kobryn, Belarus) and his son Moshe-Isaac; the merchants and large shopkeepers – the Eisenstadts, the Bachrachs, the Elkons; and others up to such toilers as the smiths Khone and his sons, and Yisroel; the bakers Efroym, Zishke, Yehoshua-Leyzer; the bookbinders Yisroel-Yankev and Moyshe; Shmuel-Ber the tinsmith; Leybel Fishbayn the tanner; Khone the bathkeeper, and others. It is interesting that among the most popular crafts among Jews, tailoring and shoemaking, the Hasidim were not represented.

[Page 152]

The above were supplemented by small shopkeepers, teachers, sons-in-law living with their wives' families, and just poor people, who were supported by the more capable, which was not considered charity, but as helping a poor man in one's own family.

Among the more prominent teachers in Grayeve were specifically the Hasidic ones, like: Simcha-Hirsh, Khaym, Berl, Moyshe-Avrom, David Krinker, my father Leybush, and others.

The Hasidic shtibl did not have any sold "seats" near the Eastern wall for the wealthy and connected families, and a "behind the *bime*" [Torah reading platform] for the masses. If there was a seat of honor it was reserved for the so-to-speak spiritual aristocracy – great scholars, "sharp Hasidim," or just more worldly men. Most Hasidim felt absolutely no need to stand at any single place during prayer. Only a few used to cover their heads with the *tales* [prayer shawl] and quietly, or in a loud voice, complain to the Master of the Universe. The rest used to walk around, or even run around the shtibl, and only by *shimenesre* [*amida*; central prayers] would they stand still at whatever spot they found. Others, at the time of public prayer, used to simply sit and study, and when the congregation had already left they would pray individually. One of these was my father, Reb Leybush the teacher. He was regularly the last one out of the shtibl. When nobody else was left there, he could concentrate on his thoughts and set himself in a corner and quietly pray. Only very rarely would he pray with the last *minyen* [prayer quorum].

A second late prayer was Yisroel-Borekh, Mordkhe the butcher's son-in-law who was still a young man, an ordained rabbi, a Domatshever Hasid. He would stand in another corner and with a voice that you could hear all around the shtibl, throw his entire body into his prayers and would fall into an ecstasy, which often bordered on hysteria.

The only ones who had their set places to sit were Leyzer Hepner, Reb Akiva and also Simcha-Hersh the teacher, an old Jew and a great scholar, who lived only with his holy books and for whom the entire outside world did not exist. I don't remember him ever sitting. I can't imagine him other than covered with his tales, standing in one place; same thing with Kalman-Moyshe Mishkavski, who died suddenly in the shtibl in his standing place, wearing his tales and *tfiln*.[5]

[Page 153]

In the community life of Grayeve the misnagdim were the dominant element; still the Hasidim insisted always to have a Hasid from among themselves among the Grayeve butchers. Earlier it was Mordkhe the butcher, and later – Moshe Mendel Mishkavski.

Around the end of the 19th century – over 50 years ago – the Hasidim over the course of several years led a strong campaign to create an office of official rabbi, in which they wanted to install the great scholar and prominent Gerer Hasid, Reb Fishel Zukert.

After the Hasidim failed to install Reb Fishel as official rabbi in a peaceable manner, several days before Passover they decided to take a "drastic step." Namely, erev peysakh, instead of "selling the *khomets*" [anything leavened] with the Grayeve rabbi, Rov Eliyahu-Ahron Milekovski, they sold it with Reb Fishel, and thereby recognized him as rabbi.

Over the course of Passover the struggle grew even more enflamed, and the climax came on the last day of Passover, when Moshe-Yosel, the *shames* [beadle], ascended the bime and called out that the khomets which was not sold with the rabbi, but only with Rov Fishel, is "khomets that was owned during Passover." That is, not only was it forbidden to be eaten after Passover, one could not even derive any benefit from it in any other way.

This enflamed the struggle even more strongly, but in the end, the Rov recalled the prohibition and the incident was ended.

* * *

Naturally, over the course of fifty years, since I left the Hasidic shtibl, many changes have come in the Jewish life in Grayeve overall. But that the Hasidim still strongly held onto their "island" in Grayeve can be seen in the letter which has been reproduced in this book, which the author of these lines received from the Grayeve Hasidim already on the path to the outbreak of the massacre which engulfed the Jewish world in Europe. The letter is signed by a number of Hasidim, children of Hasidim whom I mention in my memoirs. One knows that they further spun the thread that their elders had maintained for generations. The letter is the last echo from Hasidic Grayeve.

[Page 154]

House of Hasidim in Grayeve

Grayeve the 10th of May 1938

Very esteemed and beloved [editor: illegible] Mr. Kh. Y. Blum:

How stunned and surprised we were when reading the newspaper *Forverts* [The Jewish Daily Forward newspaper] and learning of the passing of your noble and modest father Reb Leybush, may his memory be for a blessing, whose memory and good reminiscences still remain among the old people of the local Hasidim shtibl who knew him well and always mentioned him with much honor and respect. Unfortunately our current letter of sympathy to you has been delayed by the great trouble that has happened to us in town in the meantime, which for understandable reasons we could not write. A fine young man from the shtibl by the name of Ayzenshtat, Itsik, got apoplexy from shock and died straight away. We called together everyone from the Hasidim shtibl and studied a page of Talmud every day – *daf hayomi* ["the daily page"] – and after each session said a *kadish* [a prayer sanctifying God's name and said as part of the mourning ritual] for the soul of your unforgettable, deceased father Reb Leybush. We believe that will be the finest monument and memorial for him. At the same time it was decided, since the 28 of Sivan the month, [editor: illegible] especially to honor your beloved father may his memory be for a blessing and so that the younger generation should also know and remember your father as a student of Rabbinic lore and as one of the remnants of the older generation he was a modest/humble person. He never made a fuss about himself, and he grew to be an invaluable treasure to his pupils, and then lost to them, but they carry his intellectual traits and rare character always in their hearts.

Shleyme Zalmen Tsukert —— Efroym Piel

——————☐—— son on Dovid Tankhum Bogish ☐———— Elkan☐———— son of Dovid Tankhum Bogish☐—— Tsuker Nosn — Zilberman also remember you, I was one of your father's pupils.☐When I learned the news of your father ———.☐———— Roshen, Itsik

[Editors note: many names illegible]

Footnotes

24. *Ger*: The largest Hasidic dynasty in Poland prior to the Holocaust and founded by Rabbi Yitzchak Meir Alter (1799–1866), brother-in-law of The Kotzker Rebe. He was an insightful

Torah scholar and Halakhist [*halakhah*: the collective basis of Jewish religious law, including Biblical, Talmudic and Rabbinic]
25. *Kotzk*: Hasidic dynasty founded by Rebe Menachem Mendel Morgenstern (1787–1859). The Hasidim of Kotsk focused on truth seeking rather than conformity to religious traditionalism. They were also known for their radical and controversial style of expression.
26. *Bnei Heikhala*: one of the three songs written for Shabbat by R. Issac Luria (the AR"I).
27. *skhidakes/shkidim*: editor: unknown literal translation, probably slang, play on words meant as derogatory
28. *tfiln*: Phylacteries, the small boxes filled with scripture that are strapped to the left arm and forehead for morning prayers

[Page 155]

Hepner's Suspender Factory
(In the period 1900-1905)
Hymie Shiller and Sol Shiller
Translated by Miriam Leberstein

The factory was founded in 1881 by Leyzer Hepner, his son Leybl-Moyshe, and his son-in-law Hersh Vaser; a German Jew named Zalinger was a partner. Around 1896, Leybl-Moyshe became the sole owner. He also took over Zalinger's large and splendid house.

An Unusual Factory

Hepner's factory was unique not only 50 years ago, but even today there is no other suspender factory in the world where almost every necessary part is produced on the premises. Even today, in highly industrialized America, suspender manufacturers buy all the necessary materials from other manufacturers, and sew and pack the suspenders, but the Grayever suspender factory was different. The raw rubber came from England. From *Lodzh* [Łódź] came satin and cotton thread in a natural color. Here [in *Grayeve*] they dyed the thread, spun it, and wove it on steam-powered machines. From *Varshe* [Warsaw] they got metal belts cut to a specific length, and here they would hammer out the various buckles. From local butchers they bought the hides of cows and processed them into leather in their own tannery. Their own workers cut down trees in the nearby woods, sawed them into thin boards and constructed boxes. They bought paper and cardboard in Varshe and made their own cartons.

Hepner's factory employed around two hundred workers: 120 Poles and Germans, and sixty Jews. [sic]. The Germans were the spinners, weavers, and tanners. The Jews cut the rubber, carved the leather, hammered out the buckles, sewed, and packed. Two wagon drivers employed by the factory transported the finished goods. The main office and warehouse were in Varshe, and the salesmen set out from Varshe to all parts of the Russian Empire.

[Page 156]

Working Conditions

The workers were divided into two categories: the Christians got paid a lot more and worked one hour less per day than the Jews. The workday began at 6:00 a.m. The workers had to get up at 5:00 a.m. On the dark winter pre-dawns, in order not to have to walk the two *Viorsts* [Approximately 0.6 mile/1 kilometer] outside the town alone, the workers (i.e. the Jewish workers) would gather together in one place and walk as a group. One of them would walk ahead with a lantern. The main meeting place was at Rutke the baker's. It was warm and well lit in the bakery. Rutke's reward was that the workers would buy her warm bagels.

From 6:00 a.m. to 7:00 a.m. they worked by the light of kerosene lamps and often with frozen hands. At 8:00 a.m. there was a fifteen minute break for prayers and breakfast. Since Hepner was a fervent Hasid, he saw to it that ten minutes were devoted to praying, and five to eating. The hour from 12:00 to 1:00 was lunchtime. Most of the workers brought food with them, since it would take almost an hour to go to town and back.

They worked six days a week: from Sunday to Friday, from 6:00 in the morning to 7:00 at night. Friday was a short day; in winter it ended at 3:00 p.m., in summer at 6:00 p.m., in order to give the workers time to fulfill their Sabbath obligation to bathe, in winter at the bathhouse, and in summer in the *Kosherove* [Kędzierow]. In order to make up for the shorter Friday, they worked Thursday nights and often, Saturday nights.

Many early mornings, when the workers arrived, Moyshe Hepner's wife, Ginendl, was already in the factory to make sure everyone was there; then she would go back to sleep. Often she would come in the afternoon to make sure everyone came back from lunch on time. She was never idle, but did the same work as the other girls. When a worker came fifteen minutes late, he made up for it at lunchtime. If he was more than fifteen minutes late, he was penalized for twice the amount of time lost.

[Page 157]

Wages

The beginning pay for a Jewish girl was fifty kopeks a week. If she was quick and skillful, after three years she could earn two rubles a week. A man began at seventy five kopeks a week, and after a couple of years could earn up to five rubles a week. Wages were paid every two weeks.

The Christian workers worked fewer hours: from 6:00 a.m. to 6:00 p.m., and they worked on Saturday instead of Sunday. The majority lived in houses near the factory and many came to work by bicycle. They earned a lot more than the Jewish workers.

Gradually, the Jewish workers started to protest against their longer hours and lower wages, and they organized. This was a very bold step. Hepner's was the biggest factory in Grayeve. Many workers started there as boys were already married and had children. They had never done any other kind of work. To turn against Hepner's could mean not only losing a job, but to be left with nothing to eat. Nevertheless, they decided to organize and sent a committee to Hepner with demands. Most of the committee members were young boys, about twenty years old. When they went to see Hepner in his office, he sent them home and told them to bring their fathers, because it was beneath his dignity to sit down at the same table with these young whippersnappers.

The same day, the workers returned to the factory with their parents. Hepner gave a speech, telling them they should consider themselves fortunate that he gave them work, because if not, they would die of hunger.

The Strike

The workers demanded the same work hours and the same wages as the Christian workers. Hepner wouldn't hear of it. The Jewish workers thus decided that at 6:00 on Monday evening, when the bell rang and the Christian workers went home, all of the Jewish workers would stop work. Several Jewish workers didn't show up at all on Monday morning. Several sewing machine operators remained at their machines at 6 o'clock, pretending that they were fixing the machines. The others stopped at 6 o'clock.

[Page 158]

None of the Jewish workers came to work on Tuesday morning. For the first two weeks, Hepner wouldn't even negotiate. Later, he softened and proposed a raise in wages. The workers held fast and continued to demand the same working conditions as the Christian workers. The strike lasted a couple of months. In the meantime, many workers got work elsewhere. A large number emigrated to America.

As a result of the strike, the manufacturing of suspenders stopped in Grayeve. Here they only wove the rubber, and the suspenders were fabricated in Varshe. During the First World War, production in the factory almost entirely ceased, but after the war, production started up again, and on a larger scale than before.

After Leybl-Moyshe's death, his children moved to Varshe, and from there they ran both their Varshe and Grayeve factories until the outbreak of World War II. It would appear that there were two Leybl-Moyshes: an everyday one, and a Sabbath one. All week he wore modern European clothing, was occupied with his business, travelled to Varshe, to Germany, to other countries. But when he came [to Grayeve] on *shabes* [Sabbath], he became a totally different Leybl-Moyshe. He took off his modern clothes and put on a Hasidic kaftan and hat, attended a Hasidic *shtibl* [small synagogue], and rocked back and forth while praying with fervor like all Hasidim.

His connections to the Grayeve Jews stopped there. He did not belong to any other Jewish institutions and organizations, and contributed very little to the free loan society, or to the charity that provided shelter for indigent travelers. Leybl-Moyshe Hepner's son took the same path, with one exception: he didn't even attend the Hasidic shtibl.

[Page 159]

Grajewo
(Segments of a narrative)
Dr. Tzvi Wislavsky (Jerusalem)
To my brother, to Pesach, with affection

Indeed, the crown of romance doesn't befit our town: she is young in years. Among the centuries old cities with their important historic passages and changes she will not be found; and among the ancient communities of Israel in Poland, with their long and glorious pedigree, she will not be counted. Her stormy ascent, in the last decades of the 19th century; her economic and social decline was in the days between the First World War and its counterpart, the Second World War, and its annihilation – with the annihilation and destruction of Polish Jewry by the villain, by Amalek of the last generations (not in vain was it common among the town's people to say: The Prussian-Amalekite!). When a son or daughter of Grajewo, who miraculously survived the terrible upheaval, turns the pages of Sienkiewicz's great epic novel "*Potop*,"[1] [The Deluge] he will search futilely for her of fine deeds, of great desire and of enormous lust for life and splendor, of the wonderful initiative that she possessed more than the surrounding towns –

Szczuczyn and Jedwabne, Kolno and Stawiski, Rajgrod and Radzilow and Wansosz (even this least of the nearby neighboring towns!) – all are mentioned there and pass before us, except for Grajewo. In the 17th century she wasn't in the world and didn't even exist in the 18th century; in the mid-19th century she was still out of bounds and only from the 60's of the 19th century did she begin growing and rapidly overtaking her comrades-neighbors with youthful vigor and audacity. And the quick rise came due to the important and strategic railroad that terminated there; the one that connected Odessa with its large port in Western Europe, passing through all the southwest of pre-1914 Russia, due to an important customs station – a primary source of livelihood for the town, permitted and forbidden – due to plenty of commerce that flourished between Russia and Germany at the end of the 19th and beginning of the 20th century. A border town was Grajewo, its existence in proximity throughout, with all the advantages and disadvantages, infused with three competing cultures: to Poland its allegiance, originating from Poland's influence on the town – its life and hopes; Poland's national struggle – gradually blurred with the growth of the Russian administrative base, the growth of the military (Russian cavalry and border legions), to Russia from which came an abundance of crops, livestock and poultry, and with which language, cultural, and life style influences penetrated slowly and constantly; and to Germany where many of the townspeople found their livelihood with a certain sense of freedom, imitating her language and customs, seeing her as an exalted model of civilization and culture. All the ambitions of the town's sons, their material and spiritual efforts were influenced – pulled here and there, at times one influence increases and at times another. From this emerged its greatness and from this or its social and cultural uncertainties.

[Page 160]

A.

A narrow sandy peninsula between lakes of water and peat – a continuation of the famous lakes of East Prussia – is the site of the first, original Grajewo. The nobleman's estate is stuck between the lakes and the main village. Why in fact he built his castle near the lakes, a place inflicted with bad diseases – is a riddle. Near the castle is the Polish-Catholic place of worship and around it was the broad square market with a well at its center, and this is not the place to decide the difficult historic-sociologic question that pertains to all the cities and towns of Europe: which came first – the place of worship which the market surrounded from three sides; or was the market first and the place of worship built in it? Three of the market's sides were occupied by the stores and homes of Jews (I remember only one Christian store from my childhood), nice strong walled houses and the fourth side was occupied by the place of worship and the homes of its servants. From here spread the first streets of the village, most of them toward the lakes and fewer toward the sands. The sands with their sparse vegetation, between the town and Prussia (along the Bogusze Prostki road) were a place for the young people to stroll on hot summer Sabbaths, with the pine forests closer to Goniądz and Szczuczyn, extending towards low lying hills at the foot and head of the town. Why the town's people didn't build it half a kilometer away from the valley, into which flowed plenty of rain water from all directions, miring its streets and attracting various diseases, seasonal and perennial; why they in fact pressed and crowded between the lakes – is not known to this day. The townspeople probably wanted to warm in the light of the castle, or the place of worship with its holidays and many congregations of the peasants from villages.

[Page 161]

Indeed hygienically the town's position was difficult and it had many ills and repair didn't come until after the First World War, when the government of independent Poland began to think of fixing and improving the town (the German occupation did so earlier): drained swamps (such as the large swamp next to the Pravoslavian house of worship); planted rows of trees (in the center of town near the post office); and other such repairs and improvements that turned the mud and dirt-filled town into a proper and nice place of refuge. However, this repair didn't come when the town was flourishing before Poland's independence when there was prosperity, but during the decline, when sources of livelihood were dwindling. Her sons began leaving, one by one and in groups and the Christian element began to press the Jews, with the aid of Polish society and government out of their nice homes and their emptying shops: the residents of the sand dunes began to conquer, not by storm but continuously, the main streets, and its first citizens by time and stature, her patrons, the layers of its foundations and builders of its walls, declined irreversibly.

Thus is illustrated the growth of the town, fragmented, broken, with no historical documents (because the place was young) or literary descriptions (except those of A. Ibn-Zahav, who dedicated many of his books to the town's people and their lives). Before the railroad was laid down the market was central and the streets of the Jewish residents concentrated and crowded around it. Later, when the railroad was built, the spread of construction shifted completely, matching the shift of the main source of income. The railroad and the customs house became central and new streets were built next to the station, spreading toward Szczuczyn along the strategic road; most of them Christian, Russian (officials) or Polish, and only few of the Jewish elite who had business with the customs house, settled there. The majority of Jews in the town lived on the streets near the swamps, afflicted with their diseases, a few of them becoming immune. It is well known, the hardships of climate are exhausting; I wonder if there is any town whose health was hurt like Grajewo's, mired in peat and constant mud almost year round. There were many with tuberculosis and an alarming number were demented. On the other hand, hardships develop immunity and strength. I wonder if any other town nearby was blessed with so many strong powerful men, famously self-assured, who were immunized and strengthened by the place's hardships and put fear into people, especially the gentiles who would congregate in the market on their holidays, constantly provoking arguments, conflicts and altercations. Not only the town's tar men, who would bring home their strong muscles, bored on their long "holiday" and looking for a fight (as faithfully described by Ibn-Zahav, as noted), but also its permanent residents, the famous blacksmiths, whose hands were iron bars, all the residents of the synagogue street and especially the residents of the bath house street – all of their heavy and weathered hands would thoroughly work the gentiles' faces. They were first to fight, to lift heavy loads (I remember as a child, there was one such tough who would bend under a cart loaded with flour – 100 *poods* [Russian unit of weight equaling about 3600 pounds/1600 kg] – and raise it on his back) – art for art's sake, and of course not to win any prize other than scars, cuts, bruises, for the pleasure and joy of the Jewish children and the envy of the Polish youngsters. At the end of the 90's the town began emptying of those young toughs, for whom the place became too confining. Prussia would no longer absorb them and in the town itself sources of livelihood were uncertain (as explained below). The Grajewo House in the U.S.A. was founded in those days and the Russian-Japanese war expanded the house as the Jewish force clung fondly and hopefully to this new source of life, and those who were last in social importance became first.

[Page 162]

Grajewo was surrounded on the east from three sides, among the Polish towns and villages with their lifestyles, sources of livelihood, economic and social development, attached as a final boundary link to a huge country with abundant power and authority, linked to Russia at the initial flourishing time of the young Russian capitalism and its heart in the west where many of its sons absorbed all or most of their influence, from Prussia-Germany. The town's blossoming and its material and spiritual growth were associated with the enormous blossoming of Germany in the last decades of the 19th century. From here came the mercantile and intermediary nature of Grajewo, which mediated not only between the villages and the large city as did all other Jewish towns in Poland, but mostly it mediated between great countries, facing this way and that, acting as a firm "master," extravagant and capable.

B.

It seems that Grajewo had nothing of its own: it didn't evolve unique skills like other towns that specialized in various crafts, or could boast of their products; it did not establish its own industry (other than two factories, one was Hefner's for rubber goods whose fame was mostly during Poland's era of independence, and the other for bone grinding – Bilistucki). Our town didn't have many craftsmen. There were few tailors because most of the townspeople wore readymade clothes from German factories; only a few, the elite, important landlords, the Chasidim and educated gentiles would use the town's tailors (indeed there were a few specialty tailors– Kurejwowski). They were more shoemakers, but even those became fewer with the founding of the shoe industry in Warsaw, which supplied all the shoe needs of the town and even this industry diminished and shrank early in our century.

[Page 163]

Even the rural area which relied little on the Prussian clothing products, did not establish a sector of specialty tailors and shoemakers, which were the basic trades in each and every town. There were tinsmiths (remember the tinsmith on Bogusz street who would keep all his tools outside, fence off the street and no one protested), potters, weavers, blacksmiths, locksmiths (not many of them), watchmakers, jewelers, stitchers and more, barbers, seamstresses and other such craftsmen as noted, there was no specialty in the town.

Not so was commerce. In this respect Grajewo was above the neighboring towns. Here were the big wholesalers, distributing their goods to the surrounding retailers: large merchants in flour, kerosene (with large vats to which the kerosene cars would come directly and pour the precious liquid) and other such wholesale businesses – the pride of the town. There were many shops in the town. In that its image was not unique – the same competition that destroys and doesn't build, the same jealousy that doesn't increase customers or goods; the same hatred, sometimes between brothers and members of one family; the same chase after a bit of income and a taste of decent livelihood; the same misery that would flow from among the walls of the gloomy shops; the same faces etched with worries about payments due, of a shop empty of merchandise with no goods or money in return, as told in the Jewish literature of recent generations: the great demands of life on one hand was weighed against the meager ability to fulfill them on the other. And even though this occupation was numerous, more so than other occupations, they did not characterize the town, they did not designate its image and purpose; rather it seems that the international trade was what characterized the town.

First in numbers and strength, but of course not in importance the tar men and horse traders, shouldn't be confused: the tar men would travel door-to-door among the German villages selling the farmers tar to coat their wheels (which is why they were called tar men) and leather, sewing and other such goods. Not everyone who wished for such a business could do it: only those seen as proper and honest. Their trade wasn't the easiest or cleanest and they could barely earn enough to support their families who remained in their original homes. They spent most days away from home and would return to Grajewo only for the big holidays Pesach and Sukkot, wearing suits from Titz and Wertheim (a department store in Germany), round hard hats (their unique sign) and yellow shoes on their feet. The most industrious among them would rise to the status of horse traders. But to achieve that they had to endear themselves to the townspeople who stayed year round, to act generously – after all, they had had a taste of Prussia. These, the tar men, had an important place in the town's economic and social structure. Above them were the horse traders, some of whom achieved greatness and wealth (Biloszewski, Tykocki, Worzabolowski, Poliak, Entman, Wislawski, Jamszon, Miller, Milewicz). The horse traders would venture into the depths of Russia (as far as the Ural Mountains they would go), bringing from there elegant riding horses and gigantic hauling horses, and delivering them to Germany where they had large businesses. They too were not in the town but for the holidays, behaving like landlords and great merchants, their hands open for charity and for the synagogues' needs; ambitious they were, providing their sons learning and knowledge and dedicated to excelling with the Torah. They weren't themselves knowledgeable in Torah or general learning, but they lightly hinted at such, particular about their honor and not mixing with the ordinary tar men (but the other townspeople would call them "tar men" derisively). The tar men and horse traders were a large group of the townspeople before the First World War and during the war they were absorbed into Germany.

[Page 164]

They are followed by the large wheat, geese and poultry merchants (Bufensztejn, the Marcuses, Gersztanski, Wodowski), the pillars of external commerce, the class of the town and their words were heeded everywhere. Their standing too depended on the season: some suddenly became very wealthy, others declined all at once, increasing the number of impoverished and usually working hard to make a living, diligently trying to fulfill all the demands and obligations of the wealthy, notable in their attire and demeanor at all times. Above them in every respect were the customs agents who cared for the customs matters of the large Russian businesses, which would receive machinery and machine parts for Russian industry. Their turnover reached millions per year; some of them reaching enormous wealth and greatness for a small town like Grajewo (Jazerski, Levin, Worzabolowski, Zilbersztejn, Bilistucki, Olschwanger, Fajfenzilber) – the elite of the town's elite, with the dozens of clerks, making a comfortable living, unlike the other townspeople who had no constant income. These houses also engaged in banking, lending merchants large sums at high interest (Jazerski, the biggest of these agents, was enormously wealthy, and before the First World War his wealth was more than two million rubles). And these complete the economic structure of the town.

Next to all these permanent occupations there was another transient unofficial occupation, more numerous than all the others, which would take its due from all the classes; its existence completely forbidden as it were, and sometimes being exiled to Siberia – these were of course the smugglers: smuggling Russian immigrants to Germany and smuggling German goods, world goods from Germany to Russia. This was not a respectable occupation at all, yet many engaged in it: at times of rise in this "occupation," and at times of fall to other occupations, and there were many such falls. There were frequent downturns in industry and commerce, and the town's economic structure couldn't support the whole population in legal occupations. The overseas migration from Russia increased with the frequent political crisis that affected this huge country at the beginning of the twentieth century: political migration of revolutionaries; escape from military service during the Russia-Japan war; the great migration of Jews to America who did not have passports for foreign travel (these passports were expensive and poor people could not afford them) –for all these our town was a transition point –illegally. The border smugglers were talented people, with tricks and wonderful inventions, outsmarting every decree, penetrating every crack left by the authorities – stumbling and being sent away to Siberia for a few years, or to some place far from the border, reappearing, acting legally for a few years, and then returning to their dangerous, adventurous, stimulating occupation. Along with those were hundreds who smuggled goods to neighboring towns, especially to Bialystok the large nearby city which would swallow the smuggled goods and even distribute them to other places. The goods were cheap compared to Russian goods and even the many passports and intermediaries did not raise their price so much as to make them undesirable. This occupation did not enjoy riches (except for a few); it involved dangers, fears, many failures and few successes. But what wouldn't a Jew do for his and his family's livelihood? And the needs of our townspeople were always greater than those in other towns: the life style was rich, the economic and social appetite was great, an excess of feverishness, of aspiration to wealth and social advancement, was in the blood of most townspeople and it harnessed, prodded, instilled brashness and risk in the heart, energy in arm and leg, and inventiveness in the mind. This non-occupation "occupation" would envelope all other occupations, provoke them, over-stimulate them.

[Page 165]

C.

And from the economic structure to the social structure, they overlapped almost everywhere, yet they weren't always equivalent. One of the most interesting features of our town was the abundance of eligible men from outside, from other towns, from the distant surroundings and even from far away. It seems that all those sitting at the "*Eastern*" [distinguished] wall at the synagogue, all those permitted an "*Aliyah*" [the honor of reading a blessing of the Torah] were not from the town; it seems that ours reduced themselves purposely so as not to overshadow the plentiful light emanating from the "pillars of Torah," from the nice yeshiva students, wearing tall top hats, who were all from the outside. The first residents to become rich and well off saw it as an honor and distinction to take grooms for their daughters from other towns, educated in Torah and Hebrew. One remembers the distinguished rows in synagogue and especially the new synagogue, and envisions the refined forms of learning and distinction in one place and almost all of them were outsiders. Marcus and Sterling, Rozyn and Rawidowicz (the father of Dr. S. Rawidowicz), Bialystocki and Totilman, Golombiewski and Gnachowski, Knorozowski and Greiber, Worzabolowski, Olschwanger, were the town's elite, it's wise and elders, pedants and educated – all were outsiders. The rich fish merchant who took two learned and rich bachelors (Kopciowski and Nowinski) was not alone, but set an example for the others. All tried with all their might to acquire learned and pedigreed bachelors and many succeeded, and the town that had almost nothing of its own became in one generation a town of learning and pedigree. This town of "grooms" established fine Talmud study groups ("*Chevrot Shas*"), like few in the area, with debaters who would cast fear into the great rabbis with whom our town was blessed. These bachelors, although they immediately harnessed themselves to employment and competition, would fill the yeshivas in the evenings with the voices of righteous students, who were supposedly away from studies for few hours. Among these bachelors were Torah sages (M. Bobkowski, a real "genius"), Kopciowski, Marcus, Rawidowicz, and also the Hebrew intelligentsia (A. M. Piorka from Lomza, Z. Sterling and more, and the Worzabolowski and Olschwanger families – the town's pride in general and Hebrew education, Zionism, and Jewish activism). These bachelors strove that Grajewo's teachers would be the best in five hundred by five hundred miles; that the town's rabbis would be among the great rabbis, and they succeeded: Rabbi Miliekowsi was the town's rabbi for a long time and when he left for Krakow, came Rabbi Amiel z"l, the one who the debaters, the great students, fought for weeks and refused to choose him for town's rabbi until they were all defeated, one after the other, first the small ones, then the great, and then the greatest great. Most of them also had their hearts open to the new trends that invaded the Jewish towns in those days – the Enlightenment, Zionism, Hebrew, and so on.

[Page 166] and [Page 167]

And the Enlightenment[2] – it was mostly Hebrew. There weren't many Externalists in our town – the social element that destroyed the cultural structure of Jewish towns in Russia at the beginning of the century. The most talented among the young men went to the "*kontor*" [foreign trading post] – to the customs agencies, and weren't relegated to idleness – the mother of *Externalism*.[3] Indeed these "grooms" did not pass their great Torah knowledge to their sons, did not send their sons to the great yeshivas (except for Ravidowicz), didn't continue their own dynasty, but didn't allow it to be broken completely: dunces they didn't breed, simpletons they didn't nurture, irksome intellectuals they didn't produce: the voices of fathers didn't bring heretic violations of sons. The girls received more general education than the boys, because the boys went to work, and the girls were caught up more in the modern trend of general education. A. M. Piorka was the promoter of knowledge and enlightenment for the educated townspeople and due to him, Jewish Enlightenment reached a peak that other neighboring towns did not approach. He was aided by an enthusiastic group of modern teachers (Pomerantz, Liss); and the town was a sort of center of Jewish Enlightenment for all neighboring towns. They created the Jewish environment in which arose Jewish writers and great Zionist functionaries (others will probably write about this and I touched it only in passing as part of the description of the social and cultural structure of the town). Grajewo was early with established schools before their time came in other places: Piorka's school attracted students from other towns, as did Karmin's school; and the study of the Hebrew language became mandatory in all classes and there were classes that dedicated specific hours to the language (and again Piorka was the first of those teachers). And the modern Hebrew book took over the home, and the Hebrew newspaper was not a rare guest from Sabbath-to-Sabbath (as it was with the rise of Yiddish journalism), but a permanent resident; and the volumes of *Ha'Asif* [a literary almanac founded by Nachum Sokolov] would pass from hand to hand and Sokolov – his words would be heard in every home (referring to the home-owners) and the controversies in the newspapers would even split the synagogues into factions. – The town was modern, its residents were modern and their hearts were open and their minds alert, quick to business innovations and life styles of the time. The town was blessed that its elite were learned and educated, who saw the wide world with its changes and trends and did not stagnate in their knowledge as did the elites of the older reputable towns whose past took precedence over present and future. The intellectuals did not distance themselves from the community, did not associate with the authorities despite their commercial and economic ties, but were involved with the community in everything, even in purely religious matters. I can see the image of Eliyahu Worzabolowski ("Elinka" he was called by the townspeople. By the way: The town would give popular people diminutive names and so it did with the esteemed Olschwangers), an intellectual and skeptic, who took it upon himself to build the great synagogue: he organized, collected funds, included all good people in the work, levied taxes on the town to benefit the synagogue, oversaw every detail, and it was a magnificent synagogue, and many aspired to be at the "East end" even though they didn't deserve it by their social and religious standing. And I remember the Sabbath at the end of the 19th century when they announced the collection of Shabbat donations to complete the synagogue and permitted weekday food to be eaten and all this was supervised by "Elinka" (who was by the way very wealthy and when he passed away left a quarter million rubles!).

[Page 168]

The town enjoyed a varied and rich social life only after the First World War of course, with the great community division and I cannot discuss that life because I saw it only briefly when I visited mother's home. My discussion is aimed at the days before the First World War, and even then I wasn't a resident of the town, but more of a visitor, when I would come from school to celebrate the holiday at mother's house (I studied at small and large yeshivas: Borisov, Brezin, Radin and Telz, and later Odessa and Peterburg), but Grajewo of those days is the Grajewo in its essence and greatness, as noted. It was dominated by the "grooms" economically, in religious life, education, learning, life style: they imprinted the town's signature in the material and spiritual, and they ultimately created the foundation of Grajewo between the wars, when the town shrank and moved away, and filled with a desire to change values, to leave the town and settle in Eretz Yisrael and other countries. The image that I drew above is very proper for Grajewo on the end of the 19th and beginning of the 20th century, but was not erased in the next period: it kept its character, continued its learning, and in its enlightenment exceeded its first mother (in my book "Mixed Authorities," in my article "Changing of the Guard," I envisioned our town and said what I said based on it, and I also referred to it in one of the chapters of my book "Culture Pains"). In her time of prosperity she didn't particularly chase after formal education, and only at the time of poverty did many of the townspeople get caught up in formal education; and there are many doctors and lawyers from Grajewo who live in Eretz Yisrael and America.

D.

The people of the other towns would say about Grajewo: she is a glutton, bankrupt, spending more than she earns, vain and ostentatious. Surely there is much truth in this condemnation. She craved the largest fish, the fattiest meat; her bakeries were renowned "throughout the land" (Abramski); her clothing elegant and her dresses ostentatious. But this over-eagerness to be seen, extravagant, was felt in all other activities, secular and religious: no other town was as generous as ours for all the needs of Israel in Poland. A *SD"R* [Shaliach deRabanan – a rabbi's envoy] who came to a town would spend a respectable amount for the yeshiva, and not without cause were people from

Grajewo respected by the large yeshivas, and the support they received was greater than the support of people from other towns. They were first to any charity and joint Jewish project, first in matters of Zionism and settlement of Eretz Yisrael, first to aid fire victims, etc. They were ostentatious – yes, but also ostentatious in good deeds. They were wasteful and also wasteful for *tsedkah* [giving of charity] for public needs. The town's young were not great experts in "discussions," their hearts didn't follow political debate, but public matters, of substance, were close to their alert heart, which was open throughout the year and not only on the High Holy Days or holidays. All the central committees of Polish Jewry knew our town's address: a loyal address, which deals lightly with light matters and seriously with the severe matter of national and community life. They were epicurean, but also had a good eye, quick to take from life, from the plenty of neighboring Germany, but also quick for a good deed, lending a hand, heaving a shoulder, to help an individual or the community. This writer can testify, about the young of that time, who were immersed in worldly pleasures and drank more than a sip of the world's available indulgences, that they were dedicated to the public needs. The Silbersteins, Gerstanskis, Gewirtzmans, Berenzons, etc., etc., were all dedicated to their businesses and pleasures, and how were they dedicated in their heart and soul to matters that required sacrifice. Let it be said: they liked card games (a lust that swept our brethren in Poland in all classes and social layers, the learned and the Chasids), but those in need discreetly shared in the reward of the games.

[Page 169]

My short narrative cannot encompass in the least the life, businesses, failures and successes of the town's people. I didn't even hint at the glorious saga of Grajewo's Zionism, its learning and knowledge, of its sons who traveled afar and achieved status and greatness through hard work and industriousness. It's a great saga of much interest, not only to our townspeople. Not in vain did nearby towns look upon it with envy, resentment, and fondness all at once, learning from its ways and deeds, condemning and imitating, praising and doing as she did. It seems: she was young and wanted to fulfill forcefully, independently, what it missed in time – to be a great community of Jewish Poland, of wealth and learning, affluence and intelligence, of public life and national revival.

I would like to dwell at the end upon one group, almost removed from the other groups in the town's internal life: the Chasidim. The majority of the town was *Mitnagdim* [those who were opposed to the Chasidic movement in the great religious controversy that began in the 18th century]: its rabbis, intellectuals, scholars. But a small minority, strong and assertive, of Chasidim was in the town, a group that differed from everyone in attire, even in language, and in life style. It was a minority that did not bend, its existence not disregarded. A few intrepid families, assertive, fought the majority, and usually succeeded in their fight. The Hefner, Alkon, Lipszic, Eisenstadt families fought for their status and forced the Mitnagdic town to provide their own butcher and teacher. They didn't have their own synagogues, but the *Shtieblach* [prayer rooms] were lively, following their own traditions. The battle tactics of a minority against a majority could be learned from them; preserving their image from being uprooted, their appearance from being blurred or tarnished. The Chasidim, who founded a kingdom within a kingdom, were proud of their uniqueness and separation, of standing in a sea of Mitnagdim and not being assimilated into it. And even the Chasidim who blended in on the week days in their behavior and dress would separate in looks and image on Sabbaths and holidays: a small, immune island in the sea of a different community. The majority did not impose itself on them, they imposed themselves on the majority due to their strong social cohesion, because of their stronger awareness as with any minority, a kind of Chasidic aristocracy in a crowd of Mitnagdim, and they served as a kind of conservative base in the town which knew and recognized its purpose. Over time the divisions blurred and intermixed, but in the glory days of the town they stood in their uniqueness and separation. By the way: they too were mostly outsiders and not of the long timers in town, and they also dealt in the businesses mentioned above: they were not inferior in their agility and initiative from their Mitnagdic brethren and didn't even refrain from life's pleasures; and they kept only one privilege, the privilege of a social-cultural minority which didn't follow the majority but fed from its own source, loyal to the Chasidic sects (particularly *Gur*).[4] At first they were not open to Enlightenment, to Zionism, but in the end they joined it too, in their way, by their ability. And those who were saved from the Holocaust, their hand and energy, their mind and initiative, are felt in the Jewish community in Eretz Yisrael and America. It was a vibrant town, boiling, fighting the hardships of life in its own way, weaving the tapestry of Jewish life in Poland-Russia with talent and enthusiasm, with passion of the soul and wisdom. Plenty of charm flowed from its sons with their elegant exteriors, their clothes and shoes, their manners and qualities. Someone from Grajewo was notable from afar in all of his conduct, and even the poor among them were particular about their clothes, and even those who were vapid would act as if they were knowledgeable, educated, and knew the ways of the world, dropping quotes from the old sages, the Torah, and words of wisdom. And all of this, more so on holidays.

[Page 170]

E.

The Jewish towns looked nice during the holidays – holidays being one of the most important cultural fruits that grew from humanity's cultural garden, and by which one recognizes the strength and talent of peoples not only in religion, in excess, but also in secular, essential matters – particularly in our town, which would collect the hundreds of sons who were dispersed far during all days of the year due to the necessity of distant occupations – the tar men, horse merchants, many of the grain merchants, who would bring the goods of other countries, their clothes and fashions. On those days the town would fill with tumult and noise, smiling friendly faces, the synagogues would fill with people, and the streets were full of tourists, visitors. These days were the rewards for the anguish of a whole year, the suffering of far away livelihood, the danger and indignity of illegal occupations, days of joy for babies clinging to their fathers, and days of happiness for young men and women with their long walks and lively conversations. Days of Torah study and the wonderful sermons of Rabbi Amiel, who even the agnostics of the town were quick to come and hear, days on which the cantor would sing a new tune (the tune of Avinu Malkenu that is sung in Eretz Yisrael – is from Grajewo – the cantor Chaikel composed it) and all the young ones (even the emancipated among them) would be quick to pick up and repeat it. On Passover of 1914, a few months before the war broke out, our cantor (Resnick) renewed the tune "*Vehu Yashmienu Berachamav*"[5] [from the *Kedusha*[5] prayer] and the young men and women of the town would repeat it with enthusiasm and devotion – Vehu Yashmienu Berachamav, Berachamav, Berachamav…

[Page 171]

Another "musical moment" that particularly impressed this writer also happened on Passover 1914. The Russian cavalry regiment returns from training, lines up by battalion on all sides of the market. At the head of the regiment – a handsome middle aged man sitting on his handsome horse, and the battalions pass before him, and the regiment's band plays the famous Russian march: "In the Hills of Manchuria."

As I stood and watched the march, my heart was suddenly filled with dread, a great dread for the future of the great empire Russia and for the Jewish nation: I heard both tunes: Vehu Yashmienu Berachamav, and the Russian march. Not many days passed and the Russian empire was embroiled in the world war and it completely exploded and shredded. As if the heart sensed the approaching Holocaust. Other voices were heard from the heavens, not voices of mercy but of a harsh, severe destiny, and the destiny continued to this day…

[Page 172]

Footnotes

2. *Potop/The Deluge:* written by Polish author Henryk Sienkiewicz (1846-1916) was part of a trilogy: "Fire and Sword," (1884), "The Deluge," (1886), and "Pan Michael" (1887 – 88). These epic historical fiction novels chronicled Poland's strife against the Cossacks, Tatars, Swedes, and Turks. "The Deluge," specifically covered the mid-seventeenth century Swedish Invasion of the Polish-Lithuanian Commonwealth.
3. *Enlightenment:* (18th-19th centuries) an intellectual movement encouraging Jews to assimilate both study and work in secular fields such as arts, science, arts and agriculture. This ultimately influenced the creation of both the Reform and Zionist movements.
4. *Externalism:* a philosophical doctrine held by some Jews who disassociated themselves from the shtetl's culture, religious beliefs, and lifestyle.
5. *Gur*: The largest Hasidic dynasty in Poland prior to the Holocaust and founded by Rabbi Yitzchak Meir Alter (1799– 1866), brother-in-law of The Kotzker Rebbe. He was an insightful Torah scholar and Halakhist [halakhah: the collective basis of Jewish religious law, including Biblical, Talmudic and Rabbinic]
Kedushah [holiness] is the "high" point of the Amidah, or central prayer recitation. □*Vehu Yashmienu Berachamav:* He will let us hear, in His mercy.

The administration of the town library (1920)
From right to left: Kanovitsh, Shtroysberg, Tenenboym, Sutker, Vadovski, Shimen Kolko

The administration of the Jewish Cooperative Bank

From right to left: First row (seated): A.I. Gortsitski, Tsvi Barkovski, Khaim Shmuel Mishkovski, Osher Rekhtman, Mordkhe Tikatski

Second row (standing): Eliezer Vayner, Itsik Samseber, Hershl Viernik, Opkevitsh

Third row: Efraim Vadovski, Avrom Rutkovski, Itsik Barkovski, Motke Berenzon

[Page 174]

Third Part:

The Holocaust

Nakhman Rapp **Shmuel Kaminski**

Together they visited Grayeve in 1947 in order to prepare the report for the Yizker-Bukh.

[Page 175]

History of the Grayeve Ghetto
By Nakhman Rapp (Wroclaw)
Translated by Tina Lunson

A Foreword

The history of suffering, torment and murder in the Grayeve ghetto is, in general, in its scope and contents, similar to the history of every ghetto in Poland. But the fate of the Jews in Grayeve ghetto is distinctive from other ghettos, during its existence and during its complete liquidation.

The following two points must be reckoned first as the distinction for Grayeve:

Grayeve was a border town (three kilometers from Eastern Prussia.)

The villages around Grayeve were inhabited by thoroughly hard-fisted peasants who were sharply inclined to anti-Semitism and politically influenced by "S. N.," the "Stronictwo Narodowe," an openly fascist party.

Even during the outbreak of the Polish-German war in 1939, when the Jewish population was fleeing in chaos from Grayeve to areas deeper in the interior of the country such as *Byalistok* [Białystok] and further; the direct danger of living close to a border in uncertain times became clear to the Grayeve Jews. It was already becoming apparent a month before the war that hostilities would take place. Not every Jew wanted to separate from his proprietorship, leaving everything to ruin. Only in the last days, when the government agents started fleeing and removing the archives of the administrative and communal institutions, only then did the Jews gradually begin to leave the town. There were many – and this was the majority – who simply would not contemplate such an evacuation. This was the largest part of the town's poor, who barely lived from day- to-day by labor or peddling. For them "moving from their place" would have meant economic ruin, so indeed they stayed in town and were the first to feel the Nazi "order" on their skin. Most of those who evacuated to Byalistok and further had agreed amongst themselves not to return to Grayeve, so there would be no need to flee again under similar circumstances. The decision was confirmed when they sensed the relative calm shown by the people in the towns deeper in the country.

[Page 176]

However, in two weeks time came a standstill across most of Polish soil. Except for *Varshe* [Warsaw] and *Westerplatte*,[1] which defended themselves bravely against the German enemy until the last minute, there was no fighting in the rest of the land. The Red Army took western Ukraine and western White Russia, on whose borders the Byalistok military command also settled, including the border pass for Grayeve, *Shtutzin* [Szczuczyn], *Raigrod* [Rajgród] and other towns up to the old border of eastern Prussia.

The entry of the Red Army into those areas produced joy and security among the Jewish population. The Jewish families of Grayeve who a few weeks before had fled the town in chaos, gradually returned. Every month, every week that the Soviet power was in town, reinforced the conviction that there would not be any war, because… it was enough to look at the heavy weapons, the two-story tall tanks and heavy canon of the Soviet garrison in Grayeve to be sure that the Germans would not be allowed to attack.

Along with peace came the temporary loss of the constant worry about livelihood that always pressed upon the Grayeve Jews. Every Jew without exception got work from the state and they were not paid badly.

That bound the Grayeve Jews even more to their hometown and made them completely forget the earlier danger of living in a border town and neighboring with Germany.

[Page 177]

Therefore the sudden outbreak of war in 1941 found a compact settlement of Jews in Grayeve. Apart from Grayeve itself, refugees had also come from the Polish areas that the Germans had occupied in their ambush in 1939. The new German attack found them completely abandoned by any protector, because the Soviet forces had withdrawn in great panic to the east, and the Jewish population remained in the teeth of the wolf.

That is how Grayeve, because it was a border town, had Hitler's murdering army from the beginning.

Now we come to the second point: The complete and savage liquidation of the Jewish community in Grayeve was carried out with the most active participation of the anti-Semitic neighbors of the town and countryside.

Grayeve and its region are one of the few places in Poland where almost no Jewish lives were protected or saved by their Polish neighbors (except for *Dr. Sheytelman*[2] and his wife, about whom we will write). Exactly the opposite: of the local Christian population the underworld, those previously active members of the fascist Polish organizations "Nara," and S. N. and ordinary hooligans took part, and they aided and quickened the work of the German murderer.

Since 1933 – that is since Hitler's coming to power in Germany – a wave of anti-Semitism had begun in the Grayeve area. Already in that first and second year there were organized anti-Jewish attacks, with the quiet consent of the government who generally intervened only after window panes had been broken out of Jewish houses, Jewish businesses had been robbed, and Jewish heads had been split. Every effort to organize the workforce met with extraordinary terror from the *Sanacja*[3] government. It was as though that government had specially trained the anti-Semitic Valkyries, treating the Jews as enemy number one of their lamentable regime.

True, there were Poles who did not want to make peace with the Hitler politics of murder and predation and who were prepared to actively help the Jews in their torment. Those people were gruesomely murdered by the German cutthroats after traitorous denunciations by the fascist Polish underworld.

[Page 178]

In our work we will mention some names of Poles of various strata: of the clergy, of laborers and of intellectuals, who literally sacrificed themselves in defending Jewish lives and thus paid with their own lives. May these mentions be a flower on their graves, which have until now remained unknown.[2]

Writing these lines, I see before my eyes my brothers and sisters from my hometown Grayeve, killed in agony and torment and I hear their last wish, before leaving this horrible world:

Tell about our murder! Do not let the memory of us and our suffering be obliterated! Let the mention of our martyrology be, for the few survivors of our town, a gravestone to which they come on *keyver-oves* [traditional visiting of ancestors' graves], so one may shed a warm tear and mention the tragic past. And for our people may it remain as a point that glows and flares up in a great flame of revenge that will continually awaken and demand its due:

Blot out the memory of Amelek!!!

Wroclaw, April 1948

1.
Nineteen Thirty-Nine

It happened so unexpectedly that one could hardly believe it: The German-friendly Sanacja regime had suddenly, through its press, begun pouring pitch and sulfur on Germany, in its aggressive appetite and demands on Poland for the Danzig corridor.

We read the newspapers and barely believed it. Could it be that such a "good life" would result in a war between the two "good friends?"

A "patriotic" action began in the land. To us in Grayeve came the dramatic ensemble of the 33rd Infantry Regiment in Lomzhe. The patriotic presentation "Poland – the Heart of Europe" was mounted. It made fun of Hitler, of the *bent cross* [swastika] and of his threatening a quick "lightning victory" in Poland. I went to that presentation with my friend Motl Yavko (Motl Leytshes). The presentation was organized by a civilian sponsor, headed by the regional doctor Shenkievitsh. Suddenly, right before the presentation, the doctor stood up and said to his companion, the big-whiskered German engineer, "Come, colleague, it's a shame to sit together with Jews." It was not possible to react, as many other things were not possible to do in pre-war Poland; the only thing we could do was to immediately leave the presentation.

[Page 179]

I bring out this fact as an illustration of the relationship of the Polish fascists and half-fascists to Jews, even in such a moment of danger for the country, such as the German aggression.

A week later all the military draftees, including the Jewish ones, received announcements to report to the army, in Sosnovets [Sosnowiec]. It was the first time since Poland had become a state that Jews had received an invitation to serve in the border patrol *"Kop"* in *Osovyets* [Osowiec]. We accepted that as long as the knife was at their throats, the Sanacja regime "trusted" the Jews to fight against the Germans. The Jewish youth were burning with hatred for fascist Germany and went into the army charged with a lust for fighting in the nearing clash.

Now they did not make any selection in political propriety when taking recruits into the army. Rather, the radically-minded worker was chosen especially for defending the border pass. The border formation *"Kop"* in Osovyets took the above-mentioned Motl Yavka (Motl Leytshes), a young worker who had been in prison for six years for communist activity; the left Poalei Tsion and community worker Motl Striev; the brothers Aron and Meyshe Kriskievitsh and others.

The conflict broke out on the first of September. The general mobilization that had been quickly declared three days before, did not appear in Grayeve to have time to be completed. Thursday, the last day before the outbreak of the war, the whole town, Jews and Christians, were at the train station. Heart-rending cries from the mothers, who had accompanied their sons to the front, were mixed with the shouting of the people who had not seen fit to evacuate earlier and were now perceiving their last minutes. Drunken, mobilized Poles were jumping back out of the wagons and throwing themselves on Jews, shouting with loud voices that the war was only because of the Jews and that now they would settle accounts with the Jews. Luckily there was no time to "settle accounts" on the spot, because it was already 6 p.m. and that train was the last one and had to depart immediately. At 4 in the morning that train, coming from Byalistok to Grayeve, fell to the Germans in the train station.

[Page 180]

Most of the Jews who succeeded in evacuating were left in Byalistok. From there they thought with horror and concern about the majority of the Jewish population of Grayeve who had stayed in the town. In the space of two weeks since the outbreak of the war, Grayeve had been cut off by the front-line and there was no way to reach it. Only two weeks later, when the Germans were in Byalistok, did skimpy news come out of Grayeve. No Jew had proposed to travel to Grayeve, but peasants from near Grayeve related the sad summation of two weeks of German proprietorship in the town: they had burned all the study-houses, the big beautiful *shul* [synagogue] and sent dozens of Jewish houses up in smoke.

When the Soviet powers took Grayeve, people gradually began to come back to their homes and also learned about Jews killed and about Jews whom the Germans had captured and sent to Germany.

It made everyone tremble to hear of the case of the woman Elkon, a woman not entirely in her right senses, who the Germans dragged off to near Prostken, poked out her eyes and left her blinded in mortal agony in the Bogushe forest, from where a peasant had brought her back to town in his wagon.

The Germans dragged off many Jewish young people deep into the interior, from where I recall only one came back, Khaym Fridman (a son of Feyge Malke Fridman).

The Germans dragged off the fifteen-year-old high school student Abrasha Baykovski and to this day there is still no news of him. The lonely mother Khaytshe (Helene) Baykovski, who now lives in *Bresle* [Wroclaw], still believes that her son is alive somewhere and each day she lives anew the torment of a mother who cannot find her lost child.

[Page 181]

The Germans savagely killed the seventeen-year-old boy Dovid Rapp, a son of Itsik Rapp the baker (a brother of the writer of these lines). The German sadists quartered the young man alive with swords.

A young girl ripped to pieces by a grenade, was the daughter of Khaym Leyzer the baker, who had a bakery on Shul Street. His son, Srolke Antshkovski, disappeared without a trace.

There were no recorded acts against Jews during that time on the part of the Christian population of Grayeve. Rather, there were cases when the German soldiers set fire to Jewish houses where the Polish neighbors helped to put out the fire.[2] Thus was saved the newly-built house of the tailor Itsik Grobgeld and the house of Yoske Gurovski ("Yoske the spinner" [of tales or procrastination]).

To those who disappeared and no one knows where, were added the former town rabbi *Rov* [Rabbi] Itsik Ayzik Grosman and the towns' richest man, the owner of a steam-driven mill in Grayeve, Avrom (Avromtshe) Ayzenshtat. Later it became known that the latter were horribly murdered by the Germans for ransom, in the birthplace of the rov, *Bendin* [Bêdzin].

The fighting in Poland stopped. Warsaw was conquered and in the territory of western Ukraine and western White Russia Soviet life began to take form. Gradually the evacuated Jews began to come to Grayeve, which was now part of White Russia. Besides them came a certain number of Jewish refugees from the Polish areas occupied by the Germans. Jewish Grayeve began once again to recover its Jewish face.

2.
Soviet Rule in Grayeve

That year the autumn ended very early and to our distress, an early and angry winter set in. Such a winter, with such freezing weather as in 1940–1941 had not been recorded since 1928.

[Page 182]

Life was very hard in Grayeve in the first weeks of Soviet rule. Organized noxious gangs of the former fascist Polish parties went around to the villages and agitated among the peasants not to sell grain "to the Bolsheviks." A few Jewish bakers, who had also remained in Grayeve with the Germans, got a little flour from someplace and baked black bread. The bakers were: Moyshe Pinievski (Moyshe *"smokh"*), who had fled to Byalistok before the outbreak of the war. After the coming of Soviet rule to Grayeve he baked "for himself," getting a little grain from peasants he knew.

Gradually life became easier. Several bakeries were nationalized and the "office of town welfare" took on bread baking, enough for the town and rural population. And other essential products began to come into the town, so that we lacked nothing.

From the beginning this seemed very strange to the population: Shops were open in town, bakeries were working, we had the mills, the electric station, workshops opened – and all this without owners. The people smiled and predicted that "they" would not be able to succeed in bringing about any order since without a proprietor no one could make anything. But the Jewish youth of Grayeve threw themselves into the work heart and soul. Motl Yavko, after coming back from Polish-German front, threw himself with all his youthful energy into organizing life in the town. On the cold winter days he rambled around among the villages, collecting grain from the peasants. At night he went out to track down the local gangs that did their destructive work at night. When life had stabilized after a short time, Motl Yavko became chairman of the state trade network "town welfare" in Grayeve.

Several state shops were opened, a haberdashery, knitted fabric, and others. In Etele Mishkovitshe's building in the market square, at the corner of Bogushe Street, was the central cooperative where almost only Jewish women sellers had set up stalls. The sisters Rokhl, Ore and Yehudis Mayek (daughters of Mayek the cabinetmaker) worked there and Rivke and Tshipe Markusfeld and others. The former bakery proprietors were now working in their own bakeries, which the state had nationalized. For a time, the manager of the bakeries was the former bakery-owner Shaul Bronervayn.

[Page 183]

Jews were employed in every area of economic and cultural life, so too on the town and district councils and in all institutions. A hospital with 60 beds was opened in Grayeve. The administrator of the hospital was the Grayeve doctor, Viner.

In the building of the Talmud-Torah, which was located on Powiatowe Street near the new study-house and after remodeling, a Yiddish not-full middle school was opened. Ten teachers worked there, among them Velvl (Vovak) Zilbershteyn, Dore Vapinska, Shleyme Vrontsberg, (director) and other teachers from outside. The Jewish teachers Fromer and Baykovska worked in the newly opened Polish school.

For the first time the Jewish youth of Grayeve perceived the great opportunities that the Soviet order gave the youth to develop themselves. They enrolled in the middle and high schools of the land. The teacher mentioned and many other youths began to study in various faculties. Others went off to take short and long-term courses to learn a useful specialty.

The Yiddish school in Grayeve developed very nicely. The Jewish children who came from the Polish school and the Talmud-Torah surprised them with their superb Yiddish. A circle for artistic self-realization was created at the state middle school Number Two in Grayeve, which after a short while mounted an exhibition, the likes of which Grayeve had never seen from children. The county division for popular education decided to present the heroic drama *"Bar Kokhba"*[4] by Sh. Halkin with the children from the Yiddish school. After going through a three-month "course for directors for dramatic self-realization" I was designated the leader of the group. I undertook to present the theater piece. I recall myself the great success that this show was.

From the highest balconies in town hung artistic posters, painted on big panels.

[Page 184]

The posters presented episodes from the heroic Bar Kokhba rebellion. On the site of the great shul, which the Germans had burned, had been built a gorgeous theater with 1500 seats. The presentation was performed in this theater. The hall was overflowing with a diverse audience. There were Soviet state officials, Party leaders and a large number from the Grayeve garrison. The latter, in their great appreciation of the children, gave them gifts and kissed them after the performance. (None of those children artists are alive anymore. They were, along with all the children of Grayeve, horribly murdered by the German killers, may their names be blotted out!)

The religious life of the Jews in Grayeve looked very peculiar during that time. The Germans had burned all the study-houses in the town in 1939. Now, after the coming of Soviet rule, a bit of religious life began to get established. True, for a while at the beginning, every pious Jews prayed by himself at home, in private. Later a *minyen* [prayer quorum of 10 men] was created at the home of Meyshe Pinievski ("Meyshe *smokh*") at Rutske 30 (Shul Street), where people prayed together as a community everyday, to say nothing of Shabes and holidays. When the Germans set fire to the great shul in 1939, the tailor Itsik Grobgeld succeeded in saving one Torah scroll and a small number of holy books such as Talmud volumes and others. And this was of much use in setting up the minyen.

Also in the area of religious education, the ancient Jewish tradition of the Talmud-Torah was not interrupted. True, the building of the former Talmud-Torah had been taken over by the Yiddish school, but a special place was arranged at the minyen where the Hebrew teacher Anshl Kotshak gave holy instruction to all the Jewish children who attended the Yiddish school until afternoon.

But in the darkness of the nights the noxious gangs did not rest. Among the fascists, those driven underground and the not-yet-successful home-grown fascists of the *"Narodovke"* the earnest enemy of the Polish people, Hitler-Germany, which had treacherously attacked Poland, was as if forgotten. They now released their entire poison on the Bolsheviks, who had brought in the "Judeo-commune." They relayed from ear to ear the rumors that, ostensibly, people would soon be forbidden to teach the Polish language, that all the Poles from Grayeve would be sent to labor camps in Siberia and people would be forbidden to go into the churches. Of course, the entire agitation had no basis at all and was just invented as ill will to incite the dark masses against the rulers and turn them into a tool in the hands of the princes and the reaction.

[Page 185]

Yet that dark agitation was not successful. The Polish intelligentsia sensed for the first time in its life, that it was an important and useful element in society. And those intellectuals filled all the state and the communal offices in Grayeve and worked conscientiously. The workers, or really the generally unemployed, who had earlier been for Poland, standing behind the magistrate in Grayeve and waiting for "support," got work that they could live from and were therefore loyal to the government of workers and peasants. Only the princely sinners, whose great landed estates had been taken and divided up among the landless peasants, only they could not rest and carry out their old, pre-war and well-known agitation against the "Judeo-commune."

The Soviet powers turned in a report on the noxious gangs and undertook an action to push those hateful elements away from the border town of Grayeve and send them deeper into the country.

On the 19th of June 1941, several Jewish families were sent out of Grayeve. Those sent out were: the family Baykovski, Yoysef Bialastatsky and his family, Kirshenboym and his family, the nurse Manye Kaplan. Some were ordered to reside 30 kilometers from Grayeve (Aron Leyzerson and others).

Those sent away took the fact of having to part from their old homes very badly. They considered it a tragedy and cried hard when they parted from their friends. But all in all those sent away, thanks to the fact that they had been torn away from the claws of the Hitlerists just two or three days before the war, remained alive and they regard the day of their expulsion from Grayeve as the day on which the greatest miracle in their lives took place.

In March and April 1941, those in Grayeve with military duty, including the Jewish ones, went off the serve in the Russian army. Of those who went into the army I remember: Khaym Adamshteyn, Yosl Mayek, Yankl Roymer, Gershon Gringros (a son of Zeyrekh the *katsov* [butcher]) and Shmay Markus. Those young men then bravely fought in the war against the Germans and were particularly distinguished for their bravery. Their greatest distinction however is that thanks to their going off into the army, they did not fall into the ghetto and remained alive until this day.

[Page 186]

The Grayeve youth who served in Osovyets (25 kilometers from Grayeve) shared a worse fate. They were among the first to fall into the hands of the German butchers and be killed. Of those murdered in Osovyets I remember: Yankl Rutski (a son of Falk the painter), Gershon Viernik, Meyshe Viernik (Alterke the Katsov's), Benyumin Kureyvovski, Meyshe Itsik Tobiashora, Khaym Mendl Levin, Khaym Kurzshandkovski, Leybl Zeligzon, Yosl Levin, and the 18 year-old Khaym Epshteyn. A few from the same division managed to get away and come home to Grayeve to their parents. Such was the case with Yankev Shaye Kaminski, who "merited" being killed in the Grayeve ghetto along with his mother and father.

Relatively, life was so quiet and hopeful that one could not believe that there could be such calamity as occurred, and when on the 22nd of June 1941 the Grayeve residents were suddenly torn from their sleep by powerful explosions and shooting, the first, unspoken question that lay on the lips of the frightened Grayeve Jews:

Is it possible?

Unfortunately it was possible…

3.
The Hitler Occupation in Grayeve

The German attack on the Soviet Union occurred on Sunday June 22 at four in the morning.

I had been in Byalistok for a whole week. In the city there had been nothing of note that would indicate a coming storm. Around Tuesday, a few days before the outbreak of war, I met with some Grayeve Jews in Byalistok and they told me that the Soviets had expelled some Jewish families from Grayeve. After taking care of my affairs in Byalistok, I left for Grayeve on the night of between the 21st and 22nd of June, at one in the morning.

[Page 187]

It was three o'clock in the morning when I came out of the Grayeve train station. The town was sunken in still, pre-dawn sleep. I walked from the train station with a friend of mine, Gershon Gringros, who was traveling from his military division in Osovyets for a few days leave. We talked about the lightening sky of that warm dawn and how today we could go to the beach by the Kosherova River. We agreed to meet by the river and we parted, each to his home.

My home was already on Shul Street number 24 in the building owned by Avreml Daytsh, because the Germans had burned our house on Konopsko Street in 1939. When I came in everyone woke up, father, mother, and sisters. They asked me what was new in Byalistok and why I had not brought my girlfriend back with me, whom I was shortly going to marry. We chattered on until my mother made a bed for me and said that it was time to call it a night.

Suddenly we were deafened by a terrible shriek, like dozens of factory sirens sounding right by our ears. We stood frozen and did not know what it meant. The last thing we expected was a war attack. We knew well that there was a non-aggression pact with Germany and could not imagine that the German would so suddenly, without a reason, attack Russia.

In a few minutes we came to our right senses. Every little while the air was shaken with a fresh explosion. We ran from the steps to see what was going on in the street. But just in going out of the house we soon saw that it was indeed a war in every detail and we took off running to the Byalistok Highway.

* * *

Although Grayeve was not a large district city – it had barely twelve thousand residents – it still had, because of its border with Germany, two divisions of military artillery stationed there. Therefore the war for Grayeve came with a concentrated assault from the German forces. Already in the first minutes of the war Grayeve was enveloped in a sea of smoke and fire. All kinds of weapons were trained on the town and deafened the residents with their detonations.

[Page 188]

Here is what an eyewitness related about the first minutes of the war in Grayeve:

> "I ran to the window to see what was going on in the street. A thick smoke was rising to the sky and blocked out the light. If not for the frequent shooting and explosions, one might have thought that it was not an assault on the town but that it had simply been set on fire. Unable to see anything through the window, I went out on the stoop to see what was happening. But stretching my hand in the air I soon encountered a rocket, which tore off these two fingers. I carried my wife, who had fainted, back into the house." (Yozef Kalski, a bricklayer, Rutske Street).

And beneath that same smoke and thunder the Jewish population in Grayeve lay captive and before they could grasp it, the way out was already cut off by the attacking German troops.

Soon it proved to be that the entire Byalistok region had been cut off from its center, Byalistok. The fascist underworld rose up to serve the Germans and cut the telegraph connections every thirty or so kilometers. The officials of the Soviet institutions and of the Party desperately called by telephone for help and clarification, but for naught, they were left to their own fate.

The [presence of the] fort in Osovyets was able to arouse a little hope. From there, it was reckoned, the Germans could be driven back before establishing a front, so people could evacuate deeper into the land. But that hope failed too. It was as though the Germans avoided the fort at Osovyets and gradually, from Lomzhe, surrounded it on all sides.

The German military troops did not come into Grayeve on the first day of the war. Only the German border guards came into Grayeve. They took over the train station, the post office and all the Soviet institutions. Only on the third day, that is the 24th of June, did the military establish a command, with quarters on Pilsudskiego Street (Shtutzin Street).

[Page 189]

Even on the first day that the German border guards were in Grayeve, they began to murder and violate the Jewish population. A decree was issued to the German troops that Jewish life and property was ownerless and that they could do whatever they wanted with them. Indeed on the first day mass raping of young Jewish women began. The "noble" German race was especially distinguished for biting their young victims to death and the mother of the tortured child had to stand by in horrible mindless torment and look at what they did to her child."

This is what the Polish woman Helena Nadolna related about an event which she saw with her own eyes:

> "...my neighbor from across the street barged in, in terrible desperation, [saying] that a German had killed her daughter and that she herself (the mother) must watch out that no one intruded on him. When

the German came out, he simply said to the mother 'Good mother.' What she saw later when she went into the room, she could not believe her own eyes. She called me to help her save her child, but there was no one there to save. The girl's entire body was torn open, bitten and swollen. Her mouth and breasts were smeared with blood. She was already dead, strangled, her eyes bulging out. The mother wanted to take her own life in her despair. A few days later she lost her mind and Germans killed her. Her name was Henie Shayne Bashes, Rutske Street 34. So they did with many others, whose families I don't know."

In a few days, on Wednesday the 25th of July, at ten o'clock in the morning they drove all the Jews together in the middle of the market square and the town commandant Geis read aloud for them the decree from the high command. Among other things, the decree said:

"The Jewish nation is a criminal nation and as such has earned a hard and eternal punishment of hard labor and imprisonment. They are forbidden to live free and together with other peoples, because they do not have pure blood. Sooner or later they must all die.

[Page 190]

They must be obedient to every German, under penalty of death. The Jews will be distinguished by a yellow star, which they must wear on the shoulder and breast as a sign of their shame."

As usual in the German manner, each decree was accompanied by a pointed action. After reading the decree for the Jews they drove the Jews out of the market square under a hail of blows, and arrested the two sisters Yehudis and Rokhl Mayek on the spot, took them to the old Jewish cemetery and shot them there.

An anguished fear befell the Jews gathered in the market after listening to the decree. It was an open confirmation that from today on, Jewish life was up for grabs by any German or Polish hooligan. From that day on Jews sat tense in their houses, afraid of the light of day. A rumor spread that the Polish underworld was preparing for an open pogrom on Jews. It was said that a "delegation" of Polish hooligans had presented themselves to the commandant of the Gestapo Opper, with the question of whether there was a punishment for killing a Jew and the commandant had answered that killing a Jew was without punishment. That version proved to be right, when in two days the first pogrom of the Polish underworld against the Jews broke out.

Sunday the 29th of July the first organized pogrom against the Jews of Grayeve broke out. Coming out of church, incited hooligans started robbing and killing the Jews. With specially prepared hatchets and wooden poles they set about splitting Jewish heads. The leaders of the pogrom were Aloizi Sentkovski, a young professional thief, a syphilitic, a son of the well-known

Grayeve thief Sentkovski (Konopsko Street number 6) and the knife wielders Grin, Mikloshevski, Zegarek and Stanish. The Jews who the bandits met on the street were killed on the spot, and thus Motl Striev was bestially killed by the cutthroat Aloizi Sentkovski. The photographer Efroym Vodovski fell at the hands of the murderer Stanish. The assassins were not sated with that and went into the Jewish houses, where they brought death and ruin. Today, when I happen to speak with the Christians of Grayeve about that pogrom, they take pains to avoid the subject. Mostly each of the Christians says that he helped this or that Jew. So it was interesting to get the testimony from the Grayeve Christian Yoyskovski who lived on the market square, next to the house where Yoysef Bialystocki lived. In the same house lived the ironmonger Vaynshteyn and Ukrop's son-in-law Meyshe (whose family name I have not succeeded in establishing).

[Page 191]

When the pogrom began those two Jews were out on the street. They immediately started running home to save themselves. The above-mention Christian continues in these words:

"When I saw those two little Jews running and frightened, I closed the house door and did not let them in (!) They knocked desperately on the door. But they found an ax and broke the door in and came into the house. But soon the peasants arrived and they beat the Jews. They broke Vaynshteyn's legs and the other one they chopped into his chest."

That Christian in his "innocence" tells about his own "fine action" and therewith gives a clear idea about the relationship of most of the Poles to the Jews in Grayeve in that frightful time.

But there were also good Christians, who showed their moral and human face in that bestial atmosphere. Their self-sacrifice in defending Jewish lives and their humane dignity must be mentioned by us with the greatest appreciation. First of all must be mentioned with reverence the progressive Polish worker *Henrik Sobolevski*[2] , for years a member of the Polish Communist Party, who on the day of that horrible pogrom on Jews, with word and deeds actively resisted the wild hooligans and for that, paid with his life. The Germans held him and another dozen Jews for a day in the shul, where he was horribly tortured, then taken to the old Jewish cemetery and shot.

The second beautiful spirit was the *Catholic priest Penza*[2] . He did not tire in his morning masses of calling the Christian population to reason, not to collaborate with the Germans and not to let themselves be drawn in by the Germans' provocations against the Jews. But for the hooligans it seemed as though robbery and murder stood higher than Christian morals and human love. They reported the Christian father themselves and delivered him into the hands of the German murderers, who unceremoniously shot the noble clergyman.

[Page 192]

There were rumors that right after the pogrom a Jewish delegation set out to the German town commandant Geis and requested help from him against the pogromists. Whether that fact is correct or not, we do not know. But it is correct that soon, in the first hours after the pogrom, at three o'clock in the afternoon, German police set out in a chase after the pogromists, caught three of them (Mikloshevski, Zegaret and Grin) and shot them on the spot. That was to say that the Germans were standing by the Jews and protecting them from the incited Christian population. But this was just a cunning trick by the German hangmen, who on one side organized that pogrom and when it happened, pretended not to know. And from the other side they incited the Christian population against the unprotected Jews, showing the Christians, that now they were also standing up for the Jews. This cunning game was calculated so that later, when the Germans would confine the Jews in a ghetto, the Jews would think it was a favor to them that they got to live apart from the Poles from whom they waited in terror for a similar pogrom every day.

In order to mask their true intent, it did not suffice for the Germans just to catch the three mentioned murderers. They took several wounded Jews away to a hospital where they could be "healed." From such healing Rivke Bialystocki died three days later. A horrible incident that confirmed the German provocation happened with the wounded Jew Postalski. The pogromists had beaten him so that he was unrecognizable. In the morning, as he laid half-conscious on the hospital bed, the Germans brought to him the young Polish man Lutek Remishevski and demanded from the Jew whether he recognized this young man as his assailant. In his pain and half-conscious state the Jew had the delusion that this young man was indeed the one who had beaten him and he said with tears in his voice, "Tell me, what do you have against me? Why did you beat me?" The young man went white as a sheet and stammered, "Pani Postolski, what are you saying to me? Am I capable of such a thing?" But the Germans did not allow him to speak out and took him away. That young man was a progressive Polish semi-intellectual and the Germans specially entangled him in that provocation in order to dig even deeper the abyss of hatred and distrust between the Jewish and Polish populations. In a few days the innocent Lucian Remishevski was shot by the Germans.

[Page 193]

On that day the Germans arrested, along with Remishevski, the Polish teacher Leon Klodetski, the already mentioned progressive worker Henrik Sobolevski and other progressive Poles and imprisoned them in the building of the shul. The teacher Klodetski managed through a miracle to run away at the last minute. The others were shot the same day.

The intent of the German sadists was clear: to throw the blame for organizing the pogrom onto the progressive elements of the Polish population, and use the opportunity to make a little pogrom on the communists at the same time.

The murder cellar in the shul

After a week of continual attacks on Jews, the Germans saw that the ground was ripe for the rescue of the Jews in Grayeve. Then the German hangmen, with their murderous precision, got down to their plan.

A special division of the S.S. was mobilized to catch and arrest every Jew between the ages of 15 and 45. All the captured were driven into the theater building, where the great shul had stood before the war. That was not just a regular prison where arrestees were tortured. Jews there suffered such afflictions that would make the tortures of the Inquisition seem like child's play.

They invented various tortures for their victims, but each death had to come slowly and with the greatest agony. Jews with broken arms and legs were made to perform various exercises: jump over tables and benches under the blows of the butchers' sticks.

[Page 194]

The shul until the war

The shul building.

Before the time of the Soviet regime, a theater. Now a market hall for vegetables, fish and pork. In the cellar of this building, around 200 Jews were tortured under the Nazis

[Page 195]

After three days of starving they were given salted herring to eat, and after that they were given nothing to drink for three days. The younger and stronger ones were driven to do several kinds of inhumanly difficult and completely useless work, under a hail of blows. They ordered them to carry the stone fence from the study-house back and forth. And after such a day of hard labor and exhaustion they brought them back into the shul and tortured them the whole night. Of course, since no one was able to hold out for long, 15 to 20 people died every day from the great suffering.

Before they died the butchers threw their victims into the deep cellar of the shul and let them die there. When the cellar was already half full of corpses, the German gangsters threw in healthy people and held them there until they choked out their last breath in great agony.

Here is what an eyewitness, the Christian Helene Nadolna, relates; she lived across from the shul and could see everything with her own eyes:

"They took the youth and especially the males into the synagogue and tortured them for two weeks. There in the synagogue it was a real hell. Such tortures, it would be better to die rather than suffer so much. They twisted their arms, ripped out their tongues, tore out their nails. They whipped them every day in the morning, 100 lashes each. When one of those tortured fainted, they threw him into water with chlorine and lime, and when he regained consciousness there was another new torture: jumping over various barricades, over benches, tables. After that they stood them all up in rows and each tenth person had to jump through the second-story window. If anyone jumped and lived, the Germans killed him on the spot. They twisted the Jews' hands with barbed wire, and with the same wire they twisted their heads backwards and threw them into the cellar of the shul like that, so that they would die there. The dead bodies of the tortured were only taken out a year later, completely decayed. You could not recognize who anyone was. The workers who were driven together for that work became deathly ill with several diseases. The corpses were thrown into a pit with lime that had been in the cellar."

[Page 196]

At such a "pageant," when the Germans made the Jews jump through the window of the shul, the Polish underworld was assembled below so that if someone remained alive and tried to run away, the hooligans killed him on the spot with shovels and pry-bars. So it was with the youth Velvl Piekarevitsh (the son of *Stavisk* [Stawiski] blacksmith Avrom Shleyme). After the boy jumped through the window he ran to the Jewish cemetery. The hooligans caught him and threw him alive into the full lime pit near the shul.

A horrible incident, told by Grayeve Poles, took place with the young engineer Kirshboym. The engineer was not from Grayeve, but during the outbreak of the war in 1939 he came as a refugee from Warsaw. That physically fit young man was happy to jump from the second story and tried to run away. The Polish underworld, which was standing around and taking pleasure in the Jews' suffering, caught the Jewish engineer and threw him into the big pit near the shul. The pit was a kind of big, provisional garbage pit that the Germans had made near the shul. After they threw him in, the unfortunate engineer swam around and grabbed the boards of the rim with his hands and tried to crawl out of the excrement. The hooligans were standing around and laughing at the *"zhyd"* [derogatory term for Jewish person] submerged all the while in the filth. When they saw that the young man was crawling out, the hooligans ran to him and with iron shovels split the unfortunate's head into pieces. (Testimony from Polish bricklayer Yan Kalski, Rudzka Street).

The Grayeve youth Mayer Kletski, the survivor of that bloody massacre in the shul, tells about the first night of torture this way:

"…we sat down on the earth with our feet tied together and so the night was passed. The night was very terrible. First, because they would not allow us out to urinate, people suffered a lot. Second, at such a time all kinds of thoughts occur. One says, they will set us on fire, another says something else. In the morning the overseers came in and asked with a smile, "So, little Jews? How did you sleep?"

Footnotes

6. *Battle of Westerplatte*: 1 September 1939, World War II officially began in Europe when Germany invaded Poland at the depot on the Westerplatte peninsula, north of *Dantsik* [Gdańsk].
7. *With great respect:* we would like to honor the brave Poles who helped Jewish Grayevers despite the risk to their own personal safety. They will be remembered for their acts of kindness, courage and humanity. May their memories be a Blessing and their souls bound in the bond of everlasting life.
8. *Sanacja* [Polish for sanitation] *Regime*: a term used to describe the authoritarian regime in Poland during the period 1926 to 1939.

The Bar Kokhba revolt: 132-135 C.E. This was marked by a period of hope that turned into violent anguish. The Jews believing a homeland and Holy Temple were in their site, were eventually persecuted and sold into slavery

[Page 197]

History of the Grayeve Ghetto (cont.)

Nakhman Rapp and Shmuel Kaminski, behind the shul.

In this place rest a number of murdered Jews. Here also the young engineer Kirshboym was horribly murdered.

The overseers over the Jews in the shul were the Poles, Davidovski and Stanishevski and volunteers from the Polish underworld who had served in the Polish militia, Yankovski Yanek, a well-known knifer in Grayeve and elsewhere. These overseers had to accompany the Jews every morning to their work in various places. Of course, the first assignment for the overseers was to beat the Jews with rubber truncheons and iron bars. After the Jews had worked all day without food, at hard inhuman labor, they were led back to the "theater" (shul). Arriving at the "theater," the Jews saw an inscription over the door, "Camp for Internees." It was clear that capturing the Jews and installing them in the theater was not a game for a day, but that the Jews would not be going back to their homes so quickly.

The women of the arrested Jews gathered around the theater and brought food for their husbands, sons and fathers. For a bribe the Polish hooligans took the food from the women and later distributed it among the arrestees according to their discretion. The arrestees sent the utensils back except for the bottles, which they kept to do their natural functions into.

[Page 198]

In the evening Gestapo men came in and made merry with the tormented Jews. Once they selected two old men and ordered them to kiss. When the old men kissed, the Gestapo beat them because they were kissing one another. When they stopped kissing, the Gestapo beat them because they were not kissing. So it went on for seven or eight days. By day, work under the most difficult conditions; by night in the shul, endure all the torments, humiliations and blows.

On the tenth of August 1941 the German commandant issued an order that in the space of three to five days all Jews must be concentrated on Dolne Street (Bathhouse Street). The Poles who lived there got an order to move out of there. The men who were arrested in the shul were permitted to carry or cart their things. But not all had the opportunity to move all of their things. The old Pole Antony Shelanzshek (Konopska Street) tells about a case in which the Jew Yoysef Gurovski, his neighbor for many years, worked with him for two days moving the Jew's things on his wagon. The Christian did not want to move everything, "but, when he paid me what I wanted, I carted his things into the ghetto, tipped over the wagon on Dolne Street and headed home..." What he called "what I wanted" one can presume. From that, one can also understand that the Jews took the creation of the ghetto with a little hope of rest from the side of the Polish underworld. The men who had been arrested in the shul and who had been temporarily allowed to carry their things into the ghetto were arrested again and put into the shul.

For the Polish hooligans Stanishevski and Davidovski and their helpers who had oversight over the Jews in shul, just torturing the Jews did not suffice. They sought to make a profit from their business. To that end they heard that among the arrested Jews there were some communists. The picked out twenty men from among the Jews and the hooligan Davidovski let out a shout: "A plague! These are communists!" They separated the twenty Jews behind a barrier and did not allow them to go out to work along with the other Jews. The first two days the women of the "communists" did not know what had happened with their men. They brought food for their men to the theater as before. The Polish guards took the food, but did not give it to the arrestees. The latter went hungry for two days. But later, when the women of the arrested "communists" knew about the fate of their men, is when the "business" began. They went running to the hooligan Davidovski and bribed him, so that he would allow the arrested husband or son back into the working lot and take him out from among the communists, as that would mean a certain death.

[Page 199]

And so the hooligans changed the arrestees dozens of times; let those go, took these into the communists and back again, taking from the women the last that they possessed.

At the denunciation by the Polish hooligans Davidovski and Stanishevski, the Gestapo issued a decree, and once in the morning the hooligans took the group of "communists" out, led them off, and none of the other arrestees in the theater knew where to. Only on the second day did people find out that they had been taken to the Kosherov Forest and shot.

There were also cases when the sentenced ran away and tried to hide, but the spies reported them and they were brought back to the "theater." When one of the runaways fell into the hands of the hooligans Davidovski and Stanishevski, they would take everything he had and promise him that they would not give him up, but then they would come at night and murder him.

Of the group that they took out of the theater from time to time and shot, the names of the following Grayeve Jews have been mentioned:

Shleyme Zilberman

Yoysef Abramski

Shimen Abramski

Leyzer Grinshpan

Mordechai Striev

Hersh Bukhbinder

Shaul Bronervayn

Khaym Yudl Kletski

Barash Kopl [or Kopl Barash]

Leybl Segalovitsh

Sholom Segalovitsh

Elye Kohn

Berl Sudker

Stolnitski

[Page 200]

These are some of the Jews who were shot in the woods in the time between the 1st and 25th of August, 1941.

On the 26th of August 1941 the Gestapo gave the order to arrest the women who had worked in government positions during the Soviet rule, and young women who belonged to the *"komsomol"* [a communist youth organization]. On that day the Gestapo arrested 40 Jewish women and girls. In the evening, when the arrested men were coming from work, the Gestapo and Polish militia were waiting for them at the theater and sent them right off to the horse market. The Polish hooligans from the "voluntary" militia jeered at the Jews, forcing old and young to dance over the pits that had been dug there. That torment went on for more than an hour. After that the Gestapo ordered the Jews to stand in a row and the Polish hooligans pointed out anyone that they did not like as a communist. Among the "communists" they pointed out was the old ritual slaughterer Meyshe Mendl Mishkovski. Of course, the whole bloody game was well prepared in advance by the Gestapo. The hooligans pointed out the old slaughterer as one of Stalin's good friends.

They divided off about 80 men and led them separately under heavy guard back to the theater. In the morning the Gestapo, to make fun of them, organized a "court" for the 80 men plus the women, about 120 people. The "court" lasted for two days. The Polish voluntary militia signed a paper saying that all the accused were communists. The "court" sentenced them to be shot. Hearing the sentence some of the young men leapt from the second story window in the gallery (one of Berish of *Ridzever's* [Rydzewo] sons, and others) and were killed on the spot.

Gestapo members tortured the sentenced Jews frightfully the whole night after the"court." They hit them over the head with bottles and mortally wounded many of them. The Poles dragged the wounded down to the cellar and killed, then threw the dead bodies into the cellars of the burned-out houses near the shul.

[Page 201]

That night was one of the most horrible for the arrested Jews. All night the Polish hooligans and the Gestapo dragged the old people into the cellars of the shul and bestially murdered them. The intent of the German criminals was that in the morning when they took to communists to be shot, the population, so to speak, would see that these were "real communists" and not some old Jews for whom communism could never have had any draw.

On the 29th of August a group of Jews was brought out to the Ruder Highway. In the evening coming back from work the Polish overseers, instead of going to the "theater," took the Jews to the Jewish cemetery and let them wait there. In a few minutes three automobiles full of Gestapo soldiers arrived and they indicated that the Jews should dig a pit with an area 60 meters wide. The Jews already knew very well that this was a mass grave for the 120 Jews, brothers and sisters, who were sentenced two days ago in the "tribunal" of drunken scoundrels and bloodthirsty Gestapo troops. The Jews did not want to dig the grave. The Gestapo started to beat the Jews murderously with their rifle butts and the Poles with the sticks that they held in their hands. Those who did not want to dig were promptly shot on the spot (which happen to the old Zoyrekh Elkon's son and others).

When the mass grave was ready, they led the Jews back to the theater. The drunken Gestapo tortured the sentenced Jews the whole night. They set upon the Jewish women like wild animals and raped them, thereby causing them the greatest torment. The short letter which the eyewitness survivor Mayir Kletski (now in Paris) found the same day in the shul, in the room where the arrestees spent their last moments, gives witness.

Here is what the murdered Sore Meyek wrote:

"Not enough that we must leave this world, they also raped us. The entire thing was carried out by the Gestapo men and a few Polaks. Jews! Take revenge for us and for our shame!"

[Page 202]

"The superior race" showed very vividly what it was capable of. Marrying a Jew was called a "race crime," for which one could receive the death penalty, but raping and torturing Jewish daughters that one may do."

Surviving witness Mayir Kletski tells about how the 120 Jews sentenced for communism were killed:

"At ten o'clock in the morning (August 30) they took out more than a hundred men and women, those sentenced to death for communism. Accompanied on both sides by Gestapo and Polish voluntary militia, as well as a large part of the Polish population going along the sidewalks with smiles on their lips, the Christians said, "There will be some fewer Jews…" All the Jews had to go into the pits themselves. When they were all in the grave the machine guns played and our dearest and most beloved went off into eternity…"

The 1st of September 1941 at ten o'clock in the morning the Gestapo assembled all the Jews in the area of the horse market. The civilian German town commandant arrived and delivered a speech to the assembled Jews in which he ensured that now, after exterminating the communists from among the Jews, the Jews would be able to live quietly in the ghetto, where they would have their own administration with their own leader.

As leader of the Jews in the Grayeve ghetto, the Germans on the spot appointed the Grayeve Jew Zalmen Sutker.

The Ghetto in Grayeve

Now everyone knows why the Germans created the ghettos for the Jews in Poland; the intent was to concentrate the Jewish population, cut them off from the surrounding world in order to make easier the carrying out of the criminal "end goal" of the Hitler murderers: to completely annihilate the Jewish population. But because of the German hangmen the situation before the creation of the ghettos had come to such a head, that in many towns the Jews naively believed that with the creation of the ghetto they would have peace, would be secure against incitement and provocation from the local anti-Semites.

[Page 203]

After the town commandant Geis read for the assembled Jews the decree about the creation of the ghetto for the Jews, he immediately nominated a *"Judenrat"* [Jewish Council] that would have to manage all the affairs of the ghetto residents, relative to the German powers. Nominated were:

Zalmen Sutker, president

Popovski, secretary

Itsik Voislavski, member

Tenenboyn, member

The Jews, thinking that this would really be a representative that could do something for them, chose from their side the Grayeve Jew, Leyzer (Leyshke) Grosman.

The first two orders that the "Judenrat" issued on the first day of its existence were characteristic. The first order was – at the order of the German power – to clean up the theater (shul) where only last night the arrestees had been tortured to death. The "Judenrat" chose 25 men and women with brooms and pails and sent them into the theater, to the place of the horrible bloodbath.

The surviving witness Mayir Kletski, who took part in the cleaning of the theater, provides a picture of how the building looked one day after the murders:

"The walls were sprayed with blood, like in a slaughterhouse. We had to completely wash off the blood; there should be no trace of our dearest ones. The room where the sentenced women spent their last minutes looked like the aftermath of a pogrom: torn-out women's hair was scattered across the floor along with various torn clothing and papers. We searched among the papers and found the letter which Sore Meyke had scribbled before her death (cited above, Nachman Rapp-N.R.) Weary after a day of torturous work, we could not go to sleep, but came together in the courtyard and mourned the memory of our nearest and dearest…"

[Page 204]

The second order from the "Judenrat" on the same day was to set up a guard around the whole ghetto in order to protect from the provocations on the part of the local hooligans from Davidovski's band.

The guard consisted of youths "armed" with sticks and flashlights. It is superfluous to say what kind of front the "guard" had against an attack by organized hooligans, armed ones at that. But it did give a bit of alarm security.

After a few days the "Judenrat," at the order of the Germans, created a "labor office." The "Judenrat" appointed Itsik Voislavski as the chief of the "labor office;" secretary, Liuba Fabilinska. At the demand of the Germans, the labor office of the "Judenrat" assembled Jewish workers for the German firms. The work was inhuman, 14 to 18 hours out of 24. The price of a workday was one (1!) Mark.

Jews went out to work without a guard, only with a passage permit issued by the German office.

Along with the labor office the "Judenrat" also established a Jewish militia. Members of the militia were:

Karbovski, commander (an attorney from Lomzhe)

Mayir Kletski, deputy

Berl Khilare

Ruven Nayman

Shleyme Gumovitsh

Itsik Zsharkovski

Tevl Oz-Yashirs

Yosl the blacksmith's son-in-law

Yoysef Markus

Meyshe Solvatitski

Shleymke of the blind woman

(There are no reports about how exactly the Jewish militia conducted itself in relation to the Jewish population in the ghetto. Being far from the place of these afflictions I do not feel entitled to make any sort of conclusion in one direction or another. I also do not feel entitled to bring forth any merits and good works of the Grayeve Jewish militia which were enumerated for me by the surviving witness, former deputy commander of the militia Mayir Kletski (as he represents himself as such). Bowing my head to the suffering that the latter went through, I think of him as an involved party whose evidence one cannot accept without criticism. This question will have to be left closed and so we will not mar our conscience with it in relation to our tormented brothers and in relation to the history.)

[Page 205]

In the economic sense the Grayeve ghetto was not the worst. One can say that for the time of its existence the ghetto did not starve. Of course, the devilish plan of the German murderers was thought through to the last detail in this area as well: the Jews should see, as it were, that they were cared for, so that they did not lack [food] and would not try to run away from the ghetto. But there was something else.

The German power allowed the peasants from the surrounding villages to take foodstuffs, peat and wood into the ghetto. The peasants, who drove in to the market on the appropriate days, simply drove their wagons into the ghetto, not even setting foot in the general market. On those days they set up their wagons in the narrow streets of the ghetto just as they had set them up at a fair, and the Jews bought everything they needed. A paradoxical situation was set up because of it: the Jews who were locked in the ghetto with seven locks participated in the world, had more food than the Polish population that was free. And the Poles had to purchase their needs from the Jews in the ghetto. Naturally this caused some bad blood among the rabble, who said that the zhydes were like the cats, there where you don't need them; they always land on their feet. But in truth it was a well thought-out game in German propaganda. It let them show the Polish population that the "zhydes" take everything for themselves and if they were exterminated there would be enough food for the Poles.

Under the "Judenrat" there was also an active "group to keep the ghetto clean." The leader of that group was the Pinye Suraski. Other workers in the group were: Avrom Grinberg, Sholom Zaydnberg, Goldberg, Berl Kletski and Yehude Grinberg. They cleaned up all the areas and dried out the swamp to the east of Dolne Street and sowed everything with vegetables. Almost every Jew had prepared some potatoes, wood, carrots, beets and other greens. The only hope was not to be driven out of the ghetto, or one would experience a defeat like that of Haman.

[Page 206]

The "Judenrat" also opened several workshops for the use of the ghetto. A ghetto bakery was opened to provide bread for the Jewish population. The bakery, which had once belonged to Yoysef Bialistotski, opened on Dolne Street. The manager of the ghetto bakery was Yankev Shidlo. A food store was opened too, under the management of Avrom Tenenboym. There was also a shoemaking workshop active in the ghetto that worked for the population for cheap prices.

About two weeks after the creation of the ghetto, the "Judenrat" suddenly received an order from the German town commandant to pay one million Marks into the treasury at city hall. This was a huge blow to the poor ghetto. The order also stated that if the sum was not paid, all the Jews would be sent out of the ghetto. Fear gripped the impoverished population. With no choice, they sold their last possessions to their Polish neighbors and were just happy that someone would buy them. "The poor have sold their pillows and all their furniture. The richer have bargained hard, but in the end they paid their part." (Testimony of M. Kletski)

But the belief that one would get through everything overcame the fear of dangers near and far. Despite all the troubles the ghetto was full of optimistic belief in the nearing defeat of the enemy.

A very important factor in the economic life of the Grayeve ghetto was the good relationship of the surrounding village settlements with the Jews. The local peasants were very happy selling their produce to the Jews. So, for example, a group of Jewish boys (Dovid Bunkovski, Burakovski, Khaym and others) went out of the ghetto at night and brought fish from the nearby village of *Totshelova* [Toczyłowo] and shared or sold it to the Jews in the ghetto. The peasants, who were allowed to take potatoes and wood into the ghetto two times a week, would hide chickens, fats and even whole calves in their wagons. The Jews in the ghetto were not allowed to keep cows and fowl. Yet there were always a few cows and a lot of chickens in the ghetto. All this was thanks to the help from the peasants from the surrounding villages.

[Page 207]

The eyewitness M. Kletski also tells about a *Polish woman*[1] from Grayeve who used to come to the ghetto three times a day and sell and practically for free distribute food for the Jews in the ghetto. And later, when the Grayeve ghetto was liquidated and the Jews there were driven to the camp in Bogushe, that same woman came as before and brought produce. In the proper evaluation the dealings of this noble, very brave Polish woman must be mentioned.

The Grayeve ghetto lived for one year in those circumstances, the circumstances of punitively hard labor and the struggle for a piece of bread, of keeping the spirit alive on one side, and of deep belief in overcoming the enemy and experiencing his defeat on the other side. Until the 1st [sic] of November 1942, until that day, when the German hangmen decided that they could do away with the little remnant of Jews from our town, until they had completely used up the material, economically and physically.

The Situation in Grayeve

On the 11th [sic] of November 1942 the Germans carried out the dispatching of the Jews from the Grayeve ghetto. In the night of November 11th, the ghetto was surrounded by Gestapo thugs armed with automatics, who did not let anyone escape from the ghetto. To the people who had to go to work at 4 in the morning the Gestapo laconically said, "You've already worked enough" and they brutally pushed them back from the barbed wire, into the ghetto. Soon it became known in the ghetto that something was happening. People tried to run away, but the guard of Gestapo did not let anyone out until it got light.

When it was light, the Gestapo came into the houses and amid blows and screaming chased everyone out to the plaza near Hershl Viernik's. When all the Jews were assembled with their packs and children on their shoulders, the Gestapo drove the Jews off by foot in the direction of the village Bogushe (border village between Grayeve and eastern Prussia).

Although it was already late autumn that day was very warm and the exhausted Jews could not carry with them all the things that they had hurriedly put together. All the things that they could not carry they tossed away along the highway that leads through Bogushe Street. The entire way to Bogushe was strewn with Jewish poverty. Under a hail of blows from rifle butts and sticks, with wailing and weeping, the multitude of Jews arrived at Bogushe camp.

[Page 208]

The camp in Bogushe had earlier served as an internment camp for Soviet war prisoners. The German butchers had tortured tens of thousands of Soviet soldiers who had not had time to evacuate, due to the sudden military attack by Germany. The fields around Bogushe were sown with the gigantic mass graves of the Soviet soldiers tortured in the Bogushe death camp.

The camp comprised a field fenced in with wire. On the area of the camp barracks had been "built," that is to say that deep pit had been dug and covered on top with a roof. Inside there were plank beds for the internees.

The Grayeve Jews arrived in the camp at about 11 in the morning. Until noon there was no order at all. In the afternoon, people were brought into the camp on foot and in wagons, Jews from all the surrounding towns: Shtutzin, Raigrod, *Vonsosh* [Wąsosz], *Rodzilova* [Radziłów], *Trestiny* [Trzcianne], *Ogustove* [Augustów], *Bialybzsheg* [Białobrzegi] and from the villages around Ogustove, from anyplace where there might still be any Jews. It was clear that now the Germans were proceeding with the complete liquidation of all the ghettos in the towns in the Byalistok province.

The first three or four days the imprisoned Jews were not given anything to eat. Each one ate what he had managed to bring with him from the ghetto. Only on the fifth day did the German power, at the determination of a camp commandant, create four kitchens which were supposed to feed the over 7,000 interned Jews. As commander of the camp the Germans appointed the former head of the Grayeve "*Judenrat*" Zalmen Sutker.

In the kitchens they cooked potato soup four or five times a day. Each person received a half-liter of watery soup per day. Each received 100 grams of bread. The people were so hungry that they besieged the kitchens, tearing through the potato peels and devouring them uncooked.

A group of people were assigned to work on the highway around Prostken. They considered themselves the luckiest. Going outside the ghetto they had the opportunity to buy a piece of bread, for cash or for gold. The survivor Kletski tells it this way:

[Page 209]

"A group of 15 to 20 men went around Bogushe to their work. That was good for them because through their work they encountered Poles and for gold, watches and other valuables they could get bread and bring it into the camp and sell it. The best runners were the family Kaminski (Nakhtshe the butcher). Five or six of their family went out. During the two months of being in the ghetto they became very rich in gold and dollars because people paid a couple of dollars for a kilo of bread."

On the basis of this testimony one can get a clear picture of the situation of the Jews in the camp. If a kilo of bread cost several dollars it is very clear that very few people had the several dollars. Second, as from 7,000 internees a total of 15 went out to work it is clear that they could smuggle bread into the camp, but only for an insignificant number of people.

After two weeks in the Bogushe camp the Gestapo gave permission to 15 people from the camp to go into the ghetto, take from the cellars the potatoes that the Jews had set aside for the winter, and bring them into the camp. Groups from the camp went to the ghetto three or four times. Survivor M.

Kletski, who also went to the ghetto with a group, relates how the ghetto looked after two weeks after the Jews had left it:

"One time I succeeded and I went into Grayeve, under guard by three soldiers from the Wehrmacht. We arrived in the ghetto. The ghetto looked like the aftermath of a pogrom. The houses had been robbed, the streets full of feathers. You could see Jewish holy books scattered around on the pavement. Poles had already settled in to the nicer houses. We went into the courtyard at Peysakh the baker's and found a *seyfer toyre* [Torah scroll] lying there, ripped apart. We took several wagonloads of potatoes from the cellars and our work was done. There was a baker there, the name I don't remember, (it was the baker Yan Shenkievitsh N.R.) who sold us a six-kilo loaf of bread and not at a high price."

[Page 210]

There was very high mortality in the camp because of the terrible hunger and filth. Each evening they laid the dead bodies in a pit and in the morning took them to the camp cemetery, which was the cemetery for the Russian prisoners of war who had been in the same camp a year before.

Every one of the interned Jews was subject to the sentencing of the Gestapo murderers. We were told how the Grayeve Jew Shaye Leyb Kanapsko, an invalid from World War I, was murdered. Suddenly one morning a Gestapo thug came into the camp and called this Jew out of the barrack. The invalid Shaye Leyb surmised that his end was near. With tears in his eyes he said goodbye to his friends, took from his pocket his leather gloves which he always wore because of his rheumatism and gave them to his son-in-law Leybl Sharfshteyn, and said to him, "Take them, I don't need any gloves, the world will soon end for me." He went into a prepared pit and with one shot the Gestapo thug put an end to his life.

On the 15th of December a "selection" took place in the ghetto. The Germans pressed together around 5,000 people in separate barracks. It was announced to these people that in the morning they would be sent to a camp in Silesia to work. Characteristically, a rumor had already gone around among the Jews that the Jews were being sent to Treblinka and *Maidanek* [Majdanek] to be burned in the crematoria, but if that was certain, no one believed it. So the largest part of them assigned "to Silesia for work" accepted indifferently the news of their deportation. The transporting of the people took place in the usual German way; with frightful blows and shooting on the spot, the people were chased from the barracks into the road to Prostken to the train station. The roads were soaked from the autumn rains and the crowd, weakened, could not get their footing. But the murderers were in a hurry. Those who remained in the rear were shot on the spot. The entire road from Bogushe to Prostken was lined with victims. In the morning the camp rulers ordered the Jews still in the camp to clean up the dead from the roads. On that day they collected 200 corpses and brought them to graves in the camp cemetery in the village of Bogushe (near the camp).

[Page 211]

The entire transport of 5,000 Jews – among them the camp commander and former head of the "Judenrat" in Grayeve, Zalmen Sutker and his aide Leyzer Grosman – were taken to Treblinka and killed in the crematoria. To this day no one knows of even one single person from that transport who was saved.

After the deportation of the transport of 5,000 Jews, about a thousand people remained in the ghetto. The German murderers, thinking it through and calculating in their criminal goals, wanted to create the illusion among the remaining Jews that for them, for the remaining ones, there was no imminent danger. They put the people into the better barracks, cleaner, and they even improved the "food." The survivor M. Kletski even tells about one case in which they brought geese and other birds shot by a party from the Prostke *pasharnia* [chicken coop], for the internees to eat. It was said that they might "maintain" the internees a little, mending, so to speak, and afterwards, together with their families, send them to a camp to work. The Germans then nominated an Ogustove Jew as commander of the camp and a week later ordered him to prepare the Jews for the road.

On the 2nd of January 1943, the Germans ordered the Jews to pack up and be ready to move out in the morning. In the morning – that is on the 3rd of January – the last Grayeve Jews left, forever, the Bogushe camp. Tightly packed in the wagons the Grayeve Jews traveled from the Prostke train station through Byalistok, Warsaw, Treblinke…

When the train went past Treblinke and did not stop there, a ray of hope awoke in the unfortunate ones. They did not know at the time that there were other death camps besides Treblinke. The Grayeve Jew Yankev Shidla assured his brothers, "Jews, if we are going past the Treblinke hell we will survive." Sadly this was a false hope.

The train arrived in the death camp Birkenau (Bzshezshinski) in the middle of the night. As soon as the train came to a standstill it was assaulted by S.S.-men with automatics in their hands that chased the arrestees out of the wagons. Anyone who tried to take anything with them, even a piece of bread, was shot on the spot. A selection was conducted right there. A hundred young men were selected, and the other 900 men and women were packed into heavy trucks and taken directly to the crematorium.

[Page 212]

On that same day the ovens of the death camp Birkenau swallowed up forever the last trace of the Grayeve community of Jews...

So it was

Extinct, as after a horrible flood, Grayeve was left without Jews. From every corner, from every bit of soil, rises a quiet thick cloud of just-forgotten Jewish blood: the low hills around the village Pshekopke; the muddy water of the little Kosherove River; the ruins of the houses on Shul Street; the murder-cellar in the shul; the enormous camp cemetery in Bogushe – all these places have forever locked in themselves the remembrance of a community of Jews on Polish soil.

The earth laments in Grayeve. The birds in the Greek-Orthodox garden sing a sad song. The sun is embarrassed to look on the fresh graves, because when she warms one of the graves with her glance, a stinking scream goes up from the pit, from the tortured innocents who curse the world, curse the sun, for shining on the enemies. Then the sun hides, ashamed, and a thick damp fog spreads itself over the town like a great veil of sadness and the town seems as though she wants to sit *shive*[2] at the foot of the green hills...

There is no light in Grayeve, so the dark characters crawl out from their lairs, creep and sniff; is everything done now? Is there yet some place, or someone that has evaded them? They creep over the villages and forests in search of hidden Jews. And when they don't find any, they search in all the narrow holes until... they get into the Bogushe camp... That which I tell you here happened a month after the "emptying out" of the camp in Bogushe; when on the soil of Grayeve and around it there was not one Jewish life to be found.

[Page 213]

**A part of the Jewish cemetery.
There is not one gravestone there. Houses are being built there.**

The entrance to the cemetery before the war

Several Polish hooligans from Grayeve's rich underworld had made a visit to the Bogushe camp. The barracks were empty, and much of the wood had been stolen by the local peasants. The hooligans had searched, ransacked, who knows what? They were probably digging for Jewish gold, that legendary "Jewish treasure" that every Jew "must" have. Suddenly they hit upon something soft or hard, who knows, but it was covered up; they quickly removed the earth around their feet and were astonished: a grave had opened before their eyes, a pit, in which there were two <u>living corpses</u>. The clothing on the two survivors was already rotting, only the boots were still whole. The One

God knows how the two Jews had succeeded in concealing themselves from the curse and maintained themselves for a whole month in the pit. When the hooligans, the "gold-diggers" realized that two zhydes were still alive, their "patriotic" pig's blood was inflamed in them. They dragged the two Jews out of the grave. They ordered them to take off their boots (they could be put to use!), ordered the two Jews to embrace and with one shot put holes through both skulls. The two Jews were Velvl Videnski and his young wife! (Testimony of Polish worker Yan Kolski.)

[Page 214]

Now the "Jew-free" Grayeve could rest, no more Jews in Grayeve…

But:

It would still take long, very long, for the Grayeve earth to rest. Long, very long, would sleep be taken from the eyes of those in Grayeve who helped in these great crimes. The torment of the murdered women and men, fathers and sons, would rob their peace for a long, long time. Death angst would befall them in the nights and black depressions would torment them by day for the commission of their dark work. The curse that our martyrs threw out in the last moments of the existence would follow them forever, until it would destroy them from under the heavens.

Then the blood of our martyrs will be at peace.

May their souls be bound up in the bond of life.

Footnotes

1. *With great respect:* we would like to honor the brave Poles who helped Jewish Grayevers despite the risk to their own personal safety. They will be remembered for their acts of kindness, courage and humanity. May their memories be a Blessing and their souls bound in the bond of everlasting life.

shive: Jewish mourning period of 7 days, observed by family and friends of the deceased.

[Page 215]

A Grayeve Partisan Recounts
Mendel Kayman
Translated by Yael Chaver, Ph.D

I was one of a small group of Jews who escaped from Grayeve and shtetls in the vicinity, such as Goniondzh [Goniądz], Trestiny [Trzcianne] etc.

We were lucky to be arrested by a large group of Russian partisans near Leńce [?] (Masuria region). We were jailed for only a few days, but after a series of investigations and checks, they became convinced that we had come to the forest to save ourselves from death. They let us go free and recruited us as equal fighters in their partisan groups. That day we swore an oath that our goal was to fight and take revenge for our fathers and mothers, brothers and sisters.

Even in the forest our lives were far from secure. Death lurked on all sides. But at least we knew we wouldn't be killed without resisting—we wouldn't let ourselves be led like sheep to the slaughter. The Germans often mounted raids and we had to be careful not to fall into their murderous hands. Sometimes we hid in bunkers, sometimes retreated further into the forest, but our goal was always to attack the enemy at the slightest chance and make him pay the heaviest possible price for his murders.

One rainy day, we set out, 106 partisans, to "give a lesson" to the Nazi enemy. The "lesson" was given, but only 22 members of our group remained alive. The others were killed in a battle near the village of Kopisk [?]. But our losses did not scare away or restrain the other partisan groups from continuing to fight.

[Page 216]

Now I want to recount how a group of partisans led by several guys from Grayeve, went back there to carry out a death sentence against a so-called *Volksdeutsche*,[1] who had murdered a large number of Jews.

It was May 3, 1942. We were supposed to start out of the forest at 7 p.m. The young folks from Grayeve impatiently waited for evening and constantly checked their watches. But the hands mocked us and moved slowly and lazily… The watch's ticking was dull and phlegmatic, as if it sensed that our lives were in danger of death.

The evening finally arrived. Our commander ordered everyone to prepare and carry all our weapons, ammunition, grenades and explosives. There were 43 of us. Darkness had fallen. We left the forest and avoided going through villages and on main roads. After much difficulty, we came to the first houses of Grayeve.

The first house we came to was where Brzoza had lived. The small flame of a night-light gleamed through the window. Looking at the light, a flow of memories began, reminding me of a large part of my life that had been cut off suddenly... We quietly walked behind the Jewish houses, in which there were no more Jews... The large buildings of Jewish schools stood with doors flung open, but no one went in or out... Hearts aching, we strode through the gardens behind the houses.

We carried out the death sentence against the Volksdeutsche murderer. We breathed more easily when we saw the murderer had been shot... It was dark. There were no people around. In the distance we saw the rays of a projector the Germans used to illuminate their patrols. We started to leave the house of the executed murderer and heard the heavy steps of German patrols. Now we began to hear calls in German. Bullets started flying in our direction. We slowly re-entered the forest. Forty-three Jewish partisans participated in the mission and succeeded in returning safely. But in the coming missions we were not able to return unharmed.

[Page 217]

Only a few lived to see May 9, 1945, when the Red Army and the Polish Folk Army finally drove Hitler's murderers out of Poland. These few saved themselves with the weapons they held and by being aware that they had taken at least some revenge against the enemy, in return for the dearest and most beloved of our home town, Grayeve. But all hearts were still full of grief, pain, and the desire to take revenge on our enemies many times over.

Yiskor[2] *Am Yisroel,* let the people of Israel remember the martyrs killed by the German and Polish Fascist murderers.

Yiskor Am Yisroel, let the people of Israel remember the partisans who fell in battle against the accursed Nazi Germans.

Yiskor Am Yisroel, let the people of Israel remember the heroic partisans who survived themselves and also saved many Jewish families from death.

Footnotes
29. *Volksdeutsche:* An historical term coined in the early 20th century that was used to describe ethnic Germans living outside of the Reich.
30. *Yiskor:* Jewish prayer commemorating the deceased.

[Page 218]

Shtutzin – Grayeve to the Last Breath
Khaye Golding-Kayman
Translated by Yael Chaver, Ph.D

As a child, I often heard a legend that was linked with the name of Grayeve [Grajewo]. Each time I heard the legend I liked it anew and in my imagination Grayeve grew into a tantalizing, romantic town. The legend is as follows:

In the town of Raigrod (Paradise in Polish), lived Adam and Eve. After they sinned, God drove them out. They sorrowfully walked through the fields and along the roads, not speaking a word to each other. On their way they encountered a tree: a white *vyerbe* [willow] with long, green branches like Eve's braids. They rested, and Adam fashioned a willow flute for himself. The village later built on that spot was therefore known as Vyerbove. After resting briefly, Adam and Eve continued walking. Enchanted by the beauty of their new surroundings, Adam called to Eve, "Play, Eve," (Grayeve in Polish). This is how the future town built on this spot came to be known as Grayeve.

Fourteen kilometers separated my shtetl, Shtutzin [Szczuczyn], from Grayeve. The *shtetlakh* [Plural of shtetl-small town, village] were closely connected to each other. Grayeve had a train station, which made it dominant. By district decree, other commercial and political and entities were set up in the shtetl, such as the Sick Fund and "Social Security," the district's agricultural-economic office, the PPS (Polish Socialist Party), the Veterans' Office, the examination committee for artisans' guilds, and the like. The two important economic factors – the train and the district offices – forced residents and merchants of Shtutzin to come to Grayeve. If you wanted to travel to *Varshe* [Warsaw], *Byalistok* [Białystok] or some other large city, you had to get the train in Grayeve. Anyone who wanted to smuggle themselves into the U.S. illegally through Germany by way of the border town of *Prostken* [Prostki], first had to come to Grayeve. Buses, carriages and wagons therefore went back and forth all day.

[Page 219]

Jews from Grayeve would come to fairs in Shtutzin and vice versa. Merchants and craftsmen from Shtutzin would come to pay their taxes and young men would report for the draft. Every year during *Chol Ha-Moed Peysakh and Sukes* [the days between the first and last days of the holidays] prospective brides and grooms would come to Shtutzin and Grayeve to view each other… The Jewish youths who were members of the Grayeve sports club would come for summer meets in Shtutzin. Those warm blue twilights sparkled with joy, laughter and life. Avrom and Itche Gershtonsky, Leyble Remigolsky, Simche Sarn, Izze Epstein, Gortshitsky, Gershuny Eisenstat, Chaim Friedman, Isaac Kolko, Lifshitz were all frequent guests in our shtetl.

Some young folks from Shtutzin studied in Goldlust's *gimnazyes* [secondary schools] in *Lomzhe* [Łomza]. Grayeve became the source of culture for the region. Zalmen Sutker the theater director was the first to set up a movie theater in Shtutzin and would present films twice a week. The shtetl was very grateful to him. Tsila Kolko from Grayeve would give concerts. Every winter we would arrange marvelous dances. Merry young folks from Grayeve would arrive in packed sleighs, bells ringing. The literary evenings of the professional organization in the "Perets Library," would be attended by working youths of Grayeve, who took an active part in the events up to about two weeks before their tragic death. In the summer of 1941, shortly before the outbreak of the war between Germany and Russia, the capable young teacher Miss Kolko (Shimon Kolko's daughter) and Miss Barkovska came to Shtutzin from Grayeve with their pupils and successfully presented the play "*Bar-Kochba.*"[1]

[Page 220]

The poor people of both shtetlakh had an agreement to switch shtetlakh once a week: the beggars of Shtutzin would come to Grayeve and those of Grayeve would come to Shtutzin. This worked well. They would do this during the first half of the week, so that at the end of the week each group could visit its local wealthy people and they could spend *Shabes* [Sabbath] at home. In this way the social groups of both shtetlakh were closely connected.

The Jews of Grayeve and Shtutzin had lived like this for generations. They shared a lively, vital life – up to June 22, 1941.

Just as happened to the Jewish people in all of Poland, a chain of death and destruction began to spread over our shtetlakh. Every tie between our shtetlakh was interrupted. It was very dangerous for Jews to travel, either on the main road or on side roads. At that time, we were more afraid of the Poles than of the Germans. We in Shtutzin didn't know what was happening to our friends in Grayeve.

During the second week of the German occupation, the Poles of Shtutzin went from house to house at midnight and slaughtered Jewish men, women and children. As many as 300 on the first Friday night… In Grayeve as well as in Shtutzin, they first murdered the Jewish intellectuals and householders, so as to immediately get their hands on their property. They quietly organized and used the same methods in Grayeve as in Shtutzin. All classes of Polish society took part in the slaughter: the town employees, the postmaster, the school director, the notary, lower-ranking officials and peasants. The priest sneaked away… Fifty percent of the Jews of Shtutzin were killed not by the

Germans, but by the Poles, their former neighbors, supposedly good friends, customers, and acquaintances. In *Rodzilova* [Radziłów], literally the entire Jewish population was burned alive all at once by the Poles in the largest barn in the shtetl.

Several weeks later, as the thirst for Jewish blood and property slowly decreased, news and rumors began coming from Grayeve. The word "ghetto" started hovering. Many people did not understand the significance.

[Page 221]

People struggled with it. At the time it was thought that this was only a local phenomenon of persecution and people tried to buy their way out with money and property. This went on until the Jews were suddenly driven into the marketplace without warning. After eleven hours of standing in the street without a drink of water, deathly afraid, witnessing the beating of Rov Afran (of blessed memory) and other householders; seeing shot youths being dragged around and violent assaults on Jews; we were finally driven into the Shtutzin ghetto, late on Friday night.

We lived in despair, hungry, cold and in pain. The only men in the Shtutzin ghetto were about 20 craftsmen and ten youths. All the men met with different forms of violent deaths at the hands of Poles. Here, I'm just describing in brief, the tragedy of the Jews in my hometown of Shtutzin. Like everyone, I endured that terrifying period and every horrible event etched itself deep into my consciousness; every date, every neighbor, every friend – those dear, warm, beloved people. These lines will engrave themselves into the mind of each reader. Their hearts will agonize, but they will not grasp the true concept of the profound suffering, the sorrow and pain, that overtook us.

The first rays of the sun witnessed the women of Shtutzin sneaking alongside roads into Grayeve. Some wanted to unburden themselves to family and friends; some hoped to breathe a bit more freely; some needed the services of the ritual slaughterer (the ritual slaughterers of Shtutzin had already been killed) to slaughter a chicken for a child who was seriously ill. After a few days of toothache, I made the pilgrimage to Grayeve, to the woman dentist, Barkovka.

The Grayeve ghetto was larger than that of Shtutzin. Not just one small street as we had, but several streets and not only small dilapidated house, but two or three well-constructed buildings. For a while, breathing was easier. Soon a Polish policeman who was in the ghetto stopped me: "You are a stranger," he said, and took me to the commander of the Jewish ghetto police, Karbavskin.

Abkevitch, the policeman, vouched for me, and took me to the dentist.

I took a route through yards rather than through streets to see Zalmen Sutker, the head of the *Judenrat* [Jewish Council]. All Jews did this. Jews did not dare take the main streets for fear of showing themselves to Polish or German eyes.

[Page 222]

The yards were just like those of Shtutzin and like those I later saw in the Byalistok ghetto: "the back streets." There were no more fences – all the wood had been burned for cooking. An outhouse was rare. Noisy, dark and tumultuous, like a beehive; a thick steam came from the low-lying windows. From one window prayers were heard, bearing all the acuteness of Jewish pain, sorrow, and supplication for salvation and compassion. This soared from the lowest houses to the highest of heights, believers in "God will answer you in time of trouble."

I talked with Zalmen Sutker, Julian Glatt, Leyzer Grossman, Vovek Zilbershteyn and others I met in the Judenrat. I visited several families. Everyone and everything was sunk in grief, but believed they would live through the bitter times and awaited redemption. Everyone could see what responsibility the Judenrat bore for the ghetto as a whole, and the importance of cooperating with the leaders. Individuals overcame their particular interests and became interwoven with the flame of the community. Never before and never afterwards did I see collective character so clearly, the care and struggle for each other. I wondered at the unity, loyalty and love of one Jew for another, one person for another.

Bogushe [Bogusze], the next-to-last stop for the Jews of Shtutzin, Grayeve, Ogustove [Augustów] and Raigrod [Rajgród], was united in their own troubles, common suffering and pain. Just as the two towns were strongly linked in life, so were they linked in tragic death, until the last shudder of violent death, until the last breath was drawn...

Footnote

9. *Bar Kochba* 132-135 C.E. This was marked by a period of hope that turned into violent anguish. The Jews believing a homeland and Holy Temple were in their site, were eventually persecuted and sold into slavery.

[Page 223]

The Violent Death of the Jews of Shtutzin
Translated by Yael Chaver, Ph.D

Document of the Jewish Voivodeship[1] Historical Commission, Byalistok, August 11, 1946. L. B. 46/152.

Delivered by Bashe Katsper, born in *Shtutzin* [Szczuczyn] in 1920, lived in the Shtutzin ghetto during the occupation and after the liquidation hid in surrounding villages; now living in *Byalistok* [Białystok].

The shtetl of Shtutzin (home to 3000 Jews before the war) felt the bestial hand of the Nazis beginning in 1939, when they stayed there for three weeks. At that time the shtetl lost 300 men, only a few of whom returned.

On June 24, 1941, the Germans took Shtutzin once again. The local German authorities were not established in the first few days and young Polish rowdies and hooligans taunted the Jews. Among those were Jakobcak, Dombrovski the tanner, Sviaslavski, the postmaster Jankeitis, the school principal and the town watchmen.

On June 25, 1941, at midnight on Friday, when everyone was sleeping, the Poles carried out three massacres: in the new town, at the marketplace, and on Lomzhe Street.

Among those murdered in the new town were Kaplan the photographer, with his son-in-law; Esther Kriger with her daughter and grandchild; Romorovsky the tailor, Peske Yashinsky, Meisel the head of the Yeshiva, and others.

[Page 224]

Among those murdered at the marketplace were Khane Rozental's children; Grisha Radushkonsky and his wife and infant; Beyle-Rokhl Guzavska; Zeydke Bernshteyn with Rokhke and their grandchild; Tuvia Shaynberg's children; *Rov* [Rabbi] Slutsky with his family. On Pavelke Street, outside town, they murdered Gavriel Farberovitch. Bernshteyn and Leyzer Sosnovski were shot in the slaughterhouse. The total of those murdered was 300. The Poles carried them outside on carts and did not leave them lying around, but threw them into ditches.

The Jewish women ran to the Polish intellectuals to intervene and stop the pogroms, but they didn't help. So they bribed the German soldiers at the court, and the next night the Jewish area was patrolled.

The same happened in Grayeve, Rodzilova [Radziłów], Vonsosh [Wąsosz] and Stavisk. In Rodzilova all the Jews were burned in a barn. A week before they issued the order about the ghetto, the Polish watchmen drove all the Jewish men out of their homes on the pretext of doing weeding. They drove them to the cemetery. Only women and a few men were left at home. The next day they found 100 men in a mass grave. Among those murdered were Yoyne Levinovitch's son, Panish with his son Meir, Yeshaya Kokoshko, Malkiel Lifshitz, and others. The Rabbi was beaten murderously and the *bes-medresh* [House of Study] was burned.

On July 20, 1941, the ghetto was decreed. It extended from Lapian's yard to Vilimovsky's yard. The same day, the entire Jewish population was driven out onto the streets, young and old separated, and placed in an enclosed area from which people were taken every night to be killed: Zovl Zemel, Moyshe Guzovsky, Khayim Kulinsky, Yankl Denmark, Khayim Kokoshko, Mikey Farber, Dovid Rabinovitch, Moyshe Leyzerman, the Rabbi, the ritual slaughterers, the religious judge, Kayman's father-in-law, Berman the teacher, Itche Tutelman, Skubelsky, and others were killed. Only women and children were let into the ghetto, ten tailors, Ruzshe the watchmaker, Sholem-Motl the bricklayer, three blacksmiths and others who sneaked in. Altogether there were 300 Jews there.

A Judenrat was set up in the ghetto, consisting of 15 Jews and four policemen as a Jewish security force.

[Page 225]

The president was Levinovitch, and the council members were: Notke Rabinovitch, Yisroelke Goldfarb, Mikhoel Krushbiansky, Savitsky and Friedman. In the hospital there were only Lubetsky, Leybl Dorf and two doctors. The persons mentioned above together with Dr. Vartman and Gertz, remained in Szczuczyn until the liquidation.

On November 2, 1942, the Shtutzin ghetto was liquidated and the residents were taken to Bogushe [Bogusze] (a camp outside of Grayeve). Several people tried to escape from the camp into the forests, without success. Among those murdered were Gordenberg, Lichtenshteyn, and two brothers.

Before the ghetto was liquidated, this witness worked in Grabow, in the village. After the liquidation she hid in the forests and in the house of a Christian woman in Grabow, until the liberation on January 26, 1945.

Witness--

Protocol taken by--

Chairman of the Jewish Voivodeship Historical Commission.

Mgr. M. Turek

Footnote

1. *Voivodeship:* (Polish: województwo) Province.

[Page 226]

The Violent Death of the Jews of Kolna
Translated by Yael Chaver, Ph.D

Document of the Jewish Voivodeship[1] Historical Commission, Byalistok [Białystok], June 27, 1946.

Given by Feygl Golombek (born Rozenshteyn, later Milners), born 1915 in Stavisk [Stawiski]; hid in the villages around Stawisk during the occupation.

The shtetl of *Kolna* [Kolno], with two thousand Jews is not far from the German border, so that many of the residents, including Jews, suffered from the time the war broke out on June 22, 1941. Many were killed; among them the Shklonyevitch family and many were wounded.

A few days later the villagers from Chervin [Czerwin] and Zabiele who had been released from Soviet prisons, came and killed 30 Jews. Among the victims were the Dalavitch family and Yankev Dudovitch with his wife and child.

Jews had to pull weeds in the streets for a week, where many of them were shot. Young women were raped and ordered to run around the streets naked. Among these victims was Dr. Kosovitch's sister.

On Saturday, July 5, the entire Jewish population, including women with infants, was ordered to gather near Lenin's statue, in their *tales* [prayer shawls] and with wagons, but no horses. The blacksmiths sang *Hatikvah* ["The Hope" and now the National Anthem of Israel] and were beaten. They hacked the statue to bits. They placed the pieces of the statue on the wagons that were harnessed to Jews wearing their taleysim.

[Page 227]

The wagon train traveled two kilometers from the town to the Jewish cemetery, where they buried Lenin while singing and praying. As they left the cemetery, Poles stood at the gate holding sticks and beating them over their heads.

On July 15, 1941 the Germans ordered all the young people of Kolna to assemble and bring packets of food, supposedly for work. They loaded them onto vehicles and took them to Kolimagi. There was no trace of them afterwards.

On the third day after the young people were deported, the older people were ordered to bring their valuables so they could be taken to their children. Each Jew with his package reported to the court, where vehicles with Gestapo were waiting. The packages were supposedly put in the trunks of the cars and the people entered the vehicles. Some were taken to Kolimagi and others were taken to Mściwuje and all were shot. The elderly were driven on foot to Kolimagi.

The entire process lasted three days. Only about fifty people, out of Kolna's entire Jewish population, managed to escape.

The Nitzevitch family fled from Kolna and came to Stavisk the day of the liquidation, and was then killed. The Lev family, mother and daughter (they had a printing press) were alive after the liquidation in a colony at Smirnitz, but the police caught them and took them to the Bogushe camp. The richest man in Kolna, Botchke Ayzenberg, along with Brokhe Alekh, hid in the surrounding villages. When they were in Pachuczyn (near Kolna), hiding in the house of the village headman, Lipinski, a peasant from Kolna recognized them. The headman became afraid and handed them over to the police. They were arrested and taken to Lachowo. On the way, Ayzenberg stabbed the policeman, took his weapon and fled. They lived in the forests of Grabówek until 1944, at Korwazken's. They were killed there by chance.

The only survivor was Dina Khludnievitch, who fled from Kolna to the *Lomzhe* [Łomża] ghetto and from there got to Germany, where she lived as a Christian woman.

Witness—

Protocol taken by –

Chairman of the Jewish Voivodeship Historical Commission.

Mgr. M. Turek

Footnote

Voivodeship: (Polish: województwo) Province.

[Page 228]

The Pogroms in Radzshilov [Radzilow]

Document from the Regional Historical
Commission in *Byalistok* [Białystok]
27 June 1945
L. B. 30.

Imparted by Menakhem Finklshteyn, born 1923.
Lived in *Rodzilova* [Radziłów] until the liquidation of the Jews.
He was hidden for 43 months in the region by various Poles.
Recorded by L. Rotshteyn.
Translated by Tina Lunson

After the entry of the Soviet Army into the Grayeve region in 1939, a certain wave of sabotage against the Soviet authority began. The murder of Soviet officers and officials of Soviet power often took place. After long investigations it was revealed who the bandits were. In 1940 there was a strong, armed partisan band in the forest by the village Bilineh, near Rodzilova. The battle went on for several days. As a result the bands were driven off and many were shot. From the bandits arrested, it appeared that the partisan band was made up especially of local residents who had fled because of earlier acts they had carried out. The big arrests nevertheless did not liquidate the bands completely. The acts of sabotage and the murders still continued.

In the summer of 1941, the chief of the *NKVD*[1] in Jedwabne was murdered in the woods by the village Glinki. Before the Germans came, people realized that those who carried out the murder were the brothers Bienkovski from the village Romani, Przytuly district.

[Page 229]

The authorities were preparing a new extermination of the secret organization, but just then the war broke out between Germany and the Soviet Union. The arrested bandits got out of jail and the others who were hiding were also on the loose, and they began to work officially with the Germans. Subsequently it was revealed who had carried out the sabotage and the murders. It was also revealed that a secret organization had been at work under the name A. K.,[2] which had been checking in with the Germans during the whole time of the Soviet occupation. They marched to German orders from the moment of the Germans' entry.

On the 23rd of June 1941, Aleksander Layevski, the resident of the village *Laye-Avisa*, [Łoje Awissa] along with Tadeush Piatrovskin from Rodzilova and others, went out with weapons against the retreating Red Army soldiers who were fighting by the river Biebzshe near Laye-Avisa. They disarmed the Red soldiers, took their weapons and beat them. That same day, a triumph gate was erected in Rodzilova on Lomzhe Highway to welcome the German army. Hitler's portrait was hung on it, along with the slogan "Long live the German Army, who freed us from the cursed Jew-Commune."

With the arrival of the first German tanks there were civilian Poles who stepped up to help them. So, for example, 18 Red soldiers who were hiding in the rye were uncovered by Videnetsi Piatravskin and Mietshislov Shtsheletski and his brother from Rodzilova. Baleslav Gavetski discovered 7 Red soldiers in the cemetery and turned them over to the hands of the Germans and they were shot by them.

On July 24, 1941 a group of Poles who are known to me – Antoni Kamatshevski, Yozef Kamatshevski, Feliks Moralishevitsh from Rodzilova, got weapons and drove their first tanks through the river Biebzshe in the direction of Trestiny [Trzcianne] in order to circle the fort Osowiec. After taking Osowiec on June 23, the German officers had distributed decorations to certain German soldiers and at the same time money, rewards and written thanks to the above-mentioned persons.

[Page 230]

On the 26th the German authorities distributed weapons to these trusted people in order for them to reckon with the Bolsheviks and the Jews. Their first act was the murder of the *Komsomol*[3] member Frume Derogai, 17 years old. Those who carried it out were Skrandzki, a tailor and Anton Kapmatshevski from Rodzilova. Declaring that it was a waste of such a bullet, they sawed off her head in the woods near Kolonie Kopanskes and dumped her body with the legs in Bagne.

On the 7th of July 1941 at 3 in the afternoon the Gestapo from Stavisk gathered by car in Rodzilova. At their orders, their trusted people were called together, already prepared to deal with the Jews. They called 1,700 Jews together in the market square, men, women, children and the elderly. The square was circled by the bandits so that no one could escape. Among those driving the Jews together were Yanek Valevski, the so-called "American," Yanek Mardatevski and Feliks his brother; Henrik Dzetskavski and his brother Yan; and many Gestapo-flunkies. They beat the Jews bloody. Thus, for example, they beat the old shoemaker Artel Lipinski. Blood was pouring from him, he became unconscious. They hung a heavy stone around the neck of the former policeman T. Shtshani. When he fell under the burden the persecutors beat him murderously. There were many such cases. Afterwards they told everyone to sing *Moskva-moya* and they went around and beat everyone, not leaving out small children and old folks.

After performing these gruesome deeds the Gestapo announced, "We will give you 3 days to deal with the Jews." They distributed weapons to the bandits and drove away. The executions began. The bandits, armed with machine guns and revolvers, drove the assembled into Mitkovske's barn, which is located near the village Radiviezsh. They nailed the doors shut and poured kerosene on the barn and lit it; when the barn was in flames they drove the captive Jews and forced them to go up a ladder to the roof and jump in; the bandits cut those not following the order with bayonets and threw them into the fire. The few who managed to crawl out of the fire were shot by the murderers who encircled the barn. The singing and the loud shouting of the bandits accompanied the horrifying wails and terrible cries of the unfortunates who were perishing in the fire.

[Page 231]

The spilling of blood was not enough for these creatures. They had a slogan: "Kill off every one." They started to search out Jews in the whole area. Over three days they found only a couple of hundred Jews. They killed them in a bestial way. They led many of them to the middle of the stable, poured benzene on them and burned them alive. Many of them were shot near the stable, murderously beaten before their deaths. Due to a shortage of ammunition, they allowed the splitting of small children's heads with clubs, or beat them with the club until they were dead. They cut off several limbs from living souls, violating the victims before carrying out their murder. After the fire they went into the stable and tore out gold teeth from the dead bodies.

The pogrom went on for three days, from the 7th to the 10th of July of 1941. On the third day the Germans arrived and tore victims from the hands of the bandits, saying that they had gone too far. One can imagine how the grisly acts appeared when the Germans themselves took it over.

The leaders of the above-described acts of murder were: Brothers: Yozef, Antoni and Leon Kasmatshevski; Ludvig Kasmatshevski later a gendarme; Leon Potshkovski; Aleksander Garlevski and his brother Felek from Turmeh, who got out of jail that year, 1941, on June 2nd; Lasshevitsh; a German policeman Henrik Dzekanski and his brother Yan.

Witness -

Recorder -

Chairman of the Jewish Regional Historical Commission

Footnotes

31. *NKVD* (Narodny Kommisariat Vnutrennikh Del): "People's Commissariat for Internal Affairs," in the former Soviet Union under Stalin. This was the predecessor of the KGB.
32. *A.K.* (Armia Krajowa): Polish Home Army which dominated the Polish resistance campaign against the Nazis.
33. *Komsomol*: A Communist Youth Organization.

[Page 232]

The District Jewish Historical Committee☐Bialystok, June 14 1946☐No 5/46

Reported by Menachem Finkelsztajn
Born in Radzilow, age 22
Extermination of Jews in the Districts of Grajewo☐ and Lomza in July, 1941

The war broke out on June 22, 1941. Both districts are on the border. The first wave of Germans passed through without causing harm. A week later Polish police stations were set up: Germans and Poles would enter houses. The Germans terrorized, the Poles robbed, Poles asked the Germans what the punishment would be for killing Jews and the Germans answered, "They can be killed with impunity." A week later the Germans moved on and Poles would enter the houses of Jews at night, torture and rob.

On July 5th, the Polish police surrounded the small town of Wasosz (in the district of Grajewo). Local hooligans went from house to house, murdered those both inside and outside, raped the women, cut off their breasts and smashed little children against the walls. Wives of Soviet commanders were also killed, along with a number of Soviet officials. The fingers of the corpses with gold rings were cut off, and gold teeth were torn out of their jaws; if they found both parents and children in a house, they would first murder the children and then the parents. The pogrom lasted 3 days. This was the time the Germans allowed them to murder and plunder. They dug a hole in the ground outside of the settlement and buried the bodies. About 1200 Jews were killed (some of them came from surrounding areas, because normally there were 800). About 15 people survived and remained in Wasosz until June, 1942. The German police detachment behaved properly, whereas the Poles persecuted as much as possible.

On June 1, 1942 a model farm was created in the village Milewo, located in the community of Szczuczyn and owned by a landowner from Grajewo. Everyone was transported to the farm (together with Jews from surrounding towns – approximately 500 people altogether). Work was murderous from sunrise to sunset with Polish overseers. Children also worked very hard and the accommodations were tiny and the discipline harsh.

On November 2, 1942 they were transported to the village Bogusze on the German border, where there once was an extermination camp for the annihilation of Soviet prisoners of war and Polish prisoners. They remained there until January, 1943 and then sent to their deaths in Majdanek or Treblinka.

In Bogusze there were no houses, so the Jews slept in open fields. People would throw raw potatoes and those who caught one, would eat.

Half of the Jews died right there. The talk is that the Soviet Prisoners who were interned in the barracks were continuously starved. The Jewish person Mroczek from Kolno, now lives in Lomza.

July 7, 1941: Polish hooligans, armed by the Germans with rifles and pistols, burnt about 1500 Jews in Radzilow, Bialystok (100 Jews from Radzilow, 500 from neighboring small towns Szczuczyn, Jedwabne etc.). The pogrom lasted 3 days. 22 Jews hid and survived, among them the Finkelsztajn family (father, mother and 4 children, one cousin who died later – Zina Wasersztajn). The Finkelsztajns hid in the village of Konopki-Blonie, community of Hawiski, in the district of Lomza. The other Jews remained in Radzilow and after one month they were locked up in the synagogue and forced to do hard labor to build a bridge by hauling heavy stones from the river Radzilowka. This lasted 3 weeks. The Jews ransomed themselves by paying the Polish police commander (Kiluk Konstanty). He gave them permission to stay in one of the Jewish houses on Koscielna Street, but they were summoned to hard labor (removing pavement, sweeping streets, cleaning sidewalks), this lasted until June 1, 1942. In the meantime, Kruk, Benjomin, Maraszewski, Szabsaj and others were arrested for communism. They disappeared without trace.

June 1st, everyone was transported to Milewo. Only the Finkelsztajns and Dorogoj, Mojzesz as well as his son Akiva, survived. They died on January 28, 1945, just 1 week after the liberation by the Red army in the village of Itucz, within the community of Radzilow.

The Destruction of the Small Town Jedwabne, July 11, 1941
(3 days as well)

Before the war there were 2800 Jews. They were all burnt in a barn. It was preceded by a parade headed by the rabbi and the ritual slaughterer. The rabbi carried a portrait of Stalin. The Jews carried red flags and when they passed by the statue of Stalin in the market square they were ordered to kiss his feet and raise their voices in his honor. Like in Radzilow, on the second day they went through the ashes and tore out gold teeth from the jaws. About 3300 Jews were killed – 3000 were burnt, the rest were found and killed in the next two days. 302 were left alive. They remained in Jedwabne in 3 houses until February 11, 1942. Due to some Polish provocation (they were accused of hanging anti-German banners), 15 disappeared without a trace.

November 2, 1942, they were taken to Lomza and in the same day, together with the inhabitants of the Lomza ghetto, were transported to Zambrow and then in January, probably to Treblinka.

Rescued: Zyna Cukierbraun and three men (these three are currently in Jedwabne and Zyna is in Warsaw).

Witness: Chairman of the Jewish District

Protocol reporter: Historical Commission, Mgr. M. Turek

[Page 236]

Officers of the United Grayever Relief Committee

Hyman Blum, Honorary Chairman□Isador Shiller, Chairman□Irving Klaynman, Co-Chairman□Irving Sapirshteyn, Financial Secretary□Max Cohen, Treasurer□Mrs. F. Mishkof, Recording Secretary

Executive Board

Fannie Abramson□Dr. G. Gorin□Rose Miller□William Margolis□Esther Mishkovski□Alex Sosno□Phillip Sosnovits□Sol Fishbeyn□Helen Fenster□Sylvia Shiller□Sydney Shiller

[Page 237]

From right to left. First row, seated: H. Blum, I. Shiller, A. Sapirshteyn, M.Cohen, F. Mishkovski

Second row: E. Sosne, Ts. Shiller, F.Abramson, A. Vitkovski, Ts.Koehn, I. Klayman [probably should by Klaynman]

Third row: F.Fenster, Dr. G. Gorin, I.Margolis, R.Miller, P.Sosnovitsh, Sh.I.Fishbeyn

[Page 238]

Fourth Part:

Grayeve Jews in America

A Word from the Chairman of the United Grayever Relief Committee
Translated by Miriam Leberstein

As chairman of the United Grayever Relief Committee, I take this opportunity to thank and congratulate the active members of the committee and our *landslayt* [people from the same hometown] who have helped us in the work of stretching out a brotherly hand to our Holocaust survivors, who lived through Hitler's deluge, which inundated all of Europe and annihilated six million Jews, among them our flesh and blood, our parents, brothers, sisters, and their families.

The political conflict now raging all over the world between two opposing camps and ideologies could not spare our landslayt in America. The distrust, the suspicion, which each side has of the other has spread into the realm of the work of aiding the needy survivors and has made it more difficult to organize a more active relief committee. So I would like to note, with exceptional satisfaction, that I have been able for my entire tenure as chairman to maintain the requisite balance, and through the committee to establish harmony between both sides.

It is a pleasure for me to point out that since the committee renewed its activity at the end of the last world war, not once has there occurred, for whatever reason, a clash, or even a difference of political opinion, over the collection of money or the distribution of aid. The committee functioned as one friendly family and this was reflected not only in its relief work, but also in the personal relationships among its members. In the work of the committee, the ongoing dispute was forgotten.

[Page 239]

I have the feeling, that my non-partisan approach, especially towards relief work, significantly affected the harmonious cooperation. Like other landslayt, I was impelled to engage in this work with total commitment by the tragedy that I personally experienced. The loss of my parents and my entire family that had remained in Grayeve and *Varshe* [Warsaw] turned me into a fierce advocate, devoted to helping those few Grayevers who through fortunate circumstances remained alive.

The active members of the committee worked with devotion and self-sacrifice. They were not deterred, either by the work, or by the indifference which they sometimes encountered while collecting money or clothing, or selling tickets to events.

I want to mention here at least some of the active members and officers of our committee:

Our honorary president, Hyman Blum, whose profession makes it impossible for him to attend every meeting is in constant contact with our secretary and helps us enormously in carrying out our work.

With great sorrow we note the loss of our vice-president, Ab. Mlavski, who has left us so prematurely.

Our friend and active member A. Klayman does everything possible in every area of activity.

Our treasurer, *Friend* [term of address in Jewish communal organizations] Mendel Kohn, deserves a lot of praise for his good work, and especially in raising money for landslayt.

Friend Mrs. Fannie Mishkof, our recording secretary, keeps the minutes at our meetings and whom it is a pleasure to hear speak.

Other members of our executive committee perform their duties with complete devotion.

I want to express special recognition for our tireless financial secretary, Irving Sapirstein, a truly devoted social activist who, for all the years that he stood at the helm of our relief work, has never flagged in his enthusiasm and in his practical, methodical work. It is difficult for me to imagine the relief committee without his active participation.

[Page 240]

Finally, I want to thank those who have worked to produce this great work, which we are publishing for our landslayt – the **Grayever Yizkor Book** – the monument to our martyrs and to our town Grayeve as we remember it, where our cradles stood, as it was before the two wars, but where our relatives and friends were murdered in such a horrific manner. In the work for the Yizkor Book, our friend G. Gorin was chairman and H. Blum and Sh. I. Fishbein were on the editorial committee.

I hope that our future relief work will not have to be limited to helping the needy, but will also aid in building, and in constructive endeavors that will entirely eliminate poverty and homelessness, that our landslayt, along with all the Jewish survivors, will be able to settle in new homes, where they will stand on their own feet, and will no longer require aid.

Isador Shiller, Chairman, United Grayeve Relief Committee

[Page 241]

The Editorial Board of the Yizkor Book

Sol Fishbein

Hyman Blum

Dr. G. Gorin, Chairman

[Page 242]

The Grayever Relief Committee in New York
(From 1915-1921)

H. Blum

Translation by Miriam Leberstein

Anyone who ever went to *kheyder* [Jewish religious school] is familiar with the Bible story in which our father Jacob's sons sold their brother Joseph into slavery in Egypt. It later turned out, that with this act, they saved themselves and their aged father from dying of hunger, after they had long given up hope of hearing of Joseph ever again.

A similar historical occurrence happened before our eyes with the great Jewish emigration from Eastern Europe to the new world, to America. The new Jewish settlement in America was destined to play a decisive role in the future fact of Jewish people overseas. From the beginning of the 20th century, when the economic and political condition of the Jews of Eastern Europe began to deteriorate at an ever accelerating pace, and later, when the climax came in the First World War, and the terrible aftermath, it fell to the American Jews to play the role of the long ago Joseph, to relieve the hunger of those Jews who had been unwilling or unable to leave the lands where most sources of livelihood were closed to them. And so it also was with the Grayever *landsleit* [people from the same hometown] here in America.

This writer arrived in America in 1906, during the first years of a significant Jewish emigration from Grayeve. There were then just a few Grayevers who had been here for a longer time, and even fewer of these had managed to better their economic circumstances. Almost all Grayevers here worked in the needle trades or as peddlers. They had strong ties to their home town, from which they had only recently arrived and from which they had not yet entirely uprooted themselves.

[Page 243]

It should be noted that even before the development of relief activity here in America, this writer, himself a greenhorn, after receiving news of a fire in Grayeve in 1909, called a meeting of landsleit through a notice in the Yiddish newspapers. Sixty-six dollars were collected at the meeting to aid the victims of the fire. I am including a photograph of the letter of thanks from the then rabbi of Grayeve, the deceased Rov A. Milikovski. Today this would not be considered a significant amount of money, but when one takes into consideration the small number of landsleit and their economic situation, it could be considered a great success.

But the real activity by the Grayever landsleit on behalf of their home town first began with the beginning of the First World War. As soon as the war broke out, even before the establishment of communication with the cities and towns that were occupied by the Germans, a relief committee was immediately established for the landsleit of hundred of cities and towns. The newspapers were full of notices of mass meetings of landsleit associations, and our landsleit were no exception.

Since the Grayever and *Shtutziner* [Szczuczyn] landsleit already had a shared synagogue and ladies' auxiliary, it was natural that the relief effort, which had its offices in that synagogue, should also be a joint committee. Apart from the synagogue and ladies' auxiliary, the longstanding Shtutzin Young Men's Benevolent Association and the Grayeve Young Men's Benevolent Association also joined the relief committee.

But shortly after the founding of the committee, it turned out that the marriage was not a happy one. Conflict broke out between the Shtutziners and Grayevers. The local patriotism of each group heated up. At that time there were already a significant number of prosperous Shtutziners in New York, which wasn't the case with the Grayevers, who felt like poor relations in a rich family.

Just at that time, there arrived the first appeal from Grayeve, sent on November 17, 1915. The letter was sent to Herr Khaym Katsprovski, who was a devoted community activist in Grayeve and who had just recently returned to New York. The letter, which we reproduce here, was signed by the Grayeve rabbi, M. Amiel, by the religious authority Itsik Yeshaye Rozenboym, and by Avrom Mordkhe Piurko, and called for help for the over 200 Jewish families, "who find themselves in dire straits... so that they will not die of hunger." This letter provided the final impetus for the founding of a separate Grayeve relief committee. The following were elected as officials: Aron Levintal, Chairman; Khaim Katsprovski, Vice-President; A. Rotboym, Treasurer; and Hyman Blum, Secretary. Among the other active members whose names I recall, were: Avraham Gilari, N. Kaplan, Sore Goldshteyn, Hyman Goldshteyn, S. Brikman, Dovid Litof, Phillip Morrison, Benny Bagish.

To my regret, I cannot provide the exact sum of money that was raised. The books remained with the treasurer, who died several years after the committee dissolved and the books were no longer kept. But I believe that I won't be far off the mark, if I say we raised about $8,000 during the five to six years that the committee was active.

In order to provide an idea of what it meant to raise such a sum, it is important to note that the largest sum received from a single person was $50 (from Mr. Charles Witkop-Witkovski) and three or four $25 contributions. The rest came as one, two, three and five dollar contributions. The dollar was then worth more; it was hard to earn a dollar. But for that reason, it was worth a lot when it arrived overseas.

It should also be noted that this writer conducted a correspondence with landsleit in 90 cities in 19 states for whom he helped to locate relatives, and who also sent contributions. The work of connecting relatives was difficult and many-faceted. From the beginning of the war until America also entered the bloody whirlpool, a portion of Grayever landsleit were scattered in various parts of the enormous Russian Empire and in Germany. Through various means we found out their addresses and connected them with their landsleit here in America. But that became very difficult after America entered the war. We did everything we could to maintain contacts until all the connecting threads were broken.

After the war ended, our relief work consisted mostly in helping Grayever institutions. We were in contact with the Grayever Rabbi Amiel and with a committee that at various times consisted of Eliezer Zilbershteyn, Avrom-Mordkhe Piurko, I. Papovski, Mordkhe Abramski, Mordkhe Rinkovski, and from time to time, we would receive long letters from Moyshe-Dovid Zaydberg, who would send us news from "behind the scenes" about relief work in Grayeve itself. Elsewhere in this book we reproduce a portion of the large number of letters which we received from Grayeve during that period.

[Page 244]

God's Help 21 Elul 1909 Grajewo

Aharon Milejkowski□Rabbi□Grajewo□Author of "Questions and Answers Ohalei Aharon" [Aaron's Tents]

Hyman Bloom
New York

The committee for the benefit of the victims of the Grajewo fire is honored to notify his honor that we have received through Mr. Chaim Yosef Bialaszewski of New York the sum of sixty-six rubles that was collected there for the benefit of the victims here. In expressing our thanks and our greetings for the New Year, for a Good Writing and signing for the doers and the deeds, we hereby sign with feelings of respect and gratitude.

   Eli Aharon Milejkowski / The rabbi here
   [Five other signatures-illegible]

   [A response from the Grayever Rabbi to the collection of money in 1909 for the victims of a fire in Grayeve]

[Page 245]

Grajewo November 17, 1915

Most honoured and best friend!
As the hardship and misery in our half ruined town are grievous and we do not have the ability to support the many poor, over 200 families, which are placed in dire straits we find ourselves forced to ask our friends and the charitable organizations for help.

Since we don't know, however, to whom to address in America in this matter we ask you, dear friend, to become a constant collaborator of our society and raise compassion and pity from good and merciful people or charities, so they will help us with goods or money to lessen the dreadful suffering of the poor and not let them die of hunger.

For your worries we give you our greatest thanks and send greetings to you in the name of the whole town, wishing you luck.

(Signatures of the Rabbi and other people)
M. Piurko I. Rozenbaum
Rabbiner M. Amiel

I. Rozenbaum   **Rabbiner, Moshe Avigdor Amiel**

P.S. Your family is well and sends their love.

אַ — באַ'ער, גראַ'ער א. א. זו.

או — באָו, קראָוט, מאָוו, טאָוב.

יי — (ווי מיט א רוסישן „יערי") מ"י'נען, ב"י'נער.

שוואַכבאַטאַנטער אָפענער טראָף — ע: מאַמ‌ע, טאַטע.

פאַר לאַנגער ך הערט זיך א: טישלאַך, פיסלאַך.

קיין ה איז נישטאַ: אַנט (האַנט), אַרץ (הארץ).

דער כ איז געכאַרכלט.

קיין יאַטאָציע איז נישטאַ: אידיש, איר.

דער וואָקאַליזירטער ל הערט זיך זייער אָפט:

מואַמעד גואַמפ, כאָוועע, טישו, קעפאָ, דעכו, עפו, פיסו, אידו, זעאָוטו,
זעבט, וואָכן, גואַנצן, פערדו, קאָפיטו.

דער וווייכער ן — אין די גרופן: נ'טש, אנג'ק, ענג'ק, מענטשן,
בענטשן, (ה)ענטשקע, ווינטשן, לאַנג, בענק.

דער אומבאַשטימטער אַרטיקל איז אַפילו פאַר א וואָקאַל: אַ עפל, אַ
עמער, אַ אָקס.

[Page 248]

In 1920, the Grayeve Rabbi Amiel visited London on behalf of *Mizrakhi* [religious Zionist organization] of which he was a prominent leader. We invited him to come to America on behalf of relief work. He accepted the invitation, but immediately after that, he was appointed rabbi in Antwerp and he had to give up the planned trip. Several years later, he went to Tel Aviv, where he was appointed Chief Rabbi, a position which he held until the last days of his life. (Incidentally, at the same time that Rabbi Amiel was the Chief Rabbi of Tel Aviv, the head of the Rabbinical court there was also a former Grayever rabbi, Rov Eliahu Aron Milikovski).

A kitchen for poor children in 1918. Among the leadership, we recognize (from right to left):

Alte Vilenski, Zilbershteyn, Rabbi Amiel, Sore Ziberski, Rokhl Piurko and Rabbi Amiel's wife.

[Page 249]

This period of relief work ended in 1921, when the situation in Grayeve more or less normalized. Relatives in America supported their needy relations in the old home, and interest lessened. Thus ended the first chapter of relief work in Grayeve, with the hope that it would not be necessary to renew such work. Who then could see the dark clouds that had already gathered, and predict that only a short time later the same activists would have to get back to work and continue their efforts for Grayeve. And who then could imagine the bloody deluge that inundated the world and extinguished the lives of all the Jewish men, women and children in Grayeve, in all of Poland, as in all the Eastern European countries?

I leave it to my friend, the tireless secretary of the Relief Committee, Irving Sapirstein, to write about the second period of relief work.

**A group of Jewish girl students in the city [public] school in 1917
The teachers (right to left): Stusha Kolko, Mishanznik, Papovski, and Kurievavski)**

[Page 250]

The United Grayever Relief Committee
(From 1925 to the present)
by Irving Sapirstein
Translated by Miriam Leberstein

After the situation in Poland had stabilized somewhat and the wounds of the First World War had healed a bit, the activity of the Grayever Relief Committee tapered off and during certain periods stopped entirely.

It is very characteristic of the history of the Grayever Relief Committee that most of its efforts resulted from calls for help from Grayeve, both from private individuals and institutions. Thus it was that the Committee was reactivated in 1925–26 for the first time in the interwar period. From 1926 to 1937, the committee practically did not exist. There was no solicitation of money, no programs were carried out, and the connection to the Grayeve Jews temporarily ceased entirely.

In 1937 there began a new period of activity for the Relief Committee, which continues to the present day, when the United Grayeve Relief Committee was created through the merger of the Grayeve division of the Workman's Circle Branch 35 and the International Workers Order Branch 56. The activity of this Committee continued from 1937 to 1939. Between 1940 and 1946 there was no contact between the United Grayeve Relief Committee and Grayeve Jews.

[Page 251]

Immediately after the Second World War, when letters began to arrive from Grayever refugees, the committee was reorganized. This was in 1946, and the Committee has been active from that time until the present.

We will provide here a number of details about the activity of the United Grayeve Relief Committee here in New York during the various periods noted above, as well as about the utilization of the Committee's financial resources in Grayeve. Elsewhere, we print some of the letters and documents from Grayeve institutions which will shed light on the situation of the Jews of Grayeve, especially in the last ten years before Hitler's holocaust.

***

In 1925 and 1926, a series of very sad letters arrived from Grayeve, telling of the poverty and want of many Grayeve Jews. The economic and political situation in Poland was in crisis. There was mass unrest across the country. The reactionaries responded with Pilsudski's march on Warsaw, and the beginning of a semi–fascist regime in Poland. These letters describing the situation and how it affected life in Grayeve, came from institutions, such as the *kehile* [organized Jewish community], the library and others, and also from private individuals.

A group of Grayeve *landslayt* [people from the same hometown] from Branch 35 of the Workmans' Circle organized a ball. They also collected money among themselves and from acquaintances and the proceeds were sent to Grayeve. We will here mention only some of the most active members of the group: A. Sapirstein, Sh. Fishbeyn, A. Klayman, and F. Sapnovits. But the work of this group did not continue long and between 1926 and 1937 there was no active relief committee.

In October, 1937, a call for help came to New York from the Grayeve Jewish *kehile*, to which was appended a statistical report about the economic state of the Jews in Grayeve. In response to this appeal, the United Grayever Relief Committee was established. The active members of this committee were the following: H. Blum, A. Sapirstein, S. Barkovski, Fannie Abramson, Sh.I. Fishbeyn, Max Cohen, Mr. and Mrs. Horovits, A. Mlavski, S. Krinski, A. Klaynman, M. Layzerzon, F. Sosnovits, R. Sosnovits, V. Silverman, and Y. Riba.

[Page 252]

The United Grayever Relief Committee carried out two major projects – the balls held in 1938 and 1939. More than 500 Grayeve *landslayt* attended these balls. At the ball in November 1938, many Grayeve *landslayt* came together after many years of separation, to talk about their former hometown. The committee took advantage of the opportunity not just to collect money, but also to educate people about the usefulness of frequent gatherings of Grayeve Jews from New York and its environs.

Under the leadership of the committee, Secretary A. Sapirstein (who has been secretary from its founding until the present), and a few active members, they succeeded right from the start in collecting large sums of money for relief purposes. In addition to a second ball in January, 1939, they also held a number of smaller events, concerts, gatherings, etc. The result of all this work was that the United Grayeve Relief Committee sent a total of over $2000 to Grayeve in 1938–39.

Executive Committee of Lines Hatsadik [organization providing shelter for the indigent]

[Page 253]

Even before this, the United Grayever Relief Committee had approached the *kehile* in Grayeve with a proposal that a committee be organized there, representing all sectors of the Jewish population, so that the money collected could be distributed for appropriate purposes and in a democratic manner. In November, 1937, such a committee was constituted, and the United Grayever Relief Committee in New York received an official announcement of that, which appears elsewhere in this book.

The United Grayever Relief Committee also received a list of 217 people who received aid in small amounts. For obvious reasons we cannot publish this list. We have in our possession signatures from all the people who received assistance. It is sad to note that of the 500 Jewish families in Grayeve, 217 needed assistance. The Grayever Free Loan Society had in its treasury $300 received from our committee. Our United Relief Committee asked the Joint [American Jewish Joint Distribution Committee] to review the activity of the Free Loan Society and to report to us on the need for assistance. The Joint responded with a letter, published elsewhere in this book in English.

Among the institutions supported by money from Grayever *landslayt* in New York was "Tsentas." This Jewish–Polish organization devoted itself to helping Jewish orphans, homeless children, and children of the poorest parents in the town. We publish [p.287 in this book] a description of the Grayeve Tsentas which we received from I.M.Fromer, a young teacher in the Grayever Tarbut school. This document is especially important, because it shows the great efforts made by the Grayeve Jews, despite the impoverishment of the community, to help these unfortunate children.

[Page 254]

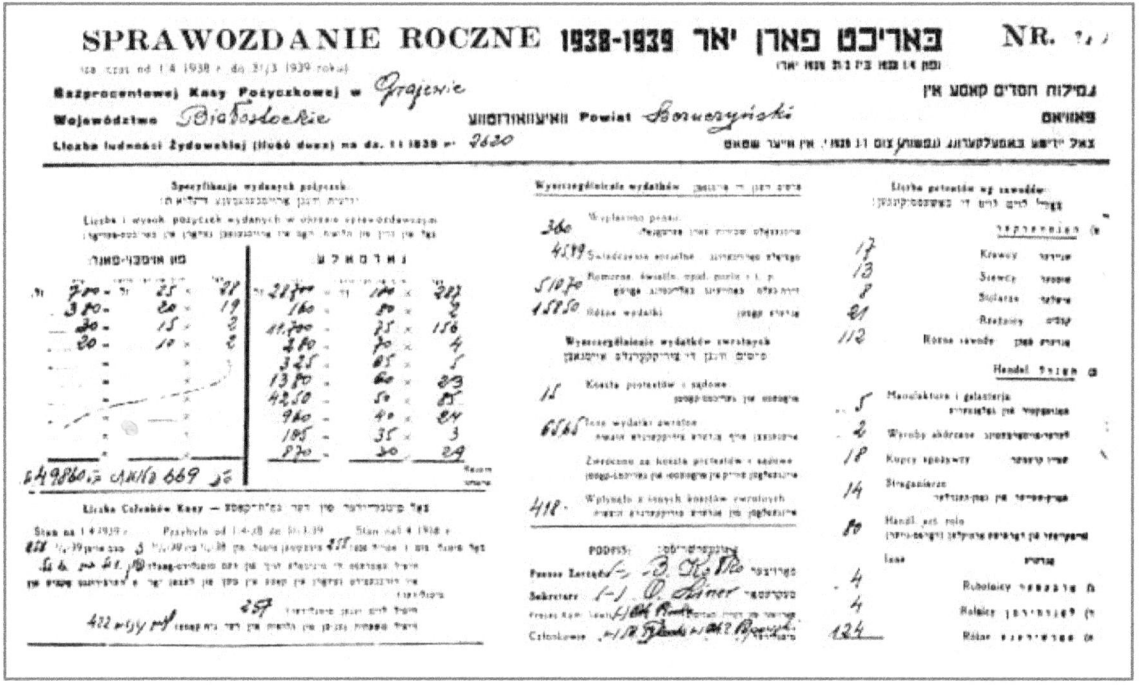

Report of the Gmiles Hesed

[Page 255]

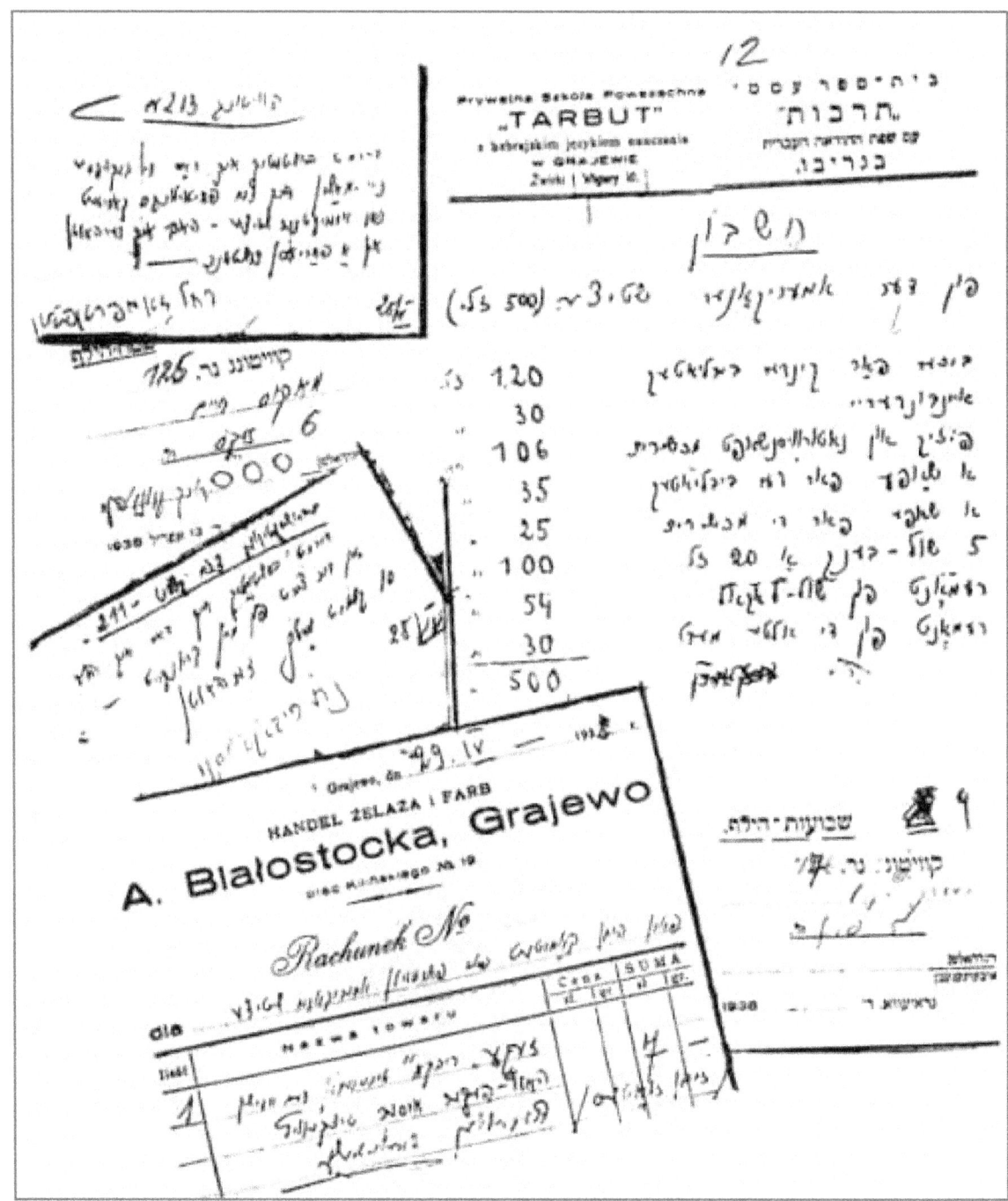

Various receipts for financial support

[Page 256]

In the summer of 1938, there arrived an appeal for help from the Grayever Jews who had been driven out of Germany. They were in the border town of Zbonshin and were living in the most horrible conditions. The letter from the Joint to the United Grayeve Relief Committee already mentioned this issue. The impoverished Jewish community in Grayeve could not help. But our Committee could not help much because of shortage of funds. The response of our *landslayt* to this appeal was weak, despite the fact that the danger of the Hitlerite storm was already looming over our native town.

***

The work of the Untied Grayever Relief Committee stopped entirely with the outbreak of World War Two. The situation of the Jews in Grayeve before the outbreak of the war was well known to the Relief Committee from detailed descriptions sent by the *kehile* and various institutions. Letters also came from individuals. We will mention only a detailed description by Dr. Nekhemie Kuravovski. As a doctor, he had the opportunity to observe, on a daily basis, the need and the desolation of the Grayeve Jews. The war oppressed and depressed the Jewish community both spiritually and materially. Also, the Jewish population diminished. From 5000 Jews in 1917, there remained in 1939 only 2500, and this number had to struggle to keep themselves and the community alive.

Absolutely no relief work was undertaken during the war years. There weren't even any preparations made to provide assistance to survivors after the war ended. The horrifying news of the Hitlerite inferno that reached us robbed us of the courage to do anything of this kind. Grayeve *landslayt* had begun to think that there would be no one left to help overseas. Not until 1946 did we begin to receive letters from Grayever refugees and we felt the impetus to revive the work of the relief committee.

[Page 257]

Several Grayever *landslayt* met in A. Saperstein's office and it was decided to reorganize the United Relief Committee. An Executive Committee was organized, consisting of the following: S. Saperstein, Sh.Fishbeyn, Helen Fenster, Volper, F.Sosnovits, A. Mlavski, Fannie Abramson, Mr. and Mrs. Max Kohn, Mr. and Mrs. A. Shiler, R. Miler, A.Sosna, V. Silverman, A. Klaynmen, and H. Blum. Later were added S. Kohn, A. Vitkovski, V. Margolis, Mr. and Mrs. Mishkof, Mrs. Don and Dr. G. Gorin.

In February, 1947, the Committee organized the first memorial meeting in memory of the Grayever Jews. A large number of *landslayt* attended. The mood was mournful. People wept quietly when the calamity of the Grayeve Jews was portrayed by the various speakers. The landslayt responded warmly. The United Relief Committee collected $1,800 at the memorial.

Encouraged by the warm response, the Committee set to work on further efforts. In November, 1947, they organized a theater event for Morris Schwartz's production of the play, "Shylock's Daughter," by the Hebrew writer Ari Ibn Zaav, a Grayever *landsman* in Israel. A thousand *landslayt* attended the performance. The playwright also attended. This event raised $1000 for the Relief Committee.

Subsequent fund raising events no longer had such a substantial response. At the memorial meeting in February, 1948, in the Grayeve shul on the East Side, fewer people attended and only $640 was collected. At the memorial in 1947 even fewer people attended and they collected only $195.

Under the leadership of A. Shiler, and with the help of a small number of active members, the Committee made various efforts to bring the Grayeve *landslayt* together at smaller events, but there was a regrettably weak response.

[Page 258]

In February, 1949, a large ball, the first since 1939, was held at the Hotel Diplomat. Many *landslayt* attended. The importance of the ball, as well as other gatherings organized by the Committee, must be appreciated from a communal perspective. These events maintained friendly connections among the *landslayt*, making it possible to carry out further, larger events. We must also gratefully mention the Grayever Relief Committee in Chicago, which donated $300 for the town's refugees.

***

We have until now described the work of the United Grayever Relief Committee in New York. Now we will provide a brief description of what was done with the money it collected.

In the last few years, the Committee has been in contact with about one hundred Grayeve refugees in various countries. Some of them wound up in the [displaced persons] camps in Germany, others in various cities and towns in Poland, Italy, France, Cyprus, and Israel. The Committee has a large number of letters from the refugees. They all contain the typical stories of shattered lives, great need, and illness, and they all contain an appeal for urgent assistance.

The aid sent by the Committee has consisted mostly of packages of food, clothing, and money. It is distributed, as far as possible, according to the needs and situation of the various refugees. In some cases, the Committee provided young people with a monthly subsidy to enable them to learn a trade and in that way to make a decent living. The trades which the young people learned ranged from shoe repair to the study of medicine. There were also shipment of tools needed to carry on a trade, and medicine, including insulin, penicillin, and even the newest medicine, streptomycin.

Finally, we want to note in this Yizkor Book, our continuing obligation to our *landslayt*, the survivors of the Holocaust, in Europe and in Israel. It is not yet too late to do our sacred duty. The United Grayever Relief Committee could do much more for the refugees. It could even organize a cooperative for the newly arrived immigrants in Israel, to build a community center named for Grayeve, etc., but our monetary resources are diminished. The Grayeve *landslayt* in America must now take a greater interest in the activity of the Committee.

[Page 259]

May this Yizkor Book, which is being published by the United Grayever Relief Committee, not only serve as an eternal monument in sacred memory of our martyrs, of our annihilated Jewish community in Grayeve, but also a reminder not to rest until all the refugees from Grayeve are settled and no longer require our assistance.

A group of schoolgirls from the Tarbut school

[Page 260]

A letter from the Grayeve Talmud Toyre

[Page 261]

Grayever Branch 35 of the Workmen's Circle
Hyman Blum
Translated by Miriam Leberstein

The Grayever Branch 35 of the Workmen's Circle was not originally founded as a branch of the Workmen's Circle. Rather, it was first founded as a *landsmanshaft* [organization of *landsleit*, i.e. people from the same hometown] organization, in 1907, by Grayever immigrants. By the time it joined the Workmen's Circle, it had already existed for 10 years as the Grayever Young Men's Benevolent Association – with over 1000 members, a fully paid-for cemetery and a significant amount of money in its treasury.

But let us begin at the beginning. It seems like only yesterday, that three greenhorn boys – Sam Krinski, Philip Buzman, and this writer – met up in Hester Park. The three of us, who had been in this country just a few months, felt the loneliness of 17-18 year old boys who had been cast out of their homes into a new world, in a city that sparkled and simmered and bustled, that had no time for anyone. We yearned for a homey environment, for friends with whom to enjoy an evening, after a hard day's work.

The landsmanshaftn associations were then in their first bloom. The "society" was for the newcomer greenhorns, both a club and a home. On the evenings that meetings were held, they would share their impressions of the new country and their sweet or bitter memories of the old home. There, people would help a greenhorn find a room or a job. At each meeting, new faces would appear, just off the boat. The slightly less green ones – those who had been here several months – would embrace the newcomers, receive greetings from the old home and demonstrate how seasoned they were by tossing off the entire dozen words of English that they had managed to learn, in a garbled and confused form.

[Page 262]

The first attempt to establish a Grayever landsmanshaft was made in 1903, when the Grayever Young Men's Association was founded. Although it had attained a membership of about 200, the association expired at the young age of about two years old, for reasons which still remain unknown to me. When we, 17-18 year old boys who had been in the country just a few months, appealed to the Grayever landsleit to join a new association, we were met with mockery and disdain from the "Americanized" landsleit who had already been here two or three years and had worked their way up, having bought a pair of yellow shoes, or moved far uptown, as far as 4th or 5th street, or even as far as Harlem. These "Americans" looked down on us greenhorns, who had gotten off the ship only yesterday.

The Greenhorns

On Friday, April 5, 1907, we held our founding meeting, at which the following were present: Hyman (Khaym Yosef) Blum, Bernard Goldshteyn and Harry Baykovksi, who were elected as the temporary committee; Shmuel Krinski; Rafoyl Kats; Yesokhar Vadovski; Sam Baykovski; Morris Lavender; Philip Buzman; Yosef Rozen; Meyer Berenzon; Nathan Lavender; Yosef Hadasa; Khaym Zimberg; Louis Bialystotski; Benny Bogush; and Meyer Vaks.

The founding meeting was continued on Friday, April 26, when the following were accepted as members and founders: Philip Morrison; Shimen Kolko; Morris Zimberg; Henekh Mishkovski; Sam Kremer; Yoyne Kohn; Harry Amsterdam; Benny Panish; Benny Vodovski; and Jake Baykovski.

Since the majority of the founders were fresh from the revolutionary movement in Russia, and many had recently been "boarders" in the prisons of Tsar Nicholas, it was only natural that one of the goals of the society was to support the revolutionary movement in the old home. We all, at that time, were living more in our old home than in our newly adopted country, America. And since we were then all quite young and unmarried, we decided not to accept as members anyone over 35. We considered a 35 year old man to be an old geezer. And it was also natural that we didn't want to admit any married men. We made an exception only for Jake Baykovski, at whose house we held the first meeting. At that time, he was already married, but we did him the favor of not forcing him to divorce his wife.

[Page 263]

Obviously, the ban against married men could not be sustained for long.

The handwritten first minutes of the Grayeve Young Men's Benevolent Association

1) Friday, April 5, 1907

Met Friday, April 5 with Kh. [Khaym] Blum as chairman. Heard a report from the provisional committee about the constitution project. Adopted the following provisions:

Name: Grayeve Young Men's Benevolent Association

Goals:

Sick benefits

Support for the unemployed (through loans)

Support for revolutionary efforts (Direct aid to strikers)

Decided not to open the fund until October 1. Made a voluntary collection for interim expenses, which brought in $2.65. Elected a provisional committee for the first month, with the following members:

Khaym Yosef Blum

Harry Baykovski

Benny Goldshteyn

"The first minutes of the Grayever Young Men's Benevolent Association."

[Page 264]

The founders themselves, one after the other, followed the example of their fathers and grandfathers. But the mere fact that at its founding the society was limited to the young, alienated large numbers of landsleit, who by then had been in the country several years and had during that time become settled young householders. They joined the more established societies of neighboring towns, such as *Shtutzin* [Szczuczyn], *Byalistok* [Białystok] *and Lomzhe* [Łomża]

At the time the Grayever society was founded, these other societies already had significant sums of money in their treasuries, paid out sick benefits, and had their own cemeteries. At their meetings, they conducted a ceremony, which was at that time very much the fashion in the landsmanshaft societies – using a password, knocking on the door a specified number of times, kneeling ceremoniously to the president and vice-president, and other such conduct – practices that seem laughable to us today, but which were then among the strongest foundation stones on which the societies rested.

The Depression Years

Soon after the founding of the Grayever society, came the difficult economic crisis of 1907-1909. The government did nothing at all to alleviate the situation. The only relief came from the breadlines, free kitchens, etc. Thus, we read in the minutes of the meeting of August 17, 1907, that when the question was raised regarding support for needy members, it turned out that the majority of the members were in need, and that with the grand sum of $79.49 in its treasury, the society could not afford to pay out any money for that purpose.

In September, 1908, the society was forced to strike 27 of its 60 members from its rolls. A portion of these paid the dues that they owed and were re-admitted; the others were out for good. And this was at a time when dues were $1.25 for three months.

Because of its founding at such an inauspicious time, the society was unable to find a firm footing for a long time. During the 42 years of its existence – 32 of them as a branch of the Workmen's Circle – it generally

[Page 265]

made little progress, and never attained a membership numbering in the hundreds. The largest number of members at any given time was, I believe, 150. It is a fact however, that the Grayever Branch 35 of the Workmen's Circle consists of over 80% landsleit, whereas many landsmanshaft societies are that only in name; their members are landsleit of other towns.

There are, regrettably, no great achievements, no important events to note in the life of the society. If I were to portray it with an image from Grayeve, I would say it was like the Kasherovke Brook, that placid stream where we would bathe as children, after we had painfully made our way over 2 *viorstn* [viorst is approximately 0.6 mile/1 kilometer] on the *Raigroder* [Rajgród] Road, where many times we were struck by blows or stones by the local Christian boys. Just as quietly, flowed most of the years in existence of the society. And perhaps precisely because of that quiet, that placidity, a number of the more active members ceased to be active, and turned their energy to other areas, where they found a wider scope for their abilities.

There are, however, a few moments in the life of the society, on which we should dwell, and these are as follow.

The Grayever Balls

The yearly balls held by the society were a gathering place for all Grayever landsleit, not just those from New York, but also from nearby cities and towns. Landsleit, young and old, would prepare for the celebration. They knew that on that evening, they would meet all their friends with whom they had spent their childhood years, and whom fate had tossed to the other side of the Atlantic Ocean. The newly arrived would come and meet the "American" landsleit who had come several years earlier, and would convey greetings from the old home. Around each of them, there would form a circle that would eagerly swallow every word, every greeting from their hometown. Young people, dressed to the nines, would dance to the music of a large orchestra, and more than one married couple has the Grayever ball to thank for bringing them together.

[Page 266]

Most memorable was the ball of 1910, in Hennington Hall, where images of Grayeve were projected by stereoscope on canvas. It appeared as if three Grayevers had swooped down into the hall, which held about 2000 people. Many people were turned away at the door, and those who had the good fortune to come inside didn't have room to move, let alone dance.

In time, the social life of the New York Jews changed. In the greenhorn years, everyone chose his friends solely from among landsleit. Later, the situation changed. New friends were made through family and business connections, with neighbors, coworkers in the shops, participation in social activities, etc. And because the landsman had ceased to play a role in the life of the Jewish immigrant, the balls of the landsmanshaft society ceased to play their former role. Fewer and fewer attended, until the event was given up entirely.

Joining the Workmen's Circle

Around 1916, the Grayever Young Men's Association already had a significant membership of around a hundred, and a fully paid for cemetery with a fence, that had cost several thousand dollars. Several members realized it was not advisable for a small society to remain autonomous, but that it must lean on a stronger, more powerful body that could help it weather a storm, should one come along. There were cases of similar organizations that fell apart when their membership got older and began to suffer more illness, more people died, and there was no new blood.

Those who supported joining the Workmen's Circle demonstrated that although the bills would be higher, the members would have a stronger foundation. They would have behind them tens of thousands of Workmen's Circle members; they wouldn't need to be afraid that when they got older the society would not be in a position to meets its obligations. They pointed to the institutions of the Workmen's Circle, such as a medical department and sanitariums, and to the organization's cultural activities as well.

[Page 267]

It took a long time for the idea to take hold among a large number of members, until finally, in 1917, the society joined the great Workmen's Circle family. Although the expectation by a number of members that entry into that organization would help the society grow was not realized, and the society did not quickly expand its membership, it nevertheless became more solid and secure. Only a few members refused to join the Workmen's Circle and remained local members. Almost all the rest became members of our branch.

Relief for War Victims in Grayeve

A fine chapter in the history of the Grayeve branch of the Workmen's Circle was written in the realm of aid to the war victims in our old home. It is true that the branch was not able to contribute a large sum from its treasury for that purpose, but through its initiative there was founded the Grayever Relief Committee, which, during the First World War and immediately after, collected and sent thousands of dollars to Grayeve. The reader will find a separate article on the committee's relief work elsewhere in this book.

In the period 1926-28, the Grayever Workmen's Circle branch, like many other branches, underwent a split based on political differences between right and left. After a series of heated meetings, it divided into two. Thirty-some members formed a separate branch of the Workmen's Circle – Branch #187- and ninety-some members remained in Branch #35.

Some time after the split, the branch established a very active women's club, at the initiative of the then financial secretary, Sam Krinski. The club carried out very fine social programs, and actively participated in relief work for Grayeve during the Second World War. The club has not been active in recent years.

[Page 268]

The Grayever Branch 56 of the Jewish People's Fraternal Order

Irving Kleynman

Translated by Miriam Leberstein

The Grayever Branch 56 of the Jewish People's Fraternal Order is one of the largest and most active branches in the Order. The branch was founded by a small group of Grayever *landsleit* [people from the same hometown] and now has more than 500 members. This is due to the unification of the landsleit from Grayevers with those from *Ostrova* [Ostrów Mazowiecka] and *Zaromb* [Zaręby Kościelne] – all of these towns being in the *Lomzhe* [Łomża] area.

Branch 56 distinguishes itself first of all by its fraternal activity, providing its members with health insurance, medical assistance, and other fraternal benefits. In addition, the organization carries out systematic programs in the social and cultural fields for its members, their families, and friends. The activities of the branch are in the spirit and best tradition of progressive Grayever youth in America.

The meetings of our branch, which take place every two weeks, are distinguished by their cultural and artistic programs. Lectures are presented by prominent speakers about social and cultural matters. There are also evenings of entertainment and artistic events, with the participation of various artists. At every meeting, various political and literary books are displayed for sale to members, and every possible effort is made to assist in the dissemination of Yiddish books.

[Page 269]

Branch 56 actively participated in all relief efforts to alleviate the poverty of the Grayeve Jews overseas. It contributed both through the Grayever Relief Committee, and through the Jewish People's Fraternal Order, and other relief organizations.

Our branch is especially remarkable for its yearly collections of money conducted by the Jewish People's Fraternal Order for the rehabilitation of Jews in Europe and Israel, as well as for the support of Jewish orphans' homes in Poland, France and Belgium. In the course of four postwar years, Branch 56 collected over $10,000 for these campaigns.

During the war against Hitler Germany, Branch 56 participated in various aid efforts for our own military forces and for those involved in the war effort. Our branch sold to its members and friends war bonds in the amount of over $150,000. We also, with our own efforts and funds, sent a gift for the heroic

Soviet fighters – an X-Ray Mobile Unit, which was donated to the Leningrad Hospital.

The aforementioned actions of Branch 56 demonstrate that, in addition to the fraternal aid and insurance which members receive, they also appreciate the importance of the organization's social and cultural work.

The achievements of Grayeve Branch 56 of the Order are the result of tireless effort by the active participants and the devoted leadership. To create such an organization, with over 500 members, and carry out its diverse activities, requires not just intelligence and responsibility, but sacrificial work and effort by the leadership. We must express recognition for the builders and leaders of Branch 56, most of all *Friends* [term of address in Jewish communal organizations]: I. Magidson, Binder, and others with whom this writer has had the honor and pleasure as well as responsibility of working with in this prolific fraternal, social and cultural people's organization.

[Page 270]

The Shtutziner and Grayever Shul in New York
H. B-M
Translated by Miriam Leberstein

On the Jewish East Side, at 242 Henry Street, near Montgomery Street, stands an unassuming building, which nevertheless stands out from its neighbors, which are tenement houses of various sizes. This synagogue building bears the inscription, "Congregation Anshe *Shtutzin* [Szczuczyn] and Anshe Grayeve – built in 1910." The building shows the signs of age and neglect, but there still remain traces of youth and beauty. One can see that not just money went into building it, but also much love and devotion.

The neighborhood is today still mainly Jewish, but practically none of those who built the shul still live there. Some have settled in Brooklyn, some in the Bronx, or in other new Jewish neighborhoods. But the majority of the first builders have already gone to their eternal rest.

Today Henry Street is old and neglected, but 40 years ago, it was one of the most aristocratic Jewish streets. A large number of Jewish doctors of the older immigrant generation, who now have their offices on Park Avenue or Central Park West, then had their offices on Henry Street, where they began their medical practices, and from which they moved after their patients had done so.

[Page 271]

The first Grayever congregation in New York was founded around 1890 and had its shul on Ludlow Street, occupying part of a floor of a building of sweatshops. The founder of the shul was Shloyme Litenberg, one of the first Grayeve immigrants, who was quickly successful and became a prominent cloak manufacturer. He had what one could call a "Grayever shop." As soon as a greenhorn tailor or aspiring tailor arrived in America from Grayeve, he was immediately brought to Litenberg's shop, where his greenness wore off, and he could decide what to do next. So, the Grayever congregation was formed in Litenberg's shop and Litenberg was for a long time its president.

[Page 272]

Also active were: Harris Rotboym and Aron Levental, who later also became very active in the Grayeve Relief Committee during the First World War (the first as treasurer, the second as vice-treasurer); Meyer Volf; Meytshe Denenmark; Gershon Zumerfeld; Max Zilbershteyn; Willy Grinshteyn; Leyzer-Hersh Berman; Leyzer and Yehude Mendelssohn; Elye Tobias; and others – there were about 40 members.

At the same time, the Shtutziner *landsleit* [people from the same hometown] also had a congregation, larger than the Grayever, with a membership of about 60. They had a shul on Forsythe Street, larger than the Grayever shul. In 1906, the two shuls merged. The Grayevers gave up their shul and united with the Shtutziners.

At first, it seemed that the marriage wasn't going to work. There was friction from the beginning. The Shtutziners felt that they were in charge. Their congregation was larger and richer. They had kept their home, their shul, and their prosperous members had the best permanent seats, got the most prestigious Torah portions to read at services, and held the most prominent offices, while the Grayevers, as "guests," had to make do with seats behind the *bime* [elevated platform in the synagogue at which the reading of the Torah takes place], with the less prestigious Torah portions, and with fewer and less important offices.

They reached the point of separating. The Grayevers wanted to break away, but the Shtutziners refused to return the money and property that the Grayevers had brought to the partnership. Both sides brought the case before a rabbinical court, consisting of three rabbis, who ruled in favor of the Shtutziners, but who appealed to both sides to make peace and coexist. The appeal was effective. Immediately after, elections were held for officers and both sides obtained appropriate representation in the administration.

[Page 273]

The peace was so well-cemented that a few years later, in 1910, they began to build the above-mentioned synagogue on Henry Street. When they began construction, the congregation had only $1800. At its completion, it cost over $36,000. The chief thanks are due to Mr. Nathan Hamer. Himself a successful builder, he gave all of his time, and found various ways and means to assure that the shul was finished.

The shul is not large, but is certainly one of the most beautiful on the East Side. In the first years of its existence, it was not only a sacred place in which to pray, but also a center for celebrations and other events. During the First World War, it was also a center for relief work.

The first president of the new shul was Moyshe Kronenberg, who held that office for two years; Max Zilbershteyn was vice-president. After that, Mr.

Harris Rotboym became president. For about 20 years in a row, the president was Yankl Burshteyn (son-in-law of Borekh-Mordkhe the bath attendant). He made it his job – and made it possible – to pay off the mortgage on the shul.

Almost all of the shul activists were workers – hard-working people who made it their goal in life to maintain a Grayever religious center in New York. Among them were: Isaac Kohn, Moyshe Goldshteyn, Avrom-Itsik Hamer, Yisroel Kleynman, Aron-Yankl Vaynberg, Itshke Rozen, Gershon Kohn, Max Zeligzon, Avrom Abot, Shmuel Brikman, Itsik Alpert, Mikhl Edelson, Alter Faynzilber, the brothers Green (one of whom, Yankl, was also president), Mates Gerson and his children, Moyshe Zilbershteyn, Max Rotbil and his son Benny.

For many years the shul also had an active Ladies Auxiliary, which helped very much with the relief work. Its main activists were Sore Goldshteyn (Sore Monzhes) and Fannie Zilberman.

The current officers of the shul are Moyshe Kohn, president; Sam Birnboym, vice-president; Annie Fayn, secretary; Max Rozentsvayg, treasurer; Yankl Burshteyn, administrator of the burial society. The new officers have recently bought a new cemetery for $3000 and paid over $6000 to renovate the shul.

[Page 274]

The Grayever Landsleit in Chicago
by A. Blushteyn □

(Former secretary and current president□ of the "Grayever Friendship Society")

Translated by Miriam Leberstein

When I arrived in Chicago in September, 1913, I found there an association of Grayever *landsleit* [people from the same hometown], to which a number of *Shtutzin* [Szczuczyn] landsleit also belonged. I immediately became a member.

At the beginning of the First World War, we began discussing raising funds to assist the victims of the war. A dispute broke out between the Grayever and the Shtutziner members over the question of where to send the money that was raised. Among the Grayevers there were two active members – Dovid

Levin, a brother of Bertshe, the *melamed* [elementary school teacher], who today lives in Los Angeles; and Frank Sevitsh, the son of the *Simner* [Simnas, Lithuana] melamed, who lives today in New York. The dispute got to the point that the Shtutziner landsleit left the association and founded a separate organization. After they left, the Grayever association died out.

In 1920, a new Grayever *landsmanshaft* [organization of landsleit; Jewish benefit society] was formed, which lasted no more than a year and a half. At the end of 1925, several Grayever landsleit met at the funeral of a young man from Grayeve, Yudl Dirmish the son of our *landsfrau*, [woman from one's hometown], Khaye-Perl Dirmish, the daughter of Zelig Smal the tailor and a sister of the Blankshteyns, a prominent family in Chicago. This encounter contributed much to the founding of the Grayever landsmanshaft organization in Chicago, which exists to the present day.

[Page 275]

"The Grayever Friendship Society" was founded on January 17, 1926 at a meeting at the Workmen's Circle Lyceum, which a large number of landsleit attended: Morris Burgler was elected president and A. Blushteyn, secretary. The following were among the first founders and executive board members: Dovid Sigel, Dzh.Sklarof, Benny Kravets, Max Sigel, Herald Grinfeld, Nathan Grosberg and their wives; Esther Sigel; the Blankshteyn family; the Silvershteyn family; the Staynbergs; the Gotlib family; the Nathan family; the Stayn family; the Fishbeyns; Jake Skaler, may he rest in peace; and Beyle-Brayne, may she rest in peace.

January 21, 1950 marked the 24th anniversary of the founding of the Grayever Society in Chicago. During that time, our landsmanshaft participated in various relief efforts on behalf of the needy in our hometown, as well as the needy Grayever landsleit in Chicago. During World War II, when it was impossible to send aid to Grayeve and also after the war, when we learned of our tragedy, we did all we could to help the Jewish institutions that devoted themselves to rescuing the surviving remnants of the Jewish people.

We must, however, express our disappointment that we were unable to organize all of the Grayeve landsleit in Chicago and to interest them in our activity. We have still not given up hope that we may yet accomplish this.

We send greetings to our Grayever landsleit in New York and all the leaders and members of the Relief Committee, on the publication of the Grayever Yizkor Book, an eternal flame in holy memory of the holy martyrs, our own loved ones from the old home. We wish you, esteemed landsleit, much happiness. Continue with your humanitarian activities, may you become even stronger, so that you may carry out your noble work of helping to assure the lives of our surviving landsleit and of the Jewish people in the land of Israel. *Am Yisroel Khay* [Am Yisrael Chai]--May the Jewish people live and outlive all their enemies!

[Page 276]

Letters and Documents from Grayeve
From the Eve of the Second World War and After the Destruction of Our Jewish Grayeve by Grayever People's Committee to the Relief Committee of the Grayever *Landslayt* in New York

Translated by Miriam Leberstein

A Letter From the Grayever People's Committee to the Relief Committee of the Grayever *Landslayt* in New York

Friends and Acquaintances!

Afflicted by hunger, need, and difficult conditions, as a result of persecution and economic extermination, we learn that you have offered aid for the impoverished Jewish population of your hometown, Grayeve.

We welcome your initiative and fraternal efforts in carrying out relief activities through all of the organizations of the Grayeve *landslayt* [people from the same hometown] in New York and surrounding areas. We—the representatives of all of the social strata of our town, who have constituted ourselves as a people's committee –consider it our moral obligation expeditiously to complete the work that you have begun.

The leadership of the Grayever *kehile* [organized Jewish community] is unfortunately not capable of doing this. Its makeup is such, that it is not able to fulfill its obligations in relation to the poor and their needs. They owe their fortuitous election only to the oppressed mood that results from our difficult living conditions. The masses regard the *kehile* leadership with mistrust.

Imbued with the necessary understanding of the social action required, and of the concerns of for our brothers and sisters overseas, we express our willingness to undertake full responsibility here, for the expeditious performance of your work until its completion.

[Page 277]

Without cutting off urgent assistance where it is absolutely necessary --no matter what happens, winter is drawing near-- the central concern must be to assure that the money is utilized not for the dole, but rather for constructive and productive purposes. Thus, the guiding principle and fundamental basis for the allocation of monies must be to rebuild the ruined workshops of the artisans and shopkeepers, thereby providing them with the means to earn their daily bread. There may also arise the need to provide for the town's cultural sphere, in which there are many needs, but that will depend on the extent and regularity of your aid.

Mindful of the goal and manner in which we expect to carry out the distribution of your aid, and not ignoring your wishes and your awaited instructions, we consider we have fulfilled our obligation to the needy workers, shopkeepers, and the indigent. We await your confidence in us.

Our temporary mailing address: M. Stryjew, Grajewo, w. Pildsudskiego 72 [in Polish]

Grayeve, 26 November, 1937

The Constituent People's Committee of all Social Strata of the Jewish Population in Grayeve:

Dr. Eli Vaser –longtime member of the town administration in Grayeve

Motl Striev –member of the town council, representative of the working class

Raye Laynberg –member of the organization for the protection of orphans and children of the poor, "Tsentas"

Hershl Kohn – representative of the *Gmiles Hesed* [Free Loan Society]

Osher Rekhtman –representative of the Cooperative Bank

[Page 278]

Hinde Leyzerzon – representative of *Lines Hatsedek* [organization providing shelter for the indigent]

A. Barshtsvetski –representative of the working class

A.Kh.Zaydenberg –representative of the working class

Leyzer Grinshpan –representative of the artisans

Yehoyshue Leyb Kanafke –representative of the artisans

Report

Constituent Committee of all Social Strata of the Jewish Population in Grayeve

To the United Grayeve Relief Committee in New York, Report, which covers the distribution of the second payment of $500 (five hundred dollars) received in the month of April, 1938, for aid to individuals, as well as the payment of $200 (two hundred dollars) received in the month of June, for aid to organizations.

Esteemed friends!

We hereby acknowledge, according to the enclosed receipts, the receipt of $500 from you, which were utilized as follows:

	Polish Gilden	Dollar equivalent
For Passover Aid	1543	295
For Shvuot Aid	1060	203
Remainder (for postage and printing)	12	2

The method of distribution was according to the system previously used: for individuals in need, small sums distributed over a wider range of social strata. As a result, 214 people benefited from the Passover program, and 195 from the Shvuot program. We permitted ourselves, however, to make certain exceptions and responded positively to the appeals of some artisans for assistance in repairing their tools (sewing machines and the like); of market sellers for aid in the vegetable season; and we had also to consider the need for larger sums for operations for those with serious illnesses.

[Page 279]

Your recent instruction that the $200 received for distribution at Passover should be distributed to organizations, was unfortunately received too late. We had already made the distribution a few days before we received your revised instruction in response to our question about this matter.

At the same time, we confirm the receipt of the most recent payment of $200, which was distributed in accordance with your direction, to the following Grayeve organizations:

The administration of the *kehila*, for fencing and repair of the fence around the cemetery – 400 gilden.

The *lines hatsedek* [organization providing shelter for the indigent], for purchase of equipment and urgent assistance –300 gilden.

The artisans' association, for aid to poor artisans to obtain certification as apprentices and masters – 165 gilden.

To "Tsentas," aid to run a summer camp for the poorest sick and frail children of school age – 120 gilden.

The money has been given to the four above-mentioned institutions, as confirmed by the enclosed receipts, with the requisite signatures and seals of the institutions.

On the other hand, because the sums provided them were too small, the following institutions did not provide receipts for the money they received:

The *gmiles-khesed* [free loan society] of Benjamin Kolko, who received 30 gilden.

The *gmiles khesed* fund of the shopkeepers association –30 gilden.

There thus remains 60 gilden, which await your further instructions. At the same time, we consider it necessary to let you know the reasons and beliefs that were the basis for the distribution committee's determination of the amounts given to the organizations above.

Why 400 gilden to the *kehile*? After an investigation by a member of our committee, along with representatives of the *kehile* administration, into the condition of the fences around the cemetery, and of the costs of materials and labor required, we determined that the sum of 400 gilden is almost sufficient to (a) erect a fence of cement blocks around the part of the cemetery that is currently unfenced (the part that borders on the new market-place (Torgavika) as well as (b) repair and complete, in stone, the destroyed portions of the fence on the other three sides of the cemetery.

[Page 280]

In giving the designated amount to the *kehile* administration, the committee considered it necessary to alert them that the 400 zlotys must be used exclusively for putting the cemetery fence in order, expressing our wish that, so far as possible, Jewish workers should be employed and that after completion of the work, an accounting of the costs should be provide to the United Grayever Relief Committee. The *kehile* should soon begin the work.

Why 300 gilden to the *lines hatsadek*? Taking into account that one should not purchase equipment and supplies in too large amounts at one time, since certain materials, e.g., rubber, can deteriorate and tin items can become covered with rust, the committee supports the position of the representatives of the *lines hatstadek* and concludes that it is appropriate to allocate no more than 150 gilden for the most needed supplies for the time being, and the remaining 150 gilden should be used for urgent assistance for cases of illness, which the *lines hastadek* is often unable to properly address with its own resources. In giving the money to the leadership, we informed them how we wish it to be allocated.

Why 165 gilden to the artisans union? The end of 1938 marks the deadline for qualifying examinations for certification as master and apprentice, without which one loses the right to work in 1939. Given the poverty that reigns among the artisan masses and the impossibility under these circumstances of their being able to acquire these certifications, the committee finds

[Page 281]

it necessary to allocate the above sum, to be used exclusively to help the poorest artisans and apprentices obtain the necessary means to assure their livelihood.

Why 120 gilden to the "Tsentas" Society? Recognizing the importance of providing a summer camp for orphans and abandoned children, where in July and August, 60 of the poorest children in our town receive better nourishment, breathe fresh air, and enjoy singing and playing during vacation time, the committee determines it necessary to aid this needy institution with the above sum, which represents the cost of ten days worth of food.

Why only 30 gilden to the two *gmiles khesed* funds? Without dismissing the social utility and value of both of these institutions, the committee does not consider it urgent to support them for the time being, since, given the limited funds, it is impossible to meet the needs of every organization. The committee also feels that although the *gmiles khesed* of Binyomen Kolko and the *gmiles khesed* fund of the artisans union should wait until further aid is received, for the sake of harmonious cooperation and mutual appreciation, they should at this time, share the remainder of the $200 payment, i.e. 60 gilden each.

This completes the financial report, up to the present, leaving 60 gilden in our possession. After disbursing these, as per your further instructions, we will transmit a financial guarantee.

As for your questions regarding [the making of] a moving picture of Grayeve, recent photos, as well as articles for the journal which you plan to publish, we advise as follows:

After inquiry of the appropriate moving picture companies and the local authorities, it would not be possible to make a film. Three hundred meters of film costs about 700 gilden. Moreover, according to new regulations governing traffic across the border, it is possible that we couldn't obtain the necessary permission from the government.

Regarding recent photographs, we will send these at the beginning of October, along with articles about socio-economic, cultural, and communal conditions in Grayeve.

[Page 282]

To accomplish this, our current committee has called together a conference of all of our skilled writers, and ten of them have committed themselves to writing [an article] by September 15.

In the hope that you will forgive us for the delay in submitting this report, we sign ourselves, with regards:

The Constituent Committee of All Social Strata of the Jewish Population in Grayeve

**Grayeve, 20 August, 1935,
Secretary, Motl Striev**

Enclosed, please find:

List #1 of the recipients of Passover relief

List #2 of the recipients of Shvuot relief

List #3 of distributions to organizations

214 receipts signed by the recipients of Passover relief

195 receipts signed by recipients of Shvuot relief

4 receipts with signatures and seals, of organizations which received aid

Secretary, Motl Striev

An Appeal for Aid
From the Administration of the Jewish *Kehile* in Grayeve to the United Grayeve Relief Committee in New York

In our previous letters, we have several times informed you that the local government is requiring us to undertake a thorough renovation of our communal buildings and institutions, such as the cemetery, baths, slaughter house, *bemedreshim* [prayer houses, synagogues], *talmed toyre*, [religious school for poor children] etc. We asked not to be required to do anything until the spring, and our request was granted. Now, however, winter is over and spring is here. Today we were visited by a committee, including the *staroste* [local official] and the mayor, and they demanded that we complete the required work within two weeks. If not, all the institutions and establishments will be closed. The renovation will cost 5000 zlotys, and the *kehile* treasury is empty—it contains not one cent. We haven't paid our officials (whose salaries amount to pennies) for several months, not to mention providing support for such institutions as the *talmed toyre*, *lines hatsedek*, and orphan care. It's been a long time since they have received anything from us. The situation in the town is truly catastrophic. The poverty is indescribable. We are unable to do anything. Our only hope is to turn to you, since, according to what we have learned, you appreciate the importance of this matter, and look upon it favorably.

[Page 283]

We appeal to you in these straitened and difficult times, asking you to turn your good will and intentions into action soon and to send us aid by wire, so that our institutions, like the cemetery, baths, etc., will not be shut down. There is not a shred of doubt that if we don't complete the renovations, the authorities will keep their word and close them. We trust in your sincere interest in this matter, and await your immediate and fraternal assistance, and thank you in advance.

Respectfully,

(Seal): Office of the Kehile of Grayeve

Chairman: Nekhemie Piurko

Yankev Mlinarski

M. Takakh

Efroyim Vadovski

Shmuel Burovski

Secretary, Y. Papovski

A Letter from the Grayever Yeshiva Bet Yoysef
With God's help, 19th day of the month of Sivan, year 5699 [civil date: June 6, 1939]

To the highly esteemed, renowned Herr Mister Y. Blum, N.Y., President of the Grayever *landslayt*, and of the Printers' Union in New York

For almost 10 years, there has been a yeshiva in Grayeve, with over 50 students who are educated on a high intellectual level. The majority are students who have finished the town's *talmed toyre* and want to continue further with their studies; they are accepted into the yeshiva and, because of their impoverished situation, are provided with food and drink.

[Page 284]

Obviously, this is very costly, and in the current economic crisis the deficit is catastrophic, without any means to sustain our holy institution. A year ago, when your letter arrived, asking that you be informed of the institutions in Grayeve requiring help, the town committee did not want to include the yeshiva or the *talmed toyre* because they were religious institutions. The several religious representatives protested in vain, that our brothers in America contribute to religious institutions as well. But because the majority opposed them, the two religious institutions were rejected. This year, thanks to your intervention, the *talmed toyre* did receive an appropriate sum. Thus, the only large institution of higher Torah learning, the yeshiva, remains disgraced and economically oppressed, alone among all the other institutions, without exception, in our town. This is so, even though the students are all poor and oppressed, and are fully supported by the yeshiva. And that it is thanks to the yeshiva that the *talmed toyre* exists, because the children there see a future for themselves after completing *talmed toyre*.

A group of students from Yeshiva "Bet Yoysef."

[Page 285]

We therefore turn to you once again to request, with God's help, that you take into consideration our holy yeshiva and treat it the same as the other institutions, and also subsidize support for the yeshiva to enable it to provide the students with at least some meager subsistence. We are certain you will fulfill our request, because the wrong that was done us was not your fault, because you did not know about it.

We wish you all good things, and success in your endeavors, and may it be given to you soon to see the consolation of Israel and the gathering of Israel on the mountains of Zion and in Jerusalem, and all that serves the glory of the Torah, and its scholars and supporters. The undersigned, the aforementioned heads of the upper and lower schools of the Yeshiva Hakatan [yeshiva for younger and post bar mitzvah aged students] of Grayeve.

The Yeshiva HaKatan, "Bet Yoysef", Grayeve☐Trustee Avrom Bekorekh☐Trustee Alter Tsukert☐Trustee Nokhem Zaytski, Shoykhet [ritual slaughterer]☐Trustee Yankev Vadovoski☐Trustee Moyse Menakhem Mishkovski, Shoykhet and Examiner [of meat for kashrut]☐Trustee Shmuel Lifshits☐Trustee Sholem Zaydenberg

An Appeal☐From the Grayever "Tsentas"☐

Grayeve, 25 August, 1938

To the Grayever *landslayt*, our brothers in America:

The administration of Tsentas, the institution for the care of orphans and abandoned children in Grayeve, turns to you with the following call for help.

For the past three years, our town has run a day-boarding home for orphans and abandoned children. [Note: The children spend the day at the day facility, eating all their meals there, but they sleep elsewhere. The term "orphan" encompasses children who have lost only one parent, so an orphan may have a remaining parent at home.] At the current time, it provides 32 boys and girls with food, clothing, school supplies and medical care. In addition, during the two-month school vacation, we run a camp for 120 of the poorest children, who recuperate both spiritually and physically, forgetting for at least a short time the poverty and gloom in their homes.

[Page 286]

The main mission of our institution is to turn the children who attend as day boarders into future productive, self-sufficient people. That means, that after finishing school, they will learn a trade and in that way, break away from their environment, which would turn them into permanent beggars.

In the beginning, we were able to maintain the day-boarding home with our own resources, but because of growing need and the difficult, even catastrophic, economic situation of Jews in Poland, and in our town in particular, it has become much more difficult to run this very important institution. For the last year, we have been running with a large deficit. At present, the situation is such, that if we don't receive material aid from our brothers overseas, we will be forced to close the warm home for these unfortunate, lonely children.

We beg and appeal to you, to help us make of these children of the poor masses into productive citizens, because only with your help will we be able to avoid sending them back to the quagmire from which we extracted them three years ago. We entreat you to send aid quickly, because Autumn is approaching and the children don't have shoes or warm clothing.

We hope our appeal will receive from you the response it deserves, and that in recognizing the importance of our institution, you will immediately undertake a fund raising campaign on our behalf. Your help is urgently needed.

At this time, we confirm the receipt of 120 zlotys, for which we express our warmest thanks on behalf of 32 children.

Respectfully:

President, N.Vasser Secretrary, Epshteyn

N.B. Please send the money in the name of our president: WMP. N.WASSER, Grajewo, Pilsudskiego 19.

[Page 287]

A Visit to "Tsentas"

I.M. Fromer

In the street a strong wind was blowing, and people were running as if they were being chased by it. I quickly ran through several small lanes and entered the white "Tsentas" building. A kitchen and three rooms. Clean, and most important, warm. A pleasant warmth struck my face and 30 pairs of childish eyes gazed at me curiously. I entered the first room, greeted the children's woman teacher, took off my coat, and sat down at a table just as they did. I wanted to make myself at home here, just as the children do.

At three long tables sat 30 children – 15 boys and 15 girls – from 6-14 years old, preparing their lessons for the next day. I approached my old acquaintances (students in our Tarbut school) and looked at their assignments. Here they feel somewhat freer than they do at school. There they are quieter, stick together, sit together and never fight. They are good students and do their work easily. I began a conversation, into which I tried also to draw in other children, especially the little ones. They boldly answer all of my questions, and watch to see what kind of impression they're making on me. They say: We feel very good here and we are content. We arrive at 7 in the morning to eat breakfast, and then go to school. At 2 P.M., we come back for lunch and we stay here until 7 P.M., when we eat supper and then go home to sleep. We don't even want to leave here, because at home it's cold, dark and gloomy. Here we have our friends; here it's warm and bright. After lunch we prepare our lessons and we play all kinds of games.

Against the wall, there's a cupboard, holding warm clothing. Today they're giving out clean, washed and ironed winter underwear. Some children receive shoes, galoshes, and even winter coats with fur collars. All are wearing heavy winter hats with earlaps to cover their ears. Chaim takes out small, colored Chanukah candles and he makes the blessing over the candles. All the children sing out "omeyn" [amen] in response.

[Page 288]

They want to sing and recite something for the teacher (me!) to hear. Please do! Hershl recites a poem by Zalmen Reyzn. He speaks well, loud and brave, and everyone claps bravo! Sorele sings a Yiddish folksong. The melody flows through the room, the lovely childish voice swaying rhythmically. The others join in the cheerful refrain and the whole room is singing. The portraits and pictures on the walls are singing, the big health posters on the wall are singing, the books and the notebooks are singing, and over it all you can hear Sorele's sweet voice. Then more songs and recitations, in Yiddish, Hebrew, Polish, and finally a rousing march, the anthem of the summer camp, full of light, sun, air, and water.

"During the summer camp, our family grows larger," says Moyshe. "More than 100 children participate. There it's lively, cheerful, pleasant. But when camp ends, and a portion of the children leave, they envy us, because we stay for the winter. They promise that they'll expand the day-boarding home but…." I go into the next room, and ask a member of the administration why they don't fulfill that promise.

"You have to understand that it's very hard for us to support even these 30 children. The town covers barely 25% of the budget. The central office of

Tsentas provides 50%, and we borrow the rest, covering our debts with promissory notes that are always being renewed.

But we don't have the heart to reduce the number of children.

"How long has the day-boarding home existed?"

"Three years. Among the children there were several who were psychologically delayed. We had to pull them out from under their beds; they were lying there like feral cats. That little girl over there couldn't even speak, even though she was five years old. Today she's in second grade, and she reads and writes and even sings"

"What happens to the children after they leave the home?"

"We try to enroll them in a trade school, but it's very difficult for us, because that costs a lot. There's no trade school here in Grayeve, so we have to send them to Bialystok."

"Are there more candidates who want to enter the home?"

"They're beating down the doors. Grayeve has recently become very impoverished. The number of poor children is growing and growing and we remain helpless. If we could accommodate even another 20 children...." sighs the woman from administration.

[Page 289]

I interrupt this sad conversation and return to the children. They're eating heartily and their faces are happy, full of holiday cheer. I approach the blackboard and read the notice: "What we're having today for lunch: soup, *kashe* [buckwheat groats] with meat...." It's truly amazing that with what meat costs these days, they don't eliminate it, but try to serve it to the children at least several times a week. I've heard in town that the administration puts in great effort and energy, and I'd like, on behalf of the children, to thank them, and entreat them, on behalf of the children who await admission, to let them join.

The meal is over. A few more songs. And slowly and reluctantly the children get up and get dressed. In the kitchen are waiting several fathers or mothers who have come to take home the little ones. Poor workers who have toiled all day and are exhausted. Now they stand and gaze as if entranced at the small faces of their clean, well fed children. We all leave together.

The snow squeaks under our feet. The children walk quickly, disperse among other small lanes, and I am left with only the sad melody of Sorele's folk song, and it plays and plays in my cold ears.

The administration of the I.L.Perets Library
From right to left, seated: Yehude Rozenboym, Rivke Kayman, Khone Bikovski
Standing: Avrom Nevadovski, Avrom Vayngrov, Perl Kaminski

[Page 290]

From American Joint Distribution Committee, Warsaw

Warsaw, October 21st, 1938

American Joint Distribution Committee, Paris.

Dear Sirs:

"The town of Grayewo numbers about 9,000 inhabitants, in this 2,500 Jews (i.e. about 500 families). Jews are mostly engaged in small trade and crafts.

The local G. Ch. Kassa was established in 1927 and has actually 252 members. The Board consists of the following 9 persons:

1. B. Kolko, chairman. 2. H. Kohn, secretary. 3. A. Abedinski. 4. S. Gurowski. 5. M. Wapinski. 6. B. Zaberman. 7. I. Tenenbaum. 8. I. Zakrzewski. 9. A. Liner.

The Auditing Committee consists of:

1. Tikocki. 2. N. Piurko. 3. I. Popowski.

As regards the actual status of the Kassa, it can be inferred from its balance-sheet on April 1st. c.y.:

The number of loans granted during the period under review was 640. On the whole, the Kassa shows an intensive activity. This can also be seen from the following statement of returns:

Working capital	Zlotys: 18.581,06
Own capital	7.335,56
Credits from J.D.C.	10.125,50
Loans granted during 1 year	46.425,00
Loans repaid during 1 year	45.498.00
Local income during 1 year	1.223,95
Admin.expenses during 1 year	1.002,01

n 1936 there were 600 loans granted tot: 49.417 zl☐In 1937 there were 699 loans granted tot: 51.077 zl☐The Kassa distributes credit to about 300 customers.☐The number of members of the Kassa is 57 customers.

[Page 293]

Fifth Part:

Grayeve Writers and Scholars

Grayeve Jews in Eretz-Yisroel
By Kh. Antshkovski[1]

Translated by Yael Chaver, Ph.D

Edited by Tina Lunson

In eternal memory of my mother Reyzl, nee Yanushevski, who died young in Grayeve, 12 Oder[2] II [March 16] 1927; and the *unknown* [emphasis in the original] graves of my father Abraham, my sisters Rivke Gortshitski and Sheyne, and my brother Levi, of blessed memory.

Near a border, near a highway, the town is small and the "wide world" lies so close. Only two or three kilometers and you are in a foreign country. Enough walking through the Bogushe woods, or swimming in the Nierotsh River. A wide world is opening, enticing and calling… The Jew of Grayeve is worldlier, more enterprising than those of other towns. They traveled the world: smugglers, tar Jews, who used to travel throughout Germany; goose merchants, who would drive the geese from deep in Russia to *Kenigsberg* [Kaliningrad]; horse traders, and others.

In this small border town, new cultural and social trends resounded loudly. Grayeve was where escapees from Czarist prisons – revolutionaries – crossed the border illegally.

[Page 294]

Forbidden literature from abroad, written on cigarette paper, would pass through here. Thirty-odd kilometers from Grayeve, in *Lik* [Ełk], David Gordon's Hebrew weekly "*Hamagid*" [The Preacher] was published. The renowned grammarian and playwright Avrom Mordkhe Piurka lived and taught in

Grayeve. He wrote and published the first Hebrew children's magazine, "Gan-Sha'ashuim;" and the first Hebrew magazine for young people, "Livnei Ha-Ne'urim." He strongly influenced the young people of Grayeve in favor of the *Khibat Tsion* [commitment to Zion] movement. Next to packed, darkened houses of study [bote-medroshim] – darkened, to avoid being noticed by an evil eye! – stood preachers describing the longed-for land that is waiting to be redeemed. Grayeve sent a delegate to the First Zionist Congress:[3] Khayim-Yitzkhok Ravidovitsh, who went to Erets Yisroel after the First World War. There, he devoted himself, body and soul, to rebuilding the land. He became a member and builder of moshav Merhaviya. (One of his sons was a founder of the new settlement of Be'er Tuvia.)

By the early years of the twentieth century, Grayeve had a strong Zionist organization, mainly *Poalei Tsion* [Movement of Marxist Zionist Jewish workers]. The first Grayever who went to Erets Yisroel not to lament the ruins, but to start a new life was Yehuda-Asher Antshkovski's son, Yisroel-Kalmen. Driven by the dream of redemption, he left his wife soon after their wedding and went away. He worked as a field-worker and a carpenter. For a while he taught crafts at the Herzliya High School, and was a founder and writer for the first Hebrew trade magazine, "*Hanagar*" [the carpenter]. He was one of the founders of Kfar-Saba, where he lives and works to this day. This was the period when Bleiberg's daughters also left, and settled in Rehovot, as well as the son of Karmi, the *Melamed* [elementary school teacher], who is now a renowned scholar in the fields of zoology, botany and biology; and teacher, author, founder and leader of the "Independent Biology Laboratories." Teperovitsh, a construction entrepreneur. Menashe Furman, who later became one of the active developers of Kupat Cholim [health care organization established by the general labor union] and organized its pharmacies, was himself a well-known pharmacist. A few more Grayever families left, but the numbers were small.

The First World War upset and ruined the economic conditions of the Jews of Grayeve. The large hinterland of Russia was now gone. The borders were closed. Young people managed to get out by various routes and went to Erets Yisroel.

[Page 295]

Yosef Karnetsky (the son of the *mashgiakh* [one who supervises the kashrut status of a kosher establishment]), known today as Yosef Karni, went through Lithuania. He held a senior position in the "*Va'ad Leumi*" [national council], the leadership body of the Jewish community in Palestine.

Leyb [Leo] Goldshteyn [who later Hebraized his name to Ari Ibn-Zahav] went through Germany. As its first secretary, he helped organize the first Hebrew University in the world. He became renowned as an author in various areas. One of his numerous literary works was an artistic, loving reflection of pre-war life in Grayeve. The Grayeve colony in Erets Yisroel slowly grew larger.

In the new Polish state established after the war, the Zionist organization in Grayeve developed, encouraged by the Balfour declaration.[4] The youth organizations "Hechalutz" and "Hashomer Hatzair" came into being, as parts of the Jewish national youth movement in Poland and elsewhere. Later, the youth organization "*Frayhayt*" [freedom] was organized by the right wing of the Poalei Tsion party. All this influenced the life-direction of Grayeve's young people. "Hechalutz" sent its members to agricultural training camps (at Abiedzynski's, in the village of Popowo) to prepare themselves for life in Erets Yisroel. *Aliyah* [immigration to Erets Yisroel] from Grayeve increased.

With the so-called Fourth Aliyah wave (1925-1927) [usually dated 1924-1928], when information started arriving about the reviving Erets Yisroel and the developing city of Tel-Aviv, entire families starting going there from Grayeve. For instance, Radom, Abramsky, Bukovsky, Yehuda-Asher Antshkovski and his son-in-law, Yitzchok-Moyshe Brustin, who became famous in Petach-Tikva as the "Grayever Rabbi," and many others. They were all distinguished by their enthusiasm, entrepreneurial spirit, and devotion, contributing to rebuilding the Jewish homeland.

Radom built an ice factory. Raphael Abramsky was a large-scale contractor; he built houses, summer camps, airfields etc.

It is worth mentioning the following early pioneers from Grayeve: Aryeh (Leybshtok) Elkon, who was a co-founder of Ein Harod [Kibbutz in Jezreel Valley]. He fell as a heroic freedom fighter on the fields of Huesca [Spain], during the Spanish Civil War in 1937.

Families sent their children to the Erets Yisroel, to prepare the ground for the rest of the family. In the late 1920s, the economic conditions of Polish Jews, especially in a small town such as Grayeve, became worse.

[Page 296]

Polish craftsmen and shopkeepers were sent to Grayeve to push out the Jews. They were quietly helped by the authorities, who gave them loans and bonuses, and set high taxes on the Jews, and the like. The small Jewish stores at the Grayeve market were soon vacant. Young people sought a way out of their hopeless, small-town lives.

The Zionist organizations of all stripes intensified and widened their activities. Pioneering activity increased. Young people from Grayeve went to the training camps to prepare themselves for the great task of rebuilding Erets Yisroel. But the gates of the longed-for land were locked. Beginning in 1932-1933 and especially in 1934-1936, mass immigration of Grayeve youth began. Hope for a new life was great. The will to realize the dream of generations was strong. The old homeland called, and the young people of Grayeve, just like the young people of all Polish cities and towns, strove to get to Erets Yisroel. They went by any possible and impossible ways, with and without immigration certificates [issued by the British Mandate authorities], legally and illegally, as students or tourists, and the like. Young people and entire families from Grayeve scattered throughout Erets Yisroel.

You can meet them at the plows in the fields of the Valley of Jezreel and in Galilee, on the construction scaffolds in Tel-Aviv or Haifa. They are in villages and cities, among the founders of new settlements and kibbutzim in the Negev or Galilee and in the first rows, front lines of the fighting forces of the Haganah.

There is quite a large Grayeve "colony" in Haifa. They meet with other Grayevers during the holidays. They are joined by Grayevers from other towns and kibbutzim at the home of Elimelech Pomerantz, the famous Zionist activist and teacher, a founder of the "*Tarbut*" [secular Hebrew Zionist] school. They have a holiday feast and reminisce about the town of Grayeve and its life.

Each Grayever in Israel contributed, according to his means and abilities, to the rebuilding of the land. Great businessmen (Elkan, Reichelson, Levine and others), agricultural workers, teachers, founders and builders of kibbutzim, literary people, scientists, doctors (Pinsky, Baravitsh and others), engineers (Furman, Eisenstadt and others) and so on. Grayevers are found in the top tier of cultural and social life. Suffice it to mention Dr. Emmanuel Olshvanger, author, folklore researcher, a delegate to the pan-Asiatic congress, translator of Dante (for which he was awarded the Tshernichovski literary prize); Dr. Zvi Voyslavski, a well-known cultural historian, author, translator of Freud and Marx's "Das Kapital" – an outstanding cultural achievement, for which he received the Tshernichovski prize; Eliahu-Moshe Genakhovski, secretary-general of the world "*Mizrachi*" [religious Zionists] organization; the above-mentioned Ibn-Zahav; Yitchak (Gortshitski) Avishai, teacher and writer of textbooks, lecturer, translator of books on music; the young novelist Khayim (Antshkovski) Reshef and others.

[Page 297]

Aboard the train that left Warsaw at 3 p.m. on October 31, 1939 – a few hours before the outbreak of the Second World War – on its way to Constanța [Romanian port] were several young people from Grayeve who were on their way to Erets Yisroel. And later when the captain and sailors of the illegal [Aliyah Bet] ship "Tiger Hill" abandoned the ship in Beirut for fear of being arrested by the British authorities it was a young man from Grayeve who took the wheel and brought the ship safely to the beach at Tel-Aviv. The later train that departed for Constanța at 12 midnight carried a larger group of people from Grayeve. Unfortunately, that train never arrived at its destination. The war had broken out and the train was forced to return to Warsaw.

The war and the Nazi beasts completely destroyed Jewish Grayeve, as they did to all of Europe's Jewish communities. The Polish army ["Anders Army"] that came from the U.S.S.R. to the Middle East, brought several Jews from Grayeve to Erets Yisroel.

At the end of the war, after the concentration camps were liberated, several young people from Grayeve arrived in Erets Yisroel by way of the Cyprus detention camps. They were a few burned embers who had undergone a long, bloody, thorny road and had been saved from the Nazi gas chambers by miracles. Carrying memories of the terrible years of suffering, with the image of the murdered Jewish Grayeve before their eyes, they started a new life. The Grayeve Jews in the country greeted them with open arms and open hearts, in the true Grayeve manner.

Let's hope that, while peacefully building Erets Yisroel, Grayevers from all over the world (and Grajevers are widely scattered...) will establish a proper monument, a cultural institution that will be a fitting memorial to Jewish Grayeve. This was a town that contributed a large number of cultural and social actors, relative to its actual size. The town is engraved in our hearts, and, regrettably, exists no more.

Footnotes

34. *Khayim Reshef Antshkovski:* a graduate of the Hebrew "Tarbut" High School in *Byalistok* [Białystok], and later – of the Agronomy Faculty in a Czechoslovak university. He is a member of Kibbutz Kfar Menachem in Israel, and active in the "*Hashomer Hatzair*" [young guard] movement. He has published a number of short stories in the "Hashomer Hatzair" and [Al Hamishmar] "*Mishmar*" [on guard] journals, and is now preparing a collection of Hebrew short stories. – *Ed*
35. *Oder II*: [Adar II, or Adar Bet]: thirteenth month of the Jewish calendar in a leap year.
36. *First Zionist Congress:* organized by Theodor Herzl and held in Basel, Switzerland on 29 Aug 1897. Its main goal was to establish a home for the Jewish people in Erets Yisroel
37. *Balfour Declaration:* It is the foundational declaration establishing the right of the Jews to a homeland in Palestine and a huge landmark in Zionist history. It was issued in conjunction with the granting of a mandate from the League of Nations to Britain as caretaker of Palestine for the next thirty years, with the stated goal of founding a Jewish State.

[Page 298]

The Three Grayevans in Jerusalem:
Dr. Emmanuel Olshvanger, Dr. Tsvi Voyslavski, Ari Ibn-Zahav

By Gershon Svet
Translated by Yael Chaver, Ph.D
Edited by Tina Lunson

The Prime Minister of Israel, David Ben-Gurion; the former Interior Minister Yitzchak Grinboim; Tabenkin, the Mapam leader; and the playwright S. Tsemach all came from the same town: Plonsk, in Poland. But there is no American-style *landsmanshaft*[1] for Plonsk. If Ben-Gurion sometimes meets Tsemach, it's not because they are from the same town, but because it's Tsemach. I mention this neither as a compliment or a rebuke, but only as a fact.

Israel doesn't have any landsmanshaftn or organizations for people from Byalistok, *Vilne* [Vilnius] or *Shklov* [Szkłów]. Neither is there a landsmanshaft for Grayeve. But it so happened that three Grayevans settled in Jerusalem and all three are more or less renowned. When they meet in Jerusalem, it is not as Grayevans, but as Jerusalemites who are all in the same class: writers and public figures.

I want to tell you about these three Grayevans: Dr. Emmanuel Olshvanger, Dr. Tsvi Voyslavski, and Ari Ibn-Zahav.

I will start with the most senior of these Grayevans: Dr. Emmanuel Olshvanger, who is now over sixty.

Dr. Olshvanger is one of those people difficult to categorize: he is a writer, speaker, scholar, public figure, and more.

[Page 299]

He is simultaneously all of these, yet the descriptions do not provide a full characterization of the human phenomenon that is Emmanuel Olshvanger.

Dr. Olshvanger is known to the Yiddish literary world as the author of the folktale collections "*Rozhinkes mit Mandlen*" [Raisins and almonds] and *Royte Pomerantsn* [Red Oranges]," which were published and printed in Latin orthography and transcription and made a great impression in non-Jewish literary circles.

These two collections of Yiddish stories, anecdotes and jokes are an important folklore achievement. After the famous collection [of Yiddish folk songs, 1901] by Ginzburg and Marek, this is the most significant and serious work to date in this field (Our friend Stutchkoff's book [Thesaurus of the Yiddish Language, 1950], to be published by YIVO, is awaited with great interest. So far it has not yet been published.)

Emmanuel Olshvanger possessed all the good qualities that a folklorist needs. First, he was a polyglot, with unusual knowledge of languages. He spoke about ten languages, I believe: Yiddish, Hebrew, Russian, English, French and Polish. He had a reading knowledge of Italian, Latin and Greek and was renowned in the world of Esperanto as one of the best masters of that language. At one of the Esperanto congresses, he was awarded first prize for his talk in Esperanto.

Dr. Olshvanger was a representative of *Keren HaYesod* [United Israel Appeal, founded in 1920] for about twenty years, if not more. He visited a number of countries and made contact with the "Bnei Moshe" community in India and with Jews in South Africa and Australia, to say nothing of Jews in all the countries of Europe. He lived in London for many years. Olshvanger attended nearly all the Zionist congresses of the last twenty-five years. With his remarkable sense of humor, Olshvanger was full of jokes, stories and anecdotes of congresses, committee meetings, Zionist delegates from other countries, etc.

This was typical of Olshvanger. He was naturally a skeptic, a man who knew that there were very few absolute truths in the world, and therefore victories should not be celebrated and defeats should not be a cause for dismay. He became a Zionist when young, but never fetishized Zionism.

[Page 300]

Obviously, Dr. Olshvanger was never a negator of the Diaspora. Mendele and Peretz were no less dear to him than Bialik and Tshernichovsky.

In recent years, Dr. Olshvanger travels for Keren HaYesod less often, and is more concerned with literary production. A few years ago he translated Dante's "Divine Comedy," from Italian into Hebrew; he has also translated Shakespeare; and rumor has it that he is writing his memoirs. Olshvanger has lived a colorful life. He has visited many countries, has met many people. He is a master of storytelling. Whenever he sits at a café table in Jerusalem, he soon becomes surrounded by listeners.

If his memoirs are published, they will certainly make a broad-ranging, interesting book. And, naturally, Grayeve will also be memorialized there.

Dr. Tsvi Voyslavski

Tsvi Voyslavski is also almost sixty. He was part of the circle of the Odessa Yeshiva, headed by Rav Tza'ir [Rabbi Chaim Tchernowitz]. Among the alumni of this yeshiva were Dr. Yehezkel Kaufmann, Prof. Yehoshua Gutmann, Shlomo Gintsberg (now Ginossar, Israel's ambassador in Italy), and others. Voyslavski has lived in Erets Israel for almost sixteen years. He lives in Jerusalem and makes a living exclusively through literature. He is one of the most serious Hebrew journalists in Israel. His books *Words of the Generation* and *Individuals in Public Space* are philosophical-sociological meditations on the essence of democracy, on the conflict between the interests of the individual and of society.

Voyslavski is a very productive translator. He has done a Hebrew translation of the memoirs of Dr. Shemaryahu Levine (printed in *Forverts* [The Jewish Daily Forward newspaper] years ago), *Das Kapital* by Karl Marx, Theodore Mommsen's *History of Rome*, and Sigmund Freud's *Psychopathology of Everyday Life*. He writes critiques on literary and scientific matters. Voyslavski is often a member of prize juries.

He has a fine reputation in the country and is an acknowledged authority in his field. People trust him. The fact that he serves on prize juries almost every year is the best indication of that.

[Page 301]

Ari Ibn-Zahav

Ari Ibn-Zahav has recently spent a few years in the United States, where he had great success with his play "Shylock, the Jew of Venice" in Maurice Schwartz's theater. Ibn-Zahav is a very productive writer. His books include novels, poems, folklore, journalistic reports, plays, research work, etc.

Ibn-Zahav was linked with the Hebrew University for over twenty years. He was close to Dr. Y. L. Magnes, and collaborated with him to find the Hebrew University Press.

He returned to Jerusalem not long ago.

He is the youngest of the three Grayevans, but he is fifty-two. Ibn-Zahav is not done with his literary work. These are his best creative years.

Footnote

10. *Landsmanshaft:* Societies created by Jewish immigrants from the same town or region to provide social, financial support and burial plot.

[Page 302]

Avrom Mordkhe Piurko
The Writer, Researcher and Teacher — Biographical Notes by one of his Pupils
By G. Gorin
Translated by Tina Lunson

Mr. Avrom Mordkhe Piurko of blessed memory was one of the most distinguished Jews in Grayeve. I will impart here a short biography of him, for which I am grateful to his son Itsik Piurko in Jerusalem.

M. Piurko was born in 1853, in *Lomzhe* [Łomża]. Up to the age of 13 he studied in *khadorim* [Jewish religious school], afterwards he studied very industriously by himself and acquired a deep knowledge of *Tanakh* [abbreviation for *Torah, Neviim, Ksuvim*; Law, Prophets, Writings, respectively], Talmud and other sources of the old Hebrew literature. While he was still a young man he was already known in Lomzhe as a master. After his marriage he settled in Grayeve, where he conducted many-branched pedagogical and literary work until the last years of his life. Piurko planted a great love for Hebrew and Jewish traditions in the hearts of the youth. Even while he was still alive he was able to see the fruits of his great work. Many of his pupils are Hebrew writers and well-known scholars in the Jewish world.

Avrom Mordkhe Piurko was also very active as a writer. He had a printing press on Rov's lane, and he did not use it to make a living, but dedicated it to the service of Hebrew literature. He wrote and published many books for children – school books and other works. In 1899 he began to publish a weekly journal for children (*"Gan sheshuim"* [1]). This was the first children's journal and was published regularly every week for two years. Many of the contributors to the journal, who were then young boys, later became famous Hebrew writers and poets.

[Page 303]

In 1907 he began to publish a monthly Hebrew journal for youth, *"Livney hanorim,"* but because of insufficient funds the journal was not published for more than six months.

In the late 1920s Avrom Mordkhe Piurko published a periodical journal for Talmud research in which many prominent rabbis and Talmud researchers participated. He complained to me many times about what he called the "spirit of competition" among the rabbis and the difficulties that he had in getting material for his periodical, but his extraordinary idealism and tact called up respect for him even among his scientific opponents in the area of Talmud research.

Avrom Mordkhe Piurko took part in various Hebrew newspapers of his generation with treatises on Hebrew and research on the Tanakh and Talmud. But his most important work and one which unfortunately was never published was his commentary on the Tanakh. After I had graduated from the Hebrew *gimnazye* [secondary schools] in Bialystok and was acquainted with the works of many Jewish and non-Jewish Bible scholars, I had the opportunity on one of my visits to Grayeve, to read his commentary on the Tanakh in manuscript form. I was many times in wonderment at how my respected teacher Piurko had written such brilliant remarks on the Tanakh without a library and without reference books. His commentary contained not only excellent linguistic treatments, but also historical explanations that in many passages were sharp-minded and brilliant.

[Page 304]

Avrom Mordkhe Piurko left behind five books in manuscript:

Mafte'ach Le'sifrey Ha'Kodesh [*An Index to the Holy Books*] - a lengthy syntaxes;

Derekh hakodesh [The Holy Way] - an interpretation of the Holy Scriptures, Torah, Prophets and Writings;

Erech - Milim Ha'chadash [The New Word-Value] - research on the scholars of the Mishne and the Gemore;

Botser Olelot [Unripe Harvester], remarks on the Babylonian and Jerusalem Talmuds;

Amirot Tehorot [Pure Sayings] - remarks and a talk on the weekly portions of the Torah.

I will never forget the patriarchal figure of Avrom Mordkhe Piurko, his sharp, clever eyes, his sedateness, nobility and fine character in general. His house was a house of culture. His children and wife had the atmosphere of their house made friendly and pleasant. It was a house where one could discuss Jewishness, Hebrew culture and general issues.

On my frequent visits to Grayeve, I would always visit my old teacher Piurko and it was a great honor for me to be considered among his friends and honorees.

Footnote

1. The journal was printed in *Lik* [Ełk], Prussia, at the press and with the same lead type of the first Hebrew newspaper, *Hamagid*.

[Page 305]

Dear Friend Mr. Blum,

I have recently written to you a few times. I wrote to our honorable friend Mr. Katzparowski in a letter of[1] which I hope has reached him, and today I come to you [both] again due to the news in the city.

Our rabbi has received the duty of rabbi in the city of Antwerp the capital of Belgium [sic] and he is leaving us perhaps before the Shavuot holiday, and therefore:

A general election to the congregation committee is being held and there is a great effort in this regard by the *Youths*,[2] The *Zionists*,[3] The *B'nei B'rith*,[4] *Poalei Yeshurun*,[5] and even the Hasidim. They will win the election without a doubt because they are bold and energetic and they are campaigning, something that those in debt and the Mizrahi cannot do.

I have another request for you: I have heard that an active company has been established in America to publish Hebrew books and manuscripts, and I have precious manuscripts worthy of being published:

Index of the Holy Books A great syntaxes, unprecedented in our literature.

The Holy Way An exegesis of the Holy Books – Torah, Prophets, Hagiography, both simple and linguistic.

The New Beit Midrash An investigation of the history of our sages, their methods and qualities (this book is now at the Mizrahi Union in Warsaw) which planned to publish a new periodical "Tachkemoni" of Jewish wisdom, and unfortunately has been delayed...

Part of a letter from Avraham Mordechai Piurka[6] to Hyman Blum

Footnotes

1. Abbreviation, "ב - ב" [Bet-Bet] written by author. We have no obvious interpretation in the context of this sentence.
2. *Youths*: The author is probably referring to the youth branch of a party of strictly Orthodox Jews called *Tze'irei Agudat Yisrael*.
3. *The Zionists*: The author is likely referring to Tzionim Clali'im, a secular Zionist party mostly representing middle class business owners. This group had an economically conservative element and eventually became part of the current Likud party in Israel.
4. *The B'nei B'rith*: [children of the covenant]. This organization, founded in 1843, has primarily focused on community service and welfare activities.
5. *Poalei Yeshurun*: We found no historic reference to this group.
6. Piurko, Avraham Mordechai (Łomża, 1853–Grajewo, Pol., 1933) intellectual, journalist, philanthropist and author, he wrote several books and founded the weekly *Gan Sha'ashu'im (1899)*, the first Hebrew-language children's newspaper outside Palestine. He founded a modern language school, thereby making Grajewo a distinguished center of Hebrew learning. Additional contributions included published periodicals in Odessa, St. Petersburg and Warsaw.

[Page 306]

Memories of Avrom-Mordkhe Piurko
By Dr. Immanuel Olsvanger (Jerusalem)
Translated by Yael Chaver, PhD

Writing these memories down is limited by the fact that I do not have the necessary materials to make a proper assessment of Avrom-Mordkhe Piurko and his prolific activities.

Fifty years ago, Piurko's books were read in *khadorim* [Jewish religious schools] all over Eastern Europe. His book *Nit'ei Na'amanim* could be found in many Jewish homes.

Piurko's weekly *Gan Sha'ashu'im* [Playground, the first Hebrew children's magazine], which was printed in the Prussian town of *Lik* [Ełk], some distance from Grayeve, brought joy into the hearts of Jewish children in all towns and *shtetlakh* [small villages].

Several Hebrew playwrights and poets, who later became famous, started their literary work on the pages of this weekly.

In his last years, Piurko started to publish a monthly *Bet Ha-Midrash He-Hadash*, dedicated to Talmudic research, with a Yiddish humor supplement.

Avrom-Mordkhe Piurko

[Page 307]

A. M. Piurko – a tall, lean person – was the central figure in our town. Who was not his student? He had a natural sense of pedagogy and knew how to explain Hebrew grammar and various complicated forms, using simple words and clear logic.

I studied with him from my childhood until age twenty. I spent a few months in his kheyder, but mostly studied with him at his home or in my parents' home.

When I left for secondary school in *Suvalk* [Suwałki] I also continued studying with him every time I came home. Years later, I studied with him every time I came home from the university at *Kenigsberg* [Kaliningrad].

I've had many teachers in my life, among them world-renowned people, but no one had such a profound effect on me as my teacher Piurko.

In later years, when I would visit him, I liked to sit at his table. He would read out loud from his commentary on the Bible. Often, he would grab my ear – a habit of his – when he wanted to emphasize the importance of a topic.

The manuscript of his commentary on the entire Bible is now in his son's house in Jerusalem. God forbid, will this fruit of his life's work be lost? Some parts of this work would be endorsed by the greatest commentators, Jewish and non-Jewish.

All those who remember Piurko, who took their first steps in the temples of the Bible and Hebrew literature, have a sacred duty to Piurko to publish this colossal work!

[Page 308]

Prof. Shimen Rabidovitsh
By Dr. G. Gorin[1]
Translated by Yael Chaver, PhD

Professor Shimen Rabidovitsh[2] was born in Grayeve in 1897. He spent his childhood years in Grayeve, where he received a traditional Talmudic education, primarily from his father Rabbi Khaym-Itsik Rabidovitsh, and writer of the book "Merkhavey-Yitzhaki" (an interpretation of Rashi's commentary).

He studied at Rav Reines' yeshiva in Lida [Belarus] for several years before the First World War. During the war he was very active in *Byalistok* [Białystok] in the field of Hebrew education and in the "*Tze'irei Tzion*" [Zion Youth] movement.

In 1919 Rabidovitsh started his studies at the Berlin University, which awarded him a Ph.D. several years later.

As a young man, Rabidovitsh exhibited great capabilities in the literary field. In 1919-1920 he was editor of the Berlin newspaper "*Undzer Frayheyt*" [Our Freedom] for the "*Ha-Po'el Ha-Tzair*" [The Young Worker] and "*Tze'irei Tzion*" organizations. From 1919-1933 Rabidovitsh was active in many areas of Hebrew literature in Berlin: he founded "Ayanot" publishing house and was one of the publishers of "*Ha-Tekufah*" and the manager of Stybel Publishing House.

[Page 309]

During the Second World War Rabidovitsh published, in England, the monthly Hebrew journal "Yalkut" and the "Metsuda" yearbook (four volumes were published and the fifth is in preparation). These two periodicals were the only Hebrew publications to appear in Europe during the war years. He was also editor in London, of "Sefer Sokolov" *(1944)*, which contained previously unpublished writings of the great Zionist leader, and writer, Nachum Sokolov, as well as critical appreciations of Sokolov.

In the near future, "Sefer Dubnov" will appear, edited by Rabidovitsh. This book includes a thorough appraisal of the great Jewish historian's work, as well as a collection of his letters.

Rabidovitsh is currently also editing "Pinkas Chicago," which will reflect the cultural life of the Jewish community of Chicago.

Rabidovitsh is responsible for articles, studies and books in Hebrew, Yiddish, English, and German (a book on Ludwig Feuerbach's philosophy, 1931).

In the field of medieval philosophy, Rabidovitsh scientifically analyzed and clarified in his own way the philosophical systems of Hebrew thinkers such as Sa'adia Gaon, Abarbanel, and especially Maimonides. He did not limit himself to theoretical studies alone, but also introduced practical deductions for the reader. His primary goal was to provide a modern approach to the bases of Jewish religion and philosophy. This new approach also emphasized the contribution of Jewish philosophy to general philosophy.

In 1947 Rabidovitsh published a new scientific edition of Maimonides' "Book of Knowledge," based on manuscripts and first editions. Part Two, sources and interpretations of the "Book of Knowledge," will appear soon.

Some of Rabidovitsh's most important work in the field of philosophy was the first edition of the works of Nakhman Krochmal (known as Ranak) in 1924. Rabidovitsh wrote a 225-page introduction in which he analyzed all aspects of Ranak. (philosophy, philology, etc.). This project, which Rabidovitsh published at age 27, elicited much respect in the Jewish scientific world, thanks to its original analysis and innovativeness. New research on Renak includes more and more of Rabidovitsh's approach to Nakhman Krochmal.

[Page 310]

The same depth also characterized Rabidovitsh's works on Moyshe Mendelssohn (Judaica 1930) and modern Jewish thinkers such as A. D. Gordon and Ahad Ha'am [Asher Ginsberg]. His strong opposition to Ahad Ha'am system of "spiritual center" was a logical result of his attitude towards

Diaspora and his important principle of cultural partnership between the Land of Israel and the Diaspora.

In 1931, Rabidovitsh, then the chairman of "*Bet Am Ivri,*" [The Hebrew Culture Center] founded in Berlin the "*Brit Ivrit Olamit,*" [The Hebrew World Union]. He gave his renowned speech "If not here – where?" at the founding session. The speech detailed the founding principles of a ramified Hebrew movement in the Diaspora. He formulated his vision of a "partnership" between the Land of Israel and the Diaspora: world Jewry has two forms – the Land of Israel and the Diaspora. Both are united in cultural creativity; one section can have no success without the other. Rabidovitsh sharply criticized the official Zionist negative attitude towards the Diaspora. He demanded a revision of the fundamental views held by Zionism, and strongly emphasized his positive stance towards Diaspora life.

At that time, Rabidovitsh was also making preparations for the creation of a central Hebrew cultural fund ("*Keren Ha-tarbut*") and for the assembly of a first Hebrew congress. These plans were interrupted by the Hitlerite turmoil in Germany.

Rabidovitsh then moved his activity to England, where he stayed from 1933-1948. In London, he was the chairman of the cultural organization and a lecturer in Jewish philosophy at London University. He was later appointed as head of the Hebrew division at the University of Leeds, England.

[Page 311]

In 1948 Rabidovitsh was invited to be a professor of Jewish philosophy at the advanced school of Jewish studies of the "Jewish Studies Midrasha" in Chicago. He has been active there ever since, as professor and chairman of the post-graduate department.

****

As is clear from this brief overview, Rabidovitsh's activity is many-faceted and nuanced. Thanks to his work he has gained a reputation as one of the most important contemporary scholars in the field of Hebrew literature.

Rabidovitsh expressed his views clearly and logically in the Hebrew periodicals "Ha'olam," "Moznaim," "Tarbiz" and in longer journalistic pieces in "Ha'tekufah," "Sefer Bialik" and "Metsuda."

In accordance with his positive attitude towards the Diaspora, Rabidovitsh is currently working in the United States. Let's hope that after his long wanderings he will succeed in building a center of Hebrew culture in the United States, to complete the construction of his philosophical-literary system and apply his great talents for the benefit of Hebrew culture.

Footnotes

1. *[Author, Dr. G. Gorin]*: I express my gratitude to Rabbi Kabakov of the Hebrew Association, for his help in describing the literary production of Shimen Rabidovitsh. I also thank my friend Dr. Eliezer Marvik, head of the Yiddish section at the Library of Congress, Washington, for the biographical details he supplied.

Professor Shimen Rabidovitsh: writer and scholar. In English sources, the name was Simon Rawidowicz; he was the father of the historian Dr. Benjamin Ravid, Professor Emeritus of Brandeis University.

Translated by Yael Chaver, Ph.D
Edited by Tina Lunson

[Page 312]

About the illustrations of A. D. Fishbeyn:

The editorial board of the Yizkor-Bukh expresses its thanks to our *landsman* [countryman], A. D. Fishbeyn for his beautiful illustrations in this book.

In the synagogue illustration, he exhibited a remarkable pictorial memory with the precise architectural details. Thirty years after leaving Grayeve, he succeeded brilliantly in conveying the marvelous beauty of the synagogue.

In the illustration, "Between *minkhe* [afternoon prayers] and *mayrev* [evening prayers], Fishbeyn portrays a typical scene of the old *bes-medresh* [house of study], where he spent much time in his childhood. The types are varied, including the gifted Talmud scholar, the artisan listening respectfully to the scholar's hair-splitting argumentation; the dreamer, reflecting on other matters – each with his characteristic expression.

A different impression is given by the illustration of the old part of the cemetery – who does not remember the mysterious fear that emanated from there and overwhelmed children, even from a distance?

The artist succeeded in precisely presenting not only the local scene, but also expressing the feelings of his and our childhood years. Once again, many thanks for this heartfelt contribution to the Yizkor-Bukh.

[Page 313]

[Page 314]

The entrance to the sports ground

The synagogue street during the German occupation of 1916
Left background shows the old *bes-medresh* and the synagogue

Meir Vaks, Yisakhar Vodovsky and Shimen Kolko.

The photo was taken in New York in 1906. Vaks and Kolko returned to Grayeve, where they perished during the war

[Page 315]

In Holy Remembrance

Translated by Yael Chaver, Ph.D
Edited by Tina Lunson

[Page 316]

blank

[Page 317]

In memory of our parents
Benjamin and Feiga KOLKO
And our brothers and sisters,
Rubin, Simon, Joseph,
And Ester (Stusza) KOLKO
Who perished

Jack KOLKO, Chicago

[Page 318]

For these I mourn For the six million of our brothers and sisters who were killed by Hitler's murderers. Philip BUZMAN	**In eternal remembrance of** Our beloved sister and brother-in-law Reyzl and Khaym MISHKOFSKY with their dear children, Motl and Esther. Honor their memory! Sadie GOLDSTEIN, Isidor LAVENDA
In remembrance of My sister Shifra and her husband Avrom Itsik BUZMAN and their five children, who perished at the hands of the Fascist murderers. Fayvl KANOVITS	**In remembrance of** Our mother Khane Gitl KLAYMAN, and our aunt Keyle and uncle KURLENDER. The KLAYMAN children
In eternal remembrance of Yechiel ZELIGMAN and family. Rachel BURSHTEYN (Raykh), Mexico	**In holy remembrance of** My brothers and sister Khaye Mirke KAHN, Itsik Mayer MISHKOF, Khenekh MISHKOF. Sister, Sere SHEYNKMAN
In remembrance of Our mother Reyzl BRIKMAN Honor her memory! Libe, Peshe, Ayda	**In eternal remembrance of** My father Yehoshua Eliezer and my mother Dvoyre. Ruven BOGISH

[Page 319]

In eternal remembrance of

Reb Elimelech, son of Rabbi Zvi VAKS,

olav hasholem [may he rest in peace]

(born 1841, died 1914).

Reb Elimelech VAKS was one of the most respected householders among the Grayeve pioneers, one of the best Talmudic scholars in the Mir Yeshiva, a well known haberdashery businessman and active for the public good. Married the noble woman Ms. Beyle Brayne, daughter of Reb Yisroel MINTZ, *olav hasholem*.

For years he served as a *gabay* [a lay person who volunteers to perform various duties in connection with Torah readings at religious services] in Grayeve and dedicated his entire life to the public good. He did not use his great talents to amass possessions, but helped create in Grayeve such public institutions as the new bathhouse, the hospitality society, the new *bes-medresh*, community butcher shops etc.

His home was always a gathering place for scholars, an open door to the needy, to immigrants from all over the world, to whom he always gave good advice and help. Hundreds of immigrants who were arrested for illegally crossing the border were freed thanks to him. Never was it too difficult for him to carry out the *mitsvah* [commandment] of freeing captives. The doors of all government offices were open for him.

Thus he lived a fine life and reserved a place in the world to come, in which he believed strongly.

We grieve for those who are gone and not forgotten. May his soul be bound up in the bundle of the living.

[Page 320]

One of the finest families with traditional lineage – son-in-law and daughter of Reb Elimelech VAKS – the great rabbi and preacher Rabbi Yosef ZAYDENBERG, *olev-hasholem*; his noble wife Ms. Tsipora; their children: 1) Borech Moyshe, 2) Brayne, 3) Sheyne Itke, 4) Elimelech and, 5) name unknown. All killed as martyrs in the gas chambers of Hitler, may his name be erased.

Max M. and Eliyahu VAKS, brothers

We grieve for those who are gone and not forgotten
In loving memory of the unforgettable:
BUFFENSTEIN's, PELTONOWITZ's & VOISLAVSKI's

Dr. W. PELTON (PELTONOWITZ), Chicago, Illinois

[Page 321]

In eternal remembrance of our beloved parents
Mendl Borech
and
Malka
TZICHATSKY,
and of our dear sisters
Reyzke, Blume and Toybe
with their families, who perished at the hands of Hitler's murderers

Hymie TZICHATSKY (SHILLER)
Benyomin TZICHATSKY
Sol TZICHATSKY (SHILLER)
Isidore TZICHATSKY (SHILLER)
and their families

[Page 322]

> **In holy remembrance of**
> My beloved mother
> Mini DON
> A devoted worker for the poor and needy Grayeve *landslayt*.
>
> An untiring supporter of the Grayeve relief committee's work to care for surviving *landslayt* who were saved from Hitler's murderers.
>
> Honor her memory!
>
> Philip DON

[Page 323]

> **In eternal remembrance of**
> Our parents
> Moyshe Yosef
> and
> Peshe MOSENZNIK,
> and sisters
> Khave and Toybe.
>
> The Brothers: Boris (Dov), Adolf (Avrom)
and Max (Mordechai) MOSSEN

[Page 324]

In holy remembrance of our beloved father
Reb Leybush BLUM
(Leybush the *melamed* [teacher]),
died in New York, 5 Tevet [January 1938]
and our dear mother
Sarah Rivke,
died in New York in 12 Kheshven [October 1941].

The children
Hyman Morris Ruven

We mourn for them!

In sorrow for our beloved sister and brother-in-law Peshe and Khaye ROTHSHTEYN, their children Yoysef and Sime Rokhl who perished in the Warsaw ghetto.

In remembrance of our brother Khenech RAICHELSON,

died in Tel Aviv

Sarah (RAICHELSON) ZAKUSKY
Dovid REICHELSON
Khaye (REICHELSON) FENSTER

In holy remembrance of

Our beloved father

Khone BUZSHIMSKY

and our dear mother

Freyde.

The children Annie ROSEN, Yeta BLOOM, Alex BUZSHIMSKY, Ayda BERNOF, Morris BUZSHIMSKY and Becky GOLDSTEIN (Milwaukee)

In remembrance of
Isaac and Khaye Mirke KOHN (Kalman Moyshe MISHKOVSKY's daughter)

Mrs. Bertha KATZ

In remembrance of
All friends and *landslayt*
who perished

Mayer BARKOVSKY

[Page 325]

With deep sorrow for our great loss of two tireless workers of the Grayeve Aid Society, Mrs. Minnie DON and our vice-president Abraham MLAVSKY May their souls be bound up in the bundle of the living
When wars, racial hatred and persecutions are abolished, Then we will forget the horror! Irving SAPIRSTEIN

[Page 326]

In holy remembrance of My beloved parents Itche and Sorke ABRAMSON, my uncle Hershl, my aunt Yehudis and my two cousins, Rokhl and Rivtshe MARATSHEVSKY Mayer ABRAMSON	**In holy remembrance of** Our parents Tankhum and Miriam Nekhe, and our brother Hershl TETENBOYM The brothers: Hyman, Charles and Morris TETENBOYM
In remembrance of The perished Sholem ZAYDENBERG, wife and family; Falk RUTSKY, wife and family; Elye Khaym RUTSKY, wife and family of Antwerp, Belgium Robert RUTSKY **In remembrance of** our beloved parents Hertske and Khaye BOGUSH The children: Rivtshe, Fishl, Khane, Feygl, Tziviye, Ester, Rokhl and Mayer	**In remembrance of** Our beloved parents Yosl and Rokhl BOGUSH The children: Becky, Minnie, Irving and Sylvia

[Page 327]

In eternal remembrance of My beloved sister and brother-in-law Sore and Shloyme VAYNSHTEYN with their four children, who perished at the hands of the Nazi murderers in the Grayeve ghetto Eliezer and Tsipe BRAMSON Sime and Shmuel GINZBURG Lina LEVIN	**In memory of** Chanina GRON's Children and Grandchildren from Warsaw and Siedlec
In holy remembrance of Those who perished: My mother Dvoyre Rokhl LEVINZON; My cousin Sheynke MOLDARSKY, her husband and children; My cousins Eliahu and wife; Yankev and family and Bashe KOHEN; The ZILBERSHTEYN and LEVINSON families; Friends, acquaintances and *landslayt* May God avenge their blood! Aaron Moshe LEVINZON **In remembrance of my family** Perished at the hand of Hitler's murderers in Grayeve Ester ABKEVITCH (BORNSHTEYN)	**In remembrance of** All the unknown martyrs of Grayeve Aaron Mayer FISHBEYN, Mexico

[Page 328]

In holy remembrance of our parents
Reb Motl Leyb and Golde MLAVSKY

Reb Motl Leyb MLAVSKY was one of the most respected householders in Grayeve. He was known as a scholar and very pious man and became beloved through his good deeds. As a young man he was the manager of POKROYSKY's suspenders factory up to 1890, when the factory was taken over by HEPNER. Later, Reb Motl Leyb MLAVSKY became a lumber contractor in the Warsaw citadel and became known as a merchant and charitable person. Reb Motl Leyb MLAVSKY was born in 1846 and was murdered at the hands of the Nazi murderers in 1943.

Honor to his holy memory!

Rose MILLER

[Page 329]

In memory of my beloved parents
Hersch and Slovi GORCZYCKI, my brothers Jacob and Szymon Leib GORCZYCKI and their families, and my sister Frume Itke

Harry GREEN

*

In eternal memory of my beloved parents
Hirsh and Slovi GORTSHITSKY, My brothers Yaacov and Shimen Leybl and their families, and my sister Frume Itke
I mourn your untimely death with deep sorrow – your memory will forever remain engraved on my heart!

H. GREEN

[Page 330]

In remembrance of Our parents Moyshe Mendl and Sore MISHKOVSKY and our brothers Shakhne, Bertshe, Aron, Tzemakh and Enekh with their wives and children Khaye SHTEYNSAFIR and Mayer VITKOVSKY	**In holy remembrance of** The GINZBURG family: Yaacov (Yankl Vigder) and Ester and their children, Sholem, Khaym and Simkhe Nekhe ZILBERMAN, Mendl GINZBURG, Rivke BERGMAN, Sore GUTFRAYND, Kalmen GINZBURG
In remembrance of My beloved parents Beylke and Mikhl VILENSKY, and my sisters Feygl and Itke and their families Alte VITKOVSKY	**In eternal remembrance of** our deceased father Nosn ZILBERMAN (18 Tevet [January 1925]), our mother Reyzl ZILBERMAN Who perished tragically (18 Kislev [December 1941]) and our brothers who perished: Borech Itsik, Abraham, Shloyme and Leybl and sisters Rivke and Mindl Leyah. Sholem, Avigdor and Yoysef ZILBERMAN
In remembrance of My beloved husband Sam and my son Abraham ROSEN Annie ROSEN	
In remembrance of My beloved husband Shayke ZILBERSHTEYN Rose and children	Reb Shloyme Halevy FRIDMAN (known as the Russian shopkeeper), may his soul be bound up with the bundle of the living; Dobe FRIDMAN (wife), Khaye (daughter), may their souls be bound up in the bundle of the living. May God avenge their blood Yehuda Zvi Halevy FRIDMAN
In remembrance of My parents Khaym Shrage and Feygl MARKUS Khaye Tsirl MARKUS	

In remembrance of
Our beloved husband and father Tevye SAPIRSHTEYN

Wife Libe and son Isidore SAPIRSHTEYN

In eternal remembrance of
The VONSOVSKY family,
the GUZIK family,
the SHKLARZSHEVSKY family,
the MARGOLIS family

[Page 331]

In remembrance of our father
Sholem Motl DORF,
Our brothers Leybl and Mayer DORF;
Our uncle Mayer and Golde Rive with their family □ Our aunt Tsirl with her husband David LEVINSON □ And our aunt Rose DORF with her children

Abraham David FISHBEYN and family;
Neytn and Betye VAYSMAN;
Royzke, Yetta and Shloyme DORF

In holy remembrance of our parents

Khaym Hersh and Feygl KALINOVSKY
And our beloved brother Yedidya KALINOVSKY
Who perished at the brutal hands of the Nazi murderers

Simon, Volf, Roze, Jean

[Page 332]

In remembrance of
My father
Shloyme RAFALOVSKY Who died in Grayeve during the First World War,
My mother Mikhle,
My brother-in-law Abraham Khaym, my sister Libe Gerzon who perished tragically at the hands of the murderous Hitlerites
Their memory will forever remain engraved in my heart!

Herman G. RAFALOVSKY

In remembrance of
Our beloved parents
Yankl and Malke KOHN The children: Dobke, Sore, Libe

In remembrance of
our parents Sam and Becky KOHN The children: Benny and Yetta

In remembrance of

My father Gershon KOHN

Max KOHN

In remembrance of
Our parents Mordechai and Rokhl VAPINSKY and our sisters Peshke and Doba, who were slaughtered by the German murderers.
Dr. Efraim VAPINSKY and family

Ida and Yankev FABRITSKY
Yafa and Yerakhmiel ZILBERSHTEYN

In memory of
the martyrs who made the
supreme sacrifice
for the Jewish people

Jacob Mordecai RAVID

In holy remembrance of
Our brothers, sisters and cousins who perished at the hands of the Fascist murderers in Grayeve:
Eliyahu KOHN and wife; Yankl KOHN, wife and children; Bashe KOHN and husband; Dvoyre LEVINZON; Leybl LEVINSON, Itse GERSHTANSKY, wife and children; Velvel LEVINE and children

Brothers Moshe, Shloyme and Mayer KOHN
Cousin, Rabbi POMERANTS and family

In holy remembrance of
Our family who perished at the hands of Hitler's murderers!

Philip SOSNOVITS and family

[Page 333]

In remembrance of
Khaym Leyb BEYLIS

Sol BEYLIS

In remembrance of
My beloved parents
Berl Hershl and Royze RUTKOVSKI

Philip RUTKOVSKI

In remembrance of
My beloved parents
Shepsl and Khaye Toybe MARASHEVSKY

Son: Dov MARASHEVSKY

In remembrance of
My beloved parents and my family!

Sam MOSS

The daughter and grandchildren of the Grayeve *khazn* [cantor], Reb Shloyme Khaym HaCohen REZNIK:
Mushke BARKOVSKY and her daughters, Soltshe, Andzshe and husband and children;
Shulamis and her son Henesh.
May their souls be bound in the bundle of the living.

The *khazn's* wife and children

In remembrance of
My parents
Leyzer Velvel and Khane Beyle ABELSKY

Tillie (ABELSKY) TOPOLSKY

In remembrance of
My brother Khaym Shloyme MARGOLIS, his wife Etki, with their three children.

Their sister Ester GALINKER

In remembrance of
My parents Avrom Itsik and Libe GARTSHITSKY

Daughter Evelyn TSHALIF

In remembrance of
Alter GARTSHITSKI

Anna YABLONSKY

In remembrance of
My beloved father Gershon KOHN

Son: Max KOHN

In remembrance of
My parents Binyomin and Feyge KOLKO, my sister Ester (Stusha), my brothers: Ruven, Shimon, Yoysef KOLKO

In eternal remembrance
ZDANOVITCH family: Moyshe Leyb, Sheyne Hinde, Efroym with his wife Polye and two children; Rani with her husband Yosak and children Sonny, Liza and Jenny

Sylvia RUBINSTEIN

In eternal remembrance
SHKLAVIN family: Shimon, Dinke; Faytshe with her family; Dushke with her family; Efroym with his family; also Rodki, Doni and Bashkie

Sylvia RUBINSTEIN

Emanuel KOLKO
In remembrance of

The VODOVSKY family: father Yankev Efroym, with his wife Rivtshe; Shmuel, his wife Royzke, their children Khaya Feygl and Bashke, Reyzl and Nekhoma

Pauline VAUDOV

[Page 334]

In eternal remembrance of
Our unforgotten parents
Zvi Yosef and Rokhl SHEVTSOVSKY,
and our sister Khane Perl

The children:
Silva SHILLER (SHEVTSOVSKY)
and Morris NATION

In remembrance of
My father
Rabbi Itsik SAPIRSHTEYN,
My mother
Moli the "female judge,"
My sister Menucha and My brothers Moyshe and Tevye

Yitzkhak SAPIRSHTEYN

[Page 335]

In eternal remembrance of

Our beloved brother Shabse Frida and his wife Peye; their children Itke and Feygl with their families Sorke, Rozke, Khaykele and Zeydke; our sister Khayke KHLUPITSKY and her husband Avrom and their children Sorele and Motele; our aunt Khane DANOVSKY and her daughter Mirl; our aunt Ester FINKELSTEYN and her family.

With deep sorrow, we mourn your early death! Your memory will be forever engraved in our hearts!

Miriam BERKOVITCH
Nosn FRIDMAN

The children and grandchildren of
Reb Mordkhei NOVALSKY, *olev hasholem*
and Rokhl Leah NOVALSKY, *oleha hasholem*,
Victims of murderous Nazism; Moyshe and his wife; ☐Itke Elkan, her husband and children; ☐Sore ABRAMSKY, her husband and children.
May their souls be bound in the bundle of the living

Borekh NOVALSKY, Costa Rica
Frida UROV (NOVALSKY), Mexico

[Page 336]

In holy remembrance of
My parents Yoel and Golde BARTSHEVSKY

Also my brothers and sister: Khaym Arie, Avrom, Getsl, Yankev and Libe with their families. Special mention of my brother Khaim Arie BARTSHEVSKY, who fell fighting in the Bialystok ghetto revolt.

Khave BARTSHEVSKY-BERK

| **In remembrance of**
Isaac and Khaye Mirke KOHN

Mrs. Bertha KATZ | **In remembrance of**
Feygl and Moyshke BEYKOVSKY
and their son Shimon Zelig
who perished in Grayeve, as well as Leybl LEV, Sore LEV
and their four sons who perished in Lithuania
They will forever live in our hearts.

Mother Rokhl LEV
and sister Sore KANTOR |

In Memory of our dear departed mother
Rivke IVRY
"Gone but not forgotten."

The IVRY family

[Page 337]

> **In eternal remembrance of**
> Our beloved brother
> Sender FRIEDMAN,
> His wife Feygl Beyle,
> Their children Meri, Avrom Moyshe, and Shloyme;
> And in remembrance of all the martyrs from our home town Grayeve, those I remember and those I do not remember.
>
> May these words be the *yortsayt* [anniversary of a death] candles in remembrance of the extinguished lives that were killed by murderous hands. Their crying out was a voice in the desert…
>
> Velvel FRIEDMAN and his family
> Shepsl FRIEDMAN and his family
> Dzsheyk [Jake] KALINSKI and family
> Khane LURYE and family
> Charlie LEVINSON and family

[Page 338]

> **In eternal remembrance**
> In remembrance of our beloved parents
> Rafoyl, son of Reb Nosn (7 Adar [April 1932])
> and
> Ester Sore, daughter of Avrom (6 Elul [September 1933]) LEYZERSON
>
> The sons:
> Mayer, Leybl, Moyshe, Yisroel
> and Abraham LEYZERSON
> Daughter Shprintse STEIN

> **In eternal remembrance**
> In remembrance of the martyrs of Grayeve who perished,
> The BOGISHes
>
> Family of Benny and Millie BOGISH

[Page 339]

An eternal memorial to
The souls of the TIKOTSKY family that fell at the hands of villains during the days of unprecedented destruction, the souls of the martyrs Tsivia TIKOTSKY and her family; Hirsh TIKOTSKY and his wife Khane Sore; Ezra TIKOTSKY and his wife Reyzl, their son Khaym and their daughter Sore; Shifra and her husband Pinkhes PAKLER and their daughter Khashke.
May God avenge their blood.

The survivors in Israel and the U. S.

In eternal remembrance of
My beloved parents.
My father Moyshe Mendl the *shoykhet* [ritual slaughterer]
And my mother
Sore Zelde.
Also my brothers: Khaym Shmuel and Yisroel Itsik, their families and children, all of whom perished as martyrs.
We will forever bear the sorrow of their lives that were cut down too early.

Mayer Leyzer MISHKOVSKY and wife
Khane Elki GLAZER
Abraham MISHKOVSKY

[Page 340]

In eternal remembrance
In remembrance of my beloved parents
Avrom MARGOLIS (died of natural causes 25 Kislev [December 1939])
and
Brayne MARGOLIS, who perished by murderous hands;
My beloved sister Leye TSUKERT, her husband Sheyme TSUKERT, their son Meylech TSUKERT (6 years old), their daughter Zisl (1 year old).
I will never forget you!

Son, Yankl Velvel MARGOLIS

Our beloved sister Tsiva with her children.

Perished at the hands of the Fascist murderers!

She will live forever in our memory

Ester SAVITSKY and David BERNSHTEYN

[Page 341]

In remembrance of All our friends whose lives the Hitlerites have murdered! We will never forget you! Eliahu and Mayer SOSNO	**In remembrance of** Our unforgettable family! Our father Mordkhe TIKOTSKY; Our brother Efroym And his wife Nekhome With their child Yudl, Who perished at the hands of the Hitlerite murderers in the Bialystok ghetto. We will forever bear you in our hearts. Henny GREENBERG (Detroit) Hannah PRESSKOVSKY (Tel Aviv)
In remembrance of My beloved parents Hirsh and Dobe BARKOVSKY, as well as my beloved sister and brother-in-law Khaye and Itsik SOLISTINSKY, Who perished as martyrs at the hands of the bestial Hitlerites. Honor their memory! Efroym BARKOVSKY	**In remembrance of** Our beloved husband and father Khaym Hersh KLAYMAN, who died July 31 1949 at the age of 53 We will always carry his memory in our hearts. Wife Dora and the children Getsl, Sheyndl and Gitl

[Page 342]

In holy remembrance of My mother Khane Bashe, my sister Zelde, my brothers: Ezra Zelig and Gedalyahu and his family; And my brother-in-law Anshl GOLDMAN Who perished at the hands of the Hitlerite murderers. Honor to their memory. P. VOYSLOVSKI	Borekh Aron and Enach MISHKOVSKY perished at the hands of the Hitlerite murderers. We bear your memory with love . Beylke FISHBEYN KUTSHIK, S. I. FISHBEYN
In eternal remembrance of My beloved father Itsik Shloyme SALISTOVSKY As well as my uncle, cousins and family. Mr. and Mrs. David H. SIEGEL, 1037 Dwersey Parkway, Chicago Ill	**With deep sorrow and anguish** We honor the holy memory of all the Grayeve martyrs. Frieda UROV NOVALSKY (Mexico)

[Page 343]

Grayeve, Ostrowe, Zarombe, Branch 56
Of the Jewish Fraternal Folk Order honors
The memory of the martyrs of Grayeve and surroundings, who perished at the bloody hands of the Fascist executioners. We salute those active in the Grayeve relief effort for their good work helping those who have suffered.
Branch 56, Jewish Fraternal Folk Order:

A. MAGIDSON, President
B. BINDER, Financial Secretary
R. BLUM, Recording Secretary
A. STEIN, Treasurer
F. GOLUB, Literature Manager
A. KLAYMAN, Director for the Sick (Manhattan and Bronx)
R. GOLDBERG, Director for the Sick (Brooklyn)
M. FRIED, Relief Director
Executive Members
B. STEIN, S. LEVINE, B. YAGODNIK

[Page 344]

To eternal memory
In memory of my beloved parents
Isaac and Sarah EIN;
My brothers Chaim, Morris and Boris; My sisters Esther and Frida.
The latter victims of Nazi barbarism.
May their souls be bound in the bundle of the living

Max EIN

In eternal remembrance Hilel and Leye TAYTELBOYM The children: Ayzik and Adam TAYTELBOYM Itke KALEKO **In memory of** My parents Leyzer Velvel and Khane Beyle ABELSKY Paul ABELSKY	**Grayeve Branch 35, A. R.** Expresses deep sorrow and pain at the murder of all Grayever martyrs who were killed by bloody murderous hands! Officers: Morris BLOOM Max KOHN Harry RUDER Sol BAYKOVSKY Sam GROSS Jack RIVA Hymie BARNOFF and all members

[Page 345]

In eternal remembrance
These I mourn!
In eternal remembrance of our *landslayt* and friends from our town of Grayeve who were killed in the great slaughter of the Jewish people by the murderous Nazi beasts in the Second World War

*

In memory of our *landsleit* and friends of our town Grayewo, Poland,
who were massacred by the Nazi murderers in the Second World War

Officers and members of the
Grayewer Friendship Society of Chicago, Illinois

[Page 347]

In memory of
our dearly beloved parents Moyshe Hersh and Khaye Sore KAYMAN and brother Yisroel, *olehem hasholem*, who perished at the hands of the Hitlerite murderers.

We will bear your beloved names in grief forever!

Khaym, Zev and Nisan KAYMAN

[Page 348]

In eternal remembrance
With love and grief I remember my sister
Itke,
My brother-in-law
Leybl KUBERSKY
And their small children Khane, Yisroel,
Khaym and Riva,
Who were tragically killed by the
murderous Nazis
Their memory will forever remain
engraved in our hearts.

Mr. and Mrs. Sam RIBET,
New York

[Page 349]

In loving memory of

Our beloved father and husband

Hyman SILVERSTEIN

Died February 9, 1949

Mrs. Dinah SILVERSTEIN
Mrs. Jeanne Roe MISHKIN

[English page III]

English Section

The Story of Grayevo

by Dr & Mrs. George Gorin
Typed up by Genia Hollander

…"that these dead shall not have died in vain –
That this nation, under God, shall have
A new birth of freedom"…
(Abraham Lincoln in
Gettysburg Address)

This chapter is written mainly for the descendants of the people, the story of whose lives and tragic end make up the contents of this book. To many of the young people who will turn the pages of this Memorial Book and look at the pictures therein, the town of Grayevo will seem a strange and distant place; and yet, these same young people carry part of it in their hearts, characters and personality makeup because Grayevo, its customs, its way of life and spirit, influenced the lives of their parents and their home environment. Indirectly, therefore, there was transmitted something intangible to the young who never saw the town.

No one can deny the law of continuity in history and civilization; and although the Jewish Grayevo was erased physically from this world, its spirit together with the spirit of Jewish life in Poland, remains an indestructible heritage.

[English page IV]

This spiritual heritage will live on and perpetuate itself by enriching Jewish life throughout the world.

Strange and unpredictable were the ways of fate which prompted some of the Grayevo inhabitants to emigrate and flee, while others remained to be cruelly destroyed by the Nazis. It is not wisdom, clairvoyance or superior intelligence that made some people emigrate; neither is it stupidity or backwardness which caused others to remain. As will be seen later in this chapter, life in Grayevo held little promise for young people and, consequently, the latter were making ceaseless efforts to emigrate – some succeeded to do so – some did not.

The desire to emigrate did not confine itself to young people only; after World War I, it was all–pervading. Any one of those here, in the U.S. today, could have remained over there had not the hand of fate guided them or their parents into the free world many years ago and before the catastrophe was in sight.

I. The Old Ways

This is the story of a town – a town which lived, created, grew and perished. It is a part of a sad pattern in Jewish history for the past 2000 years; the growth of Jewish communities in some countries and their destruction as a result of political, religious and social upheavals.

It was a typical small town which grew over a period of several hundred years from a small village, with dirt roads and unpaved streets into a community of ten thousand people – the majority of who were Jews.

[English page V]

Grayevo was located in the North–Central part of Poland, at the southern border of East Prussia. This location as a border town was an important factor in its economic and cultural life. Lying on a main highway, it has risen in importance over the neighbouring small towns long before World War I.

In 1795, the Kingdom of Poland was partitioned for the third time and Grayevo became part of Czarist Russia. A railway running through Grayevo was built by the latter and by that time, the town had already a good sized Jewish population although no new Jews were allowed to come in by prohibitive order of the Czar. This order was rescinded later and the Jewish population of the town grew considerably through the influx of Jewish merchants, shipping agents and tradesmen from all over Russia.

The volume of commercial traffic between Russia and Prussia going through Grayevo was considerable, and brought prosperity to its inhabitants. Also, by virtue of the town's position, the people of Grayevo had, it seemed, through those commercial transactions, an easier access to the wider world. They travelled extensively to Prussia, Greater Germany and Russia and that made the Jew of Grayevo more of a man of the world. Those who did not have the good fortune to travel themselves always received first–hand information about the world at large from the businessmen returning home. Some of the information thus conveyed was frequently inaccurate and exaggerated, but it all contributed to giving the people of the small town a dream of a free and bright world outside of Grayevo.

The strategic importance of Grayevo as a border town brought to it a large garrison of Czarist troops which also constituted a source of revenue and increased business to the townspeople. Grayevo had the appearance of a hustling town with many freight trains unloading ware to be transferred into Russia and many products from Russia going into Prussia. Some of the Jews of Grayevo were an Integral part of this important commercial activity and some even enriched themselves at it. Others profited indirectly by rendering services, selling food, housing transients, etc.

[English page VI]

On the whole, the economic situation of the Jews of Grayevo was quite good until the outbreak of World War I in 1914. Yet there was a constant stream of emigration from Grayevo to the United States. The reasons for this exodus of people in the last decade of the 19th century and in the beginning of the 20th century were several: The most important one was the pogroms to which the Jews of Russia were subjected from time to time. And, as the immigration to America was unrestricted then and Grayevo had easy access to transportation facilities, many young Jews left for America.

To describe Grayevo of the period before World War I would require a translation of this whole book into English. But, to make the older generation and their background better understood to the readers of this chapter and their children, a few salient features of life in Grayevo ought to be described.

The economic life of Grayevo was partly touched upon before. But it was not all big business as the previous description might lead to believe. The bulk of the Jewish population consisted of small shopkeepers and artisans and they eked out a meagre existence in the midst of prosperous business activities which were being carried on through their town.

The commercial phase of life in Grayevo was predominantly in Jewish hands. They were the business people who supplied the whole population with goods and services.

As in all the towns of old Russia, religion was a dominant factor in the life of the Jews of Grayevo. Religion was also the background of education; it began its influence when an individual was born and carried on his education through the old fashioned "Kheder" under the supervision of old scholars whose function it was to indoctrinate the young generation in the precepts of the Torah and the Talmud. From the grown–ups, daily visits to the synagogue for prayer were expected and, in general, religion was the important and directing force in all situations of life.

[English page VII]

The Jewish community had its own court of justice – the Rabbi. He used to settle all litigation among Jews by arbitration. He also had the power to grant divorces and to settle various problems within the family. All this led to a way of life which was isolated from the non–Jewish community and explains partly the preservation of customs and traditions and their passing on from generation to generation.

Education confined itself solely to the studies of Jewish learning. It began early in life, at the age of 4, and continued until maturity. Education was directed at menfolk only. Women needed to learn their prayers only. There was little secular education available and every attempt to introduce it was considered an act of heresy. However, Grayevo could not resist the trend of the times and new ideas did infiltrate into the life of the community. Among these new ideas was primarily Zionism. Professor Rawidowicz, a native of Grayevo, describes in this book the beginnings of the Zionist movement in Grayevo and the opposition of the orthodox Jews to it. An attempt was made to discredit Zionism as a movement of heresy and the fight was quite bitter. Likewise, several attempts were made to teach Hebrew as a language for daily use and not just as the Holy Language of the Scriptures.

In the field of Hebrew culture, Grayevo gained renown through several of its outstanding citizens: Mr Abraham Mordecai Piorko was a great Hebrew scholar of the period of Renaissance in Hebrew literature. Mr. Piorko published the first Hebrew periodical for children and also a Talmudistic periodical as well as a brilliant interpretation of the bible.

Another one of Grayevo's outstanding citizens – Professor Simon Rawidowicz, is known as a brilliant Hebrew scholar in the field of old as well as modern Hebrew literature. He has written many important volumes of Hebrew learning and is presently editing and writing in the Hebrew field. He has honoured this book with an interesting chapter.

[English page VIII]

Another personality of whom Grayevo is proud is Mr. Ari Ibn Zaav who has made a reputation for himself in America with his book: "Jessica My Daughter". He is also the author of many Hebrew novels which have Grayevo as their background, and which earned him renown as one of Israel's leading novelists. He also has honoured this book with a chapter from a novel yet unpublished.

Mention must also be made of Dr. Zwi Woyslavski, now residing in Jerusalem, where he is known as an eminent literary reviewer, highly respected in Israel and also Dr. Emanuel Olschwanger, an outstanding Hebrew writer, who is also becoming known to the English reader public through his collection of folk tales and anecdotes in the book: "Roite Promerantzen".

To make the description of life in Grayevo accurate, one must not confine it to the few outstanding personalities. There were others who "stood out", though their names have no renown. Some left their families and embarked on the arduous road of pioneering in Palestine, others espoused the cause of Socialism for which they paid with years of imprisonment, and many others that travelled from one Centre of learning (Yeshiva) to another, living in the most destitute conditions, while trying to acquire mastery in the knowledge of the Talmud.

All the foregone is evidence that Grayevo was a thriving and intellectually alert little town which mirrored in its confines the strife between progress and backwardness in Jewish life everywhere.

[English page IX]

II. During and After World War I

There came the fateful day of August 1914. The news about the declaration of war struck the small town like thunder from the clear sky. Confusion was great; people were running towards rail lines leading away from their border town and towards the larger city of Bialystok.

At first, the Russian armies invaded East Prussia and the bulk of the troops passed through Grayevo. It was a steady stream, day and night for weeks. Then came the Hindenburg victory near the town of Tannenberg where the Russian armies suffered severe losses and retreated. In their wake came the Germans who occupied Grayevo and held it until the end of the war.

The Germans were no strangers to the Jews of Grayevo who had travelled into Germany for numerous reasons. Some used to go there for business purposes, some to consult doctors and many Jews of Grayevo used to spend the greater part of the year at work in Prussia, returning home only twice a year for the Passover and the High Holy holidays.

The Germans, during the period of occupation of the town, imposed various obligations and hardships upon the population. Forced labour and high taxes were some of these obligations, but there was no discrimination between Jews and non-Jews; all were oppressed alike and no acts of murder or brutality were committed against the civilian population.

The Jews of Grayevo realized that the economic prosperity of pre-war days was gone forever and they were reconciled to just earning a meagre livelihood.

At the end of the war, the Polish Republic came into being and Grayevo became again a border town between Germany and Poland on the latter's side of the border.

And then a strange thing happened. The Poles of Grayevo, so terribly oppressed by Czarist Russia over a period of 125 years, embarked upon a course of persecuting the Jews as soon as Poland regained its freedom and independence. Those were years of political instability in the new Polish state, and during this period, the Jews of Grayevo lived in constant danger and fear for their lives and safety.

[English page X]

Then, in 1920, during the Soviet-Polish War, again a period of troop movements and severe fighting developed around Grayevo. The town was cut-off from the rest of the world and for several months, no one knew what was going to happen. Finally, the Soviet troops retreated and the Poles took over Grayevo, ushering in their rule with reprisals against the Jews whom they accused of sympathy to the Soviets. A few Jews were murdered on the outskirts of the town and the whole Jewish population lived through a very dark period. It was then that a terrible tragedy occurred. Fifteen young Jews were caught by the Poles while attempting to flee Poland. All 15 were murdered and their mass grave remained as evidence of fascist brutality.

The Polish government embarked upon a campaign of economic oppression against the Jews in spite of the fact that it had signed agreements at the Peace Conference in Paris, guaranteeing minority rights, and in spite of the fact that its new constitution guaranteed freedom and quality to all its citizens. The oppressive measures consisted mainly of high taxes designed to ruin Jewish commerce (there was practically no Polish commerce in the small towns and besides subsidies were given to the Poles to enable them to compete with the Jews). Laws also were passed excluding Jews, indirectly from various trades; Government jobs were closed to them practically and admissions to high schools and universities were governed by a rigid quota system.

In view of this situation, the only hope and future for young people was emigration. But, the field of immigration deteriorated considerably after World War I. The large mass immigration to the U.S. was put to an end by the passage of the Immigration Law of 1924, restricting considerably immigration from Eastern Europe by the introduction of the Quota System. To the Jews of Poland, it meant cutting off their avenue of escape from a situation which was becoming more and more desperate. Some Jews, realizing the ever increasing oppression, had foresight of impending disaster and liquidated their affairs and immigrated to Palestine. But even that was wrought with difficulties and only a small number were able to leave and rebuild their lives. The majority were trapped in a situation in which they could not carry on and from which they had no means of escaping.

[English page XI]

The young Jewish people of Grayevo did not accept this situation without revolt. They did not sink into apathy. On the contrary, they joined movements and organizations in the hope of finding strength and solutions to their problems through collective efforts.

Some joined Socialist organizations which advocated liberation of the masses from oppression and thereby offered hope of solving the Jewish problem. The majority, however, joined the various Zionist Pioneer organizations and prepared themselves for life in Palestine. Animated by the Zionist ideal to rebuild Palestine as a Jewish homeland, they hoped to reconstruct their lives in a free and better world. Vocational training along completely new lines became necessary and training centres which were established for that purpose had many young people from Grayevo among their members. There was also a Zionist scout organization in Grayevo which prepared teenagers for future pioneering. The older generation, though it dreaded the eventual separation from their children, realized that the solution to the problems of the future was to be found for their children in Palestine and they cooperated in these activities.

Religion ceased to play an important role in the lives of the young Jews of Grayevo. Many prejudices and restrictions were thrown overboard and though it aroused the anger of the orthodox elders of the town, the young generation did succeed in winning greater freedom and ceased to be hampered by many religious taboos and prohibitions.

[English page XII]

Similarly, changes occurred in the field of education. Although the old fashioned religious schools continued to exist, they were modernize, somewhat, but the majority of children and young people attended secular schools in Grayevo or went to nearby larger towns. Grayevo also boasted a number of students at universities throughout the continent of Europe.

The economic situation was deteriorating but their cultural life did not suffer; new ideas penetrated and gave interest, strength and hope to the young people. Extensive reading was popular and, in general, the life and activities of the young centred on the various organizations. The older generation still clung to the synagogue and the various places of prayer. They also realized the need for various community institutions which they established to make life easier: a cooperative bank, an "Appliances for the Sick" institution and Public Baths.

The public baths were needed because there were no bathtubs or showers in the home. There was no running water – it had to be carried from a well in a bucket.

Grayevo had no electricity until after World War I. During the winter months, all windows were locked and nailed and all cracks and crevices were stuffed with cotton and pasted over with paper to keep the cold air from entering. The arrival of spring coinciding with Passover was an occasion for thorough cleaning, airing and general overhauling of the household. It also marked the end of the gloomy winter which was whiled away with card playing, visiting, amateur theatricals by the young people and cultural meetings and lectures.

Like all small towns in Poland, the Jewish Grayevo had its social strata according to wealth, education or ancestry. Grayevo had its customary towns' idiot, a few freaks and some eccentric individuals who are well remembered by the older generation.

[English page XIII]

Despite the lack of comfort and the low standard of living, hygienic measures were maintained; health standards were higher than among the non–Jewish population and mortality rates were lower.

The Jews of Grayevo had a certain amount of autonomy in conducting their own purely Jewish affairs. This was accomplished through an official body (kahal), recognized by the government. This body had authority to impose taxes upon the Jews and the moneys thus collected went towards the upkeep of communal institutions.

The disintegration of the Jewish community in Grayevo began as a slow and gradual process during the period following World War I. The Jews lived there in a hostile world and anti–Semitic outbreaks increased in intensity and frequency in the late thirties. Life became unbearable, not only because of discriminatory and oppressive policies of the Polish government, but also on account of brutal actions on the part of their Polish neighbours. The Poles imitated the persecution of Jews taking place in Germany at that time and they waited for the opportunity to deal with the Jews cruelly and freely. This fateful day came on September 1, 1939.

III. The Catastrophe

After the Munich Pact in September 1938, the Jews of Grayevo knew that they were being delivered into the hands of Hitler and that dark times were ahead. Yet, undying optimism which always supported them in dark hours of their history, did not allow them to sink into despair. They lived through a whole year on the brink of disaster and hoped that a miracle would save them.

[English page XIV]

On September 1, 1939, the hordes of Hitler swept across the border from East Prussia and within hours were in possession of Grayevo. The Jews of the town were panic stricken; they were trapped by the enemy. From their hiding places, they watched with fear the goose–stepping Nazi march into Grayevo. They were trapped by the Nazi and by the Poles and there did not seem to be the slightest chance of escaping death.

A reign of terror began immediately. While the Nazi were busy setting up their headquarters and military installations, the anti–Semitic Poles went on an orgy of brutality. They dragged Jews from their hiding places and murdered many of them. First they killed those who owned real estate property in order to take over their homes. Then they set upon the intellectuals. Many Polish criminals armed with hatchets and iron bars walked from house to house and did their cruel work in the darkness of the night. Before the Nazi had time to begin their own programme of extermination of the Jews of Grayevo, Soviet troops occupied the town as a result of the Russo–German pact which gave Grayevo to Soviet Russia. The Jews watched with relief the withdrawal of the Nazi from their town.

The period between September 1939 and June 1941, during which the Jews of Grayevo lived under Soviet rule, was only a breathing spell.

The Soviet regime restored order in Grayevo and brought a measure of security to its Jews. In many instances, the situation of the population at large was much better during that short period than it had ever been under Polish rule. Jews were admitted to places and positions hitherto barred to them. For the first time in many centuries, they were treated with equality and without discrimination because of race. This fair treatment did not apply however to the so–called "bourgeois" element among the Jews and there began a large scale deportation of Jewish business men, Zionists and all those suspected of opposition to the Soviet regime.

[English page XV]

This deportation of Jews deep into Asiatic Russia oddly enough was responsible later on for the survival of a certain number of Polish Jews and among them, some of the Jews of Grayevo. As the number of the bourgeois element in Grayevo was small, it is obvious that most of the Jewish population remained in their town and enjoyed the short period of relative freedom under the Soviet occupation.

The fateful day finally came at daybreak on June 22nd, 1941. German bombers swooped down on Grayevo and bombed the town indiscriminately. Shortly afterwards, German mechanized units took possession of the town.

This time it was unmistakably clear to the Jews of Grayevo that they were trapped. The Soviet troops retreated in disorder or were captured as a result of the surprise attach by the Nazi. The Poles, who angrily watched the Jews during the period of Soviet occupation, embarked immediately on an unrestrained campaign of murder. They accused the whole Jewish population of collaborating with the Soviets and helped the Germans in the initial stages of their extermination programme. Many Jews were dragged from their houses, shot in front of their families and buried in the streets. Jewish girls were raped by the Poles and the Nazi and were murdered in cold blood afterwards.

A large number of Jews were rounded up and placed under arrest in the synagogue. They were kept there for several days without food or water and were finally murdered. Other Jews were taken to the cemetery, lined up in front of one large grave, dug by fellow Jews, and mowed down into it with machine guns.

The German intentions were to extract first every ounce of energy and every valuable possession from the Jewish population before destroying them. And so they proceeded to order the Jews to organize a governing body – the so–called "Judenrat" whose only function was to receive orders from the Germans and to relay and enforce them upon the Jewish population.

[English page XVI]

The remaining Jews of Grayevo were driven from their homes and herded together into a Ghetto in one of the poorest and shabbiest streets of the town.

A Jewish militia was organized to keep order inside the Ghetto which was closed upon all sides and guarded day and night be armed Polish guards.

The Ghetto was very crowded. Many families were herded into one room. Privacy and basic comforts of life were done away with. Yet, the Jews did not lose their courage and by a common effort, as if by tacit agreement, carried on even under these horrible conditions. At no time did the Jews of Grayevo lose their dignity in spite of the physical degradation and the total abject living conditions. Those who had some money shared it with others; various activities were organized within the Ghetto. The Judenrat opened up a grocery store, a bakery and a few other establishments through which were distributed the most important and basic necessities of life.

The punitive taxes and forced labour drained the meagre earnings and exhausted the energy of the dwellers of the Ghetto. At times, they used to pool all their resources and valuables so as to meet the exorbitant demands of the Germans. They knew that non–compliance meant death and hoped that they would survive in spite of these horrible conditions. As time went on, the purchasing power of the Ghetto was dwindling rapidly. The sanitation problems were getting increasingly worse.

The young Jews were forced to do hard labour for the Germans who paid them in food rations which were not enough to sustain life.

The policy of the Nazi was to degrade and humiliate the Jews, but in this respect, they seldom succeeded. The Jews of Grayevo never turned against each other; on the contrary, there was a feeling of brotherhood and devotion encompassing all the Jews in the Nazi clutches.

[English page XVII]

As the extermination policy of the Germans entered its next stage, the horrible sight of the big "death vans" rolling through the streets began to appear. The Jews of Grayevo knew what the contents of these vans were and surmised with horror that their turn was approaching.

Soon after the occupation of Grayevo, the Nazi established a large concentration camp (Bogushe) where they held and then exterminated thousands of Russian prisoners. When this task was completed, they then herded into this camp all the Jews from surrounding towns including the Jews of Grayevo.

Living conditions in this camp were horrible – beyond description. Sheltered in flimsy tents, exposed to the elements, subsisting on meagre rations and crowded into a small space, the Jews were being ravaged and decimated by hunger and disease.

A few individuals managed to escape into the surrounding woods and join the partisan bands; but the majority of the Jews had not hope left but to wait for the day of their deportation to the death camps. This happened early in

1943 when the Bogushe concentration camp was liquidated and its occupants transported to the Treblinka death camp where they were burned in the Nazi fashioned crematoria.

Grayevo remained a town without Jews. The physical part of the town remained practically intact, but the Jewish Grayevo had perished and disappeared from the face of the earth. Only a handful of refugees out of the whole population survived the D.P. camps and managed to continue their broken lives in the U.S., Israel or elsewhere.

It is to the memory of all those lives and death were described in this chapter that this book is dedicated. Their death is a horrible tragedy but we ought to perhaps find consolation in the fact that this wholesale slaughter awoke the Jews of the rest of the world as well as international conscience to the realization that the Jews must be redeemed as a nation in Israel. Let us then remember our martyrs – let us keep their memory forever sacred in our hearts and may we all find consolation in the thought that they, by their dying, have given the nation a new birth of freedom and have not, therefore, died in vain.

[English page XVIII]

[English page XIX]

History of the Grayevo Ghetto
by Nachman Rapp (Wroclaw)

While writing these lines, I see before my eyes my brothers and sisters of my birthplace Grayevo, who died under torture and in great pain. I hear their last desire unspoken as they left the horrible world: *Tell of our deaths! Let not our memory and the memory of our sorrows be forgotten! Let the memory of our martyrdom remain as a headstone for the few survivors of our city where they may come to weep and recall the tragic loss. And for our people, let it remain as a spark which ignites a great flame of revenge, a constant reminder: Erase the remembrance of Amalek...*

Nineteen Thirty Nine

......It happened so suddenly that it was almost impossible to believe; the pro–German reactionary government of Poland began, through its press, to attack Germany, its aggressive appetites, its demands on Poland for the Danzig corridor.

[English page XX]

We read the papers in wonder. Can it be that a war is imminent between two such "good friends"?

....A "patriotic" fervour swept the country. The dramatic ensemble of the thirty–third infantry division of Lomzhe came to Grayevo and performed the patriotic play: "Poland – the Heart of Europe". The play lampooned Hitler, the swastika and his threats of a blitz victory over Poland. I attended this performance with my friend *Mottel Yabko* (Mottel Laitche). The performance had been sponsored by a citizen's group under the leadership of the District doctor, *Sienkiewic*. Suddenly, before the curtain rose, the doctor stood up and said to his companion, the thickly be–whiskered German engineer: "Come, friend, I can't stand sitting near Jews..."

It was impossible to react as it was impossible to react to too many things in pre–war Poland: all we could do was leave the theatre immediately.

I present this fact as an illustration of the attitude of the Polish fascists and semi–fascists even in such a dangerous situation as the threatened German attack.

Within a week, all men eligible for military service, including Jews, were ordered to report in Osowiec.

For the first time since Poland had become an independent state, Jews were allowed to serve in the "head" border guard at Osowiec. It was felt that since the noose was already on its neck, the reactionary government could trust the Jews to fight the Germans. Among the Jewish youth, anti–fascist feeling ran high and they joined the army with an enthusiastic anticipation of the coming encounter.

Now there was no longer a loyalty test for recruits. To the contrary, radically inclined workers seemed to be specially chosen for border duty. In the "head" border guard at Osowiec were included the afore–mentioned Mottel Yabko, a young worker who had served a six–year prison term for Communist activity – the left Paole–Zionist, *Mottel Striev*, the brothers *Aaron* and *Moishe Krimkiewich*, and others.

[English page XXI]

War broke out on 1st September. The general mobilization which had been hastily called three days earlier was not completed in Grayevo. On Thursday, the day before war broke out the entire population was at the railroad station. The heart–rending cries of the mothers whose sons were leaving for the front mixed with the shouting of those who had not been able to leave earlier and were now in panic. Drunken Polish solders leaped from the cars into the Jews, shouting that the war had come because of the Jews and that now they would get even. Fortunately, there was no longer time to "get even" on the spot because it was already 6p.m. and that train was the last and was scheduled to leave immediately. At 4a.m. the next morning, the train which had come from Bialystok to Grayevo was captured by the Germans in the station...

Most of the Jews who had managed to escape remained in Bialystok. There they worried about the majority of the Jewish population which had remained in Grayevo. During the two weeks since the outbreak of the war, Grayevo had been cut off by the front line and it was impossible to receive any news from there. Only when the Germans occupied Bialystok did some information arrive about Grayevo. Though no Jew had yet dared to go there, peasants from the neighbourhood related the sorrowful total of two weeks of German rule. All the synagogues had been burned together with a number of Jewish homes.

When the Soviets took over Grayevo, Jews slowly began returning home and learned of killings and of Jews who had been deported to Germany.

Particularly horrible was the case of the woman *Elkon* – a mentally unbalanced person whom the Nazi had dragged into the Bogusha woods. They put out her eyes and left her blind and dying. A peasant had found her and brought her home in this wagon.

Many Jewish young people had been deported. Of these I remember only one returned. *Chaim Friedman*, son of *Malke Friedman*.

[English page XXII]

The 15 year old high school student, *Abrasha Bykowski* was taken by the Nazi and to this day, we know nothing of him. His mother *Khaiche*, (Helen) *Beikowsky* now in Wroclaw, still believes that her son is alive and relives every day the pain of a mother who cannot find her lost child.

Brutally, the Germans killed 17 year old *David Rapp*, son of the baker *Isaac Rapp* (brother of the author). The German sadists quartered the live body of the young boy with their swords.

An exploding grenade killed the young daughter of *Chaim Lazer* whose bakery was on the synagogue street. His son *Srolke Antchkowski* disappeared without a trace.

During this time the non-Jewish population of Grayevo took no part in anti-Semitic actions. To the contrary, there were cases in which German soldiers set fire to Jewish homes while the Polish neighbours helped quench the flame. In this manner, the newly-built home of the tailor *Isaac Grobeld* was saved as well as that of *Yoske Gurovske* ("Yoske the Spinner").

Among those who disappeared were also *Rabbi Yitzkhok, Isaac Grossman* and the well-to-do owner of a steam mill in Grayevo, *Abraham (Avramtche) Eisenstadt*. Later it was learned that they had been horribly killed as hostages in Bendin, the home town of the Rabbi.

The war in Poland had stopped. Warsaw had been captured and in the areas of Western Ukraine and Western White Russia, Soviet life began to establish itself. Slowly the Jews began to return to Grayevo which had become part of Western White Russia. In addition, a number of Jewish refugees began to arrive. Jewish Grayevo slowly regained its Jewish appearance.

[English page XXIII]

Soviet Rule in Grayevo

Autumn ended early that year and a fierce winter set in. A winter such as in 1940–41 was unprecedented since 1928.

Life was hard in Grayevo during the first weeks of Soviet rule. Organized hoodlums of the former Polish fascist parties roamed the countryside and agitated the peasant to refrain from selling wheat "to the Bolsheviks". Several Jewish bakers who also remained in Grayevo under German rule were able to obtain flour somewhere and baked black bread. One of these was the baker *Moishe Piniewski* who fled to Bialystok before the outbreak of the war. When the Soviets arrived in Grayevo, he baked "for himself", obtaining small amounts of wheat from peasant acquaintances.

Slowly life became easier. Several bakeries were nationalized and the "City Supply Department" began to bake enough bread for the urban and rural population. Consumer goods began to flow into the city so that shortages no longer existed.

At first, it seemed ridiculous: business was going on in the city; bakeries were operating, mills and the electric plant were running, workshops were opened, and all of this without bosses! People smiled and predicted that "they" would not be able to establish order because it could not be done without a boss. The Jewish youth in Grayevo, however, threw themselves into the work with heart and soul. "*Mottle Yabko*", after returning from the Polish-German front, threw himself with all his youthful energy into the establishment of order into the life of the city. On cold winter days he would wander through the countryside collecting wheat from the peasants. At night, he would trace down the roaming marauders who did their nefarious work under cover of darkness. When life became stable, a short time later, he became chairman of the State Distributive Trust in Grayevo.

Several State dry-goods and knit-good stores were opened. A cooperative store was established in *Ettele Mishkowski's* building in the market place on the corner of Bogusha Street. Jewish salesgirls were almost exclusively employed there. Among them were the sisters *Rachel, Sarah, Yehudis Mayek* (daughters of *Mayek* the *carpenter*), *Rivke* and *Chipeh Marcusfeld* and others. The former owners were no working in their own bakeries which the State had nationalized. The manager of the bakeries was for a certain period of time, the former bakery owner, *Saul Bronerwein*.

[English page XXIV]

Jews were employed in all phases of economic and cultural life in the city and district councils, and in all subordinate institutions. A 60-bed hospital was opened in Grayevo. Its supervisor was the Grayevo doctor *Wiener*.

A Yiddish junior high school was established in the re-modelled Talmud Torah on Powiatowy Street near the New Synagogue. Working in this school were some ten teachers, among them: *Velvel (Vovak) Silberstein, Dora Wapinska, Shlome Wronsberg* (director) and several others from outside Grayevo. Two Jewish teachers, *Fromer* and *Beykowski*, were on the staff of the newly-opened Polish school. The Jewish youth of Grayevo saw, for the first time, the many opportunities which Soviet rule offered to young people. They flocked to the high schools and colleges of the country. The above-mentioned teachers and many other young people began to study in many fields. Others left for a wide range of short and long-term courses to become useful specialists.

The Yiddish school in Grayevo developed wonderfully. Jewish children who had come from the Polish schools and Talmud Torah startled their teachers and parents with their rapid advance in Yiddish studies. The Junior High School in Grayevo established a dramatic group which was able to present a performance by children never before witnessed in the city. The District Education Administration decided to sponsor the performance of the epic drama: "Bar Kochba" by *Sh. Halkin*, with the participation of the pupils of the Jewish School. After a three-month "Course for Stage Directors", I was appointed the leader of this group. I immediately began rehearsals for the production.

[English page XXV]

From the highest balconies in the city, hung huge placards depicting scenes of the heroic Bar Kochba uprising. On the site of the old synagogue burned by the Germans, a beautiful theatre seating 1500 was built. Here the show was staged. The hall was packed with a diverse audience including Soviet officials, party leaders and a large part of the Grayevo garrison which rewarded the children after the performance with gifts and kisses. (Not one of these young performers survived the war. They, together with all the children of Grayevo, were slaughtered by the Nazi beasts).

The Germans had burned all the synagogues, so now a communal prayer house was established in the home of the baker, *Moishe Piniewski*, where a *minyen* would gather daily and, of course, on Sabbath and holidays. When the Germans set fire to the large synagogue *Yitshok Grobgeld* succeeded in saving one Holy Scroll and a number of prayer books which were of great use during this time.

Religious education was also not neglected in this period. Though the building which had housed the old Talmud Torah was no occupied by the Yiddish School, a part of the communal prayer–house was set aside for *Anshel Kotchak*, the Hebrew teacher who taught religious subjects to all the Jewish children who attended the Yiddish junior high school in the mornings.

But in the dark of night, the marauders didn't rest. These were the unregenerate home–grown Polish fascists who had been driven underground. Hitler's Germany which had betrayed and attacked Poland was not considered an enemy. They vented all their hate against the Bolsheviks who had established: "Jewish Communism". From mouth–to–mouth, the evil rumour spread: teaching of Polish would soon be forbidden: All Poles would be exiled from Grayevo to hard labour in Siberia and church–going would be forbidden. Of course all this agitation had absolutely no basis in fact but was maliciously fanned in order to arouse the illiterate masses against the government and to convert them into a weapon in the hands of the feudal lords and reactionaries.

[English page XXVI]

The agitation was, however, doomed to failure. The Polish intelligentsia felt for the first time that it was a vitally useful element in society and was utilized in most State and community positions where it laboured conscientiously. The workers and especially the permanently unemployed, who had previously existed on charity, received jobs which provided them with a livelihood. Only the sons of the large landowners whose estate had been divided among the landless peasants were unable to rest and maintained their old familiar pre-war agitation against "Jew Communism".

The Soviet government was very well aware of the damage being done by these groups and had undertaken to remove the inimical elements from the border city of Grayevo to points further in the interior. On 19th June, 1941, a number of Jewish families were also sent out from Grayevo. They were the *Beykowskis, Yosef Bialostocki* and family, *Kirshenbaum* and family and the nurse, *Mania Kaplan*. Some were ordered to move to thirty kilometres from Grayevo (*Aaron Leizerson* and others).

These families regretted deeply the need of leaving their old home. They considered it a tragedy and were very mournful in bidding their friends farewell. Actually, all those who were sent out two or three days before the war, were thereby saved from the Hitlerite murderers and they now consider that that day as the one in which they experienced the greatest miracle of their lives.

In the months of March and April 1941, all men of military age were called up into the Red Army. Of the Jews who went, I remember *Chaim Adanstein, Yosel Mayek, Yankel Roimer, Leibel Dorf, Gershon Gringross* (a son of *Zorach* the butcher) and *Shamai Marcus*. These young men later fought heroically in the war against the Germans and were in various ways decorated for their bravery. Their personal accomplishment, however, was that by serving in the Red Army, they did not experience the horror of the Ghetto and are now alive.

[English page XXVII]

A worse fate befell those young people of Grayevo who served in the Polish army in Osowiec (25km from Grayevo). They were the first to fall into the hands of the German beasts and the first to die. Of these, I remember: Yankel Rutski (son of the painter Falk), Gershon Viernik, Moishe Viernik, Benyomen Kureyvowski, Moishe Yitzhok, Tobiashora, Chaim Mendel Levine, Chaim Kurzhondkowski, Leibl Zeligson, Yosel Levitt and the 18-year old Chaim Epstein. Some members of the same unit were able to escape and to return home to their parents in Grayevo as was the case for Yakov Shia Kaminski who "escaped" to die later in the Grayevo Ghetto with his father and mother.

Life was so peaceful and with so strong a feeling of security that it was impossible to believe that a tragedy such as occurred on 22nd June, 1941 could really happen. When, in the early hours before dawn the inhabitants of Grayevo were torn from their sleep by loud explosions and sounds of firing, the first unasked question that came to the lips of the frightened Grayevo Jew was: "Can it be possible"? Unfortunately it was…

Nazi Occupation in Grayevo

On 22nd June at 4a.m., the Nazi began their invasion of the Soviet Union.

The previous week, I had been in Bialystok. There was nothing in the city that indicated the coming storm. Around Tuesday, a few days before the outbreak of war, I met a number of Grayevo inhabitants in Bialystok and they told me that a number of Jewish families had been sent out.

[English page XXVIII]

Having completed my business in Bialystok, I left for Grayevo at 1a.m. on the morning of 22nd June.

It was 3a.m. when I arrived at the Grayevo station. The City was sunk in quiet pre-dawn sleep. I strolled from the station with my friend *Gershon Greengross* who had come home on furlough from his detachment in Osowiec. We spoke of the clear blue sky and of the warm pre-dawn and that that day there would be strolling on the beach near the Kosherove Lake and decided we would meet near the lake. We then parted, each to his own home.

My home was on Rutske Street n°24 in Avreml Greenberg's house since our former home on Konopska Street had been burned by the Germans in 1939. The entire family was awakened by my arrival: father, mother and sisters were up. Questions flowed: "how is everything in Bialystok, and … why I didn't bring back a girl I was to marry"… Everyone chattered until mother made my bed and announced that it was time to "call it a day".

Suddenly, we were deafened by a horrible shriek, as if scores of factory whistles had begun wailing. We were stunned and did not understand the meaning of all this. Least of all did we expect an invasion. We knew very well that there existed a non-aggression pact with Germany and we didn't expect the Germans to attack without the "formality" of some provocation.

But several minutes later, there was no longer doubt. Every few moments another explosion shook the house. We ran down the steps to see what was happening. But as soon as we reached the street, we realized that this was really war and we headed for the Bialystok highway.

Though Grayevo wasn't a large city with barely twelve thousand inhabitants, two artillery companies were stationed there because of the proximity to the German border. Therefore, the war came to Grayevo in a concentrated German attack. In the first moments, the city was wrapped in a sea of smoke and flame. All sorts of arms began firing at once deafening the frightened populace. It was, therefore, impossible to think of escaping by fleeing the city. Here is what an eye-witness tells of these first minutes of war:

[English page XXIX]

"I ran to the window to see what was happening. A thick column of smoke rose to the sky blocking out the light. Were it not for the constant firing and explosions, one might have thought that the city was not being attacked but merely put to the torch. Not being able to see anything through the window, I went out onto the porch. But as soon as I put my hand outside, I was hit by a piece of shrapnel which tore off these two fingers. I fainted and my wife carried me indoors". (*Yosef Kalski*, bricklayer – Rutske Street).

And in that maze of smoke and noise, the Jewish population of Grayevo lay trapped. Before one could even think of escaping, the roads had been cut off by the advancing German troops.

It immediately became obvious that the entire area had been cut off from Bialystok its centre. The fascist underground placed itself immediately at the service of the Nazi and cut all telephone connections in an area of some thirty odd kilometres. The officials of the Soviet institutions and of the Party tried desperately to establish contact with central headquarters, but to no avail. Some hope was based on the Osowiec fortress. There, we thought, the Germans would be driven back and before the front would be established, we might be able to escape to the rear. But this hope, too, turned to nought. The Germans by-passed Osowiec and slowly encircled it through the Lomzher region.

German military units did not enter Grayevo on the first day of the war. Only the German border–guard occupied the city. They took over the railroad station, the post office and all Soviet institutions. Only by the third day 24th June did a German military kommandatur arrive, setting up its headquarters on Pilsudskiego Street (formerly Shtutchiner Street).

[English page XXX]

On the first day of the German border–guard occupation, the soldiers immediately began murdering the Jewish population. An order was issued to the German troops declaring Jewish lives and property open to whatever actions they might decide upon. So that, in the very first day, there were mass rapes of young Jewish girls. The "gentle" German race excelled in biting its young victims to death while the mothers of the tortured children were forced to stand by and witness these horrors.

Here is what the Polish woman, *Helena Nadolna* tells of a scene that day.

"....My next-door neighbour came running into my house screaming that her daughter had just been murdered by a German and that she, the mother, had been forced to stand by and see that no one disturbed him. When the German left, all he said to her was: "Nice Mama". When she went into the room she could not believe her eyes. She begged me to come and help save her child's life, but there was no longer any life to save. The girl's flesh was torn, bitten and bruised. Blood foamed from her mouth and breasts. She was dead – choked – her eyes bulging from her sockets. Her mother wanted to commit suicide. In a few days, she went out of her mind and the Germans killed her. Her name is Henie Shine Bashed, 34 Ruska Street. The same was done to many others whose names I do not know".

A few days later, Wednesday 25th June at 10a.m., all the Jews were driven into the marketplace where the Stadt-Kommandant *Geiss* read the order of the kommandatur. The order read in part:

"The Jewish nation is a criminal nation and as such, it merits the eternal punishment of hard labour and enslavement. They may not live freely and among other people because of their impure blood. Sooner or later, all must die. They must obey every German under pain of death. Jews will be designated by yellow stars which they will have to wear on their backs and chests as a sign of their shame".

[English page XXXI]

As usual in German practice, every order was accompanied by "direct action". After reading the order, the Jews were driven from the marketplace under a hail of blows and two sisters were arrested on the spot – *Rachel* and *Yehudis Mayek*. They were led to the Jewish cemetery and executed.

Great fear gripped the Jews in the marketplace after the reading of the order. It was open proof that as of this day, Jewish life is free to any German or Polish hoodlum. From that day on, Jews sat locked in their homes fearing even the light of day. A rumour spread that the Polish underworld was preparing a pogrom. It was said that a "delegation" of reactionary cut-throats had visited Gestapo commander *Opper* to determine whether the murder of Jews was punishable by law and that *Opper* had reassured them that they had nothing to fear. This rumour turned out to be true when the first pogrom by the Polish reactionaries took place two days later.

Sunday 29th June, the first organized pogrom took place in Grayevo. Leaving the church, the incited hoodlums ran to rob and murder the Jews. With previously prepared axes and clubs, they left on their task of splitting Jewish heads. The leaders of the pogrom were: *Aloise Stenkowski*, a young professional thief, a syphilitic, a son of the noted thief – *Stenkowski* (Konopska

Street n°6) and the cut–throats: *Green, Mikloszewski, Zegavek* and *Stanisz*. The Jews whom the bandits caught on the street were murdered on the spot. In this manner, *Aloise Stenkowski* killed *Mottel Striev*. The photographer *Ephraim Vodowski* fell at the hands of the murderer *Stanisz*. This was not enough for the pogromists who then brought death and destruction to the Jewish homes.

[English page XXXII]

In the present day, when speaking with Christians of Grayevo about that pogrom, most try to avoid the question entirely. Many say that they helped one Jew or another. It is, therefore, interesting to note the personal testimony of the Christian *Zyskowski* who lives in the marketplace next to the house where *Yosef Bialystotski* once lived. In the same house, there lived the hardware–dealer *Weinstein* and *Ukrop's* son–in–law, *Moishe* (whose family name I have not been able to ascertain).

When the pogrom began, these two Jews found themselves in the street and ran home in an effort to save themselves. The narrative is here as taken up by the above–mentioned *Zyskowski*.

"When I saw the two zydki (Jews) running down the street, I locked the house door and didn't let them in (!). Terrified, they banged on the door. They found an axe and smashed open the door and ran to their own apartment. Soon the 'boys' came and beat up the Jews. *Weinstein's* legs were broken and the other was merely bruised".

On the other hand, there were many Christians who, despite the bestial atmosphere, retained their moral and human values. Their self–sacrifice in defending Jewish lives and human dignity must be accorded the greatest recognition. In the first place, we must mention with great honour, *Henryk Sobolewski* – a progressive Polish worker and a long–time member of the Polish Communist Party who, on the day of the horrible pogrom, bravely fought with word and deed and prayed for his struggle with his life. He was arrested together with some ten Jews and after being held and tortured for one day in the synagogue, he was taken to the Jewish cemetery and executed.

The second heroic figure is that of the Catholic priest – Penza. Tirelessly, he preached daily masses calling the Christian population to regain its senses, not to cooperate with the Germans and their anti–Semitic provocations. The hooligans, however, held robbery and murder dearer than Christian morality and brotherly love. They reported the Catholic priest to the Germans who unceremoniously shot the gentle priest.

[English page XXXIII]

There are rumours that immediately after the pogrom, a Jewish delegation went to the German commander Geiss to ask for protection from the pogromists. We do not know whether this rumour is factual or not. It is a fact, however, that exactly one hour after the pogrom – at 3p.m. German police began hunting the pogromists. They caught three: (Miklasevski, Zegarek and Green) and shot them on the spot. This was supposed to have indicated that the Germans sided with the Jews and protected them from the enraged Christian population. But, this was only a wily trick of the German hangmen who, on the one hand organized the pogrom, while on the other, they wanted further to whip up feeling against the defenceless Jews by showing the Christian population that even now the authorities sided with the Jews. This was also intended to convince the Jews later on when the Ghetto was being formed, that it was in their favour to live apart from the Poles.

In order to further hide their real aims, the Germans did not stop at "punishing" the three murderers. They also took a number of wounded Jews to the hospital where they were "treated" and as a result of these treatments, *Rifke Bialystotski* died within three days. Particularly horrible and revealing of the fascist type of provocation, was the case of the wounded *Postolsky*. He had been savagely beaten by the pogromists and was only half conscious the next morning when the Nazi brought the Polish youth, *Lutek Remiszewski* to his bedside and demanded that he identify his attacker. In his pain and semi-consciousness, the Jew thought that this was actually the man who had beaten him and despite the tearful protests of the youth, he identified him. The young man was a progressive Polish student whom the Germans had purposely implicated. Within a few days, the innocent young man was executed.

[English page XXXIV]

That day, the Germans also arrested the Polish teacher *Leon Klodetski*, the above-mentioned progressive worker, *Henryk Sobolewski* and a number of other progressive Poles who were imprisoned in the synagogue. *Klodetski* managed to escape while the others were shot the same day.

The Death Chamber in the Synagogue

After a week of systematic attacks on the Jews, the Germans decided that the time for starting the extermination of the Jews in Grayevo was now ripe.

A special SS group was mobilized for the purpose of catching every Jew between the ages of 15 and 45. The prisoners were brought to the theatre which had been the large synagogue before the war. This was not merely a prison where inmates were tortured – here, Jews were subjected to inhumanities besides which the tortures of the inquisition seemed no more than child's play.

Jews with broken hands and legs were forced to perform exercises; to leap over tables and chairs, driven by blows from their tormentors. After three days' starvation, they were fed salted herring following which they were deprived of water for three days. The younger and stronger ones were driven under a hail of blows to perform inhumanly hard and totally useless labour. They were forced, for instance, to carry the stone archway to and from the cemetery. After such a day's labour, they were brought back to the synagogue where the night–long torture began. Between 15 and 20 people died daily.

Before death came, the Germans would throw the dying into the deep cellar of the synagogue, leaving them there to expire. When the cellar was half–filled with corpses, healthy people were then thrown in and kept there until the odour of death engulfed and claimed them too.

[English page XXXV]

This is the testimony of the Christian woman, *Helena Nadolna* who lived opposite the synagogue and was able to see what went on:

"The young people and particularly the men were put into the synagogue and tortured for two weeks. Such tortures that even death would be a blessing. They twisted out their arms, tore out their tongues and fingernails. Every morning they received on hundred lashes. When someone fainted, he was thrown into infested water and when he revived, was subjected to new tortures: leaping over various obstacles, tables and chairs. Then they were forced to line up and every tenth man had to leap from the second story window. Those who leapt and remained alive were killed on the spot. The Jews' hands were tied with barbed wire which was then wound around their necks and in that condition were tossed into the cellar to expire. The corpses were removed from the cellar a year later, almost completely decomposed. The workers who were forced to remove the bodies became fatally infected. The corpses were thrown in to a lime–filled ditch near the cellar".

On those occasions, when the Germans ordered Jews to leap from the window of the synagogue, the Polish fascists were gathered below and it was they who killed the ones who remained alive. Such was the case with the young lad *Velvi Piekarevitch* (son of the Stavisker smith, *Avrom Shlime*). After leaping from the window, the boy ran until he reached the Jewish cemetery. There, the hoodlums caught him and threw him alive into the lime pit near the synagogue.

The prison guards in the synagogue were the Poles *Davidowski* and *Staniesewiski*, volunteers from among the Polish reactionaries who served in the militia, *Yanek Yankowski*, a well–known cut–throat in Grayevo and others. These overseers led the Jews, each morning, to slave labour in various places. Of course, their first responsibility was to beat the Jews with truncheons and iron rods. On returning from the first day's labour, the Jews saw above the door a sign: "Internment Camp". It became clear that their imprisonment was not a caprice but that it would be long, if ever, before they returned home.

[English page XXXVI]

The women assembled about the theatre (synagogue) with food for their husbands, sons and fathers. For graft, the guards took the food and distributed as they saw fit among the prisoners who later sent out the dishes, keeping the bottles for their own biological needs.

On 10th August, 1941, the German kommandatur issued an order that in the course of some three to five days, all Jews must move to Dolna Street (Bod Street). The Polish residents were ordered to evacuate. The prisoners were permitted to help their families move their belongings. Many were not able to move all their things. A psychosis gripped everyone, driving them to the Ghetto where they thought they might escape the native hoodlums. The men who were temporarily released were then rearrested.

The Polish overseers, Staniszewski and Davidowski and their accomplices were not content with merely torturing the Jews in the synagogue prison. They evolved a plan to gain personal profit. They had heard that there were Communists among the prisoners. They chose some twenty Jews at random and the beast Davidowski shouted at them "Cholera! To byli Komunisci!" (The devil take you! These were communists!). These 20 Jews were separated behind a barrier and were no longer permitted to leave on the work brigades with the others. For the first two days, the wives of the "communists" did not know what had happened to their men. The guards continued to take the food but did not distribute it so that the "communists" starved for two days. When the wives of the "communists" learned of their fate, The overseers profiteering began in earnest. The wives ran to the beast Davidowski and bribed him to release their husbands from the "communist" cells which meant sure death.

[English page XXXVII]

And so the beasts kept alternating their victims; freeing one and placing another among the "communists" taking the last remaining money from the wives.

At the instigation of Davidowski and Staniszewski, the Gestapo issued an order and one morning, the beasts took out the group of "communists" and none of the other prisoners knew what had happened to them. The next day it was learned that they had been taken to the Kosheruvka woods and shot.

Among the groups which were periodically taken from the prison and shot were the following individuals:

Silverman, Shloime. *Abramski*, Yosef. *Abramski*, Shimen. *Greenspan*, Lazar. *Striev*, Mordehe. *Buchbinder*, Hersh. *Bronervein*, Saul. *Kletski*, Chaim Ydel. *Barash*, Kopel. *Segalovitch*, Leibl. *Segalovitch*, Sholom. *Cohen*, Elia. *Sudker*, Berl. *Stolnitski*.

This is a partial list of the Jews who were shot in the woods from 1st–25th August.

On August 26th, 1941, the Gestapo ordered the arrest of all women who had worked at government jobs during the Soviet rule and all young girls who had been members of the "Komsomol" (communist youth organization). Forty Jewish women and girls were taken away that day.

At night, when the captive men returned from work, they were immediately taken to the horse market. There, the Polish reactionary hoodlums "took over", forcing old and young alike to leap over ditches. This torture lasted an hour. Then the Gestapo commanded the Jews to form a line and the Polish hoodlums pointed out the "communists" at random. Among the "communists" they also included the old *shokhet, Moishe Mendl Myshkowski*. Of course all this had been arranged by the Gestapo. The hoodlums pointed to the *shokhet* saying: "this one is Stalin's comrade…"

[English page XXXVIII]

The Grayevo Poles tell of a horrible experience which befell the young engineer *Kirshbaum*. The young man was not an inhabitant of Grayevo but came to the city as a refugee from Warsaw at the outbreak of the war. He was physically fit and managed to land safely after leaping from the second-story window. When he tried to escape, he was caught by the Polish hoodlums who generally stood about enjoying the tortures which the Jews underwent. They threw him into the large ditch near the synagogue. This ditch was actually a large, temporary latrine which the Germans had dug.

After being thrown in, the miserable engineer swam to the side trying to climb the boards which shored up the ditch. The hoodlums stood by, laughing at the attempts of the young man to rescue himself from the filth. When he had almost reached the top, their laughter turned to rage and they attacked him with their spades, splitting his head open. (Eye witness report by the Polish bricklayer, Jan Kalsik, Rudzka Street).

Some eighty men were then taken from the line and separately led back to the theatre under heavy guard. On the morrow, the Gestapo mockingly organized a "trial" of the eighty men and the forty women. The "trial" lasted two days. The Polish militiamen signed affidavits asserting that all the accused were communists. The "curt" sentenced them all to be shot. Upon hearing the verdict, a number of young people leapt from the second story windows to instant death.

The night after the trial, the Gestapo brutally tortured the condemned Jews. Their heads were beaten with bottles and many were fatally wounded. These were dragged to the cellar and murdered and the corpses thrown into the cellars of the burned houses nearby.

[English page XXXIX]

That night was one of the worst for the prisoners. All night the Polish hoodlums and Gestapo men dragged the old people to the cellar to be brutally murdered.

On 29th of August, a group of Jews were put to work on the Ruder Highway. In the evening, the Polish overseers brought the Jews to the cemetery instead of to the theatre and left them standing there. Within several minutes, Gestapo men arrived and ordered the Jews to dig a 60 meter hole. The Jews understood only too well that this was to be the mass grave for 120 Jews – their brothers and sisters who had, two days earlier, been sentenced by a "high court" of drunken hoodlums and blood-thirsty Gestapo agents. The Jews refused to dig this hole. The Gestapo beasts began at once to murderously club the Jews into submission and the Poles made use of the sticks they held in their hands. Anyone who refused to begin digging was immediately shot (as was the case of *Zorach Elkon's* son and others).

When the mass grave was ready, the Jews were brought back to the theatre. The drunken Gestapo tortured the sentenced Jews all night. Like wild beasts, they threw themselves upon the Jewish women. Proof of this horrible episode can be found in a short letter found by the survivor, *Meyer Kletsky*, that same day in the synagogue room where the prisoners spent their last minutes. This what Sarah Mayek wrote:

"It doesn't suffice from them to merely see us die. They had to rape us in addition. Gestapo men and some Poles did the job. Brother Jews! Take revenge for us and for our shame!..."

Thus, the *Herren folk* brazenly proved its "abilities". Marry a Jew – and you have "shamed your race", to be punished by death but rape and torture of Jewish women can bring only glory!

Meyer Kletsky tells how the 120 Jews finally met their death.

[English page XL]

"At ten in the morning (30th August) the men and women who had been sentenced to death for being "communists" were taken out. Flanking them were Gestapo men and Polish militia volunteers as well as a large segment of the Polish population. All followed the prisoners through the streets with smiles on their lips saying: "So there will be some fewer Jews...". All the Jews had to enter the graves on their own. When all stood inside, the machine guns let loose and took from us forever our beloved and dear ones...."

On September 1st, 1941 at 10a.m. the Gestapo gathered all the Jews in the horse market. The German Stadt-Kommandant arrived and spoke to the assembled Jews assuring them that now that they were cleansed of their "communists" they would be able to live peacefully in the Ghetto, would have their own management and their own president.

The Ghetto in Grayevo

The reason for the establishment of ghettoes for the Jews throughout Poland by the Nazi is now self-evident! The Nazi wanted to concentrate the Jewish population in specific areas, cut-off from the world in order to simplify the final criminal objective – the complete annihilation of the Jews. At the time of the creation of the ghettoes, however, the German hangmen had so well prepared the groundwork that in many cities, the Jews naively believed that they would find refuge there, being protected from the provocations of the native anti-Semites.

This was also true in Grayevo.

On reading the order establishing the Grayevo ghetto, Stadt-Kommandant Geiss simultaneously proposed a *Judenrat* for the administration of all internal problems and for a liaison with the German government. Those proposed were: 1. *Sutker Zalman*, president; 2. *Popovski*, secretary; 3. *Voyslavski, Yitzhok*, member; 4. *Tennenbaum*, member. The Jews, believing this to be in reality a representative body, added *Lazer (Leishke) Grossman* to the *Judenrat*.

[English page XLI]

The first two orders issued by the *Judenrat* are in themselves revealing. The first order – at the insistence of the Nazi – was to immediately clean the theatre (synagogue) where the prisoners had been tortured to death the night before. The *Judenrat* selected 25 men and women whom they sent with brooms and pails of water to the site of the awful blood bath.

Meyer Kletsky, who was one of the 25 and has remained alive to tell the story, describes the interior of the building:

"The walls were completely flecked with blood, as in a slaughter house. We had to wash the blood clean so that no sign of our dearest ones would remain. The room, in which the condemned women spent their last minutes, gave the appearance of a recent pogrom. Torn out strands of hair were strewn about the floor together with ripped items of clothing and papers. We searched among the papers and found a note which *Sarah Mayek* had left (see above, N.R.). Exhausted after a horrible day's work, we were nevertheless unable to go home to sleep. We gathered in the yard and mourned the remnants of our dearest ones".

The second order which the *Judenrat* issued that same day was to post a guard around the ghetto for the night to prevent provocation by the native hoodlums of Davidowski's gang.

The "guard" was composed of young people "armed" with....sticks and flashlights. It is obvious what little good this "guard" would have done against organized and probably armed hoodlums. Still, they might serve to spread an alarm.

[English PageXLII]

Several days later, the *Judenrat*, under German orders, created a labour bureau headed by *Yitshok Voyslawski*, with *Luba Fabilinska* as secretary. At the behest of the Germans, this labour bureau supplied Jewish workers for German firms. The workday was from 14hr to 18hr and the wages per day was 1Mark!

Jews were permitted to leave the Ghetto for work without guards but with a pass issued by the German authorities. At the same time, the *Judenrat* formed a Jewish militia which included/

1. *Karbowski*, commander (a lawyer from Lomzhe); 2. *Meyer Kletski*, vice-commander; 3. *Khilare, Berl*; 4. *Neiman Reubin*; 5. *Gumovitch, Shloime*; 6. *Zharkowski, Yitzhok*; 7. *Tevel Oz–Iosher*; 8. A son–in–law of *Yosel the smith*; 9. *Marcus, Joseph*; 10. *Slovatitski, Moishe*; 11. *Sholomke* of the "blind".

(There is no accurate evidence as to the conduct of the Jewish militia in relation to the ghetto population. Having been personally far removed from the tragic scene, I do not feel justified in coming to any conclusions, one way or another. I also would not feel justified in repeating all the virtues and good deeds related to me by the eye–witness, *Meyer Kletsky*, admitted vice–commanded of the militia. While respecting the great pain which the former experienced, he must nevertheless be considered an interested party and therefore not the source, in this case, of objective testimony).

Economically, life was not of the worst in the Ghetto. It can be said that during its existence, there was no starvation there. Of course, the satanic plan of the Nazi murderers had been worked out to the last detail: let the Jews see that they are cared for, that necessities are provided and they will not try to escape. There was, however, more to the plan.

[English page XLIII]

The Nazi authorities permitted the peasants of the surrounding villages to bring food, peat and wood into the ghetto. The peasants who had come to market on the specified days would drive straight to the ghetto without even stopping at the general market place. On these days, the streets of the ghetto would be choked with wagons as at a fair in the old days, and the Jews would buy out all the produce. This created the following paradox: the Jews, who were walled–in the ghetto, completely isolated, had more essential commodities than the Polish population outside. The latter were forced to buy these essentials from the Jews in the Ghetto. Of course, this led to more hatred among the Polish population who compared the Jews to cats, saying: "no matter where you throw them, they'll always land on their feet...." Actually, this was a well–planned manoeuvre of the German propagandists. They were out to convince the Polish population that the "zhides" take all for themselves and only when they will be wiped out will there be enough food for the Poles.

A group was also appointed by the *Judenrat* to keep the ghetto clean. *Pinyeh Suraski* headed the group. Working with him was: *Abraham Greenberg, Sholem Zaidenberg, Goldberg, Berl Kletski* and *Yehudah Greenberg*. Everything was kept clean – the swamps on the east end of Dolna Street were drained and vegetables planted in all parts of the ghetto. Almost every Jew had stored some supply of potatoes, wood, carrots, beets and other vegetables. The only hope was that if only they would remain in the ghetto, they would somehow manage to live to see the "downfall of Haman".

The *Judenrat* also established a number of workshops for the ghetto's needs. A bakery was opened to supply the population. The bakery, once the property of *Joseph Bialystotski*, was on Dolna Street. The manager of the ghetto–bakery was *Jacob Shidlow*. A food–store, under the management of *Abraham Tenenbaum* was also established. A shoe workshop was also in operation in the Ghetto producing at low prices for the population.

[English page XLIV]

About two weeks after the creation of the ghetto, the *Judenrat* suddenly received an order from the German Stadt–Komandant to pay one million marks into the Magistrate's treasury. This was a terrible blow to the impoverished ghetto. The order threatened that if this sum were not paid, the Jews would be sent out of the ghetto. Fear gripped the ghetto inhabitants. Having no other alternative, they now sold whatever was left to the Polish population, rejoicing that they were willing to buy. The poorer ones sold pillows and all their furniture. The rich Jews bargained closely, but finally paid their share. (Eye–witness account by M. Kletski).

But the hope of survival outweighed the fear of immediate and future dangers. Throughout all these troubles, the ghetto was filled with optimistic faith in the approaching defeat of the enemy.

A very important factor in the economic life of the Grayevo ghetto was the good relations between the near–by communities and the Jews. The peasants eagerly sold their produce to the Jews. For example, a group of Jewish young men (*David Bunkovski, Chaim Burakovski* and others) would leave the ghetto at night and bring back fish from the near–by town of Tochelova and either distribute or sell it to the Jews in the ghetto. The peasants, who were permitted to bring potatoes and wood into the ghetto twice a week, would hide chickens and even whole calves in their wagons. The ghetto–Jews were not permitted to keep animals or fowls. Nevertheless, the ghetto always had a number of cows and quite a few chickens. All this was thanks to the help of the peasants from near–by villages.

The eye–witness account by M. Kletski also tells of a Polish woman from Grayevo who would come three times a day to the ghetto and sell or partly distribute food to the Jews in the ghetto. When the Grayevo ghetto was liquidated and the Jews driven to the camp in Bogusha, this same woman came, as before and brought produce. Let us accord due respect to this fine and warm–hearted Polish woman.

[English page XLV]

Under these conditions – conditions of hard labour and struggle for a piece of bread, for survival and abiding faith in surviving the enemy and living to see his downfall – the Grayevo ghetto existed for a period of one year. The ghetto was allowed to exist until 1st November, 1942 when the German hangmen decided that they could now put an end to the few remaining Jews of our city, after they had fully used them materially, economically and physically.

The Camp in Bogushe

On 11th November, 1942, the Germans evacuated the Jews from the Grayevo Ghetto. The previous night, the ghetto had been surrounded by gestapo men armed with machine guns and who permitted no one to leave. The people who were supposed to report to work at 4a.m. were laconically informed: "you've worked enough" and were then brutally shoved back into the ghetto. The ghetto immediately became aware that something was afoot. Some tried to escape but the gestapo guards allowed no one to leave until dawn.

When it grew light, the gestapo entered the houses, driving everyone to the square with blows and shouts. When all the Jews had assembled, carrying bundles and children, the gestapo began driving the Jews in the direction of the village Bogushe (border village between Grayevo and East Prussia).

Though it was late fall, that day was very hot and the tired Jews were unable to carry all which they had so hurriedly put together. Everything they were unable to carry they dropped along the highway. The whole length of the road from Grayevo to Bogushe was littered with Jewish poverty.

[English page XLVI]

Under a hail of blows from gun-butts and sticks, with cries and sobs, the pitiful army of Jews arrived at the Bogushe concentration camp.

This camp had previously served as an internment camp for Soviet prisoners of war. The German beasts had tortured to death tens of thousands of Soviet soldiers who, because of the sudden German attack, were unable to escape. The fields around Bogushe were full of huge mass graves of Soviet soldiers, murdered in the Bogushe Death Camp.

The camp consisted of a large fenced-in field with barbed wire. Barracks had been "built" – that is, ditches had been dug and covered with make-shift roofs.

The Grayevo Jews arrived at about 11a.m. In the afternoon, Jews were brought into the camp afoot and in wagons from all surrounding cities: Szczucizn, Raygrod, Vonsosh, Radshilovo, Trestena, Augustow, Byalibzberg and villages around Augustow, wherever Jews still remained. It was clear that the Germans had begun the complete liquidation of all ghettos in the towns of the Bialystok region.

The first three to four days, the Jews remained entirely unfed. Everyone ate whatever they had managed to bring with them from the Ghetto. Only on the

5th day did the German authorities, having appointed a commander of the camp, establish 4 kitchens which were to feed over 7,600 interned Jews. The German chosen commander was the former president of the Grayevo *Judenrat*, Zalman Sutker.

The kitchens produced little more than potato soup. The daily ration per person was half a litre of watery soup and a hundred grams of bread. Jews were so starved that they would besiege the kitchens – fight over the potato peelings and gulp them down raw.

A group of Jews were assigned to work on the highway around Prostken. These were considered the luckiest. Outside the ghetto, they were able to buy a piece of bread, paying in hard cash or gold. The survivor, *Kletski*, relates the following:

[English page XLVII]

"A group of some 20 men worked outside the camp. They had it good because at work, they met with Poles and for gold, watches and other valuables, they received bread which they brought to the camp and sold. The biggest speculators were the *Kaminsky* family (of *Nachtche* the butcher). Five or six members of the family participated. During the two months they spent in the camp they had amassed a huge hoard of gold and dollars since a kilo of bread went for a few dollars".

On the basis of this eye–witness account, one is able to clearly picture the life of the Jews in the camp. If a kilo of bread cost a few dollars, it is clear that very few could afford it. Secondly, of the 7,600 internees, only some 20 were able to leave camp so that at best, only an insignificant amount of people benefited from the smuggling.

After the first two weeks, the gestapo permitted 15 persons to return to the Ghetto for the purpose of obtaining the potatoes which the Jews had stored in the cellars. Such groups made three to four trips. Mr. *Kletski* relates:

"Once, I succeeded in getting into one of the groups which went to Grayevo under a guard of three Wehrmacht soldiers. We entered the ghetto. It looked as if another pogrom had struck it – houses robbed, streets full of feathers. On the street, one sees various Yiddish books. Poles already occupy the better houses. We enter Pesach the baker's yard and find a torn Holy Scroll. We took a few wagon–loads of potatoes from the cellar. There was a baker there whose name I don't remember (this was the baker *Ian Sienkiewich* – N.R.). He sold each of us a six–kilo bread at low prices".)

A very high death–rate existed in the camp because of the horrible starvation and filth. Every night, the dead bodies were collected in a ditch and removed in the morning to the camp cemetery which was the cemetery of the Russian prisoner of war.

[English page XLVIII]

Every one of the interned Jews was at the mercy of any one SS guard. In relation to this, it is told of the Grayevo Jew, *Shaie Leib Konopko*, a casualty of World War I. One morning, a gestapo came into the camp and called the Jew out of the barrack. The invalid, *Shaie Leib*, realized that his time had come. With tears in this eyes, he bid farewell to his friends, took from his basked the leather gloves which he had always worn due to his rheumatism, gave them to his brother–in–law, *Leibl Sharfstein* and said: "take them. I don't need gloves anymore". He entered the prepared ditch…and the gestapo extinguished his life with one shot.

A "selection" was made in the camp on 15th December. Some 5,000 people were closely packed in separate barracks. They were told that they would be sent to a Silesian labour camp the next day. It is interesting to note that at that time, there was already rumour that the Jews were being sent to crematoria of Treblinka and Maidanek but not one believed the rumour. Therefore, the majority of those selected for "labour in Silesia" calmly accepted the news of their transfer. The transportation was carried out in the usual German manner: terrible blows and shootings on the spot drove the people out of the barracks to the railway station in Prostken. The roads were soaked by the fall rains and the mass of people were too tired to walk. But the beasts drove them on; those who lagged were immediately shot. The road from Bogushe to Prostken was littered with the dead and dying. The following day, the camp administration ordered the remaining Jews to collect the corpses from the road. 200 bodies were collected and buried in the camp cemetery.

The entire transport of 5,000 Jews, among whom were the camp commander and former president of the "Judenrat" *Zalman Zutker* and his aide, *Lazar Grossman*, were taken to Treblinka and destroyed in the crematoria. (To this day, we do not know of a single person who managed to escape from that transport).

[English page XLIX]

Some thousand persons remained in the camp. The German murderers, who had carefully laid their criminal plans, wanted to create the illusion among the remaining ones that they were no longer in any danger. They were placed in the better and larger barracks and were even better fed. M. Kletski tells about one instance in which a number of killed geese and other fowl were brought from the Prostken pasture for the internees. It was intimated that the internees would be allowed to "recuperate" and then be sent to labour camps. The Germans then designated a Jew from Augustow as camp commander and a week later, ordered him to prepare the Jews for their journey.

On 2nd January, 1943, the Germans ordered the Jews to pack up and prepare to leave the next day. On 3rd January, the last Grayevo Jews left the Bogushe camp forever. In jammed cars, they left the Prostken railway station and rolled on through Bialystok, Warsaw, and Treblinka....

When the train passed Treblinka and did not stop, a ray of home shone among the unfortunate. They did not yet know that there were other death camps besides Treblinka. .... So the Grayevo Jew *Jacob Shidlow* consoled his brethren: "Jews, if we have passed the hell of Treblinka, we shall survive..." Unfortunately, this was a false hope.

At midnight, the train arrived at the Birkenau death camp, adjacent to Auschwitz (Oswiencim). As soon as the train stopped, it was attacked by SS men with tommy guns. They drove the prisoners from the carriages. Whoever tried to take anything with him, even a piece of bread, was shot on the spot. Alongside the rails, a selection was made, some 100 young men were taken out and the other 900 men and women were jammed onto trucks and taken down the long road to the crematorium. That same day, the oven of the Birkenau death factory swallowed forever the last remnants of the Grayevo Jews.

[English page I]

Thus it was

Dead, as though following some horrible flood, Grayevo remained without Jews.... A quiet, thick cloud of recently–shed Jewish blood seemed to rise from every corner, from every bit of earth. The flat hills around the village of Przekopke, the shallow waters on the Kosherufke brook, the ruins of the houses on Synagogue Street, the murder chamber in the synagogue, the huge cemetery near the Bogush camp – all these places contained for eternity the remains of a Jewish community on Polish soil...Sobs shake the earth of Grayevo. The birds in the church garden sing a dreary song. The sun is ashamed to look upon the fresh graves because, when she warms such a grave with their contents, a choked cry rises from the innocently tortured victim who curses the world – curses the sun for having shone on the enemy...Then, the shamed sun hides and a thick, damp fog settles over the city like a great shawl of mourning and the city appears then to be sitting *shive* at the foot of the "green mountain..." There is no light in Grayevo! So the dark souled creatures crawl from their holes, sniffing; Is everything done? Have we somewhere overlooked someone? Jews – and, not finding any, they seek everywhere until....they came to the Bogushe camp....

That which I am about to tell, happened a month after the "emptying" of the camp in Bogushe, when, on the soil of Grayevo and its environs, there rested not one Jewish foot.

Some of the Polish hoodlums from among the Grayevo's rich store of the underworld went to visit the Bogushe camp. The barracks were empty, partially dismantled by the peasants for firewood. The hoodlums searched and rummaged. Perhaps they were seeking buried Jewish gold – that legendary "Jewish treasure" which every Jew "must" have. Suddenly, they struck on something soft or hard. Who knows? But it was suspicious. They quickly began digging at the earth under their feet and were stunned at what they found. Before their eyes, they opened a grave – a ditch in which *two living corpses* lay...The clothes on the two had already rotted away. Only the boots remained whole. One can only guess how these two Jews managed to hide during the liquidation and how they managed to stay alive in the ditch for an entire month. When the treasure hunting hoodlums saw that the two Jews were still alive, their beastly "patriotic" blood was inflamed. They dragged the two from the ditch, ordered them to remove their boots and to embrace each other so that one bullet penetrated both skulls. The two Jews were: *Velvl Videnski* and his young wife! (Eye–witness account of the Polish worker, *Yankolsky*).

[English page II]

Now Grayevo – "Juden–rein" can sleep peacefully. No more Jews in Grayevo....

But:

The earth of Grayevo shall not rest for a long, long time. Long – very long shall sleep be taken from the eyes of those in Grayevo who helped in the great crime. The pain of the murdered women and children, fathers and sons, shall long disturb their rest. Mortal fear shall grip them by night and black melancholy shall torture them by day for the awful deeds that they have done. The curse which our martyrs cast in the final moments of their being shall pursue them eternally to the end of their days....

Then, the blood of martyrs shall be quieted...

Table of Contents of the Original Yizkor Book

Translated by Tina Lunson

Foreword	7

First Part: Once, once…

Nakhman Rapp: Midnight (poem)	9
Sh. Y. Fishbeyn: Grayeve from the Past	11
Mayer Vaser: Our Hometown, Grayeve	19
Prof. Shimen Rabidovitsh: Grayeve, the Aspiring and Dreaming	35
Dr. G. Gorin: Images and Figures of Grayeve	47

Second Part: Community and Life-Style

Itsik Gartshitski: The Zionist Movement in Grayeve	71
Sh. Y. Fishbeyn: Workers' Organizations in Grayeve	105
Abutsh Kolko: An Encounter Between Grayevers in Siberia	119
Ari Ibn-Zahav: Grayeve *Dzshegtshares* [tar sellers]	123
Heyman Blum: Hasidism in Grayeve	147
Haymie and Sol Shiller: Hepner's Suspender Factory	155
Dr. Tsvi Vislevski: Grajewo [In Hebrew]	159

Third Part: The Holocaust

Nakhman Rapp: History of the Grayeve Ghetto	174
Mendel Kayman: A Grayeve Partisan Recounts	215
Khaye Golding-Kayman: Shtutzin – Grayeve to the Last Breath	218
The Violent Death of the Jews of Shtutzin [Szczuczyn] (Document)	223
The Violent Death of the Jews of Kolna [Kolno] (Document)	226
The Pogroms in Radzshilov [Radzilow] (Document)	228

Fourth Part: Grayeve Jews in America

Our Students: A Word from the Chairman of the United Grayeve Aid Committee	238
H. Blum: The Grayever Relief Committee in New York	242
Irving Sapirstein: The United Grayever Relief Committee	250
Heyman Blum: Grayeve Branch 35 of the Workers' Circle	261
Irving Kleynman: The Grayever Branch 56 of The Jewish People's Fraternal Order	268
H. B–M: The Shtutziner and Grayever Shul in New York	270
A. Blushteyn: The Grayever Landsleit in Chicago	274
Letters and Documents from Grayeve	276
From American Joint Distribution Committee, Warsaw	290

Fifth Part: Grayeve Writers and Scholars

Kh. Antshkovski: Grayeve Jews in Erets Yisroel	293
Gershen Svet: The Three Grayevans in Jerusalem	298

Dr. G. Gorin: Avrom Mordkhe Piurko	302
Dr. Emanuel Olshvanger: Memoirs of Avrom Mordkhe Piurko	306
Dr. G. Gorin: Prof. Shimen Rabidovitsh	308
About the illustrations of A. D. Fishbeyn	312
In Holy Remembrance (Necrology)	315

English Section

Dr & Mrs. George Gorin: The Story of Grayevo	III
Nachman Rapp : History of the Grayevo Ghetto	XIX